Selling to the Masses

Pitt Series in Russian and East European Studies
Jonathan Harris, Editor

Selling to the Masses

Retailing in Russia, 1880-1930

MARJORIE L. HILTON

University of Pittsburgh Press

Published by the University of Pittsburgh Press, Pittsburgh, Pa., 15260

Copyright © 2012, University of Pittsburgh Press

Manufactured in the United States of America

Printed on acid-free paper

10 9 8 7 6 5 4 3 2 1

Hilton, Marjorie L. (Marjorie Louise), 1961–

  Selling to the masses : retailing in Russia, 1880–1930 / Marjorie L. Hilton.

    p. cm. — (Pitt series in Russian and East European studies)

  Includes bibliographical references and index.

  ISBN 978-0-8229-6167-3 (pbk. : alk. paper)

  1. Retail trade—Russia (Federation)—Moscow—History—19th century. 2. Retail trade—
Russia (Federation)—Moscow—History—20th century. 3. Retail trade—Soviet Union.
4. Consumption (Economics)—Russia (Federation)—Moscow—History—19th century. 5.
Consumption (Economics)—Russia (Federation)—Moscow—History—20th century. 6. Consumption (Economics)—Soviet Union. 7. Shopping—Russia (Federation)—Moscow—History—19th century. 8. Shopping—Russia (Federation)—Moscow—History—20th century. 9.
Shopping—Soviet Union. I. Title. II. Series: Series in Russian and East European studies.

  HF5429.6.R8H55 2011

    381'.1094709041—dc23   2011039624

For my parents,
Betty and Edward

Contents

Acknowledgments

Although I have spent many solitary hours completing this book, numerous people and organizations have contributed to it in various ways. I am delighted to thank them for their support and encouragement.

I conducted research in Russia and Ukraine with the support of a grant from the American Councils for International Education (ACTR/ACCELS) and a fellowship from the University of Illinois. The Department of History at the University of Illinois provided support for research and writing in earlier stages of the project. The Russian and Eastern European Center at the University of Illinois also provided financial assistance at various phases.

Diane Koenker read the chapters and provided detailed, insightful feedback and encouragement, and the book has benefited immeasurably from her keen, critical readings and wide-ranging knowledge of the field. I am also deeply appreciative of the wise advice and support she has offered. Mark Steinberg also read several drafts, offering invaluable insights that helped me to interpret retail culture more inventively and to demonstrate its relationship to other aspects of Russian society. Christine Ruane lent her expertise in Russian consumer culture and likewise provided rounds of incisive commentary. I am also grateful to Chris for her support and counsel over the years. Clare Crowston's insights into consumption in the early modern European context challenged me to consider more carefully the use of certain terms and concepts and thereby contextualize the project more creatively. I am also deeply grateful to Larry Holmes, who provided my first model of research excellence and taught me the ropes at Russia's archives and libraries. Larry's unflagging love of research and his enthusiasm for new adventures in Russia continue to inspire me.

I also wish to express my appreciation to the two anonymous readers for the University of Pittsburgh Press for their helpful suggestions and comments on the manuscript as a whole. Their ideas provided the inspiration for my final revisions. Sally West, Christine Varga-Harris, David Fisher, Jennifer Nelson, Kathleen Feeley, and Dorene Isenberg also read portions of the manuscript and offered constructive ways to make my arguments stronger and clearer. Colleagues and friends in Russia and Ukraine made my research trips more productive and interesting. During my stay in Odessa, I was lucky to have the assistance and companionship of "fellow Southerners" Valeria Kukharenko, Maria Zavgorodnaia, and my dear friend Lena Igina and her husband, Viktor. I owe great thanks to Lena and her students at Odessa State University for making my stay in Odessa a memorable experience, for welcoming me into their homes, teaching me about everyday life there, and preparing for me a special Thanksgiving dinner. I am indebted to Patricia Herlihy for putting me into contact with this wonderful group of people. In Moscow, Varvara Masiagina made a place for me in her home and smoothed my path every day. From Varya I learned how to traverse the city and to enjoy the small niceties of daily life. I also received assistance in Moscow from Nikolai Kotriakhov and also from Galina Ulianova and Mikhail Zolotarev, who generously shared with me their knowledge of merchant Moscow.

At the Press, Peter Kracht, Alex Wolfe, Amberle Sherman, and Ann Walston ably assisted me at various phases of the publishing process and patiently answered numerous questions. Maureen Creamer Bemko's skillful editing resulted in a more polished text. Claire Morales assisted with the book's cover design and preparation of photographs for publication. Daniel Albert assisted with the preparation of the index.

Finally, family and friends have sustained me throughout the research and writing of this book, cheering me on and keeping me grounded. To my parents in particular I am enormously grateful for their support and confidence. It was going to the grocery store with them that generated my curiosity about the relationships and meanings that people form over a sales counter.

Selling to the Masses

Introduction

When I first visited Moscow, in 1995, I made the obligatory trek to Red Square. Standing in the center of the square, I was captivated by the Kremlin's spires and St. Basil's multihued curves and peaks, but the enormous, ornate retail arcade directly opposite the Kremlin—the famous GUM (Gosudarstven-nyi universal'nyi magazin), the State Department Store of Soviet times—held my attention. As I scanned the lines of this sprawling neo-Russian fantasy, I puzzled over the incongruity of a shopping center, the ultimate symbol of consumer capitalism, in the center of Red Square. To my then-uninitiated mind, Red Square signified communism, and communism meant small, dingy shops bereft of goods, not this fantastical monument to consumption. As I soon discovered, GUM had not always been GUM; the arcade dated to the late nineteenth century, not the Soviet era. At the time of its completion in 1893, this complex went by the rather prosaic name of the Upper Trading Rows (Verkhnye torgovye riady). In 1918, the Soviet government nationalized the Upper Rows and reopened it for business in 1921 as GUM. The spot occupied by the Upper Rows and then GUM has an even older pedigree. Prior to the completion of the Upper Rows arcade in 1893, four previous structures at that location had borne the same name, and the site had served as Moscow's central marketplace since the 1500s. As it turned out, the opulent arcade was as much a part of Russia's history as the Kremlin and St. Basil's, GUM being only the latest incarnation.

What interests me about the Upper Rows, GUM, and other landmarks of Russia's retail landscape is not so much their institutional history but the culture that grew up within and around them—the customs, practices, rituals, symbols, idioms, and discourses that over time became attached to the daily routines of buying and selling. In this book, I explore the creation, contestation, and re-creation of the retail sector across society and its exchange culture in the period from 1880 to 1930. This work demonstrates that retail and trade culture stood at the center of debates and also helped to structure the transformations taking place in the late imperial and early Soviet eras. This exploration of the retail sphere as a cultural system proceeds from the idea that the exchange of goods for money is not simply an economic transaction but a "form of socialization" and, further, that society as an "absolute entity" does not exist and then create exchange but that exchange itself creates the bonds of society.[1] Buying and selling were not just routine activities with little impact beyond the sales floor. These seemingly commonplace activities helped to constitute and signify state power, discourses of morality, ethnicity, civil rights and citizenship, the construction of social and gender identities, and codes of public behavior. As a public and symbolic site that engaged all sectors of society and represented their divergent agendas and aspirations, the retail sphere became deeply intertwined with the state, urban society, and the individual.

The argument developed throughout the chapters that follow is that stores, shops, retail arcades, and marketplaces were not simply sites where buying and selling took place but also agents and mediums of political transformation, social organization, and cultural training. Three major themes are important to note. The first involves issues of state power and the state's relationship to merchants and policies toward the retail sector and consumption. The retail sphere fit into the structures of tsarist and Soviet power, and although commercial and political interests sometimes conflicted, more often they supported and promoted each other. Moreover, both the tsarist and Soviet states adapted the tactics of the mass market to represent themselves, communicate with subjects and citizens, and further political goals. The second theme relates to the relationship of the retail trade to the city and the role of trade in creating urban mass society. Several lines of inquiry are pertinent here, particularly the contributions to the development of retail culture by diverse groups of individuals, including merchants, consumers, retail workers, activist journalists, trade union leaders, state and municipal officials, intellectuals, and artists. A related issue is the degree to which various individuals and groups identified with, appropriated, or rejected the culture of the urban retail marketplace and used its structures, symbols, practices, and language to define themselves, mediate their lives in the city, and assert their agendas. The third theme is cultural transformation. In the years immediately after 1905, in the 1920s, and then again in the 1930s, new campaigns promised a beautiful, democratic, efficient, and cultured society through both the reinvention of relationships among merchants, retail employees, and consumers and the reform of buying and selling. These campaigns sought ultimately to transform society by installing a system of modern mass retailing, promoting consumerist values, and reeducating subjects and citizens.

The research on mass retailing and consumption in Western Europe and the United States is vast, although until recently the topic has received relatively little attention from scholars of Russia and the Soviet Union.[2] Since the mid-1990s, several fine works have explored Russia's nascent urban commercial culture, which began to develop in the mid- to late nineteenth centuries. Historians have focused especially on the extent to which an urban mass culture challenged social hierarchies and established traditions and beliefs. Louise McReynolds argues that new urban leisure industries offered Russians an entirely "new set of cultural referents," which helped them construct new identities and construe their lives.[3] Sally West's work on the Russian advertising industry finds that advertisements promoted self-aspirational ideals and consumerist values. In contrast to McReynolds, however, West argues that Russians' engagement with consumption was complex, since the advertising industry's discourses of modernity and tradition both promoted and undermined accepted values. She concludes that in many respects a culture of consumption "happily" coexisted with Russian autocracy.[4] Christine Ruane has argued that the capitalist transformation of retailing was never quite accepted in Russia and was largely viewed as a "foreign import."[5] Still, her research on the history of Russia's fashion industry, which details its origins in the reign of Peter the Great and developments such as the establishment of a ready-to-wear industry and a fashion press, demonstrates the extent to which modern forms of urban culture, including those that promoted fashion, recreation, and consumption, had been created.[6] The varying conclusions reached by these scholars suggest that philosophies of and attitudes toward mass retailing and consumption were variegated and contested and that the rise of the leisure and advertising industries, mass manufacturing, the department store, fashion magazines, and other vehicles of an urban mass consumer society in themselves constituted important sociocultural conflicts.

The previously neglected roles of retailing and consumption in Soviet society have also begun to be illuminated. The excellent body of work produced thus far demonstrates that whether or not a Soviet version of a consumer society existed, consumption was a primary concern, even a preoccupation, of daily life. In his pioneering work on the so-called NEPmen of the 1920s, Alan Ball establishes that the Bolsheviks' policies toward private enterprise alternated between tolerance and repression. The quest to eliminate private industry and commerce, however, ultimately took precedence and, Ball argues, ended up mostly hurting consumers, who resorted to extralegal measures in order to obtain basic goods.[7] Several works on the 1930s show that as shortages, rationing, buying on the black market, and queuing became prevalent, the Soviet population obsessed over the process of consuming. Elena Osokina contends that Soviet society was actually organized around consumption, with its social structure denoted by a hierarchy of rationing, privileges, and entitlements.[8] Julie Hessler's work has shown that shortages were not just a characteristic of the Soviet economy but its primary organizing principle. Shortages, queuing, and other traits of the consumer goods sector induced in the state and consumers behavioral patterns that over time, she argues, coalesced into a uniquely Soviet "exchange culture."[9] Amy Randall has interpreted the Stalinist campaign for a cultured, socialist retail network as a campaign comparable to industrialization and collectivization, which mobilized and engaged the population, especially women, with its promotion of model stores and luxury goods.[10] Scholars of the Soviet period have also taken up topics of travel and tourism and the party's and state's renewed efforts to address issues of consumption during the cultural thaw of the Khrushchev era.[11]

One of the major outcomes of the research on commerce and consumption in the first decades of Soviet power has been the discovery of compelling continuities between the era of the New Economic Policy (NEP, 1921–1928, years during which state and private enterprises competed) and the Stalinist 1930s. Instead of interpreting the NEP as a "golden age" of limited private enterprise, relative economic abundance, and cultural experimentation and pluralism, several scholars have turned a spotlight on the NEP's darker aspects, highlighting state policies that limited choice, caused material deprivation, and led to high levels of anxiety and social conflict.[12] Further, as opposed to a conceptualization of the NEP years as a period when leaders tried to peacefully resolve the "complex social and cultural residues of prerevolutionary Russia, implicitly at odds with ongoing social and cultural goals of building a socialist of communist order," scholars like Osokina and Hessler contend that Stalin's political agenda of the late 1920s and early 1930s fulfilled NEP goals of centralization, social differentiation, and the liquidation of private enterprise, thus laying the foundations for a restructuring of the retail economy and society.[13] My approach draws on both models of the NEP. While the NEP era was experimental in, for example, instituting state-run model retail firms to sell popular goods to workers and peasants, establishing a formal procedure for consumer complaints, and attempting sociocultural transformation through education and persuasion, it was also a period filled with tension and conflict as previous retail practices and conventions clashed with the goals of building a worker-centered socialist retail sector staffed by efficient employees and patronized by conscientious citizens who consumed in purposeful ways.

I draw connections between the 1920s and 1930s but also bridge existing research on the late imperial period and the 1930s, thereby teasing out broader trends across the late tsarist era, the seven years of war, revolution, and civil war between 1914 and 1921, the NEP 1920s, and the turn to Stalinism at the end of the decade. To that end, I posit an expanded timeframe in Russia's pursuit of a modern, cultured retail sector, what contemporaries and scholars of the 1930s have labeled the "campaign for cultured trade."[14] While most historians identify the 1930s as a turning point in the invention of both a socialist retail trade and a distinctive Soviet exchange culture, the Stalinist-era campaign fits into a longer historical timeframe and broader sociocultural context. I treat the entire period between the 1880s and the 1930s, therefore, as one continuous period of socioeconomic and cultural transformation, exemplified by recurrent attempts to revolutionize the retail sector and its culture. The years between the 1880s and 1914 were pivotal in the development of Russia's commercial industries, especially with the advent of mass production, the advertising industry, and new retail formats such as arcades and the department store, which operated according to new philosophies of merchandising and retailing and promoted material acquisition, pleasure, leisure, and an urban lifestyle. Whereas some Russians perceived in mass-produced consumer goods and stylish stores frivolous temptations or threats to native traditions and Russian autonomy, others saw promise and hope. In the years following the revolution of 1905, a sector among the merchant elite launched a campaign to revolutionize the retail sector. In the 1920s, the Soviet state embarked on a similar campaign. Although both campaigns sought to remake the retail sphere by introducing Russians to modern methods of retailing and ideals of beauty, cleanliness, technology, and civil interaction, established customs, traditions, and behavioral patterns nonetheless persisted.

Although I do not examine in detail the retail reinvention campaign of the 1930s, primarily because several excellent works on the topic already exist, my decision to begin this study in the late imperial period and to end it in the late 1920s indicates that the structure the Soviet retail economy assumed and the characteristics of its culture owed as much to the nature of the pre-1917 retail sphere and the NEP-era attempt to revamp it as to the state-directed campaign for cultured trade of the 1930s. And even though I do not consider 1917 a logical starting or ending point, political events spurred changes in retailing and consumption. The 1905 revolution, which resulted in a constitutional monarchy, the establishment of a Russian-style parliament (the Duma), and increased freedom of the press, for example, galvanized some among the merchant communities of Moscow, Odessa, and St. Petersburg to launch a movement to recast the commercial world as the site of a rebirth of Russian society, with merchants as its leaders. The 1917 Bolshevik revolution also brought substantial changes to the retail economy and culture. The new socialist state continued and expanded the process of nationalizing and municipalizing large-scale manufacturing and commercial enterprises, which had been initiated under Nicholas II, and undertook its own campaign to remake the retail sector by creating a state network of model retail stores, rescripting the retail transaction, and promoting constructive attitudes toward consumption.

My exploration of Russia's retail culture also seeks to elucidate a series of developments that were more complex than can be captured in the term *consumer culture,* which has conventionally denoted a structural and mental shift in the West from societies preoccupied with the production of goods to societies focused on consumption. In this formulation, the emergence of a consumer culture entails the mass production of standardized goods for widespread purchase, the development of mass forms of retailing, as well as promotional techniques and attitudes that glorify the acquisition of consumer goods as the means to achieving happiness and establishing identity. A consumer culture also presupposes a society in which a large proportion of the population has both the income to consume goods above a subsistence level and the luxury of selecting one good over another.[15] Given the various large-scale and long-range developments encapsulated in this definition, the term *consumer culture* seems something of a misnomer in that it suggests that the transformations that took place primarily involved the consumer and consumption. Moreover, as indicated above, there are disagreements about the extent to which the socioeconomic developments in Russia and the Soviet Union amounted to a consumer culture, at least in the terms set out by historians of the West. Although I fully engage the historiography on consumer culture and situate the introduction of modern, mass forms of retailing and the promotion of consumerist values in Russia within a broader European context, showing that developments in the late imperial commercial sector roughly paralleled those elsewhere on the continent, I am less concerned about judging whether or not the culture attached to buying and selling in Russia conformed to a Western version of the phenomenon. Instead, I am more interested in investigating the culture that in fact existed and in explaining its constitutive role in Russian and Soviet society and its role in shaping the changes that took place during roughly fifty years of momentous change. The introduction of methods of modern mass retailing provoked a search for meaning in late-nineteenth- and early-twentieth-century Russia. Analyzing Russia's brand of commercial culture is less about asserting

Russia's comparability to the West or, for that matter, declaring the victory of modern retail venues and practices or the virtue of traditional, customary ones. As I argue, Russia's retail sector melded modern and customary structures and practices into a kaleidoscopic landscape that allowed traditions and innovations to coexist, albeit not without conflicts and tensions. The syncretism of the retail sphere and of urban public life in the Russian Empire and Soviet Union symbolized neither social chaos nor economic backwardness but a society grappling with its multiple and diverse, although not necessarily incompatible, sociocultural legacies.

The culture of Russia's urban retail sector arose not only from the consumption of material goods but also from the protocols of buying and selling, advertising, the building and renovation of stores, media coverage, intellectual debates, and political imperatives, among other things, and the process involved merchants, retail employees, activist journalists, and state, municipal, and trade union officials, as well as consumers. Therefore, I employ terms like *retail culture, exchange culture, culture of the retail marketplace,* or even *commercial culture* more often than *consumer culture.*[16] In preferring these terms, I am trying to designate a culture that is broader in scope, one that captures the wide-ranging political, social, and cultural functions of the activities surrounding the core ones of buying, selling, and consuming and one that indicates the participation of multiple sectors of society. As the various chapters illustrate, commercial culture was not all about consumption or the consumer. The context within which consumers consumed incorporated a range of diverse influences and various relationships. Consumption was only the end point in a series of interrelated acts that might begin with a consumer becoming aware of a store or product, perhaps through childhood experiences or from a newspaper advertisement, and then entering a shop to inquire about the price of a tin of Chinese tea or being coerced into a neighborhood shop to have a look at the wares on display and venturing an opening bid in a haggling match for a pair of boots. The ways in which individuals made meaning from these various influences and routine public transactions by constructing identities, forming relationships with other city dwellers, merchants, and political authorities, imagining their role in the city and society at large, and carrying out political change through the prism of daily encounters are, of course, enormous, complicated issues. I hope, however, to begin to illuminate them in this book.

This conceptualization of commercial culture is not intended to deny the significance of the consumer or to de-center consumption. Mass production and retailing were driven by increasing consumer demand, and the consumer was an active participant in the creation of Russia's exchange culture. Yet consumers and acts of consumption were embedded within a society whose members, in various productive, promotional, intellectual, and symbolic capacities, contributed to the elaboration of a culture organized around the key activities of buying and selling. Merchants of the late imperial period presented themselves, their businesses, and merchandise in ways that reflected their personal beliefs, social status and aspirations, and business philosophies and that had been developed in association with the state and other merchants and that were consonant with their religious convictions. Journalists and urban chroniclers interpreted changes in the retail sphere for a reading public, pondering the implications of new retail structures, policies, and business tactics, alongside established, traditional ones, and constructing visions of urban life and Russian society based on their interpretations. Through their daily rounds of shopping, consumers formed identities, such as city dweller, subject, or citizen, immersed themselves in the spectacle of urban life, and, in the Soviet period, lodged complaints against the new regime. The tsarist state acted as both regulator and patron. The Soviet state became primary merchant in the 1920s, infusing the retail sphere with concepts of political struggle and, through its priorities and policies, introducing shortages and rationing. The press promoted the firms and agendas of retailers who advertised in their newspapers. Thus, the activities leading up to, attached to, and following the exchange of goods for money engaged individuals at all levels of society. Moreover, no one group dominated the development of such activities or the meanings assigned to them.

This broadly inclusive designation of an urban retail culture engages reconceptualizations of the relationship between state and society, or the concept of civil society.[17] Some of the initial research on Russia's civil society focused on merchants' social status and the extent to which they developed a middle-class consciousness or contributed to the formation of civil society in late imperial Russia.[18] Scholars who pursued this line of inquiry ultimately centered on the issue of the middle-class failure to mobilize politically in 1917. They acknowledged changes within the merchantry, but most came to the conclusion that late imperial civil society was small and fractured and, as a result, never gave rise to a middle class capable of defining and defending its political interests. A couple of recent works, including the book *Merchant Moscow*, which explores Moscow's last prerevolutionary generation of elite merchants, continues this line of interpretation. Although the majority of its essays paint portraits of a self-assured, energetic merchant elite whose political philosophies, commercial architecture, and modern dress signaled merchants' position on the cusp of modernity, the introductory essay casts doubt on the depth of their ideas and activities, arguing that the "deeply rooted" impediments of an autocratic state and static social structure ultimately inhibited the development of a "modern entrepreneurial bourgeoisie."[19]

However, other scholars have challenged the idea that civil society and entrepreneurship did not develop in imperial Russia because of the authoritarian nature of the tsarist state. As Joseph Bradley and others have pointed out, European rulers "enabled, if not purposefully created, civil society," and merchants and other professional groups existed in a relatively harmonious, rather than contentious, relationship with the state.[20] Historians of mass culture argue that Russia's middle classes were not, in fact, "missing" but, for instance, played a significant role in the emergence of the urban mass media and leisure and entertainment industries.[21] Others whose research focuses on commerce and merchants conclude that the authoritative role played by the Russian state in public and commercial affairs does not necessarily mean that its relationship with civil society or merchants was an exclusively adversarial one. The tsarist state approved the creation of business firms and subsequently regulated their activities; however, the state also encouraged commerce and rewarded merchants for excellence and innovation.[22]

The evidence presented in this book supports this more complicated view of the relationship between the state and professional groups. Successful, socially prominent merchants who owned large-scale retail businesses in the late imperial period more often operated in concert, rather than in opposition to, the state, at least until 1905, and to a large extent even thereafter, cooperating, for example, to carry out the rebuilding of the Upper Rows and symbolically melding their business firms with the imagery and rituals of state power. At the same time, their methods of modern retailing challenged established conventions by providing spaces where individuals could carve out identities and roles that subverted traditional social and gender hierarchies. Their advertisements cut across socioeconomic, gender, and ethnic strata in an idiom that conveyed messages of acquisition, elegance, and pleasure. Finally, reform-minded merchants who were influential in municipal politics and associational life began to showcase their aspirations to political, social, and cultural leadership. Some among them undertook agendas of commercial reform that challenged established authorities and structures, even as they were embedded within a limited political system and "vocabulary of social description" that they themselves helped to articulate.[23] Clearly, merchants and the retail sphere stood in a complex relationship to state power and to other social groups.

The relationship between state power and professional groups like merchants became even more complex in the 1920s, when the state established its own model retail stores to compete in the marketplace against private merchants. Private retailers continued to serve consumers, by all accounts much more effectively than state retail enterprises, but merchants lost the autonomy they had previously had to organize public life. State model retailers instead took the lead in revolutionizing the retail sphere, applying similar ideals of beauty, justice, technology, and civil interaction that the prerevolutionary commercial trade press had advocated and that the merchant elite's retail firms had promoted, although they introduced the class struggle into the marketplace and privileged the retail worker. The state also institutionalized a formal complaint process, which gave consumers the opportunity to vent their frustration with the state's management of the economy. The establishment of a complaint process allowed state retail firms to function as public places where citizens could express an opinion and, in short, exercise a limited kind of citizenship. Thus, even as state retailers carried out the regime's agenda of transforming the retail marketplace by squeezing out private retailers and creating a socialist retail economy, they provided a forum in which citizens could expose the state's dysfunction and unfulfilled promises.

Just as political regimes influenced developments in the retail sector, the methods of modern commerce influenced the state's exercise of power. The tsarist and Soviet states both adopted the methods of mass retailing, marketing, and merchandising to present themselves to and communicate with a public that was becoming more accustomed to buying material goods in order to express their affections and loyalties, thus developing a sort of urban spectatorship. In the last decade or so of the empire, the tsarist regime had begun to commodify its symbols and imagery through the sale of common household goods emblazoned with pictures of the court and royal family and through the propaganda poster, a medium that, in Russia and in other countries, became a government tool to rally support during World War I.[24] The state expanded its use of commercial techniques in the Soviet period as the Bolsheviks embarked on a full-scale campaign to sell socialism to the public. Recognizing the potential in modern marketing and retailing strategies to wage a struggle against capitalism, state retail firms employed artists to create agitational advertisements that recommended shopping at GUM at the same time they harangued consumers about shopping at private stores. Product packages and wrappers featuring socialist slogans and symbols of the new regime praised the accomplishments of the Red Army and denigrated capitalism. As the Bolsheviks recognized, the mediums and idioms of modern commerce that were so effective at selling chocolate, cigarettes, tea, and soap could also be used to sell politics.

The introduction of mass marketing and retailing also gave rise to new conceptualizations of femininity and masculinity. In European countries throughout this period, urbanization and the commercialization of culture and leisure made women increasingly visible on city streets.[25] New kinds of retail venues brought with them new cultural referents and values and gave rise to reconceptualizations of masculinity and femininity. Although consumption has been conventionally conceived of as uniquely connected to constructs of femininity, as Rita Felski notes, competing myths of modernity emphasized both masculine and feminine qualities, although masculinity was most frequently associated with rationalization and productivity and femininity, with sensuality and passive hedonism.[26] Most of the literature on gender and consumption has replicated the focus on discourses that connected women in the cultural imagination to the department store and fashion. Much less attention has been devoted to constructions of masculinity based on men's relationship to retailing and consumption.[27] When the male consumer appears in the historical literature, he often distinguishes himself through inconspicuous purchases designed to display his sobriety, restraint, and political virtue or through individuated consuming activities.[28] The exploration of such icons of restraint and modes of purposeful or extraordinary consumption has permitted scholars to incorporate masculinity into interpretations of the emergent world of urban mass consumption, although in my mind they have limited understanding of the ways in which men actually consumed and have thus reinforced cultural stereotypes. What has been largely missing is the identification of masculine consuming identities that situate men within the daily context of buying and selling and that portray their purchasing habits as an aspect of their routine activities and nonextraordinary identities.

This book furthers the conceptualization of the male consumer, balancing constructed images with practice. The male consumer appears in the pre-1917 period in the guise of the haggler and, in the ads of state model retailers, as the novice peasant male consumer, the primary beneficiary of the new Soviet retail sector.[29] In practice, men, as well as women, struggled to supply themselves with basic goods during the civil war and lodged complaints against the state's model retailers in the 1920s. These findings suggest that men and constructions of masculinity were as deeply embedded in the processes of buying, selling, and consumption as were women and constructions of femininity, and such findings also accord with the tendency of late imperial period advertisers to pitch ads to men as frequently, if not even more often, than they did to women.[30] Perhaps men's limited scope for autonomous, independent political action in Russia partially explains the creation of more numerous representations of masculine consumption. In the Soviet era, the politicization of retailing and consumption may also have made these activities seem appropriately masculine arenas of action. However, I doubt the Russian case was extraordinary.

Finally, this book is also about the relationship of the retail trade to the city, particularly Moscow, and to urban culture. Certain centrally located retail venues, including the Upper Trading Rows, the Muir & Mirrielees department store, Eliseev Brothers, Odessa's Passazh and Petrokokino Brothers, as well as

GUM, Mostorg, and department store and other retailers, were landmarks on the urban landscape. I trace through 1917 the ways in which these retailers operated and the ways in which Russians perceived them and interacted in them. These and several other retail sites provide focal points not only because their rich, recorded histories transcend 1917 but also because they had a literally towering presence in the city. Many served as cultural touchstones, with their appearance, products, business strategies, and employees and with Russians' memories of them being constitutive of self, society, and history. These retail venues also evoked much social commentary and private rumination. Urbanites mediated the city in part through their relationship to the merchants and retail employees they encountered and the routines they performed in stores and shops. For some Russians, becoming an urbanite seems to have been just as important as, if not more important than, thinking of themselves as a subject of the Russian Empire. In the Soviet period, the emphasis on becoming an urbanite may have been superseded by the struggle to understand what it meant to be a Soviet citizen, although new arrivals to the city no doubt continued to try to navigate the urban landscape by learning how to shop in downtown stores and markets. Moreover, Moscow was at the center of efforts to construct a socialist retail network, and Soviet leaders privileged urban centers, particularly Moscow, over other cities and the provinces.

Although the primary focus in this book is Moscow, it does include some comparisons to Odessa, as a way of testing the power of mass retailing to absorb, accommodate, and subsume ethnic and religious differences. Moscow's population was largely Russian Orthodox, and although foreign merchants were conspicuous, Russians dominated every sector of commerce, a fact that reflected that city's demographics. By contrast, Odessa, a Ukrainian city located at the margins of the Russian Empire on the Black Sea, prided itself on its ethnic diversity and its independent, commercial spirit. Odessa's ethnic profile may have provided a more cosmopolitan outlook and corps of activist commercial editors more willing to directly challenge traditional conceptions of the merchant, consumer, and the retail marketplace and, by extension, political authority. However, even though merchants in the two cities conceived of themselves and the role their city played in the empire differently, the culture of the marketplace may to some extent have subsumed ethnic and religious differences beneath a façade of beauty, material goods, technology, and middle-class culture. This idea is merely a suggestion, however. The degree to which Odessa's merchant classes, and those in other regions, created an alternative public culture or altered the dominant one merits further exploration. Roshanna Sylvester, for example, argues that in Odessa a "secularized Jewish culture" became dominant and that Odessa's own "brand of modernity" was a function of the "reciprocal relationship" between Russians and Jews of the middle classes.[31] Certainly, the important work being conducted on empire could help to illuminate the interplay between Russian Orthodox culture and the variations on urban commercial culture that ethnic and religious minorities provided.

Russia's Retail Landscape, 1860s–1890s

Upon his return to Moscow in 1864, Nikolai V. Davydov, a lawyer and legal scholar, recalled the remarkable changes that had taken place in the city's commercial landscape during his five-year absence: "Moscow was unrecognizable; so much had its appearance changed. It had taken on an almost European appearance. A drastic change had happened. Everything felt new. New streets had sprung up. The new street lighting was magnificent. Streets were livelier. The *magaziny* on Tverskaia and Kuznetskii Most presented the most elegant appearance, with splendid shop windows, tempting displays, and understated shop signs."[1] Davydov linked changes in the city's appearance, brought on in part by the emergence of new kinds of retail stores, to a shift in attitudes, emotions, and behaviors. As he perceived it, artful displays of desirable goods, handsome façades, and graceful shop signs created an air of European sophistication that animated the population and the city itself. He realized, however, that the physical makeover of the fashionable business district did not mean that the city's entire commercial landscape or its retail culture had been transformed. His description of other business quarters affirmed that traditional store structures and customary ways of buying and selling persisted throughout much of the city: "The majority of establishments and small shops on other streets have retained their ancient signs for the illiterate, frequently amusing inscriptions or pictures that crudely represent the line of business. . . . Most of these are crude drawings, clumsy and unattractive."[2] Davydov also noted the appearance of a "giant and beautiful" building on Red Square, the Upper Trading Rows, but seemed disappointed that a nearby "Asiatic-type" bazaar marred its magnificence. In those areas untouched by innovation, he perceived primitivism, ugliness, and the coarseness of Russian life.

Davydov's differentiation between beautiful new emporia and small, modest shops captured the eclectic nature of Russia's retail marketplace, a realm where *lavki* (small shops) and open-air markets stood in proximity to elegant arcades and *magaziny* (from the French word for stylish stores, *magasins*). The eclecticism of the retail marketplace signaled Russia's position as a country in transition from a rural, agricultural, peasant-based economy to an industrialized and commercialized one centered in burgeoning cities. Indeed, the innovations reshaping the retail sphere constituted enormous, tangible changes, which themselves provoked tensions and conflicts, as well as optimistic hopes. As a rising merchant elite built vast, grand stores that operated according to contemporary methods of retailing, the position and methods of small shopkeepers and vendors, who conducted business according to customary practices, were called into question. Observant spectators such as Davydov struggled to absorb the physical changes taking place around them and reconcile these new elements into a coherent vision of urban life. As his narration suggests, the city juxtaposed tradition and innovation, producing a landscape of diversity, contrasts, and spectacular sights.

Between the 1860s and the beginning of the twentieth century, the retail sector expanded and diversified to such an extent that contemporaries meditated and reflected on the impact of the changes. Customary and modern modes of retailing existed alongside each other and even influenced each other, although not always without conflict. Images of merchants that circulated in late imperial Russia reveal a change in the nature of public critiques developed by a new urban mass media. Even as Russia's retail sphere was growing and becoming more diverse, the images of retail trade and of the merchant remained largely negative. At the turn of the century, then, Russia's retail marketplace lay at the heart of conflicts in society, revealing the stigma of decades of resentment toward merchants and commerce, even while technological innovation and new practices emerged and retailers appealed to a larger section of the population with messages of leisure, pleasure, and acquisition.

Russia's Customary and Modern Retail Systems

The retail marketplace or retail sphere refers to the collection of public spaces where merchants and consumers transacted sales of manufactured goods; it also connotes a cultural system through which merchants, consumers, the press, and members of educated society developed philosophies, idioms, practices, customs, rituals, and prescribed codes of behaviors that structured exchange transactions and social relationships. Of course, the retail sphere did not exist in isolation from the rest of society. Russia's political, economic, social, and cultural milieu influenced its shape, but the retail sphere nevertheless had its own internally logical and self-perpetuating culture. At the same time, the retail sector did not constitute a unified, monolithic entity. Practices and prescribed behaviors varied widely among a diverse group of retailers ranging from large department stores, arcades, and magazins to small shops, markets, and street vendors.

Russian retailing exhibited a path of development roughly similar to that of many countries in western parts of Europe, even though expansion occurred slightly later. Until the mid- to late nineteenth century, there were very few retail venues at all across Europe. Most people, particularly the majority living in rural areas, produced many of the goods they needed and made trips to towns to buy other goods at fairs and weekly markets; they also occasionally bought items from itinerant peddlers. Small retail shops were more common in urban centers. In the late eighteenth century in many European cities, including Paris and London, as well as Moscow, shops appeared that were large and tastefully appointed and that catered to wealthy urban dwellers. The owners of these luxury boutiques pioneered new sales and merchandising methods, ushering in what historians refer to as the "consumer revolution."[3] Urban centers thus offered a larger variety of shopping venues, among them stationary retailers, including shops, luxury boutiques, booths, and stalls, and weekly and seasonal markets. Episodic vending continued to prevail in rural areas well into the mid-nineteenth century, although many villages, including those in Russia, had by that time a few small, permanent retail shops.[4] By the 1850s, in major cities in western parts of Europe and also in the United States, a phenomenon called "consumerism" had emerged, together with a mass-retailing apparatus.[5] After Russia's defeat in the Crimean War and the emancipation of the serfs in 1861, but especially in the 1880s and 1890s, as industrialization got under way, Russia's industrial and commercial sectors began to develop rapidly.[6] The innovations in retailing, which had altered the ways that goods were displayed, bought, and sold in western Europe and the United States and had already altered the appearance of Russia's most fashionable shopping quarters, began to more thoroughly transform central retail districts in St. Petersburg, Moscow, Odessa, and other cities.

By the turn of the century, two distinct retail models, broadly defined as customary and modern and typified by the *lavka* and the *magazin,* respectively, coexisted in Russia. The terms *customary* and *modern* are meant to distinguish between existent and emergent philosophies of retailing and to signify two different clusters of physical attributes, which include size, exterior and interior appearance, operational policies, sales and merchandising techniques, and models of the merchant-customer relationship, all of which defined a retail space and created (consciously or not) a particular regimen and aesthetic. In using these terms, I intend no value judgments about superiority and inferiority. The fact remains, however, that in the late nineteenth and early twentieth centuries, one retail model was already in place and rooted in long-established physical structures, customs, and business practices; the other was relatively new and incorporated contemporary business and merchandising philosophies, new technologies, and mass communications. Further, Russians perceived differences between the lavka and magazin and attached meanings and value judgments to those differences. It is important to keep in mind, though, that while the terms signify discrete and important differences, there were not always clear, precise divisions between customary and modern retailers, and it was not unusual for a lavka or magazin to exhibit features of both.

Dating to at least medieval times, the lavka represented the quintessential Russian retail shop, and lavka owners, along with other small-scale operators, constituted the overwhelming majority of individuals engaged in the retail trade in Russia.[7] Lavka owners ranged from petty traders who worked from modest shopfronts to proprietors of spacious premises who cultivated extensive business contacts. Most lavkas, however, generally displayed some standard physical features and observed common business practices. Typically a small, unheated shop that was open at one end to the street, a lavka allowed customers to enter, although there was little maneuvering room inside and few comforts or amenities. Lavkas stood either as individual units in neighborhoods and on city streets or connected in a series of rows organized according to products sold. In the city's center, lavkas usually carried a fairly limited and specialized inventory, especially in textiles, apparel, and food, or in leather goods, tobacco, tea, sugar, icons, and other relatively inexpensive basic goods, but it was not unheard of for a tobacco lavka, for example, to also sell harmonicas and guitars. On the outskirts, lavkas served as general stores and stocked a wider assortment of goods. Proprietors usually displayed their merchandise simply, if sometimes haphazardly, and seldom devised elaborate displays. Most did not place advertisements in newspapers or other mass media. Instead, they attracted customers by "calling" (zazyvat') to passersby, pressing them to enter their shops, and then haggling with them to arrive at a price. Traditionally, owners had recruited shop clerks as young boys, offering them a place to live in their homes or shops and training them as apprentices. By the late nineteenth century, however, the apprentice system had begun to break down, and many shop clerks were no longer bound to their masters by the paternalistic ties of apprenticeship.[8]

The open-air market represented another long-established retail space where vendors operated from relatively simple premises and according to customary practices. Set up in large, open spaces, markets attracted peasants from the surrounding areas, who came to sell their produce and handcrafted items, as well as urban traders, who retailed food and drink, clothing, and other everyday wares. These sellers conducted business from booths, stalls, and open stands or carts or roamed the grounds carrying their wares or displaying them on trays. Although the relative importance of markets had declined by the beginning of the twentieth century, they continued to meet the basic needs of many urban dwellers. In 1840, more than forty open-air markets, accounting for 12.5 percent of retail sales, functioned in Moscow. More than thirty years later, there were at least that many turning approximately the same volume.[9]

Some markets were large and extensive in their offerings, others small and specialized, but whatever their characteristics, they were important sites of exchange and social interaction in Russia. Permanent markets met regularly on specified days of the week, structuring people's weekly routines. Sunday trade at Smolensk Market had been carried on since the late eighteenth century. The market on Trubnaia Square also operated on Sundays. Special occasion markets appeared seasonally and included, for example, Moscow's Mushroom Market, which was held during the first week of Lent and stretched from the walls of the Kremlin to the Moscow River, and the Palm Sunday Bazaar, held on Red Square the week prior to Easter. Both markets attracted locals and residents from surrounding areas, who flocked to the stalls to purchase fresh produce and holiday items and to stroll the grounds eating and drinking, riding the swings and carousel, or watching a street performance. Over time, some markets even achieved local notoriety and legendary status. Moscow's Sukharev Market had a reputation as a place where city dwellers could go for bargains on secondhand clothing or to locate items that had been stolen. Sukharev had been established after the War of 1812, when the governor-general of Moscow published an order decreeing that any item, no matter its origin, was the inalienable property of the person who possessed it at the present. The governor-general authorized those who possessed such property to sell it, but they could do so only once a week, on Sundays opposite the Sukharev Tower. From that time on, the market became associated with crime and theft, although that apparently did not stop crowds of people from descending on it each Sunday.[10] Other cities had a similar collection of markets. In 1890, thirty large and small markets operated in Odessa, among them the Greek Market, Novyi Bazaar, and the Staryi Bazaar, as well as Privoz (meaning "carted here"), the largest and busiest, which specialized in food products. Odessa's flea market, Tolkuchnyi (from the verb *tolknut'*, meaning to shove or knock about), was widely renowned as a colorful place where one might encounter all kinds of people—Greeks, Tatars, Germans, Jews, Russians—as well as swindlers, the riffraff of the city, and flaneurs. Like Sukharev, Tolkuchnyi had earned a reputation as the place to go to reclaim stolen items.[11]

Street vending represented another well-established mode of retailing. Vendors, the majority of them male and of peasant origin, could be found at busy street corners and squares or at various markets hawking food, drink, books, clothing, ribbons, lace, tobacco, toys, balloons, and other popular, inexpensive items, either from trays or their hands. Others offered services such as shoe repair or knife sharpening. Vendors tended to gather in commercial districts at particular spots; for example, at the Pie Exchange, a group of vendors hawking *pirozhki* (savory pies) congregated near the front entrance to the Upper Trading Rows on Red Square. Vendors also walked the streets of Moscow's Zaryad'ye (meaning "beyond the Rows"), a quarter of the city where petty tradesmen and craftsmen, many of them Jews, lived and worked. Estimates of the number of street vendors in prerevolutionary Moscow vary from forty-four hundred to six thousand, although it is possible that the number was higher since many vendors worked without licenses.[12] Municipal authorities were concerned about the number and location of free-standing vendors and repeatedly attempted to regulate their number and fix certain places for public vending. These repeated attempts suggest that they were not entirely successful in their efforts.

Larger retail establishments that required more working capital and assumed a more formal appearance and complex organizational structure, including the magazin, arcade, and department store, first appeared in Europe and Russia in the late eighteenth century. Various economic, technological, and social processes conspired to facilitate their emergence, including innovations in the mass production of textiles, clothing, and other consumer goods, the breakdown of guild restrictions, and real rises in the standard of living of the middle and working classes, especially after 1850, as well as urbanization, improvements in public transport, and the rise of the advertising industry and new marketing techniques.[13] The first *magasins* reportedly opened in Paris in the decades following the French Revolution and bore such names as La Petit Matelot, Au Grand Mogol, and Au Pavillion d'Or. These new kinds of retail venues exhibited physical characteristics, operating policies, and sales and merchandising strategies that distinguished them from shops and are generally considered the hallmarks of modern retailing. Magasins were much larger than shops. Many occupied entire permanent buildings rather than shop space within a building. They further differed from shops in their large storefront windows with elaborate displays of merchandise, their luxurious interiors, mirrors, spacious counters, ample selection of goods, and policies of fixed pricing, cash payment, and polite, noncoercive service.[14]

The magazin debuted in Russia at roughly the same time, during the reign of Catherine the Great. The first proprietors were German and French merchants, who set up elegant stores to sell fashion goods and toiletries in Belyi Gorod and Kuznetskii Most, the latter a street in Moscow's central business district that thereafter became known as the city's au courant shopping quarter. A few Jewish merchants also opened stores on the same street, although evictions removed them not long afterward.[15] The magazin also appeared in other Russian cities at about the same time, lining Nevskii Prospekt in St. Petersburg and DeRibas, Rishel'ev, Torgovaia, and Aleksandrovskii streets in Odessa.[16] Most specialized in high-quality, high-priced fashion goods, including textiles, ready-to-wear apparel, dry goods, and jewelry, or in furnishings, china, and crystal; others focused on specialty food products, such as tea, sugar, and coffee, as their primary business. The magazins cultivated a reserved, discreet atmosphere by instituting policies that encouraged passersby to enter the store and browse without any pressure or obligation to buy. Most accepted only cash as payment and adhered to a prix fixe policy meant to assure shoppers that they would not have to bargain with a clerk to settle on a price and also that the price paid was true. Sales clerks, trained to speak in courteous and deferential tones, stood by attentively, ready to show customers goods, which were displayed to their best advantage in glass cases, and to assist them in making a selection. The magazins also advised the public of their offerings and policies through signs posted in front windows and advertisements in newspapers and journals. The magazin became more prevalent in Russia in the post-emancipation period, especially during the 1870s and 1880s, when prominent and successful Russian merchants opened their own luxurious magazins on Kuznetskii Most alongside German, French, and other foreign merchants' establishments. V. Perlov & Sons Tea Company, furriers Pavel Sorokoumovskii & Sons, and Abrikosov & Sons confectioners were among the first Russian firms to establish stores there. Despite the presence of these and other well-known Russian businesses, however, the magazin continued to be regarded as a foreign import and Kuznetskii Most, a foreign domain.[17] Approximately 10 percent of the founders of corporations in the Russian Empire in the century prior to 1914 were foreign citizens. Foreign citizens who operated retail businesses made up a portion of that figure. It was not the sheer numbers of foreign merchants in Moscow that created this impression that the new retailers were foreign but simply their concentration in the city's new, fashionable districts.

The retail arcade or *passage* also appeared in several European cities in the late eighteenth and early nineteenth centuries, when technical innovations made their construction possible. Arcade design and construction typically included an iron frame and a pitched glass roof. Inside, stores of various kinds, all of which displayed a uniform storefront, lined long, elegant corridors. By the end of the nineteenth century, there were new arcades throughout the world, including Australia, South America, and South Africa, as well as in western and eastern Europe. Paris had more than thirty arcades, most built in the years after 1822. Russia's first *passazh,* the Gostinyi Dvor in St. Petersburg, opened in 1785, at roughly the same time that arcades first appeared in western Europe; most of Russia's arcades, however, were built after the 1840s. By 1914, Moscow boasted at least ten arcades, including the Upper Trading Rows on Red Square and the Petrov, Popov, Golitsyn, Golofteev, Postnikov, and Solodovnikov arcades. Arcades in Russia varied in size and appearance. The Golitsyn Passazh, completed in 1841 and designed by Mikhail Bykovskii, a pioneer of the Russian arcade, was a neoclassical- and Renaissance-inspired structure with space for twenty-four shops. St. Petersburg's passazh on Nevskii Prospekt, completed in 1848, was a neo-Renaissance style building that accommodated sixty stores. The Passazh in Odessa, a four-story building completed in 1899, exhibited neoclassical motifs and housed a hotel as well as commercial enterprises and offices.[18]

The department store represented the culmination of trends in the retail industry, which, along with the commercialization of leisure and culture and the appearance of restaurants, music and concert halls, sports arenas, and museums, transformed downtown districts into commercial landscapes where men and women sought entertainment and pleasure.[19] It is difficult to pinpoint precise dates for the establishment of some of the first department stores because many originated as haberdasheries and drapers' shops and gradually expanded, but some of the first generally recognized department stores were established in western Europe and the United States between 1850 and 1890. Examples include the Bon Marché, Louvre, and Le Printemps in Paris, Whiteley's in London, and R. H. Macy, Marshall Field & Company, and John Wanamaker in the United States. Hermann Tietz, Wertheim, and Kaufhaus des Westens were founded in Germany in the late nineteenth and early twentieth centuries. Distinguished by their enormous size and extraordinary variety of goods for sale, department stores built on principles employed by magazins, inaugurating polices such as *entrée libre* (freedom to browse without a requirement to buy), return and exchange privileges, and sales commissions. They also operated on principles of mass retailing such as volume sales, lower profit margins on items, and rapid turnover of merchandise. They should not, however, be confused with discount outlets. Proprietors took great care to cultivate an image of fashion leadership, beauty, and cultural refinement, erecting fantastically opulent buildings with tasteful, inviting interiors that often included museum-quality works of art. Colorful cascades of silks and calicos or artfully staged scenarios of home life or travel, replete with the essential consumer accessories, filled their giant plate-glass display windows. Inside, large assortments of ready-to-wear apparel, fashion accessories, home furnishings, and other goods awaited the inspection of customers. This new breed of retailer aimed not only to impress customers with its imposing size, beauty, and abundant stocks but also to make shopping pleasant and more convenient, a new kind of urban adventure. Information desks helped customers navigate their way through the store and provided information on the city, while home delivery services offered to ease the burdens of weary shoppers. Reading and writing rooms, lavatories, and telephones mimicked the comforts of home. Many department stores also consciously rejected the apprentice system, which had become synonymous with tyranny and abuse, and tried to show concern for their employees' well-being through paternalistic policies and benefits such as free lunches, housing, and a credit union. Finally, department stores relied on various media, including newspaper advertising, publicity, and in-store promotional events, to attract the public's attention and to create a stir of importance and newsworthiness around their businesses.[20]

With the opening of Muir & Mirrielees on Theatre Square in Moscow in 1885, the department store made its official debut in Russia. Like some of the department stores in France, the United States, and elsewhere, Muir & Mirrielees began as a haberdashery and millinery shop. Established in 1847 by British citizen Archibald Merrilees, the store expanded over the next few decades, and, by 1914, it operated forty-three departments, as well as a restaurant, and employed more than a thousand workers.[21] Billing itself as "The Leading Department Store in Russia" (Velichaishii v Rossii Universal'nyi Magazin), the store was unrivaled within the Russian Empire in size, scope of operations, merchandise selection, and amenities. Its exceptional status brought it fame, especially after it was rebuilt following a fire in 1908. Architect Roman Klein was behind the three-story style moderne and English gothic edifice.[22] Russians visited Muir & Mirrielees not only to browse and shop but also to eat lunch, take a ride on one of the two elevators, and luxuriate in the marvelous interior, which featured a sweeping double staircase and sculpted ceilings. Customers could also receive assistance from the store's bureau for information on Moscow and currency exchange and find comfort in the snack bar, reading room, lavatories, and clinic, which had a female medical attendant. Like other department stores, Muir & Mirrielees catered to middling and upper-middle-class urban consumers, although its marketing strategies suggest that management aimed to communicate the firm's name to a wider audience and to extend the firm's influence to the farthest reaches of Russia. Mailings of fashion catalogs circulated throughout the Russian Empire and carried offers to send samples of fabrics to interested customers and to deliver purchases of 25 rubles or more free of charge to European Russia and COD purchases anywhere.[23] These strategies helped to draw crowds of visitors, many no doubt just to look, and attracted buyers from places far away from Moscow. In 1899, the firm reported that ten thousand people visited the store daily and that every year it mailed approximately sixty thousand parcels to out-of-town customers.[24] Net profits rose steadily. In the last five years of its operation, net profits increased from 936,452 rubles (1912–13) to 2,334,957 rubles (1916–17).[25]

Although Muir & Mirrielees was the only true department store in Russia, several larger specialty stores exemplified a similar model of retailing and strived to achieve far-flung economic influence and cultural stewardship. The Department Store of the Moscow Guards Society, which opened in Moscow in 1913, Kunst & Al'bers, which was a large retail enterprise based in Vladivostok that operated branches throughout eastern Asia and in other cities of the empire, and Odessa's Petrokokino Brothers, William Wagner's English magazin, and Bellino-Fenderikh, large specialty stores of "foreign merchandise," also aimed for name recognition and excellent service. Petrokokino's boasted a palatial neoclassical façade, a luxurious interior graced by a fountain on the main floor and double staircases, twenty departments selling a choice selection of luxury goods, a custom logo, frequent advertisements, promotional activities, and general and specialized catalogs. The store did a brisk business. By 1914, the firm reported sales of one million rubles a year.[26]

Although large, profitable, and fashionable stores such as Muir & Mirrielees and Petrokokino Brothers garnered a great deal of attention, the lavka and magazin still dominated Russia's retail sector, together accounting for nearly 90 percent of all estimated sales volume on the eve of World War I.[27] Moreover, lavkas outnumbered magazins, even in urban areas. In St. Petersburg's *guberniia*, or administrative district, where in some places magazins accounted for as much as 27 percent of retail establishments, lavkas still constituted 59 percent of all retail enterprises.[28] However total per unit sales of magazins exceeded that of lavkas throughout this period. Even though the number of lavkas rose at a faster rate than the number of magazins, growth did not translate into a proportional share of sales. Overall, lavkas accounted for about 83 percent of all retail enterprises and 39 percent of total retail volume. By contrast, magazins, which accounted for between 13 and 15 percent of all retail outlets, took in 47 percent of all retail sales.[29]

As much as the lavka and the magazin represented two distinct retail models, in practice they were not completely diametrically opposed. In fact, they shared many traits, and each influenced the other. Some lavka owners engaged in decidedly modern practices. Several proprietors who operated lavkas in the Upper Trading Rows, for example, printed business cards with their names and the names of their shops, often in both Russian and French.[30] Owners of large lavkas sometimes advertised in newspapers. And if we are to believe one source, lavka owners pioneered the concept of clearance sales, which became popular events at fashionable stores in the late nineteenth century.[31] Likewise, proprietors of magazins did not always follow the cardinal tenets of modern retailing. Many, for instance, failed to adhere to their publicized policy of fixed prices. Despite mutual influences, however, physical and philosophical differences between the lavka and the magazin were apparent to contemporaries, who perceived in their distinctive appearances, merchandising and sales strategies, and operational policies intrinsic merits or flaws.

The Image of the Merchant and Retail Trade in Russia

Although the retail sphere was undergoing major and perceptible change, popular negative images of the merchant and retail trade remained largely unchanged. In fact, new mass media circulated negative representations of merchants and the retail sphere among a wider urban audience. Traditionally, merchants and the retail trade had inspired little admiration in Russian society. The proverb, "If you don't cheat [someone], you won't sell [anything]" (ne naduesh'—ne prodash') captured the long-standing assumption that the kupets (merchant or trader) was a swindler and the retail trade, a degraded, parasitic profession.[32] In contemporary parlance, the word kupets referred to an old-school, lower-class male merchant, probably not too far removed from his peasant origins, who kept a lavka and transacted sales by haranguing shoppers and engaging them in haggling matches. The term kupets also carried a significant amount of cultural baggage, signifying dishonesty and a willingness, even an eagerness, to cheat customers. Stereotypes of the merchant as a dishonest trickster and pretentious philistine abounded in many societies in Europe in which Christian values prevailed and the socioeconomic structure privileged land as the source of wealth and status. In such societies, merchants did not pray, fight, or work, or at least work the land or produce craft or artisanal goods. Instead, they profited from the exchange of goods for money, a business that earned them reputations as self-interested and morally compromised. In Russia, these stereotypes and biases proved extremely durable. By the early twentieth century, several sectors of society had developed critiques that reflected contempt or ambivalence toward the kupets and the retail trade.

These negative conceptions proceeded from the highest levels of Russian society. Despite a close regulatory relationship with merchants, the tsarist state had traditionally downplayed the significance of commerce and consumption.

In the 1890s, Minister of Finance Sergei Witte attempted to reform Russia's economy through a state capitalist system that sponsored industrialization and entrepreneurship. His campaign eventually ran up against a coalition of opponents led by Konstantin Pobedonostsev, a close adviser of Nicholas II. This coalition rejected Witte's plan on the grounds that agriculture and conditions for the peasants would deteriorate as a result of economic imitation of and integration with the West.[33] The role that commerce and consumption should play in Russia's economy had been raised within this context, but most high-ranking political leaders and advisers regarded these two economic activities as secondary or even tertiary priorities and ranked industry as a higher priority. In Russia, agriculture occupied a privileged place, despite the fact that commerce accounted for a larger proportion of the population's employment in many of the largest cities. As a matter of fact, some of the ambivalence toward commerce can be attributed to the fact that commerce was becoming increasingly important to the economy. The nation's agrarian orientation, however, reflected the socioeconomic reality of the Russian Empire as a whole. Even though more than 20 percent of Moscow's population worked in commerce at the beginning of the twentieth century, as late as 1913 agriculture still accounted for more than half of Russia's national income and three-fourths of its employment.[34]

Regarding commerce primarily as a political and economic issue, Russian rulers and their ministers and advisers failed to see the role that an expanding mass market was playing in reframing established traditions and reshaping Russian society. Indeed, even as Nicholas II used film as a political tool to present himself and his family to his subjects and allowed his name, likeness, and the imperial seal to be reproduced on various kinds of consumer goods, he and his advisers apparently thought little of the impact of their actions from a sociocultural standpoint. In trying to channel the power of the retail marketplace to political ends but limit its role within the national economy, the state alienated many leaders of the merchant community and helped to sustain a gap between thousands of small-scale, struggling shopkeepers and a smaller number of prosperous entrepreneurs who headed large-scale firms.

Some members of the business community themselves struggled to accept the retail trade as a legitimate occupation and often gave priority to industry and the state's industrial needs over commerce and Russians' eagerness to obtain consumer goods. For example, members of the Association of Industry and Trade, a group in existence from 1905 to 1917, consistently prioritized production over consumption and the needs of the industrial consumer over the private consumer. This tendency was based on the belief that industrial growth, not consumer demand, would provide the catalyst for improvement in the population's well-being.[35] To some extent, this attitude also reflected the division within the business community between merchants and industrialists, a divide based not only on the generally higher level of wealth, education, and activism that industrialists had achieved but also on ethnic, regional, and religious affiliations. Even within a city and even when members of the commercial-industrial community belonged to similar social, religious, and ethnic groups, however, a clear demarcation between commerce and industry persisted.[36]

Members of the intelligentsia, as well as some among the aristocracy, likewise scorned merchants for what they perceived as their base relationship to money and its possibly deleterious effects. Many intellectuals worried that the emergent mass market and urban entertainments encouraged self-indulgent materialism and threatened authentic folk traditions and culture. Slavophiles and populists were the most outspoken on this issue, although they approached it from different ideological vantage points. Both envisioned an economy founded on the peasant commune and held that agriculture, a socially productive kind of labor and the primary source of national wealth, rather than industry or commerce, should support Russian society. Following from this worldview, both groups faulted wealthy capitalist entrepreneurs for their purported imitation of the West and adoption of Western ideas, trends they deemed irreconcilable with Russia's traditions of rural community.[37] Among the cultural intelligentsia, writers and playwrights gave literary and dramatic life to the kupets, creating characters that mirrored the material and social realities of the lives of many small-scale merchants. They also reinscribed the commercial stigma. The plays, stories, and novels of Aleksandr Ostrovskii (*A Family Affair* and *The Storm*), as well as Nikolai Dobroliubov's influential interpretation of Ostrovskii's plays as depictions of a "kingdom of darkness," plus those of P. D. Boborykin (*Kitai Gorod*) and Prince Aleksandr Sumbatov-Iuzhin (*The Gentleman*), painted unflattering portraits of merchants as obese, wily, tyrannical, and narrow-minded shopkeepers or, conversely, as rich, swaggering, obtuse merchant-industrialists.[38] Some members of the clergy evinced a similar hostility. The *popovichi* intelligentsia, or sons of Orthodox clergymen who in the late nineteenth century worked in secular professions and developed a self-consciously anti-aristocratic, anticapitalist critique, considered the commercial profession to be the most dangerous for one's soul. They admonished merchants to guard against the temptations of lying and cheating and reminded them of their obligation to use their wealth for the general good. Their critiques conformed to Ostrovskii's and Dobroliubov's stereotypes, portraying the merchant as a tyrannical, ignorant, and greedy philistine in mortal danger of damnation.[39]

Not everyone among the educated classes, however, denigrated or lampooned merchants. Nostalgic chroniclers often warmly memorialized the kupets in recollections of bygone Moscow. The writer Nikolai Teleshov, who came from a merchant background, evoked the harsh conditions that lavka merchants in the Upper Trading Rows endured. Even if he romanticized these characters, he enshrined the image of hearty Russian merchants sitting in frigid, dim little shops, bundled in heavy raccoon coats belted around the middle or repairing to a neighboring inn to warm themselves and drink tea with male colleagues.[40] Other writers produced similarly fond, if somewhat patronizing, images of the old-style Russian merchant in the last decades of the empire as profound socioeconomic changes transformed the urban landscape. A longing for the past tinted their images of the kupets, rendering the figure a quaint and lovable, if pitiable, character.[41]

The urban boulevard press, a new medium that developed in the late nineteenth century, further publicized the negative image of merchants as crafty operators and the retail trade as a profession that relied on deception and shifty tricks. Columnists for *Moskovskii listok* (The Moscow Sheet), *Petersburgskii listok* (The Petersburg Sheet), *Odesskii listok* (The Odessa Sheet), and other popular daily newspapers entertained readers with feuilletons and daily "popular justice" or "social life" columns that regularly relayed the frustrations and predicaments urban residents experienced as they went about their daily shopping routines.[42] Such columns, which simultaneously shamed merchants by name for their rude behavior and dishonest practices and indulged readers with tales of merchants' social and personal lives, held up the retail sphere to scathing, satirical public scrutiny, exposing its flaws to middling and lower-class readers.[43] Common offenses cited in these columns included sanitary infractions, insolence, shoddy merchandise, overcharging customers by tipping the scales when weighing items, and harsh treatment of employees. One typical item in *Moskovskii listok's* regular column titled "The Diary of Mayor Brevnov," written by A. A. Sokolov, alerted readers to devious practices at a hat store on one of Moscow's side streets. According to the column, the store displayed a sign in its window advertising a 25 percent discount, an offer that supposedly enticed one gentleman to enter the shop. When the man picked out a fur hat and inquired about the price, however, the shop assistant informed him that the price marked on the item already included the 25 percent discount. Sokolov reported that when the customer objected to the disingenuous offer, the doorkeeper unceremoniously threw him out of the store.[44] In the same column, readers were warned to beware of the sellers at the Okhotnyi Riad (Hunters' Row) meat and fowl market, who, they claimed, frequently passed off pigeons as hazel grouse and partridges.[45] Another column, titled "What They Sell at Our Little Shops," named a fish seller working from a tent at Bolotnaia Square who sold salted pike completely unfit for eating and a flour merchant at Smolensk Market whose flour was rife with worms.[46] Odessa's boulevard press treated readers to similar tales. One writer reported that, after purchasing a pound of butter, he discovered that the several sheets of paper in which the "Mssrs. Odessa dairymen" had wrapped the butter weighed half a pound themselves, leaving him short a half pound of butter.[47] Another faulted shopkeepers who wrapped groceries, vegetables, and tobacco in old, grimy paper and left food on counters, where it lay exposed to insects and customers' hands.[48]

Alongside these caustically humorous tales of deceit and unsanitary conditions, boulevard newspapers published details of official inspections. One columnist revealed that an inspection of a *traktir* (tavern) on Bol'shaia Butyrskaia Street in Moscow had resulted in citations for dirty floors, ragged wallpaper, and the use of dirty rags, instead of napkins, on the tables.[49] *Odesskii novosti* (Odessa News) vigilantly reported infractions. One column exposed the "filthy conditions" at the Aleksandrov Bakery, citing the comments of the inspector, who reported finding piles of dough heaped on dirty floors, where two boys were occupied with twisting them into pretzels, while workers ate their lunches sitting on the slab used for mixing dough.[50] A report filed by Odessa's police chief also made its way into the newspapers. The chief's report of his rounds noted that meat sellers at the city's bazaars wore soiled aprons and covered the meat for sale with dirty sheets.[51] Even the most popular spots in the city did not escape the scrutiny of the press. The kitchens at two cafés, Fankoni and Robina, favorites of the city's middle classes and business leaders, were deemed unsanitary, their prices outrageous, and their environment vulgar.[52]

The public airing of complaints about dirt, deceptive advertising, and ill treatment of customers, as well as inspection reports that confirmed the existence of such problems, implied that these conditions were no longer acceptable and that consumers should expect and demand higher standards of cleanliness, quality, and service. Journalists surely intended to entertain readers by publicly ridiculing merchants, but the complaint columns cannot be dismissed as mere entertainment. The editors of the popular press were astute managers who tried to fill their newspapers with stories and information that appealed to their targeted audiences and spoke to their concerns. As new stores and shops, as well as cafés and restaurants, movie houses, dance halls, museums, and pleasure gardens, sprang up and as more and more people came to live in the city, the boulevard newspapers became an important medium of urban socialization. They introduced readers to the delights of the city, alerted them to its hazards, and instructed them on how to negotiate the range of experiences and characters that awaited them on city streets.[53] Moreover, in the absence of any systematic effort to attend to the material concerns that occupied millions of Russians on a daily basis, columnists for the popular dailies became consumer advocates of a sort. In the pages of these newspapers, consumers found a public forum where their interests were taken seriously, even if peppered with satire and gossip. Besides giving readers important information about which shops and vendors to avoid, the airing of complaints implied that merchants should care about their customers and that customers should not patronize businesses that did not show them respect or deal with them fairly. While columns sometimes targeted large, successful, and popular establishments, small-scale merchants, vendors, and café owners came in for the most criticism, perhaps because editors wanted to promote and protect the firms whose owners regularly advertised in their papers. In any case, the willingness to cite sellers and firms by name conveyed the message that merchants and businesses who failed to transact business honestly, keep a tidy shop, and show consideration for their customers were not meeting the needs of consumers.

The boulevard press also reported on scheming retail employees, shoplifters, pickpockets, con artists, and other assorted ne'er-do-wells who operated in and around shopping districts, sending the message that the retail sphere provided the space and enticements for various kinds of social transgressions. The publication of reports on acts of petty crime drew attention to the perils lurking in retail districts, turning them into stories that reflected anxieties about the temptations and liberties the retail sphere presented to men and women, even those of apparently good character. Shocking stories of "elegantly dressed young women" and "properly dressed men" stealing lace, gloves, handkerchiefs, pieces of cloth, and jewelry filled the newspapers.[54] Such petty crimes were certainly nothing new, but reports that people who presented a respectable middle- or upper-class appearance were perpetrating crimes suggested that new kinds of retailers were blurring class lines, either by attracting criminals or, alternatively, by leading astray respectable people. Indeed, as the popular dailies depicted the situation, simply being in the proximity of buying and selling posed dangers. In Odessa, thefts of gold watches and Astrakhan fur hats were repeatedly reported in 1898, a fact not lost on the editors, who advised readers that wearing an Astrakhan fur amounted to an invitation to thievery.[55] Of course, we cannot discount the desire of publishers to make a profit from satisfying the reading public's appetite for titillating tales of good men and women gone bad in the cities, but the stories played on an undercurrent of social concern about the power of new retail venues and consumer goods to tempt people to commit crimes or engage in morally dubious behaviors. The message was that all who entered the retail sphere became vulnerable to the lure of luxury, as well as to criminals masquerading as respectable men and women.

In the decades between the 1860s and 1900 then, Russia's retail sector underwent enormous change. The popular image of the merchant and the retail trade remained primarily negative, although issues relating to retail trade and consumption were routinely highlighted in the mass media, an indication of a new awareness about the importance of these activities to urban dwellers. The introduction of new retail venues and a new model of retailing, as well as the establishment of a mass media that both advertised retail firms and aired public concerns about questionable practices, elicited unease about the role of the retail sphere and the nature of its exchange culture. Some among Russia's merchant community began to reconsider how business should be transacted not only in their own stores but also in society at large. In particular, they wondered how to create a beautiful, clean, just, and cultured retail sector without sacrificing cherished customs, beliefs, and relationships. The attempts of Russia's new merchant elite to achieve this goal resulted in the creation and promotion of model institutions, the reinvention of rituals, and construction of a new ideal of the merchant. In seeking to reconstruct the retail sector and its culture, the merchant elite did not reject established authorities and traditions; instead, they blended them with technology, principles of the mass market, and new ideals of beauty, material progress, business integrity, and civility.

2

Palaces of Retailing
and Consumption

No single event captured more succinctly the conflicts inherent in Russia's retail sphere than the reconstruction of the Upper Trading Rows on Red Square from 1886 to 1893. More than a plan to transform Moscow's largest retail venue into an enormous arcade, the renovation signified a self-conscious attempt to aesthetically capture the meaning of contemporary urban life, to reconcile past, present, and future into one grand architectural statement. Situated in the city's centuries-old commercial center across from the Kremlin, the empire's political center, the Rows acquired a symbolic significance far beyond their commercial importance. As the rebuilding was proposed, debated, implemented, and then assessed, the Rows became a conspicuous, contestable symbol that different groups manipulated and mythologized in pursuit of their aspirations and agendas. As constructed, the Rows served as a monument to both modern retailing and urban modernity, as well as to the rising power of Moscow's merchant and political elite, Russian nationalism, and empire.

The reconstruction project symbolized different things to different groups. The merchant-investors, municipal authorities, writers, and journalists who initiated and publicly supported the Rows' rebuilding saw it as a chance to exhibit the superiority of modern methods of retailing. They cast the project as a signal step in the transformation of the city's retail sphere into a bright, beautiful, orderly, efficient, and technologically advanced realm that would accustom urban residents to modern, transparent business practices, culture, and civility. Some also identified the reconstruction as an opportunity to fashion a landmark to assert Moscow's preeminent role as the heart of Russian Orthodox commerce. The completion of a project that expressed this set of interrelated assumptions and goals indicates the rising confidence and hopes of members of Moscow's civil society, who worked in alliance, although not always in agreement, with the tsarist state. Late imperial Russian civil society, particularly the middle-class merchantry, has conventionally been interpreted as politically fractious and ineffectual and ultimately incapable of serving as a counterweight to tsar-ism or Bolshevism.[1] The rebuilding of the Rows challenges this interpretation. The project demonstrates the successful efforts of merchant-investors to collab-orate with various other professional and political groups to accomplish a com-mon goal. The position of the state vis-à-vis civic proponents of the rebuilding, however, was complicated. While the tsarist state supported the project in vari-ous ways, some of the state's aspirations were at odds with those of the project's merchant-investors. The new arcade provided the tsarist regime with an arena in which to further legitimize the Russian autocracy and to uphold discrimi-natory policies toward foreigners and Jews, projects that did not necessarily accord with the modern society that some envisioned. Still, merchant-investors and tsarist authorities agreed on the overriding goal of modernizing the Rows. Not everyone involved in or affected by the reconstruction, however, viewed it optimistically or believed it was necessary. Objections issued from numerous quarters, but especially from a group of Row merchants who attempted to halt the project. The backlash against the rebuilding nevertheless contributed to a developing discourse of civil rights and likewise suggested a fledgling move-ment among the middling classes to assert political and personal rights.

The Rows project did not represent the only conceptualization of modern retailing, urban life, and empire. Building projects in St. Petersburg and Odessa presented alternative visions. The builders of Odessa's Passazh (1898–1899), for example, attempted a similar architectural expression. Like the sponsors of the Rows, they intended the new arcade to model the principles of modern retail-ing and exhibit ideals of beauty, rationality, technological superiority, business integrity, and civility; however, Odessa's self-recognition as a multiethnic city influenced the design. As a result, Odessa's arcade muted any ethnic divisions, celebrating instead cosmopolitanism and links to western Europe and classical culture. As constructed, Odessa's Passazh represented the city's position as the cosmopolitan center of non-Russian, non-Orthodox merchants on the empire's periphery and conveyed the ideal of a modern retail sector and urban center that drew its vitality from diversity.

The contrast between Moscow's and Odessa's arcade projects highlights the conflicting ways in which city dwellers in two geographically and culturally distinct parts of the empire conceived of urban modernity, reminding us that there was not a single vision in late imperial society. A spectrum of ideas existed about how economics, social relationships, and culture informed public life, with the representation of public life being dependent on the city, the composition of a city's residents and political, business, and professional elite, and a conceptualization of the city's status in the empire and relationship to other cities. In essence, structures such as the Upper Rows and the Passazh were constructed, both literally and figuratively, to express these ideas visually.

The story of Odessa's Passazh has not been chronicled.[2] However, the history of the Upper Trading Rows has been treated by a few Russian writers, most notably A. S. Razmadze, who authored a jubilee volume to mark the occasion of the Rows' grand reopening in 1893.[3] Brief accounts have also appeared in various histories of Moscow.[4] Several memoirs and literary chronicles of the city also recall the Rows, both before and after the reconstruction, and provide some of the best descriptive evidence of the culture of the Old Rows.[5] More recently, scholars have drawn attention to the reconstruction of the Rows in surveys of Moscow's commercial landscape, interpreting the project as part of a period of modernization that signaled the passing of the old era of Moscow trade, the "victory of modern, impersonal commercial organizations over the more traditional personal forms," and "a cultural institution emblematic of prosperity and progress."[6] These scholars have disagreed over the extent to which practicality or aesthetics guided the building of the Rows. Irina Paltusova, for instance, argues that functional considerations such as rationality and economy overruled aesthetic considerations.[7] One Soviet scholar takes the opposite view, contending that the needs of commerce took second place behind concern for the appearance of the building and maintenance of the historical integrity of Red Square.[8] William Brumfield finds "disjunction" between the functional demands of commercial architecture and the desire for a Russian style.[9] The characterization of the new arcade as representative of the transition from customary to modern retailing in Russia is apt. Judgments of the building as either too functional or too laden with symbolism, however, miss the point that conflicting aims and ideals were consciously juxtaposed in the building. Or, perhaps more accurately, such interpretations overlook the fact that the merchants and municipal and tsarist authorities who collaborated on the rebuilding did not view the aims and ideals as oppositional. They sought a design that exhibited both traditional and modern styles precisely because such a design reflected Moscow's variegated commercial landscape.[10] Further, assessments of the façade neglect the social conflicts that lay beneath the reconstruction project. The analysis presented here brings these aspects into focus. The 1893 rebuilding symbolized a triumph for Moscow's emergent middle-class merchantry and for civil society. The new arcade, however, did not bring an end to customary modes of retailing or secure the victory of modern retail practices. Instead, the entire sequence of events—the closure of the old Rows and eviction of proprietors, the formation of a joint-stock company to manage the reconstruction project, the search for an appropriate design for the new building, the festive events surrounding the reopening, and the aftermath of the rebuilding—exposes social alliances and rifts and illuminates the melding of customary and emergent values and practices amid significant conflict and controversy. In the discourses, myths, and images constructed to support the rebuilding or to oppose it, one finds optimism, hope, anxiety, prejudices, and nostalgia and, more importantly, attempts to reconcile established customs and practices with contemporary business trends.

The History and Culture of the Old Rows

The decision to reinvent the Upper Trading Rows in 1886 was not a novel one. In fact, the Rows had been rebuilt four times over the previous four centuries.[11] Until the mid-sixteenth century, trade in Moscow had been conducted inside the Kremlin's walls. In 1546, Ivan the Terrible decreed that the market be moved outside the Kremlin, and he ordered the building of new commercial premises on the opposite side of Red Square in a section of the city known as Kitai Gorod, which thereafter became the central commercial district. The new Red Square market accommodated a collection of mostly wooden stalls and small shops and spaces for traders, who sold all kinds of odds and ends from benches, vats, and sleighs. The new market had room for roaming peddlers. Over time, traders converted their stalls to lavkas and gradually arranged them into lines, or trading rows, with narrow passageways between them. By sometime in the seventeenth century, this conglomeration of lavkas had split into three separate complexes of rows, called the Upper, Middle, and Lower Trading Rows. The Upper Rows, the largest of the three, stretched along Red Square from Nikol'skaia Street to Il'inka Street. The Middle Rows stood next to them, to the south, running between the Il'inka and Varvarka gates. The Lower Rows extended from there to the Moscow River embankment. Together, all three blocks of rows covered about fourteen acres and made up the city's main commercial center. By the nineteenth century, the Upper Rows had earned a reputation as a center for elegant shopping, while the Middle and Lower Rows specialized in wholesale, food, and heavy items.[12]

The Rows were originally organized and named according to the type of goods sold, a format that suggests some attention to rational organization. Adam Olearius, a German diplomatic envoy dispatched to Moscow in the 1630s, described the market as the largest and best in the city, where male and female tradespeople, shoppers, slaves, idlers, and prostitutes passed their days. The arrangement of the Row vendors, however, impressed him most. He noted that shoemakers, tailors, furriers, belt and girdle makers, hat makers, and others each had their "special streets" where they sold their wares, an arrangement the visitor found "very convenient, for everyone knows where to go to find [what they need]."[13] The number and kinds of rows varied over time. In the seventeenth century, there were ninety rows, including several bread and fish rows, three honey rows, a salt, garlic, and mushroom row, as well as rows dedicated to the sale of icons, boots, fabric, secondhand clothing, soap, bells, knives, candles, needles, and books. Despite the appearance of a well-organized scheme, however, a strict order never reigned, and row names did not always correspond to the products sold in them. Paper and sealing wax, for example, could be found in the Vegetable Row. Stacks of books and fresh fish could be found in the Seed Row. Thus, while merchants strived for organization and association with colleagues engaged in the same trade, the systematic classification of merchandise was not a prime concern.[14]

The first renovation of the Upper Rows came in 1626, when Tsar Aleksei ordered the building of stone rows after a fire destroyed the wooden ones. In order to finance the project, Aleksei compelled each merchant to pay a fee for stones and brick. These rows lasted more than 150 years, being demolished in 1789 due to dilapidation.[15] The following year, the state sold the Rows to private investors, who commissioned the St. Petersburg–based architect Giacomo Quarenghi, noted for designing, among other buildings, the Academy of Sciences and Aleksandr Palace in Tsarskoe Selo, to renovate them. Quarenghi submitted a plan for a neoclassical, two-story, trapezoidal-shaped structure that differed from previous designs in its attempt to present the Rows as a single, coherent unit through the device of an open exterior arcade. Three Russian architects assumed direction of the rebuilding, although they diverged from Quarenghi's original plan and by 1805 had only partially completed the building. Merchants did not seem to mind, though, and began to set up shop. The harmonious façade that Quarenghi had planned, however, concealed a discordant interior. Inside proprietors built lavkas according to their own needs, adding to their shops as business grew and finances permitted, spreading out to the left, right, or above, and over time producing an irregular floor plan. This iteration of the Rows lasted only a few years. Along with most of the other shops in the Kitai Gorod area, they were destroyed in the 1812 fire. The following year a plan to resurrect the Rows surfaced. Osip Bove, the architect commissioned for the job, patterned his design after Quarenghi's neoclassical arcade. Perhaps some kind of orderly parceling out of interior space existed in Bove's plan, but, by the mid-nineteenth century, a façade of symmetrical unity once again camouflaged an improvised maze of shops of various sizes, shapes, heights, widths, and appearances, leaving intact the proprietor-centered system that had previously allowed merchants to modify their shops as needed without the extra expense of bringing them into structural conformity with the larger building or neighboring occupants.[16]

In the decades following the 1814 rebuilding, and especially in the 1860s and 1870s, the Rows attracted a growing number of merchants and consumers, a trend that reflected the arrival of more people, especially newly liberated peasants, in the city and their entry into the retail trade, as well as growing consumer demand. At midcentury, tenancies in the Upper Rows numbered 768. Together with the Middle and Lower Rows, the number of tenants reached 1,318, double the number in 1701.[17] In 1862, the number of tenants in the Upper Rows alone had jumped to 1,139.[18] By the 1870s, the Upper Rows comprised approximately 60 rows spread out over four quadrants, with each quadrant divided into parcels of shop floor space, measuring about 14 by 17.5 feet each, with a cellar for storage. On average, a lavka took up about 2.6 parcels of space, although it was also common for a lavka to take up 4 or more parcels.[19] Some lavkas were rather large units whose proprietors engaged in both wholesale and retail trade and maintained commercial contacts outside of Moscow. The Russian fur-trading firm Pavel Sorokoumovskii & Sons, for instance, maintained a sizable shop in the Rows. By contrast, other lavkas were relatively small and unassuming. Petty traders who did not own a shop also conducted business in the Rows, crowding the narrow aisles to sell stationery, ribbons, lace, buttons, and other items from cupboards. Outside, lining the square in front, were numerous vendors, many of them women selling handcrafted and household items. By the third quarter of the nineteenth century, the Rows had garnered a reputation as Moscow's central marketplace. As the writer Nikolai Teleshov put it, at the Rows you could buy anything, "from a spool of thread to pearls and diamonds, from a glass of kvass to a fashionable tail coat or a sable coat, from autographed books to velvet rugs."[20]

In the decades prior to the Rows' destruction in 1886, the disorderly physical layout of the sprawling complex had become one of its most striking features, at least according to those who penned narratives about life in the Rows. One Muscovite described the convoluted internal floor plan as "an enormous, labyrinthine gallery of walkways, passages, and lines."[21] Another called it a "confusing, unending [series of] rows, alleys, and passageways."[22] In his memoir of mid-nineteenth-century commerce, Row merchant Ivan Slonov testified to the lack of standardization and the ensuing collection of irregularly shaped rows and shops. He remembered that proprietors built lavkas without any overarching plan, remarking that "everyone did what he wished, when he wished, and according to his own judgment."[23] As a result, he observed, the individual rows were crooked, one being higher, another lower, with lavkas differing from each other, one large and another small. While such comments often reflected the negative impression the Rows made, they also suggest that Row merchants valued some degree of independent shopkeeping and decision making.

The dirt, darkness, and general disrepair inside the Rows also struck many urban chroniclers. Although amazed by the abundance of goods inside, Muscovite Vera Kharuzina characterized the Rows as an ancient and neglected structure filled with a "dank, peculiar air." To her, the Rows' bleak, dark passageways, dirty glass roof panes, "clammy, damp air [that] reigned everywhere," and gutters that ran down the middle of the passageways amounted to an "uncivilized filth."[24] Even the Row merchant Slonov thought that prior to its demolition, the old structure "resembled dark ruins." Conceding that Row merchants had not been known for cleanliness or orderly shopkeeping, Slonov maintained that customers had to use caution when traversing the uneven floors of the passageways, taking care to avoid the crates, bales, and heaps of trash that lay alongside shops.[25] At least one narrator delighted in the grimy, harsh scenery. In evoking the harsh conditions of the Rows, Teleshov endowed the lack of comforts and conveniences with a quaint, romantic charm. He described temperatures so frigid that ink froze in the inkwell, compelling merchants to breathe on their feather pens to soften the "black snow" in order to write a promissory note.[26] Photographs taken in the 1880s confirm the physical deterioration of parts of the structure. The Rows lining Red Square and those along the two sides of the building on Il'inka and Nikol'skaia Streets, where the upscale shops were located, appear to be in fairly good shape. However, photographs of the Secondhand Clothing Row and the Icon Row, situated in the middle and rear of the building, respectively, show uneven, worn stones in precarious-looking passageways with boards laid down the middle to serve as drain covers. The camera also captured cracked and poorly patched walls and ceilings and low-hanging or even wide-open roofs.[27]

Not all lavkas were small, dark, dreary hovels devoid of cleanliness and comfort. Shops fronting Red Square were larger and better appointed and partitioned off from interior passageways by glass doors and windows, effects that gave them the semblance of a magazin. According to Slonov, these shops did a brisk trade and constituted the most novel (original'naia) section of the Rows.[28] Kharuzina considered these shops "a little better" (polushche), an apparent reference to their physical appearance as well as their more fashionable goods.[29] Also, testaments to clutter and disorder disguise the fact that some degree of organization actually governed the Rows. In the 1860s, various rows still carried names that designated the kinds of merchandise sold, and even though row names did not always correspond to the merchandise carried in each shop, many merchants selling similar products were still situated on the same rows. The publication of guidebooks to the Rows, which listed occupants alphabetically and/or by rows or goods, also suggests a concern with systematizing lavkas and orienting shoppers.

Over time, the Rows had developed a distinctive culture that, while connected to the customs and practices of the larger retail sphere, also grew out of the social relationships forged among a community of (largely) male Russian Orthodox merchant-proprietors. Observers rarely wrote about the Rows without remarking on the peculiar ways that held sway there, and thus the Rows acquired an image of being a distinctive realm unto itself. It is testimony to this statement that one commentator referred to the Rows as a "city," a word that imparts autonomy and collective identity, a place with its own customs, practices, rituals, symbols, and idioms.[30] Russian males dominated among the Rows' proprietors, although female vendors were not uncommon. Of the 1,139 tenants listed in an 1862 guide, for instance, women accounted for 175 or 15 percent; several of them were widows continuing a late husband's business.[31] Family ties also characterized business in the Rows. Brothers, sons, and other relatives sometimes occupied adjoining properties. Most Row tenants also came from the lower and middling strata. In 1862, one year prior to an 1863 decree that deregulated the merchant estate, the majority of Row merchants belonged to the ranks of the merchant *soslovie,* although shopkeepers from the *meshchanstvo* (urban middling) and peasant *sosloviia* were common. Honored Citizens and Hereditary Honored Citizens also operated shops in the Rows, although they made up only about 2 percent of proprietors.[32]

Various forms of masculine conviviality served to strengthen the social bonds among male merchants. According to the merchant Slonov, an air of casual familiarity reigned among Row merchants. On a typical day, merchants and their assistants spent much of their time talking and playing checkers as they awaited customers and gathered in groups at Bubnov's, a nearby inn, to have lunch, drink tea, and talk over business.[33] Contemporaries had very little to say about the female Row merchants who operated businesses, although Kharuzina made reference to the women who sold their handcrafted wares outside the building. She remembered them "walking the pavement, inviting shoppers with touching appeals to examine their wares."[34] Her sympathetic portrayal suggests the deprivation of these women, but their experiences as street vendors do not tell us much about the status and experiences of female merchants inside. There is no reason to assume that female Row merchants did not take part in most aspects of Row life, for example, the prayer services and public rituals, alongside their male counterparts. Male merchants, however, excluded their female associates from the regular rounds of drinking and feasting. Inns and taverns were primarily places of male sociability and drinking, an activity that men engaged in with each other as a rite of passage and ritual of male bonding.[35]

Religion played an important role in the lives of the Orthodox merchants who dominated the Rows and, consequently, in Row culture.[36] Merchants openly displayed their religiosity by mounting religious images throughout the passageways and in individual shops. These images reminded merchants to be pious and dutiful in their daily religious observances. Merchants also believed the presence of the images would ensure divine protection and favor. Large, gilded icons hung over the passageways and decorated the canopies outside, where Row merchants regularly gathered to pray as a group. They also held prayer services, religious rituals, and processions throughout the year, the most celebrated of these observances being the fall prayer service, to which the public was invited. Rituals of reconciliation between merchants, shop assistants, and apprentices conducted on religious holidays also brought those employed by Row merchants into a patriarchal bond cemented by the Orthodox faith.[37]

Perhaps the most notorious feature of Row culture was the customarily physical, aggressive style of transacting business. Although this style was not unique to Row merchants, they acquired a reputation for their wile, for their importunateness in "inviting" customers into their shops, and for haggling with daunting ferocity. Almost all accounts of the Rows include a description of the merchants' business skills, practices that will be explored more fully in later chapters. Narratives written in the decades between the mid-nineteenth and early twentieth centuries invariably portrayed the Row merchant ensconced in a tiny, dim, shabby lavka awaiting the next unsuspecting customer. According to Slonov, Row merchants spent little time arranging displays of merchandise and instead either sat beside their shops calling out to passersby to come inside and examine their merchandise or sent their apprentices out to Red Square to "catch" shoppers.[38] Shopkeepers and market vendors throughout the city conducted business using these same methods, but the concentration of such shopkeepers and the fame that the Rows engendered in narratives of the city, especially after the rebuilding, imparted to Row merchants the semblance of a shared identity and culture.

Despite the centrality of the Rows and the vital culture that prevailed there, reports of the structure's decay and talk of its renovation had begun circulating in Moscow as early as the late 1860s. New commercial districts lined with elegant stores and arcades had been appearing in other parts of the city. In the 1870s, many prosperous Russian merchants moved their retail establishments from Kitai Gorod to Kuznetskii Most and other more fashionable streets. New commercial centers on Moscow's outskirts served an expanding lower-class urban population. Although shoppers continued to visit the Upper Rows, by the late 1880s they had lost their reputation as Moscow's undisputed, premier retail center.

The Struggle to Rebuild the Rows, 1869–1886

The plan to rebuild the Rows would involve tearing down not only the old structure but also eradicating the culture of the Rows. To the merchant elite and state and municipal authorities who advocated its rebuilding, the Rows epitomized all that was wrong with retail trade in Russia. They deemed the Rows an outdated eyesore and a public danger that hindered the implementation of more efficient and cultured modes of business. Conflating physical deterioration with irrationality and immorality, they also perceived the structure as an external manifestation of the inefficiencies and corruption inside. To them, the building bore the outward effects of the vices inside and symbolized the slothfulness and the underhandedness of merchants in Russia. In their view, modern, ethical businesses could not possibly operate in such demoralizing physical surroundings. These proponents of demolition and renovation intended to construct a beautiful, brightly lit, clean, heated, and commodious venue powered by new technologies and retail principles and governed by restrained, civil interactions. Only such a physical environment, they believed, could foster a rational, honest, and sophisticated retail culture.

The entire reconstruction project actually lasted several decades and consisted of four contentious attempts to craft a plan to which all parties could agree.[39] Not everyone greeted the basic proposal enthusiastically. Some Row merchants feared the loss of their livelihood and autonomy and protested government coercion and impingement on their civil rights. The first attempt to rebuild the Rows came in 1869, when Moscow's governor-general, Prince V. A. Dolgorukii, proposed the renovation to the city duma. Worried that they would lose control of the project and their property, Row merchants petitioned the duma to approve the rebuilding only if they gave their permission. The duma agreed and entrusted to proprietors the task of presenting their own plan. A commission of Row merchants submitted a proposal to the duma requesting that the city grant them additional property to compensate for the widening of passageways between the rows, something municipal officials had deemed a necessary improvement. The merchants' proposal failed to win approval, and plans to rebuild proceeded no further at that point. Two other attempts to initiate reconstruction, in 1875 and 1880, failed as well. Conflict surfaced again over the widening of passageways and subsequent loss of property, as well as when Row merchants objected to the plan to form a corporation to fund and supervise the project. In the 1880 attempt, duma members became impatient and even tried to bypass Row merchants by asking the state to intervene and compel merchants to create a joint-stock company with the stipulation that the property of those owners who refused to join the corporation would be expropriated. This tactic failed, and the project languished once again.

The failure of the duma and the Row merchants to come to an agreement reflects the conflicting interests at the center of the project. Although Row merchants failed to win concessions from the duma in these three rounds, their success in stalling reconstruction signaled their role in the realm of civic participation. As early as 1869, Row merchants were contributing to a developing liberal discourse of civil rights and private property. In their proposal to the duma, merchants asserted that their "right to property" (*pravo sobstvennosti*) was "inviolable" (*neprikosnovennoe*).[40] On that basis, they succeeded in forestalling the project. Their assertive statement indicates that some Row merchants were savvy operators familiar with liberal legal concepts, or at least the rhetoric, and were prepared to use it to present their demands. The use of such language suggests that despite a political culture that had regulated the commercial sector through paternalistic corporate laws, a new generation of merchants was developing, one that was familiar with the liberal discourses, active in municipal politics and the professions, and conscious of their positions. While most Row merchants probably did not belong to this educated, liberal set, those who found themselves in conflict with the duma and municipal authorities nonetheless appropriated the ideals and language of civil rights and private property to articulate their interests and appeal to them in terms they would find compelling.

Given their inability to come to an agreement with Row merchants on three previous occasions, municipal authorities and duma representatives apparently decided to force the issue, although they still found it necessary to proceed cautiously and with some attention to protocol and consensus. In 1883, Governor-General Dolgorukii ordered a formal inspection of the Rows. Inspectors filed a report condemning the building, claiming that many of the rows were so dilapidated that they were in danger of falling down or catching fire. The report also concluded that the "extremely unsanitary condition" of the Rows posed a "great danger to the health of those conducting business there and to the public."[41] In 1885, the duma delegated to N. A. Alekseev, Moscow's activist mayor from 1885 to 1893, the task of convening a general assembly of lavka owners to discuss establishing a joint-stock company to oversee the rebuilding.[42] Meanwhile, the governor-general's office ordered another round of inspections, which, like the first ones, pronounced the Rows "a public calamity" (*obshchestvennoe bedstvie*), an assessment with which the Moscow mayor, the minister of internal affairs, and the Moscow Stock Exchange Committee concurred.[43] The assembly of lavka proprietors met in January 1886, almost a

year after the duma had requested its convocation. Of the more than 1,000 proprietors then occupying the Rows, a mere 135 showed up, an indication that
the reconstruction plan was unpopular among Row merchants. The meeting
nevertheless proceeded. The majority of those assembled approved the formation of the Committee for the Reconstruction of the Upper Trading Rows,
authorized to work out in six months' time a draft of the statutes of a joint-stock
company and to draw up a financial plan to rebuild the Rows.[44] A published
draft of terms of membership in the new corporation stipulated that anyone
owning a lavka in the Rows had until March 1, 1886, to submit a written statement to the Moscow Merchants Board signaling his or her intent to join the
corporation. Property not voluntarily ceded to the corporation would become
the property of the city, a stipulation that the city duma approved.[45] Following
this announcement, a third team of inspectors examined the Rows, concluding that, while many lavkas presented a tolerable appearance, the building was
structurally unsound and dangerous.[46]

Despite all of this activity, no definitive action was taken until Dolgorukii
ordered the almost immediate closing of the Rows in July 1886. In response,
Row merchants petitioned for and won a postponement until October, during
which time they unsuccessfully appealed to Tsar Aleksandr III to rescind the
governor-general's order. In October, the city published announcements of the
impending closure in newspapers and pasted notices on the walls of the Rows.[47]
On the appointed day, police began to forcibly evict Row merchants. In the
meantime, the Moscow municipal government had begun building temporary
retail premises on Red Square to house merchants ousted by the closing, but
when the Rows were closed, the temporary structures had not been finished.
In the absence of available facilities, Row merchants began to move to other
locations throughout Moscow.

Despite notification, some Row merchants reacted indignantly to the
forced evictions. Slonov wrote disapprovingly of the actions of the municipal
authorities, who, he claimed, swooped down on merchants unexpectedly. As
he portrayed the situation, Row merchants were the victims of arbitrary decision making and the police, who, he wrote, appeared in the Rows "one fine
morning" and commanded the Row watchmen to immediately board up the
passages and doors to the Knife Row. Maintaining that the merchants had not
anticipated such "drastic measures," he declared they were so startled by this
draconian police action that at first they did not know what to do or whom to
petition.[48] Slonov further asserted that many Row merchants considered themselves ruined and some even lost their minds, although this last claim is probably an exaggeration, given that he cited only the example of sixty-year-old P.
A. Solodovnikov, who in fact became so distraught that he slit his throat in the

Arkhangel'skii Cathedral.[49] In truth, dissenting merchants did not stand idly by. Still hoping to forestall the closing, a group of them petitioned the governor-general and Moscow's police chief. This time, they received no response, and evictions continued.

Proponents of the rebuilding treated the closure as a difficult but obligatory step toward progress and public welfare. In his official history of the Rows, Razmadze confirmed Slonov's assertion that merchants reacted negatively to evictions, although he justified the measures taken. Acknowledging that the closure had elicited public censure because of the bad timing and inhumanity of it, Razmadze nevertheless called it "to a great extent, reasonable" and "a necessary measure."[50] As he explained it, the reconstruction had been bogged down for decades and would have continued to drag on without decisive action. Further, the Rows had become so badly decayed that they were ready to fall down, a condition that necessitated their closing.

Dramatic characterizations of the closure and sound justifications for rebuilding notwithstanding, a considerable amount of hostility and hardship did in fact result from the events that transpired. Most Row merchants, conceding the imminent loss of their retail premises, rented new space elsewhere in the city. One month after the October closing, 72 percent of lavka owners had established shops in new locations, although a significant minority struggled to reestablish themselves.[51] One estimate puts the number of shopkeepers and assistants thrown out of work by the closing at five hundred.[52] Some Row merchants perceived the municipal government's methods as coercive, heartless, and illegal, and they expressed anger that the temporary retail premises were not ready for occupancy at the time of the Rows' closing. Petitions sent to the Moscow governor-general and Moscow Merchants Board reveal the difficulties that some merchants and shop assistants faced. One group of 33 prikazchiki (shop assistants) complained to the governor-general that the shutdown had left them without positions and, with families to support, desperate for a way to make a living.[53] A brother and sister by the name of Telepeev protested to the elder of the Moscow Merchants' Soslovie, an organization consisting of first- and second-guild merchants, that the closing of their lavka in the Secondhand Clothing Row "deprived [us] of our sole means of livelihood."[54] Another petition submitted to the minister of internal affairs by two female and two male merchants protested the formation of a private corporation.[55] The Moscow Merchants Board extended financial relief to some petitioners.[56] The duma also tried to alleviate distress by voting to allot five thousand rubles for members of the Society of Shop Assistants.

Opposition to the closing, however, did not so much reflect the conflict between rank-and-file merchants and the progressive merchants allied with political leaders, as proponents would have it, as it did the fact that nagging issues pertaining to property had not been settled in a manner entirely satisfactory to some Row merchants. The plan to take some of the merchants' property in order to widen passageways had continued to generate hostility, and the issue remained unsettled until November 1886, when the municipal government agreed to relinquish the land to the corporation as a free grant, on the condition that ownership of both the land and building would revert to the city in seventy-five years.[57] Still, some found this solution unjust and self-serving. The decision to expropriate land not voluntarily surrendered to the corporation also generated resistance. In February 1887, a group of seventeen lavka owners submitted to the governor-general's office a petition expressing their dissatisfaction with "municipal swindling" and demanding that collective and individual rights override profit motives. The petitioners presented themselves as contemporary shopkeepers open to new ideas and methods of commerce but opposed to the corruption and social injustices occasioned by the reconstruction. They acknowledged that the closing of the Rows, while difficult, was a "necessary sacrifice in the interests of the improvement [blagoustroistvo] of the city." But they deplored the duma's decision to seize dissenters' land, asserting that the plan to eventually grant to the city the entire property overrode the "collective will" (kollektivnoi voli) of lavka owners in the interests of securing a handsome profit for the city. According to the petitioners, "The new Rows should be well built and beautiful, but no less than that, they should not be built on the violation of rights and justice, nor on the sacrifice of the welfare of the mass of people, who have the right to expect that their small interests and rights are protected by the full force of the existing laws."[58] This petition does not appear to have been issued by stubbornly old-fashioned petty traders mired in tradition and clinging to outdated business practices. It is not written in the language of supplicants. These merchant-petitioners recognized the benefits of a new retail arcade but opposed what they considered municipal officials' legal maneuverings and infractions of the law, and they resented the suffering that particular methods had occasioned. They demanded an agreement ensuring merchants would be provided for during the transition, that property would be equitably assessed, and that lavka owners would be allowed to represent their interests. In putting forth these demands, they were not operating out of ignorance or fear of the new but out of an awareness that conflicts of interest existed. They were asking for an arbitration process that would allow them an equal voice in the process.

Even as complaints and petitions continued to be filed, the constitution of a private company to finance and guide the reconstruction proceeded. On May 10, 1888, almost twenty years after the initial attempt, in 1869, to inaugurate the project and a year and a half after the closing of the Rows, Aleksandr III approved the statutes of the Corporation of the Upper Trading Rows on Red Square in Moscow.[59] The corporation's statutes formalized the agenda of the project's advocates, who included several prosperous Row merchants, municipal authorities, and duma representatives, as well as the tsarist state. Terms of membership stipulated that the new rows be completed within four years. Lavka owners would be allowed to convert their property into shares, the value of which would correspond to the value of their shops, as determined by municipal appraisal. Owners who did not cede their lavkas to the corporation voluntarily and who did not present reasons for their refusal to the Moscow municipal government within one month would forfeit their property to the city, which would then assume ownership of their shares.[60]

The fact that leaders from Moscow's duma, municipal government, and merchant community, in alliance with the state, chose to constitute a joint-stock company to direct the reconstruction suggests the scale of the undertaking and the trend toward corporate forms of business in Russia, as well as state-society cooperation. The assets of the corporation consisted of the land, which provided the collateral for a bond issue to raise money. Five million rubles worth of 5 percent bonds were issued in three installments between 1889 and early 1892, and investors bought these bonds at face value.[61] Shareholders numbered more than nine hundred, with the cloth merchant I. S. Titov, who formerly occupied the largest retail shop in the Rows, being the largest shareholder and the Moscow Merchants Society, the second largest. In addition, more than nine million rubles worth of shares were issued to previous lavka owners. Businesses and municipal organizations, including the First Moscow Merchants' Credit Union Society and the Moscow Municipal Society, as well as churches, monasteries, and charitable societies, also held large shares.[62]

The composition of the company's board and council, elected by the general assembly of shareholders, reflected the significant role that Moscow's entrepreneurial elite played in the reconstruction project. Many individuals elected to posts on the council or board also held membership in the Moscow Merchants' Soslovie. The company's statutes also stipulated that the director and members of the board must hold no fewer than one hundred shares in the company, a provision that guaranteed the election of more prosperous merchants.[63] The general assembly of shareholders elected as its first chairman of the board Aleksandr Grigor'evich Kol'chugin, a second-guild merchant and Hereditary Honored Citizen whose family operated the Kol'chugin Copper Works. Kol'chugin had also distinguished himself by twice serving as *starshina* (elder) of the Merchants' Soslovie and in the Moscow duma. For director of the board, the assembly chose Petr Mikhailovich Kalashnikov, also a second-guild merchant and Hereditary

Honored Citizen, who ran a family watch business and served in the Moscow duma and on the boards of various philanthropic organizations. The cloth merchant Titov served as the third board member. Like his two colleagues, Titov was a prosperous, prominent Row merchant, a Hereditary Honored Citizen, and active in municipal and community affairs. Most of the men elected to the council also came from established, wealthy merchant-industrial families, and many held offices in merchants' and philanthropic organizations and served in municipal posts.[64]

Shortly after the company's constitution, new problems exposed a gap between leaders' desire to implement contemporary business practices and the realities of doing business in Russia. Enrolling merchants in the corporation or allowing them to sell their space in the Rows required an assessment of the value of their lavkas and the issuance of stock shares of comparable value. This process necessitated that proprietors accept a new concept of ownership, one based on a paper certificate, representative of shares in a corporation's profits and risks, and not on physical property. The logistics of conversion also turned out to be a complicated and arduous task, contributing to the resentment that reluctant Row merchants already felt. The major obstacles in converting property to shares turned out to be tracing and transferring individual titles, processes complicated by cases in which ownership was not clear or in which no documents of ownership could be found. In some instances, assessors established ownership by referring to municipal plans and taxation records, leaving some lavka owners confused, suspicious, and hesitant to enroll as shareholders.

Razmadze's history portrayed the resistance to joining the corporation as a feminized, old-world mentality, a tactic that appears to have been a way of discrediting and downplaying complaints. Drawing on cultural conventions that associated women with backwardness and ignorance, the author claimed that female lavka owners as "decrepit as the Rows themselves" predominated among those merchants who found the process of converting lavka space to paper shares bewildering and considered it a forceful seizure of property. As he reimagined it, elderly female shop owners, "touching in their good-natured helplessness," understood only that "the Rows were closed by orders from above, that their lavkas no longer brought income, and that someone was taking away the lavka and giving God knows what for it."[65] Razmadze's rendering of dissenting voices as distressed and female differs from the strident, confident tones that both male and female Row merchants registered in their petitions of protest. His depiction of dissenters as aged, ignorant women who could not comprehend the devices of the modern marketplace and, as a result, required the gentle, indulgent guidance of the project's male leaders implied that no substantive opposition was raised. Such an image framed the reconstruction as a

modern, rational reorganization project led by men, who would shepherd backward women into a new world.

Disagreements over property values and membership in the corporation
dragged on for years. Five years after the closing of the Rows, nine merchants,
six men and three women, still declined to join.[66] The Merchants' Soslovie
tried to settle, offering to compensate them for their expropriated property,
but negotiations stalled. One of the dissenters, Nikolai Lukoshkin, expressed
his objections and demanded justice against municipal tyranny in two angry
letters to Stepan Alekseevich Protopopov, starshina of the Merchants Soslovie.
Lukoshkin regarded as "unlawful" (bezzakoniie) the taking of his lavka (which,
he claimed, legally belonged to him according to "His Imperial Majesty's com-
mand" and the laws of May 19, 1887) for use by the city of Moscow. To him,
membership in the corporation would be a contradiction. Lukoshkin expressed
his displeasure with the settlement offered him by the Merchants Board by demanding twenty-five thousand rubles in cash. He furthermore tried to override
the decisions of local authorities by requesting that the state council, and not
municipal officials or the corporation, decide his case. And he also warned the
starshina that despite the contrivances of interested parties, "I will receive as established by the Monarch, the compensation based on the laws of May 19, 1887,
and no other, which is just and proper."[67] Although money was clearly an issue,
the language of this petition shows Lukoshkin's objection to what many Row
merchants perceived as a ruthless misuse of political power and trampling of
property and civil rights, which he believed were protected by the tsar. The final settling of accounts with the nine hold-outs, Lukoshkin among them, came
only in 1897, eleven years after the closing of the Rows and four years after the
opening of the new structure.[68]

Demolition represented the final phase of the Rows' closure, and it was
marked by a dramatic, ritualized finale. On September 20, 1888, alongside the
façade of the Upper Rows, on a specially erected platform decorated with carpets and adorned with icons of the Mother of God and Saints Basil, Kosima,
and Damian, a religious service marked the solemn occasion. Following the
service, a priest sprinkled holy water on the spot where demolition crews would
begin their work. After the blessing, a choir sang the national hymn, and then
Kol'chugin, along with members of the board and council and with the aid of
workers, pulled a rope. One section of the wall came crashing down.[69]

Refashioning the Rows

The next phase of the reconstruction entailed choosing a design for the new
structure, a process that necessitated reconciling the various agendas of merchant investors, municipal authorities, and the tsarist regime, each of whom

sought to make a statement through the building. The merchants who sat on the corporation's board and council wanted, above all, to refashion the Rows as a retail complex that would assert the superiority of modern retailing and reflect the important roles that merchants and commerce had played in Russian history. Moscow's merchant elite had already begun to demonstrate their rising wealth and influence through civic activism, such as sponsoring hospitals, churches, and schools, and building showplace homes, offices, and retail stores, many in the fashionable style moderne.[70] This project gave the corporation's merchant leaders the chance to leave their imprint on Red Square, the city's most venerated historic site. Municipal authorities emphasized creating a building that would bring the city credit and provide residents with a handsome and safe place to shop. Several members of the merchant elite who served on city governing organs and in the duma concurred with these motives. The tsarist state's desire to project an image of power that reflected its vision of the Russian past also informed the choice of design. During the reign of Aleksandr III, a conservative coterie, which included Mikhail Katkov of *Moskovskie vedomosti* (Moscow News), and Konstantin Pobedonostsev, Aleksandr's former tutor and closest adviser who in 1880 was the chief procurator of the Holy Synod, constructed national myths and symbols that vaunted Russia's traditions and native structures as part of a strategy of political representation. These image makers styled the tsar a patriarchal ruler who acted with force and decisiveness, ruling over a united Russian Orthodox empire. In this "scenario of power," ancient Muscovy represented the conceptual origins and foundational site of the monarchy.[71] As part of this strategy, Aleksandr embarked on a building campaign intended to capture in monumental style his vision of Russian national identity.[72] Aleksandr's desire dovetailed with a broader movement already under way among architects to develop an artistic form to represent Russian identity, which led to the invention of Russian revival, an ornate, historicist style inspired by the Kremlin and other medieval monuments. Russian revival became particularly popular in Moscow. Several large buildings in and near Red Square, including the Historical Museum (1874–1883) and the Moscow duma building (1890–1892), were built in this style.[73]

In November 1888, the Upper Trading Rows Corporation announced a design competition. Twenty-three architects from within and outside the empire submitted entries, which were put on display at the Historical Museum for public inspection prior to and following the announcement of the winning design. The panel of judges included prominent specialists in art, architecture, and engineering, as well as municipal officials, Moscow's mayor, and members of the corporation's board and council. In February, after the tsar confirmed the judges' decision, they declared Aleksandr Nikanorovich Pomerantsev, professor of architecture at the Academy of Arts in St. Petersburg, the winner. Pomerantsev received six thousand rubles for his arcade design, executed in Russian revival style.[74]

Judges evaluated entries on how well the designs met the needs of modern commerce while preserving the historical integrity of Red Square. They sought a design that employed the latest in engineering and technology, which they believed would give merchant-occupants a competitive edge and demonstrate that Russian commerce was current and innovative. To that end, they placed priority on adequate storage space and room for deliveries, attributes they considered necessary for efficiency. They also deemed comfort and convenience for both merchants and shoppers a necessary ingredient for commercial success; as a result, the widening of passageways and construction of convenient staircases became requirements. The judges also factored in aesthetic concerns, which did not mean simply choosing an attractive design but also selecting one that conformed visually to the historic surroundings. As the chronicler Razmadze presented it, the planners who formulated the contest's criteria wanted a building that would be an "adornment" (ukrashenie) to the city, one worthy of its place on Russia's most famous square.[75]

The panel's assessments of the entries make clear their intention of balancing the need for structural integrity and commercial suitability with aesthetic considerations. Structural defects doomed some designs. Judges found one entry impractical because the architect failed to provide a plan for removing snow from the roof. Another unsuccessful submission lacked an adequate lighting system, while another did not satisfactorily connect the staircases between floors.[76] Other plans failed because judges found them unattractive, unsuitable for a commercial structure, or unrepresentative of a national style. That last criterion meant rejecting designs derived from western European architectural styles. The panel faulted one entry conceived in the Renaissance style, for example, because it "inadequately expresses the character of a commercial structure and does not conform to Red Square." They reproached another for "inadequately [executing] the lower floor and corners of the building in the spirit of Russian style." Another plan, designed in neoclassical style, was considered disharmonious with the buildings on Red Square because of the "unfortunate curved shapes of the cupolas on the two sides of the building projecting onto the square."[77] Pomerantsev's winning entry satisfied the critical criteria, displaying a high level of technical proficiency and successfully blending the contemporary arcade design with distinctively Russian exterior motifs.

Contractors and workers transformed Pomerantsev's plan into a building unsurpassed by any other in Russia in size or engineering skill. The main building, bounded by Red Square, Il'inka, Nikol'skaia, and a new street, Vetoshnyi, was a vast three-story structure (with two basement levels) that provided 253,036 square feet of commercial space and room for more than a thousand retail shops, restaurants, and other businesses. A smaller, secondary building behind the main building furnished an additional 13,095 square feet of space. The quantity of manufactured materials used suggests a large-scale mobilization of resources and labor. In all, forty million bricks were laid during construction. Red Finnish granite covered the Red Square exterior and a bluish Don granite, the exterior facing the side streets. A broad, asphalt pavement circled the building. Inside, three lengthwise galleries intersected with three shorter crosswise passageways. Bridges of reinforced concrete and wrought iron spanned the galleries on the second and third floors connecting opposite sides. An iron-and-glass arched skylight that allowed sunlight to penetrate the length of the galleries topped the entire structure. Marble stairs were placed at intervals throughout the Rows, and stairs of Finnish granite were at the main entrance. Floors inside shops were laid with decorative parquet. The building was also fitted with electric lighting and central steam heating. It also boasted an artesian well and relied on a system of convex mirrors and prisms to direct light to the basement. Loading docks were constructed underground to save interior space and conceal the mechanics of business.[78]

The new Rows presented something more than a pleasing façade to its planners and admirers, who lauded the monumental arcade as a beautiful, immaculate, luxurious, and technologically progressive building that afforded Muscovites a new kind of civic space where merchants could pursue an enlightened, ethical trade and residents, a civilized way of life. It was as if the new physical surroundings would elicit changes in behavior and mentality and, ultimately, bring happiness to Moscow's residents. Razmadze predicted enormous change for the merchants who would occupy the new Rows, contrasting the "luxurious, bright, and warm magazins equipped with all imaginable conveniences" to the "dim, cold, broken down little lavkas" that had dominated the Rows previously.[79] A journalist writing under the pseudonym Moskvich also celebrated the reopening of the "Palace of Moscow Commerce" as the herald of a bright future. In an article for *Moskovskie vedomosti,* he contrasted the spacious and luminous new arcade to the cramped spaces of the old Rows. Recalling the shops in the former Rows as "narrow, open to the four winds, cold little lavkas crammed from top to bottom with merchandise," he claimed that space inside shops had been so limited that there was not enough room for the seller or the shopper to even turn around. In his view, confining spaces and dim lighting not only created an unaccommodating atmosphere but also made it impossible for a customer to shop for and choose an item. Promoting the idea that customers' comfort and pleasure should be taken into consideration, Moskvich wondered at the amount of patience and endurance that customers had to summon to frequent such places. By contrast, he praised the capacious magazins of the new arcade, dwelling on the sunlight afforded by the glass roof, on the electricity, heat, and latest store fixtures designed for optimal examination and selection of merchandise. Such comforts and conveniences, he asserted, had been "unthinkable" (nemyslimo) in the old, dark, and cold structure. In particular, Moskvich saw in the renovated Rows an extension to the public sphere of the demand in private life (chastnaia zhizn') for convenience and comfort. However, he also expected that retailers would outpace these demands, spurring further innovations.[80]

To supporters such as Moskvich, and to the corporation's major investors and executives, the rebuilding was nothing less than a revolution that promised to usher in a new society. These optimists expected that a spacious, attractive, clean, bright, and warm environment would inculcate desirable behaviors in merchants, customers, and workers and discourage objectionable ones. As they envisioned it, Row merchants would invite customers to revel in the beauty of their new stores, receiving them and attending to their requests respectfully. Shopping would no longer be a struggle of wills between merchants and shoppers but a pleasant excursion, akin to a visit to a museum. In their imagining, customers would sweep through the broad passageways, appreciating the elbow room and public lavatories, admiring elaborate displays of merchandise, and browsing and selecting items at their leisure. Workers' health would benefit from the air, sunlight, cleanliness, and warmth of their new workplace, and they could relax in tastefully appointed employee lounges decorated with comfortable furniture, authentic ancient Russian drawings, and mosaic floors. Their work would also become easier thanks to new mechanical devices and equipment that made storing and displaying merchandise easier. In short, people and behaviors would be transformed underneath the great, bright canopy of the Upper Rows.

Moskvich and others like him put faith in the physical structure itself, but they also believed that a new breed of Row merchants would dramatically change the ways business would be conducted. The majority of proprietors who had kept shops in the old Rows chose not to return to the Red Square location after the rebuilding, either because they had already relocated to other premises and did not wish to move again or because they disapproved of the new arcade and its operational policies. Several large- and medium-sized Russian firms that had occupied space in the old Rows, however, did reopen in the new venue. These included Pavel Sorokoumovskii & Sons, M. P. Shcherbachev & Sons Textiles Company, and the firm belonging to the director of the corporation's board, Mikhail Kalashnikov & Sons Watch Company. Slonov and his partner also reopened their precious metals business there. Despite some continuity with these tenants, however, a different group of merchants defined the style and methods of retailing in the new arcade. Firms such as A. & V. Sapozhnikov Company exemplified the new order of business in the Rows. Established in 1852, this firm had built a reputation on their luxurious, high-quality silks, velvets, and brocades, which were worked with Russian Orthodox imagery. These products had earned first-guild merchants Aleksandr and Vladimir Sapozhnikov several medals at national and international exhibitions. Such was the renown of their work that they counted among regular clientele the high clergy and members of the court, who ordered brocaded robes for special occasions and upholstery for their palaces. The firm also crafted banners and standards for the military and received orders from the Dalai Lama and fashion houses in Paris and London.[81] In Moskvich's estimation, the Sapozhnikovs' store was a paragon of retailing, and he praised the firm's bright, roomy premises, exemplary displays, and international standing. In profiling a Russian-owned firm that made goods embroidered with Orthodox symbols and relied upon the state, church, and military for much of its business, Moskvich played up the image of the Rows as a patently Russian enterprise firmly rooted in tradition. At the same time, his profile depicted an exemplary modern Russian business capable of producing the highest quality products for discriminating customers in Russia and abroad and of providing an attractive, organized store and excellent customer service. In essence, his profile of the Sapozhnikov Company conveyed the impression that Russian firms could be large, internationally successful entities that could adopt contemporary methods of retailing without losing their Russianness.

Other journalists wrote similarly admiring features, one predicting that the arcade would provide a new kind of civic space, one where Muscovites would go not only to shop but also to attend meetings, concerts, and social events. The new structure, in fact, housed several halls for precisely these purposes, and one of the rooms could accommodate a thousand people. Not long after the reopening, *Moskovskii listok* reported on a glittering charity event held in the Rows that represented the kind of life that Moskvich and the Rows' planners had envisioned. Hosted by the Grand Duchess Elizaveta Fedorovna, patroness of the Municipal Guardianship of the Poor in Moscow, this event was described in rapturous detail: galleries illuminated by multicolored lanterns, a string orchestra, balalaika players, and choirs of gypsy and Russian singers. Moving among it all, an elegantly attired public (*publika*) strolled the Rows listening to music and treating themselves to champagne, fruit, and candy. The journalist-author took pride in the fact that the Rows afforded such a suitably grand venue for such sparkling events, intimating that, without the rebuilding, such events would have been impossible.[82]

Despite the Rows' thoroughly modern features, the new arcade harkened back to the old Rows and celebrated Russian traditions and history. To be sure, the arcade was patterned after the then-fashionable style for such shopping centers and thus presented the latest trend in commercial architecture. But the interior design remained true in spirit to the row arrangement that had developed in Russia over the preceding centuries. The three lengthwise and crosswise passageways lined with shops were reminiscent of the layout of the old structure in which blocks of shops formed rows. The tradition of naming each row also remained, although the appellations no longer indicated commodities sold but paid tribute to significant events in Russia's past or to important Russian cities and personalities. The Kazan', Il'inka, Middle, Vladimir, and Ivanov rows ran parallel to Red Square on the first floor. The Minin, Pozharskii, and Central rows ran crosswise.[83]

The internal layout of stores was not completely standardized or uniform but maintained the irregular occupancy patterns of the old Rows. While blueprints of the new building show an interior divided into uniform parcels of retail space, shops actually differed from each other in size and shape, with the result being a less regular apportionment reminiscent of the individually improvised arrangement of lavkas in the old Rows. Some tenants, desiring more space than a single parcel afforded, rented two or more spaces in configurations of their own making. The Sapozhnikov Company, for example, occupied seventeen spaces on the second floor, fifteen on one side of the third floor, and five more across from them. The company's premises thus assumed the shape of a large rectangle, topped by a smaller one, with an adjunct smaller space across the way. Abrikosov & Sons confectioners rented the four front corner spaces on the Il'inka side of the building, forming a mid-sized, square-shaped shop. P. V. Uskov's textile store occupied an L-shaped area comprising three spaces on the first floor. To be sure, such occupancy patterns were not the result of the spontaneous and idiosyncratic expansion that had characterized the old Rows, and the shapes that stores assumed were limited by the rectangular shape of individual parcels of space. Still, the tailoring of space to suit individual proprietors contradicted the impression that the new Rows had been built according to a precise, uniform floor plan in which each store occupied a standard amount of space. The new edifice also did not completely abandon the small-scale, freewheeling kinds of trade that had flourished in the old Rows. The mezzanine on the second floor provided space for many booths from which small-scale vendors conducted business, thus constituting, in essence, another floor. Several *shkafchiki*, vendors who sold items from cupboards, also occupied spaces at three different points in and around the building.[84]

Items retailed in the arcade also did not change dramatically. The majority of businesses continued to sell those items for which the Upper Rows had become known: textiles, ready-to-wear clothing, haberdashery items, jewelry and watches, gold and silver items, icons, perfume and cosmetics, tobacco, and confections, although fewer merchants than previously dealt in grocery items. Well-known firms such as K. & S. Popov Brothers and Abrikosov & Sons sold sugar, tea, coffee, candy, and other inexpensive luxuries, but merchants who dealt in produce and other foodstuffs were noticeably absent.

Religious imagery and rituals also carried over into the new Rows, preserving links with Russian traditions and manifesting the new Row merchants' attachment to Orthodox beliefs and institutions. The well-known firm of Frolov, which had formerly been located in the Rows, created three mosaic-style icons to adorn the building's exterior. An image of the Savior decorated the space over the main entrance and the Kazan' Mother of God icon, the Nikol'skaia entrance. One of the entrances on Il'inka Street featured an icon of Nikolai the Miracle Worker, patron saint of merchants.[85] Religious observances also continued to commemorate important phases of the rebuilding. Public prayer services marked the demolition of the old building and the beginning of construction of temporary lavkas, as well as their subsequent opening, and the laying of the cornerstone on May 21, 1890.

The gala festivities that celebrated the reopening in December 1893 showcased the role that Moscow's civil society had played in establishing this monument to modern commerce and urban life. No less important, they also demonstrated the bonds among entrepreneurial, political, and professional elites, Orthodoxy, and the tsarist state.[86] The Grand Duke Sergei Aleksandrovich and his wife, the Grand Duchess Elizaveta Fedorovna, representing the royal family and the state's ties to the project, showed up to witness the event, as did Moscow's governor-general, vice-governor, and various municipal officials and civic leaders, including the starshina of the Merchants' Soslovie, members of the municipal board, and the director of the post office. Representatives from the world of art, architecture, and education, such as the chairman of the Historical Museum, the French artist F. Fevr, Pomerantsev, and other professors of art and architecture, also attended. The importance of accentuating the building's cutting-edge design and enmeshing its contemporary functionality with established symbols of authority showed in the decorations and festivities. Russia's national flag decorated all four façades of the arcade and all of the bridges and galleries inside. An icon was placed over each of the twelve entrances to the arcade. At precisely twelve o'clock, three clergymen stood in the meeting hall on the *belle étage* in front of a wall draped with brightly colored fabrics and hung with icons sacred to Moscow to conduct a public prayer service. The service ended with the customary proclamations of a long life to the tsar, tsarevich, and the royal house. According to the *Moskovskie vedomosti* and *Russkie vedomosti,* a resounding acclamation arose after the proclamations. Following the service, the clergy sprinkled the entire premises of the Upper Rows with holy water. Afterward, guests repaired to another hall, also decorated with Russian flags, for breakfast, during which another round of toasts to the tsar and family were reportedly received by shouts of "Hurrah!" and followed by the playing of the national hymn, "God Save the Tsar." Attendance at the service was limited due to space; however, an estimated sixty thousand people stood in the galleries of the Rows or outside the entrances to witness the ceremony and performances by seven different orchestras.

Such an elaborate reopening ceremony and attentive press coverage suggest that the event was staged to communicate the idea that the rebuilding was a significant public event in which all sectors of urban society played a role. In the hands of the merchant investors who led the reconstruction project and with the involvement of the press, the reopening signified a new way of configuring urban life, one with Moscow's merchant elite and its modern retail sector at the center, supported by the rituals and symbols of the tsarist state and Orthodox faith and consumed by the public. Participants symbolically celebrated the potential to infuse society with beauty, orderliness, technology, consumption, and civility, while paying obeisance to God and ruler.

The Russian Rows

The desire to pay homage to Russian traditions and established authorities also meant the reinforcement of prejudicial policies toward Jews and foreign subjects. Statute 15 in the corporation's charter explicitly forbade either owning shares in the new venture or acquiring them later. The statute declared, "Shares of the Company may be transferred only to Russian citizens who were born of the Christian faith, the State Bank, the Moscow Merchants' Bank, the First Credit Union Company, and the Moscow Commercial Bank, and also to Orthodox churches and monasteries, as well as charitable and philanthropic institutions for persons of the Orthodox faith, zemstvo, municipal, and soslovie societies. . . . Any further transfer of shares to other persons and institutions, except the above-mentioned credit institutions and from those institutions to Russian subjects not born into the Christian faith, are prohibited."[87] This statute devolved from Reform Era policies that had aimed to promote the "activization" of Jews and their "selective integration" into the empire, but, by the 1880s, these policies had sparked attempts to limit Jews' economic influence.[88] The influx of non–Russian Orthodox merchants into Moscow, St. Petersburg, and other places where Jews had once been forbidden to reside had begun only in the 1860s, after a decree in 1859 gave Jewish merchants, bankers, and heads of industrial-commercial firms, as well as foreign subjects, permission to register in the first guild of merchants and carry out business in any city in the empire. A decree in 1865 extended the right of permanent residence to all guild-registered artisans. Following the issuance of these and similar decrees, a stream of Jewish merchants and professionals left Minsk, Kiev, Odessa, Vil'no, Riga, and other cities where Jews had been settled and headed for cities throughout the empire. By the end of the century, more than three hundred thousand Jews were living in places previously off limits to them. The largest number of them settled in St. Petersburg. Moscow, a major commercial center, also attracted a great number of them.[89] In fact, despite the declaration of Moscow as the Russian Orthodox center of commerce by many contemporaries and the acceptance of that claim in much of the scholarly literature, Jews' share of commerce in Moscow steadily increased in the last decades of the nineteenth century. Records show that, in 1865, only 1.1 percent of Moscow's first-guild merchants' capital came from Jewish sources, but, by 1898, that figure had jumped to 29.3 percent. In all, according to one historian of Jewish entrepreneurs, almost 60 percent of the capital of first- and second-guild Jewish merchants was recorded in Moscow.[90]

According to Benjamin Nathans, migration from areas where Jews had traditionally been allowed to settle reflected a plan, formulated by the tsarist state in consultation with a group of twelve wealthy first-guild Jewish merchants, to manage the "Jewish question" by first integrating into the existing corporative structure those Jews believed to possess sufficient education and skills to make valuable contributions to the economy or civic life.[91] Even as the plan succeeded in drawing Jews into Russia's interior, it elicited anxiety and resentment among the Russian Orthodox populations in St. Petersburg, Moscow, and, presumably, other cities. Many of the Jewish migrants who settled in Moscow, for example, were involved in wholesale operations, especially textiles, which had traditionally been an important industry for Moscow's merchants. Moreover, several attained high levels of success, some even garnering the titles of Honored Citizen and Hereditary Honored Citizen. The influx of Jewish entrepreneurs into Moscow, therefore, intensified competition in the wholesale textile industry, threatening the position of influential Russian businessmen and prompting them to file complaints with city and tsarist officials about Jewish business practices.[92] One anonymous letter, labeled "Secret" and sent to the governor-general's office in 1889, typified the anxieties that Moscow's Russian

Orthodox merchants frequently expressed, including the allegation that Jews conducted business without obtaining the requisite documents and evaded paying taxes, thus giving them an unfair advantage.[93]

In the 1880s and 1890s, when Aleksandr III sat on the throne and less tolerant-minded municipal authorities governed Moscow and St. Petersburg, such accusations provoked a series of prohibitive decrees that undermined the earlier goal of Jewish integration and allowed prejudice to prevail.[94] One decree authorized the minister of finance to organize a committee tasked with uncovering illegal businesses operated by Jews. A statute issued in 1891 gave Moscow's governor-general, who at that time happened to be the tsar's brother, Sergei, the power to expel Jews who had been permitted to reside in the city temporarily during the era of reforms. The campaign against Jewish corporate influence culminated in Aleksandr's decree of 1892 that all corporate charters would be required to prohibit Jewish employees from managing an enterprise's real estate and that Jews, as well as foreigners, would not be permitted to participate in the formation of corporations.[95] A later imperial decree, issued in 1899, restricted the number of Jews permitted to register in the first guild in Moscow and in Moscow's guberniia. These measures had the intended effect. Prior to 1891, approximately thirty-four thousand Jews lived in Moscow. Over the next few years, the majority, most of them artisans rather than wealthy merchants, were forced to depart the city; by 1897, only eighty-two hundred Jews remained.[96] In St. Petersburg, the city governor, Petr A. Gresser, put harsh measures in place in the 1880s and 1890s, including a campaign of random searches of Jewish artisan shops, thus further reducing the number of Jews in the capital.[97]

Within this context, the authors of statute 15 revised the language several times in order to ensure that its meaning was clear and that no loopholes remained that might allow stock shares to fall into the hands of Jews. While the statute technically barred both foreigners and Jews from acquiring stock in the corporation, organizers clearly worried more about Jewish infiltration. One Row merchant, who helped frame the corporation's statutes, recommended the addition of the phrase "by birth" to the statement that only Russian citizens could hold shares in the corporation. Justifying the amendment, he noted that foreigners (*inostrantsy*) living in Russia, particularly Jews, often would go abroad to live and, once there, would change their citizenship. Therefore, in order to "eliminate this alien element" (*chuzhdyi dlia nas element*) and prevent it from subsequently acquiring shares, he recommended that the statute specify *"that only persons born and remaining from the time of birth Russian citizens, i.e., native residents [korennye zhiteli] of our native land can own shares."*[98] The language of the statute reflected a "rightist nationalist" position, which held that, in the words of one historian of empire, "Russia belonged to Russians" and that, although non-Russian peoples should be allowed to reside in the empire, they "had to remember the 'reigning' nationality was, is, and would always be Russian."[99]

Other nationalist writers approached the issue of property from another angle, evoking legends of the Rows and of Moscow's merchantry to construct an image of Moscow as the heart of true Russian commerce; in doing so, they created a discourse that implicitly justified the exclusion of non–Russian Orthodox shareholders. Razmadze's commemorative volume, for example, presented the Red Square marketplace as a venerable national institution, a citadel of history and tradition, by skillfully interweaving its history with the history of Moscow. Razmadze opened his chronicle with an account of Moscow's founding by Iurii Dolgorukii and the city's subsequent attainment of its "historical destiny" as the "heart of Russia."[100] Within the context of Moscow's ascendance to power, the author depicted the Rows as witness to crucial historical events such as the Polish and Napoleonic invasions and the crowning of Mikhail Romanov. Because of its immediate proximity to Red Square, one of the key sites where these historic events played out, the Rows assumed a certain sacrality and shared in the mythic aura of Russia's past, becoming, in Razmadze's telling, a revered historical site in its own right.

The image of the Rows as a national preserve of Russian Orthodox merchants requiring protection from foreigners also appeared in an anonymous treatise published in the year prior to the company's incorporation. Written to protest the trading of the corporation's shares on the stock market, the treatise suggested that the Russian Orthodox merchants' exclusive privilege of occupying the Rows had been guaranteed in an ancient pact between Ivan the Terrible and Moscow's merchants. According to this legend, when Ivan built St. Basil's Cathedral, he invited merchants from the Gostinyi Dvor to a banquet. Upon arrival, each of the guests bowed to the sovereign and presented him with something magnificent—sable, damask, brocade—to adorn his new cathedral. Seeing the merchants' zeal and realizing the significance of commerce to Russia, Ivan supposedly granted to the merchants "a place for eternity where they could conduct their trade." Thus, the author concluded, "since antiquity this place [Red Square] has belonged to the native Russian Orthodox population."[101] The legend of this sacred compact, in which Russian Orthodox merchants embellished the newly built church in exchange for trading privileges near the Kremlin, made clear that it was only because of their pious beneficence that the tsar granted them commercial favor. The implication was that such devotion, performed on behalf of the Orthodox Church, automatically excluded those who did not profess the faith from enjoying the same privilege. As this author argued, only "full-blooded" Russians were entitled to occupy this "sacred place," and he considered it the "greatest injustice" to allow this "legacy of the Russian people" to fall into the hands of foreigners by allowing the sale of bonds.[102] The veracity of the tale of Ivan and the Moscow merchants is unclear, but its publication attests to the fact that some saw it as a duty to defend and preserve the Rows for Russian Orthodox merchants, who in their rendering stood as sentinels of the Russian nation.

Assertions of Moscow's position as the center of Russian Orthodox commerce surely reflected both nostalgia on the part of Russian Orthodox merchants and officials as well as anxiety about an increasingly diverse city and merchantry. Some writers for the boulevard press also fostered such emotions. The columnist Moskvich embroidered his celebratory feature of the Rows' reopening with phrases asserting Moscow's timeless essence as "not only the capital of tsarism, the heart of Russia, but the capital of Russian commerce." Although his article did not call for the exclusion of foreigners or Jews, the journalist emphasized Moscow's pivotal role in commerce, using hyperbolic language that accorded sacrosanct status to the arcade and the city. Calling the rebuilding of the Upper Rows "an event" that "resounds throughout all of Russia," his words, in effect, asserted that this national landmark was purely and exclusively Russian.[103]

Unmoved by emotional nationalistic appeals, shareholders protested statute 15 and unanimously voted to petition for its amendment, but they ran up against state and local officials, who endorsed the image of the Rows as sacred ground in need of protection from the non-Orthodox population. In 1894, a shareholders' assembly voted unanimously to petition Minister of Finance Sergei Witte to request an amendment that would allow all credit institutions operating under state-approved statutes to obtain shares.[104] Board chairman Kol'chugin drafted a petition explaining that shareholders, most of whom did not have at their disposal large amounts of capital, wanted the change in order to have access to more lines of credit. The Moscow governor-general, however, intervened, writing to Witte to convey his objections. Declaring that statute 15 served as a guarantee that the "high value and historical significance of the land" on which the Rows sat would not end up the property of foreign citizens or non-Christians, he argued that since most private financial institutions were owned by Jews, adding all credit institutions to the list of approved lenders and shareholders would give Jews the opportunity to obtain shares in the company. He went on to chide the shareholders for privileging profit potential over the "social significance" of the property and advised them to deal only with those banks and credit companies whose boards were located in Moscow and composed of purely Russian capital. For the governor-general, Jewish ownership of land in Red Square equated to the destruction of Moscow as the Russian heartland, a turn of events he considered would constitute an "irreparable and unforgivable mistake."[105] He also communicated his concerns to the minister of internal affairs, writing anxiously that "the Upper Rows, which occupies the most precious place in all of Russia, could fall into Jewish hands."[106] Predictably, the tsar ruled against the shareholders' petition. As Witte explained in a letter to the minister of internal affairs, "His Imperial Highness" found it "impossible" to agree to the proposed change, since most private credit institutions are "in Jewish hands."[107] The issue, however, did not go away. Again in 1913, the board complained that shareholders found themselves in a financially difficult position because of the confines of statute 15. This petition resulted in the addition of the Moscow Discount Bank, a bank founded by German-born entrepreneurs, to the list of approved credit institutions, but banks owned by Jews still could not transact business for Row merchants or obtain shares in the company.[108]

Despite such restrictions, several foreign-owned firms and even a few Jewish ones leased retail space in the Rows, although the Rows remained largely the preserve of Russian merchants. In 1895, approximately 90 percent of firms were operated by ethnically Russian proprietors.[109] Some well-known foreign firms, including the French perfume and cosmetics firms Brocard & Company and A. Ralle & Company and Einem, the popular German confectionery company, all maintained stores and together made up about 8 percent of the shops in the Rows. Jewish firms accounted for only about 1 percent.

Reception of the Rows

Reflecting the divisions that had rent the reconstruction project from the start, the new Rows received a mixed reaction from the merchant community. One year after the opening of the Rows, approximately 720 of the more than 1,000 available retail spaces had been rented by a total of 285 firms. Shop space on the first floor, especially fronting Red Square, was considered prime retail property. Of the 322 spaces on the ground floor, 305 were rented. Space on the second and third floors, however, proved a harder sell. That same year, only 146 and 107 spaces on the second and third floors, respectively, were rented.[110] The corporation's board tried to overcome merchants' resistance to renting upper-floor spaces by offering discounts to tenants who signed long-term contracts. In this way, the board managed to persuade the Sapozhnikov brothers to sign a six-year contract for a sizable block of space on the upper floors. Board members hoped that the presence of such a highly respected firm would serve as an anchor and attract other retailers, but this tactic proved unsuccessful.[111] The board's report of 1895 revealed lingering problems attracting tenants to the upper galleries. Board members blamed the city's abundant available commercial space, as well as the general assembly of shareholders' too-strict system of rental rates and refusal to allow concessions. The board recommended that it be given more leeway in negotiating contracts.[112] The general assembly relented, and the following year the board reported some success when it finalized an agreement to bring the Mart'ianov tavern to the Rows.[113] The board continued to struggle not only to attract merchant-proprietors but also to retain them. Although total rent monies had increased by 1895, several firms, including some large ones such as L. M. Ruzhentsev & Company and V. Vitaliev and I. A. Slonov, had given up their spaces in the arcade.[114] By 1902, more firms had set up business on the hard-to-rent second and third floors, although slightly fewer occupied the first floor.[115]

The Rows did not attract more businesses because, for one thing, many merchants had relocated to other commercial districts in the city, and, once settled in their new locations, they were reluctant to move again.[116] Others simply disliked the new building. The merchant Slonov, who occupied both old and new incarnations of the Rows, claimed that the builders' primary concern had been the façade and arrangement of the internal galleries and passageways. Even though he acknowledged that the builders had turned out a beautiful and stylish structure, he argued that "they lost the most important thing—the construction of a commercial venue that was not only for show, but convenient for trade."[117] Merchants such as Slonov did not necessarily disapprove of the handsome arcade, but, as practical men of business, they also expected the structure to serve their business needs. Slonov also complained that the structure impeded comfort. The stores on the first floor, he argued, all had low ceilings, and colossal stone pillars and arches encroached from all sides—a faulty design, he contended, that prevented air and light from reaching the shops. Customers, he pointed out, never went up to the second floor because the "winding iron stairs inside the stores are so narrow and awkward that not everyone can climb them."[118]

Beyond structural concerns, Slonov hinted that the new Rows lacked life and vitality, qualities he believed had characterized the former building: "Whereas commerce in the old rows was conducted in a lively and gay manner, now it is conducted in a quiet and lifeless fashion in the new, beautiful building of the Upper Trading Rows."[119] Slonov's assessment, tinged as it is with nostalgia, suggests that he—and others like him—missed the lenient rules, customary business methods, and male camaraderie that had reigned in the old Rows and that they disliked the regulations dictated by a new community of businessmen. For the Rows to live up to its image as a modern retail center, the management stipulated in contracts that tenants must meet certain obligations, which required that merchants dispense with the more informal methods of operating in the old structure. For example, all tenants had to agree to use only electric lighting in their stores. They were also obliged to keep the premises clean and tidy and not to obstruct pavements, galleries, staircases, and loading areas with merchandise and materials. Permission to put up a sign required prior approval from the board.[120] Merchants also related to each other differently than before, mostly remaining inside their shops, instead of standing around outside chatting with each other and playing games. Sales tactics also changed. Merchants were explicitly prohibited from chasing after customers and pleading with them to enter their stores or engaging them in haggling matches. Slonov perceived the tidy orderliness, restrained modes of contracting sales, and lack of traditional kinds of merchant fellowship as hindrances to the operation of a retail business. To him, the establishment of new rules and protocols meant an antiseptic and lifeless world, devoid of the clutter, chatter, and camaraderie that had previously made the Rows not simply a place to work and shop but an amiable, colorful community.

Urban residents and social commentators also registered mixed reactions to the new arcade. A snippet from an issue of *Moskovskii listok* in January 1896 poked fun at the Upper Rows' empty galleries, remarking that in the absence of shops and customers, pigeons had taken up residence there.[121] The newspaper's jab was apparently not far from the mark. That same year the company's report for 1895 acknowledged that customers had not readily taken to the arcade, but it also reported that business had picked up and that the "public is getting used to [*privykaet*] the arcade and visiting it more frequently." Council members attributed the increase of interest to the "livening up" of the Rows, in particular the staging of concerts, a marketing tactic that other arcades in the city used to attract customers.[122] The report adopted an optimistic tone, although the statement that "now complaints of dissatisfaction are not heard" was hardly a strong endorsement of the Rows' popularity.[123] The following year, a writer for *Moskovskii listok,* however, found reason to remark favorably upon the arcade. Although vendors at the Palm Sunday Bazaar (held despite snowy weather) were disappointed in the small turnout, the journalist reported, store owners at the Rows delighted in the throngs who eagerly visited the warm, dry arcade.[124]

As a result of merchants' and customers' lukewarm reception, the corporation took in smaller-than-expected dividends, at least according to one observer.[125] Ten years after the reconstruction, returns totaled between 3 and 3.5 percent per annum. Still, the Rows turned a profit almost from the beginning, netting 180,704 rubles in 1895 and more than 385,000 in 1904, dipping in 1909 to approximately 350,000.[126] Further, some of the largest retailers maintained shops in the Rows, right up to 1918, the year the Bolsheviks nationalized the arcade. In May 1917, in a show of satisfaction with and confidence in the arcade, the Sapozhnikov brothers' firm, the largest retail occupant, renewed its lease for six years and, by this time, had increased the total area it occupied on the upper floors.

Commercial Cosmopolitanism in Odessa's Passazh

Seven years after the Rows' grand reopening, the Passazh, Odessa's first arcade, opened at the corner of DeRibas and Preobrazhenskaia Streets. Like the Rows, the Passazh stood as a monument to modern retailing and symbolized a vision of urban life, the merchantry, and the city's position within the empire. The Passazh, like the Rows, also juxtaposed historical legacies with city leaders' aspirations and vision of the future. Unlike the Rows, however, the Passazh represented an ethnically diverse merchant community and Odessa's cultivation of itself as a city, in Patricia Herlihy's words, "on the fringe of empire, filled with free spirits and far from the stern gaze of Moscow and St. Petersburg."[127]

Political, business, and professional leaders, writers and journalists, and other image makers had long made virtues out of Odessa's youth, its geographic location on the Black Sea in the southwestern corner of the empire, its role as a commercial center linking Russia to Europe, and its large, diverse population. Dubbing the city the "Southern Palmyra," the "Jewel on the Sea," "Little Paris," and the "Capital of the South," among others, the official and informal leaders cultivated for the city a reputation as a young, international, cosmopolitan commercial and leisure center. Professor A. I. Markevich, who contributed a chapter to a hundred-year anniversary volume on Odessa's history, connected the city's commercial significance to a spirited and cultured lifestyle. Asserting that manufacturing had always been of relatively little importance to Odessa, he argued that commerce had enabled the city to become one of the "most well-appointed" (blagoustroennyi) cities in Russia and indeed in all of Europe. He further argued that the city's commercial knack had raised the standard of living for residents and attracted a stream of "people of the cultured class," who enlivened the city and made fashionable the idea of vacationing in Odessa.[128] Markevich's boasting about the vitality and significance of Odessa's commercial sector differed from the notion that agriculture, buttressed by industry, not commerce, was the strength of the empire's economy, a view held by most of the empire's political and business leaders, although some officials recognized the city's value as a grain exporting center. Many foreign visitors concurred with Markevich's assessment. Several found Odessa intriguing and wrote of the colorful clothing one could see on the streets, the fezzes and turbans, and the pleasures of the city, including "bargain" prices on foreign luxuries, although some complained that Odessa lacked an agreeable society.[129]

Many who lived in Russia's interior shared the professor's view of Odessa, although they advanced a different interpretation. To be sure, Grigorii Moskvich, who wrote a guidebook to Odessa, represented the city as prosperous, lively, and stylish and the "essential Odessan" as "immaculately dressed, with an expensive cigar in his teeth," riding in his carriage to one of the stylish downtown cafés accompanied by his fashionably dressed wife. To Moskvich, however, the emphasis on fashion and café society signified a preoccupation with external appearances instead of an abiding interest in intellectual or "spiritual development."[130] In short, in Moskvich's opinion, Odessa's commercial focus overshadowed cultural and intellectual affairs, making Odessa inferior to other cities in Russia. In other works published in Russia's interior, commerce in Odessa was explicitly linked to Jews, who, writers claimed, routinely violated laws in order to make money, thus making Odessa a corrupted city.[131]

Thus, to both admirers and detractors, Odessa represented commerce and the commercial classes, leisure, and cosmopolitan values and lifestyles. Beholden to this image, the men who invested in the Passazh, as well as its builders and designers, envisioned a different style of retail arcade for Odessa. The architects commissioned to design the arcade, L. L. Vlodek and T. L. Fishel', fashioned a structure that mixed neoclassical and Italianate styles and was unconnected to the Russian state or Orthodox religion in any perceptible way. The absence of such visual referents also had something to do with the fact that the Passazh did not sit on a historic site considered sacred. Perhaps more important was the fact that the heirs of Moisei Iakovlevich Mendelevich, a Jewish first-guild merchant and grain exporter, financed its construction. In contrast to Moscow's determined search for a Russian national style, the decision to blend two European-derived architectural styles paid homage to Odessa's distinctive historical trajectory and the influences of classical and western European styles. The neoclassical-Italianate structure omitted any semiotic representation of ancient Muscovy, the Russian nation, or Orthodox faith, juxtaposing instead the city's classical roots and pre-Christian legacy with the modern world of urban commercial culture and industrialization.

From its founding by Catherine the Great in 1794, Odessa was viewed as a beautiful "window on Europe," an image that Odessa's political leaders, business community, and opinion makers cultivated. The Black Sea northern coastal region had a longer, more diverse legacy, however, one that stretched back as far as the seventh century BCE, when colonies there served as trading outposts of the Greek city-states on the Aegean. Thus, Odessa could claim a tie to classical Mediterranean civilization. After a period of Polish rule in the early modern period, Cossacks and Tatars vied for power in the region, a circumstance that perhaps contributed to its image as a free-wheeling frontier. Russia defeated the Ottomans in 1774 and subsequently annexed the Crimean peninsula and Black Sea north coast. Catherine allegedly named Odessa after Odysseus, as part of her so-called Greek Project. She sought to populate the newly acquired territory by offering settlers free land and tax exemptions. Her offer attracted a large number of non-Russian and non-Orthodox peoples, among them Greeks, Italians, Turks, Armenians, Albanians, Serbians, Romanians, Swiss, and Germans, many of whom were Mennonites, as well as runaway serfs from the central provinces. In its first decade of existence, Odessa experienced economic growth from commerce, and, in the following decades, Odessa grew to become the Russian Empire's most important commercial port. Catherine's liberal policies in relation to Black Sea commerce, including reduced import and exports duties, spurred further growth. By 1796, Odessa had established a stock exchange, as well as an office of censorship, both being indicators of its commercial and cultural significance.[132]

The city retained its reputation for ethnic diversity over the next century. In the 1897 census, 58 percent of the city's population reported one of the Slavic languages—Russian, Ukrainian, or Belorussian—as their native tongue, while 33 percent claimed Yiddish, 4 percent Polish, 2 percent German, 1.5 percent Greek, and smaller percentages claiming Armenian and French. Jews, who had lived in the region even prior to the establishment of New Russia and had never been forbidden to reside in Odessa, constituted the second-largest ethnic group in the city. Odessa's merchant community was particularly diverse. In 1799, more than 40 percent of merchants and traders had come from abroad, with Greeks and Italians predominating. Jews made up an even larger percentage of the merchantry than they did of the city's population; by the 1850s, Jews constituted 53 percent of those engaged in trade, a figure that increased in subsequent years.[133] Odessa was also unique in that Jews were allowed to play a role in municipal affairs. The wealthy merchant-industrialist Avram Brodskii, for example, was among the six men who founded the executive committee of Odessa's general municipal duma in 1873. Jews were also permitted to hold positions in the duma, although they could not occupy more than one-third of the seats.[134]

During Catherine's reign, classical references were in vogue, a trend reflected in the neoclassical structures that Catherine and her grandson, Aleksandr I, sponsored. They were helped in this project by a few men of European origin, considered the chief architects of the city, including Don Joseph de Ribas, born in Naples of Spanish/Irish stock, Franz de Voland, a Dutch engineer, and the Duc de Richelieu, a French émigré and great-nephew of Cardinal Richelieu who served as the city's chief for more than a decade. In the early nineteenth century, Odessa's merchants took the lead in embellishing the city's streets, sponsoring, among other projects, the building of the neoclassical Exchange Building in 1829. Throughout the following decades, many other classical and neoclassical mansions, hospitals, and orphanages, as well as the Italian Renaissance– and baroque-inspired opera house (1883–1887) and the new Exchange Building (1894–1899), were built in the city.[135]

The four-story, L-shaped Passazh, which opened in January 1900, channeled Odessa's classical and European cultural heritage and representations of the city as a commercial-industrial urban center, combining neoclassical architecture and pre-Christian images with symbols of modern technology. The arcade's exterior and interior emphasized classical ideals of symmetry and pure forms in the regularly placed columns and statues that adorned the walls and doorways, the gracefully curved arches framing the windows, and the stone-tiled floor laid out in geometric patterns. Instead of Orthodox icons, large statues of Mercury (the Roman god of commerce and one of Odessa's mythical protectors), flanked by two female demigoddesses, embellished the arcade's two central entrances. Atop the cornice of the glass-and-iron skylight, illuminated in the evenings by electric lights, sat another figure of Mercury perched on a steam engine. The building also showcased technological and engineering innovations, including gas lighting, an elevator, and a sophisticated underground merchandise delivery system.[136] Thus, investors and builders rejected the Russocentric iconography that Moscow's merchant-investors and state and municipal authorities had endorsed for the Upper Rows. And although they did not overtly celebrate ethnic diversity by, for instance, creating a self-consciously multicultural style, they relied on an architectural style and motifs that, while not symbolizing ethnic diversity, muted Russian nationalist tendencies and exhibited instead the city's historical legacies and, surprisingly, given Odessa's commercial fame, the promise of industry.

From the start, the Passazh operated near capacity, its occupants epitomizing the retail sector as an international community of merchants. An advertisement announced the opening of, among others, the following stores and shops: G. Gezelle's stationery store, Iakov Gal'perin's haberdashery, R. Zak's toy store, Gentleman (a men's clothing store), Georgi Brothers' Special Greek Store, G. Eishiskii's frame store, E. D. Weinberg's shoe business, Leon Zinder's barbershop, Nelly (a store affiliated with the Nelly Corset Factory), and Faberzhe jewelers, purveyor to the Royal Court.[137] Other merchants set up shop in the Passazh soon after its opening, including Antonopulo's photography studio, Pervushin & Sons wine shop, Moisei and El'ia Poliakin's hardware store, Maria Desmarey's clothing store, and Rudnianskii's nondispensing drugstore.[138] Of course, some of the proprietors whose firms carried foreign-sounding names may not have been foreigners at all but may have named their firms "Nelly" or "Gentleman" in hopes of cultivating a stylish cachet. Still, the concentration of non-Russian and Jewish merchants departed from the model of the Upper

Rows, where presenting a Russian face was of paramount importance. Besides retail stores, the Passazh also housed public institutions, private dwellings, professional services, and cultural amenities, including the Hermitage restaurant, Raspopov's bookstore and public library, various professional offices, including the office of S. Fainshtein, professor of mnemonics, elegantly decorated apartments, Bel'ts and Stavraki, a girls' gymnasium, and the Hotel Passazh, which occupied the third and fourth floors. Such a diverse range of occupants suggests that the new venue was meant to function as something more akin to a sociocultural center rather than merely a retail center.

The merchants of the Passazh, like those of the Rows, strived to disassociate themselves from the negative reputation of merchants and the retail trade and to present the arcade as a model retail enterprise committed to fashion leadership, honesty, customer satisfaction, and urban civility. A couple of months after opening, proprietors sponsored an advertisement that announced a collective code of business ethics. The ad broadcast the message that all stores in the Passazh sold goods "conscientiously" and at fixed prices, and as a show of their determination to enforce this policy, proprietors pledged to collectively impose a fine on any merchant who gave a shopper a price reduction.[139] This policy sought to assure customers that they were being treated fairly and would receive the same price as the next customer. Merchants also tried to distance themselves from the image of the merchant as a dishonest vendor of shoddy goods by promising to sell only new, fashionable, good-quality merchandise and by urging customers to bring complaints about poor-quality merchandise to the management's attention. These pledges aimed to bring integrity and dignity to the retail trade and to foster a more restrained kind of shopping experience for those who disliked aggressive merchants, haggling, and other customary business practices.

To many urban observers, Odessa's arcade also showcased ideals of beauty, order, civic interaction, and a cultured lifestyle. Once the Passazh was complete, prominent Odessans proclaimed the arcade a marker of progress. The mayor proudly declared the arcade an "adornment" (ukrashenie) to the city and "the pride of Odessa," and he pointed to its presence as "evidence of the level of development of our commerce."[140] Guidebooks to the city likewise praised the building's "graceful architecture and beautiful decoration" and its "richly adorned interior," "handsome, unbroken line of elegant display windows," and "beautifully paved tile floors."[141] One guidebook also singled out the Passazh as a model of cleanliness and order.[142] Municipal boosters named the arcade one of the city's finest attractions and an indicator of its status as a modern, progressive urban center devoted to the pursuit of both business and pleasure. Admirers also conceived of the new venue as a public space that brought together fine consumer goods, civic activism, and high culture. Not long after the opening, a fête to benefit the Odessa Society for the Physical Education and Protection of Children was held in the arcade. *Odesskie novosti* featured several enthusiastic reports on this "grandiose charitable bazaar" and "outdoor festival" (*gulian'e*). Journalists reported that the event had attracted a great many members of the "public," who moved among the green garlands, multicolored electric lights, Chinese lanterns, banners, and flags, enjoying performances by orchestras and the opera star Oskar Kamionskii and demonstrations of gramophones, phonographs, and movies. According to one account, the event attracted more than six thousand people and earned thirty-two hundred rubles for the charity.[143]

Despite the diversity of occupants and the nods to cosmopolitanism in the Passazh, however, images of the Russian nation and Orthodox ritual and symbolism still played a role in the public inauguration of the new retail complex. Although only a minority of the merchant-occupants professed the Orthodox faith, those who participated in official opening ceremonies paid obeisance to the tsar and the Orthodox Church in a formal ceremonial blessing. Judging from press accounts, the ceremony closely resembled the one held to consecrate the Rows and consisted of an Orthodox prayer service before an array of icons and a sprinkling of the arcade with holy water, followed by a breakfast at which a roster of distinguished guests proposed toasts to the tsar's health and family and listened as an orchestra played "God Save the Tsar" three times.[144] Slight variations in protocol occurred, however, which gestured to Odessa's non-Russian heritage. Russian and Greek Orthodox clergymen jointly performed the rite of consecration, and a Ukrainian choir troupe performed alongside the Orthodox cathedral's choir. The ritual blessing incorporated some Greek and Ukrainian elements, but despite the presence of many non-Russian merchants in the Passazh and its financing by a Jewish merchant family, the Russian state remained the symbolic patron and Russian Orthodoxy, its public moral focal point. The Mendelevich brothers themselves did not attend the opening festivities, and manifestations of the Jewish faith, or any faith other than Eastern Orthodoxy, were conspicuously absent.

It might be tempting to argue that this peculiar staging of the blessing indicates that, although merchants of various ethnic backgrounds and religious dominations could freely operate in Odessa, there were still limits to how far public ceremonies could deviate from the dominant national narrative or that public demonstrations of non-Orthodox religiosity would serve only to point out divergence from a self-consciously Russian Orthodox empire. Perhaps the concepts of empire and Jewish integration and acculturation, rather than nation or Russian nationalism, provide more compelling interpretive keys.[145] To contemporary observers, as well as to scholars of Odessa and of Russia's Jews,

Odessa's Jews appeared to be more integrated into society than Jews in many other cities in the empire. Stephen Zipperstein argues that because Odessa was located in a "frontier setting" and because there were clear economic, social, and cultural benefits to involving themselves in the life of the city, Odessa's Jews participated more fully than did Jews elsewhere in Russia. He points out, however, that as such "acculturation" took place, Jews tended to identify more with commerce and materialism, for which Odessa was well known, and less with traditional values and religious ritual.[146] Odessa's Jews may not have been entirely unique, however. In his study of the Jewish elite in St. Petersburg, Nathans argues that the capital's Jews "exhibited remarkable adaptation to their new surroundings and abiding separateness," a phenomenon he terms "selective integration."[147] Moreover, he argues that certain wealthy Jewish merchants adopted prevailing styles of fund raising, restricted their religious observances, and played instrumental roles in the economy but did not necessarily distance themselves from the larger Jewish population. In fact, a wealthy young St. Petersburg cohort that included the Gintsburgs, Poliakovs, and Avram I. Zak carved out for themselves roles as spokesmen for the Jewish people and consultants to the tsarist government on the "Jewish question."[148]

Together, the work of Zipperstein and Nathans provides important context for understanding the construction of the Passazh as a public event in the life of an empire. Although a study of the role played by Odessa's Jewish merchant community remains to be done, it is safe to say that Odessa's Jewish merchant elite, like St. Petersburg's Jewish merchant elite, engaged in a process of selective integration, one in which the exhibition of modern entrepreneurship and civic leadership trumped adherence to public forms of religious ritual, at least in a commercial venue. In the 1870s, for example, about 90 percent of Jewish-owned shops apparently opened for business on the Sabbath.[149] Moreover, and perhaps more importantly, Jews lived in an empire that, according to John Klier, "made a great external show of Christian belief, and in which the institutional church was deeply involved in public life."[150] To the extent that some prosperous Jewish merchants and professionals may have been, at the least, indifferent to external forms of religious observance and that displays of the tsarist state and Russian Orthodoxy were de rigueur, the ceremonial blessing of the Passazh is not entirely surprising.

The building and dedication of St. Petersburg's first synagogue, the Choral Synagogue, at roughly the same time as the reconstruction of the Rows and the building of the Passazh, provide an illuminating parallel. Discussions about an appropriate architectural style and debate about whether there was an authentically Jewish style dominated planning for the synagogue in the years leading up to its opening in 1893. At issue was whether the structure should reflect an

Arabic heritage or the style of Berlin's synagogues or whether the synagogue's architecture should reflect its location within the Russian Empire and adopt the style of Russian Orthodox churches, only without Christian images. The opening ceremonial dedication included customary prayers for the royal family, in line with all public ceremonials, and the "El male rahamim" was recited in memory of Aleksandr II, who had been tsar at the time the project was initiated.[151]

Such evidence suggests that the Passazh reflected a multiethnic cohort of proprietors, investors, and builders, as well as city officials, and their selective integration into the empire. Its investors and architects made conscious choices about the external appearance of the arcade, which conspicuously departed from the Russian revival style and displayed Odessa's unique legacy and vision of itself, but nonetheless scripted the opening ceremonies to conform to the arcade's location within the European part of the Russian Empire, albeit with a few local adaptations.

Modern Commerce and Progress in Odessa

Following the opening of the Passazh, few, if any, complaints about its design, structural integrity, or place in the city emerged, at least in the press, although unabashed jubilant veneration did not last for long. Ambivalence toward Odessa's emphasis on commerce and its purported role in fostering progress surfaced the following year when a fire broke out in the Passazh, claiming the lives of two firefighters and a young female student from the gymnasium located inside. In covering the fire, journalists and residents who wrote letters to the editors eschewed the rhetoric of beauty and progress that had been employed earlier and instead asked whether the city leaders' preoccupation with commerce and the beautification of the city distracted them from their responsibility to protect citizens' welfare.[152] Newspaper reports recounted terrifying tales of the escape of young female pupils, who had to jump from the school's third-floor balconies into the arms of people standing below. In the wake of this incident, Odessans came forward to savage the Passazh and the city's frivolous delight over its presence in the city. They particularly objected to the idea of locating a school inside a shopping center, deeming commerce a corrupting influence completely at odds with education and the upbringing of young children, allegations that contradicted the image of the Passazh as an adornment to the city and a multipurpose cultural center. One such letter to the editor chided city leaders for the "delight" and "rapture" they exhibited upon the opening of the "pride of Odessa." The letter writer urged Odessans to "sober up" and think of public safety and children's education in a serious manner.[153] Another expressed outrage that the city had allowed a school to be inside a shopping arcade without first acquiring certification that the building had adequate ventilation and access points as well as the recreation yard necessary for a school.[154]

A. Fedorov, a writer for *Odesskie novosti*, likewise deplored the decision to put the school inside the Passazh. He labeled that move a "crime" that challenged the city's conception of itself as an advanced center of culture and commerce. Pointing out that this "auto-da-fé" had happened in broad daylight, in the center of a "European city," he argued that accidents, while unexpected, should not be completely unforeseen and that the level of development, of the "culture [*kul'turnost*] of a city" depends on that foresight. As these and other similarly outraged writers made clear, the fire in what many considered a modern structure in a city on the order of a western European metropolis raised issues about Odessa's priorities and its actual level of material and cultural progress. These critiques also revealed that not everyone believed that retail venues such as the Passazh endowed a city with productive traits and values. Some apparently thought that instead they endangered residents and detracted from projects that brought true progress, such as education and public safety. Making these points poetic, Fedorov mocked the classical and non-Christian images in the Passazh's interior. Describing the fire, he focused on a statue of "the little idol of buying and selling," the merry Mercury reigning over the chaos, "playfully stand[ing] with his right leg raised upward." His rendering of the god of commerce as a reckless imp symbolized the callous and destructive folly of commerce. Calling the devastation a "sacrifice to the short-sighted mercenary-mindedness of the city," Fedorov ended his report with an ominous image of the blaze stealing up from behind Mercury and, "in a sinister cloud of fire and smoke," swallowing up the idol.[155] The insinuation was that rather than commerce offering Odessans a new way of life, commerce would consume itself and perhaps Odessa along with it.

Despite enthusiastic public acclamations, ambivalence about the nature of the retail trade and about large, multistory venues that combined commercial and civic purposes existed among sectors of society, even in a city that had built a reputation on commerce and leisure industries. The negative publicity surrounding the fire, however, did not stop enterprising individuals from capitalizing on the tragedy. Merchants organized after-fire sales, and a local photographer offered for sale postcards featuring pictures of the building in flames. A book entitled *The Fire in the Passazh* and containing the personal reminisces of the author sold for fifteen kopeks. These products found an audience among curiosity seekers, who reportedly traveled from the provinces just to have a look at the burned structure.[156]

Considered together, the Upper Rows and the Passazh clearly were attempts to represent different brands of modern commerce and urban modernity within the Russian Empire. The history of both structures reveals the optimism and the anxiety inherent in the search for ways to reconcile established authorities, traditions, and beliefs with contemporary ideals, symbols, practices, and technologies. As constructed, Moscow's Upper Rows exhibited one version of modernity, endorsing values of beauty, rationalization, industry, civility, and civic collaboration while displaying fidelity to the Orthodox faith and the idea of a Russian nation. Odessa's Passazh projected the same values within a different stylistic mode that referenced classicism, Europe, industrialization, and cosmopolitanism and that incorporated notions of the tsarist state and Orthodox faith only in a ceremonial form. Despite these differences, both projects demonstrated that creating model commercial enterprises did not mean a complete rejection of previous systems of organization, ethnic and religious affiliations, or ties to the state but an updating or reblending of them with contemporary engineering and technology and newer ideals of restrained, rationalized business practices that admirers believed promoted civic activism and cultured living. The reimagining of Russian urban life as organized by Moscow's and Odessa's merchant elites, in association with municipal and state authorities, also contributed to the development of emerging discourses, including the rhetoric of legal and civil rights and the idea of external beauty supported by technology as indicative of progress, morality, and culture.

3

For God, Tsar, and Consumerism

The day that Grigorii Eliseev opened his fine foods and wine emporium in a renovated palace on Tverskaia Street in Moscow in 1901, a crowd formed in front of the store in anticipation of the noontime opening. As the occasion was by invitation only, the crowd gathered not so much to enter the store and make purchases as to simply witness the event: to admire the building's newly lavish façade and enticing window displays of caviar, lobsters, wine, and exotic fruits, to catch a glimpse of the stunning, gilded interior, and to watch as elegantly attired guests arrived. According to Vladimir Giliarovskii, the popular Moscow journalist and writer, the doors of the store swung open exactly at noon and a porter appeared at the entrance to receive the elect. Men festooned in the glittering ribbons of official orders, generals suited in white trousers and plumed, tri-cornered hats, and members of the clergy enrobed in expensive violet cassocks filed into the store to be greeted by Grigorii Eliseev himself, a blond, fair-eyed man in an impeccable tailcoat who was also wearing the Order of St. Vladimir and the honorary Order of the French Legion. Inside, "something fantastical" awaited the guests. Eliseev had completely transformed the historic mansion, demolishing its white marble staircase and replacing it with aisles stocked with wine for sale. Tremendous crystal chandeliers hung from the richly ornamented ceilings. A bay set into the wall resembled a theater box, alongside which hung a rare English clock with an enormous golden pendulum. At the appointed time, the main event commenced. Priests donned gold brocade chasubles and conducted a religious service, the highlight of which was a blessing of the premises and sprinkling with holy water. Following the service, guests took their places at a table, their positions determined by social rank, with the Archbishop Parfeniia occupying the highest place of honor. During the meal, various notables proposed toasts, the first to the health of the tsar and royal family, and an orchestra played the hymn "God Save the Tsar."[1]

Eliseev was not only one of the most prominent retailers in Moscow but also one of the most astute purveyors of the commercial ritual known as the ceremonial blessing (*torzhestvennoe osviashchenie*). The blessing was a long-established popular tradition, which prominent, enterprising merchants like Eliseev reinvented as an urban spectacle to showcase their relationship to tsarist power and the Orthodox faith and to exhibit a vision of urban life made possible by modern forms of retailing. There were many interconnected relationships among tsarist power, religion, and an expanding culture of mass retailing and consumption, and they were evident in the promotional strategies and commercial rituals of the merchant elite. Large, luxurious retail venues served as monuments to modern retailing and consumerism, but they also provided public spaces where merchants gathered local dignitaries, retail employees, journalists, and the public to orchestrate a performance based on a new merchant ethos that prescribed elegant buildings and interiors, transparent business practices, spectatorship, and benevolent, patriarchal relations. Merchants drew on the imagery and symbols of court and church to promote this vision, even as their promotion also commodified these representations. In the process, merchants such as Eliseev constructed alternative communities based on commercial relations but tied to religious and political loyalties, thus blending dominant beliefs, values, rituals, and symbols with emerging secular ones and papering over social, political, and religious differences.

The symbols and ceremonies of the Orthodox religion and tsarist court might seem incompatible with such a seemingly trifling affair as the opening of a retail store. It might be tempting to point out the contradictions among the various elements of the ritual blessing celebrations and allege disingenuousness and cynical calculation on the part of merchants. The outward incongruities, however, are largely due to Western conceptions of and discourses about the "modern" or "modernity," which maintain dichotomies between, for example, religion and modernity, and are less the result of the worldview or endeavors of many Russian merchants, who did not conceive of the contemporary world without religious traditions. Indeed, one of the most striking things about the ritual celebrations is that merchants like Eliseev apparently found few contradictions between the stewardship of their firms and their devotion to Orthodoxy and tsarism. Or perhaps it is more accurate to say that they found more complementarity than contradiction. To them at least, the modern business world was neither secular nor officially independent of the state; therefore, their use of the imagery of church and court for commercial purposes was an extension of their religious and political fidelity. That is not to say that the utilization of religious and political images and rituals was not calculated or that such usage did not have commercial value. Indeed, even as merchants may have earnestly paid obeisance to God and tsar, they drew the images and symbols of church and state into the commodifying realm of mass retailing and urban culture, and they profited from the association. Yet, as Vera Shevzov has wisely pointed out in her study of the "sacred centers" of Russian Orthodox life in the late empire years, it is difficult to separate "insincere" from "sincere" motives on the part of believers, who may have calculated, for example, that the construction of a chapel to honor the Romanov dynasty might bring favor to a petition or request. As she argues, "It is reasonable to assume that in some instances at least, rural believers genuinely assigned sacred meaning to political events and to events in the life of the imperial family."[2] Likewise, while not ignoring the apparent conflicts and business calculations made in orchestrating blessing ceremonies, my analysis tends to emphasize affinities among the various elements. In the Russian case, consumption, religion, and tsarist politics symbolically reinforced and promoted each other.

A consideration of the complex relationships among the three suggests several compatibilities. First, merchants shared a long, intertwined history with both the state and the Orthodox faith. Throughout Russian history, the state had acted as patron, regulator, and competitor in the commercial realm. Religion intersected with the commercial sphere in numerous and various ways, most apparently in Orthodox merchants' personal devotion to their faith, the integration of religious images and rituals into their daily business routines, and in the connection between the celebration of religious holidays and consumption of retailed goods. The public display of these affiliations was, therefore, not extraordinary; the blessing made them manifest and celebrated them. Second, the tsarist state, the Orthodox Church, and the retail trade had all historically relied on performance to present themselves to and communicate with their consuming publics. Of course, the purposes and goals of the three differed. Merchants sought a profit, the church, spiritual devotion, and the state, political and social stability, but the objectives of inculcating loyalty to and affection for an institution were essentially similar. The means each employed, particularly the production of awe-inspiring displays of power, wealth, and splendor, were also similar. Just as Nicholas II and his ministers began to update and enhance the tsar's methods of presenting his power to Russian subjects (for example, by allowing the royal family to appear on film), so prominent merchants like

Eliseev used contemporary merchandising and marketing strategies to aggrandize their public image. In doing so, the exhibition of their affiliations with church and state became a public spectacle befitting the age of mass media and retailing. Finally, Orthodoxy and tsarism, like most other ideas, persons, and institutions commonly considered inviolable or intractable to the marketplace, were in fact easily commodifiable.[3] The symbols and personas that represented them could be marketed and sold just like any other commodity. Recognizing the potential resonance of religious and political images, merchants packaged and integrated them into their firms' advertisements and publicity events. Although the relationships among merchants, church, and state were deeply intertwined and mutual, certainly the balance of power was unequal. The state and church held a far-reaching, formal kind of power that merchants did not. Nevertheless, merchants were not completely reliant upon these institutions for inspiration or direction. As much as they depended on and courted the patronage of church and state, they commodified their imagery and adapted some of their performance strategies for their own ends. In return, the state and church gave at least the appearance of endorsing or sanctioning mass retailing and the values of consumption.

The spiritual and commercial motives of the merchant elite intersected with the aspirations and interests of many urban consumers. The ritual festivities appealed to certain segments of the public, especially those who sought entertainment in urban public venues. Such consumers apparently attended these events because they viewed them as noteworthy local events of which they wanted to be a part, even if only as spectators. Attendance gave them the satisfaction that comes from "just looking," providing the chance to consume the spectacle of a grand event that combined pageantry, beauty, and local celebrities, and the familiar symbols of the Orthodox Church and Russian Empire.

Merchants and the State

Historically, rulers the world over have played an active role in the commercial economy. The exchange of goods generates a great amount of revenue for states in the form of customs, duties, taxes, and tribute, and, because of the profit potential, states and governments considered certain aspects of trade, especially foreign trade and the domestic production and sale of certain valuable or essential commodities, their exclusive domains. As a result, rulers have often formulated commercial policies and regulations that first of all serve the interests of the state but that nonetheless protect and further the interests of private merchants.[4] In this regard, the Russian state conformed to a global pattern among emerging states in the early modern period. Prior to 1650, for example, the Russian state claimed a monopoly on the production and sale of vodka and caviar; by 1705, salt, too, had come under the state's exclusive control. State-sponsored commercial enterprises also directly competed with merchants in the exportation of goods that were not deemed monopoly items, for example, furs, fish, cloth, and wax. Moreover, it was not only large-scale domestic and long-distance commercial operations that interested Russia's state officials. They also deemed the retail trade an important economic activity, and, until sometime in the eighteenth century, the state operated retail shops in Moscow's historic commercial district, the Kitai Gorod, just beyond Red Square.[5] Besides acting as primary merchant, the state regulated the retail trade. In the Muscovite period, rulers designated commercial sites, and state officials closely supervised them. Until the mid-sixteenth century, Moscow's main market was located inside the Kremlin. After Ivan the Terrible had the market stalls removed from the Kremlin, merchants still remained in close proximity to the seat of power, most moving across Red Square to the streets beyond, in the Kitai Gorod.[6] At times, the state also attempted to regulate retail prices, especially on staple items such as grain, although officials were not always able to persuade merchants to comply with their requests.[7]

The Russian state had also orchestrated commercial life through merchant guilds. Enacted in 1724 during the reign of Peter I, the guild system required merchants to register in one of three guilds, each of which accorded rights and privileges, as well as tax obligations. Reforms in 1863 under Aleksandr II ended the connection between registration in a guild and the merchant estate. After that year, the state required anyone wishing to engage in commerce, no matter his or her status, to buy a certificate each year.[8] Socioeconomic developments and emancipation ushered in a new age of commercial activity, and as new forms of business ventures, including joint-stock companies, appeared in the 1830s, the state continued in its role as regulator. In 1836, the tsarist state issued a corporate law code, which established a concession system requiring a merchant desiring to start a business to submit a charter to various ministries for approval and then to the tsar for his signature. The law further stipulated that once a charter had been approved, no changes could be made without first obtaining permission from the government.[9] The number of incorporations increased apace in the 1850s and 1860s and especially in the 1880s and 1890s as capitalist ventures formed to fund the building of railroads and the establishment of financial institutions and manufacturing enterprises. Despite these new financial arrangements and business formats, corporations continued to operate under the increasingly outdated and rather onerous and arbitrarily enforced Corporate Law of 1836. At the turn of the century, the corporate code remained

nearly unchanged from the time of its enactment, except for the addition of
several provisions in the late nineteenth century that restricted the rights and
influence of foreigners, Jews, and Poles.[10]

The advent of the advertising industry also stimulated the state's monitoring impulses. Until 1828, the state reserved for itself the right to print almost
all official and commercial advertisements, a privilege that guaranteed a significant amount of revenue. In contrast to its role in the incorporation process,
the state began to decentralize its supervision of advertising, although it began to explicitly define its interest in content. The censorship statutes of 1828
and 1865 proscribed offending the Orthodox Church or Christianity and the
tsar or royal family, as well as the personal honor and morality of individuals.
The 1828 statute also mandated that posters and small print ads be submitted
to local police authorities for approval. This delegation of censorship meant
that the process relied on the individual interpretive skills and judgment of
local officials, who, over time, became overwhelmed by more sophisticated
ads in a greater number of publications. According to Sally West, however,
even though advertisements had to first pass official muster, the statutes did
not seriously circumscribe commercial activity, although they did create confusion and logistical problems, especially for censorship offices. As a result,
the censorship of ads was often arbitrary and ineffective. Laws on advertising
continued to exist, but they were routinely ignored, although authorities could
punish offenders post-publication through the courts.[11] Censorship laws also
applied to retailed printed goods, and local officials conducted regular searches
of retail stores and marketplaces for items that violated the codes. Police in
Odessa confiscated from vendors at the Staryi Bazaar pictures considered offensive, such as one of the tsarevich standing on a mound of skulls, as well as
postcards of a reclining Empress Aleksandra, whose head, when viewed from
another angle, resembled that of Aleksandr II.[12]

By the start of the twentieth century, although the tsarist state retained the
corporate code, it had delegated many of its supervisory and regulatory tasks
to municipal authorities. Nevertheless, or perhaps as a result, the regulation
and supervision of commerce expanded. Furthermore, local authorities adopted
new guises as moral arbiters and defenders of the public, setting rules and standards and thus finding new ways to assert their own authority. In 1897, Odessa's
municipal government set up special divisions within the police department
and the office of the *gradonachal'nik* (city governor) to survey commercial establishments. The corps of commercial police in the gradonachal'nik's office
consisted of inspectors and the bazaar elder (*starosta*) charged with broad responsibilities for surveillance over markets, bazaar squares, and all commercial
establishments. Acting as consumer advocates, these local officials were to carry

out health inspections in shops and markets in an attempt to ensure some level of quality, safety, cleanliness, and accuracy in weighing and measuring goods. The gradonachal'nik's office also established regulations for street vending, setting, for example, the legal age of vending, the number of vendors allowed to operate in the city, the kinds of goods permitted for sale, and areas off limits to street vending.[13] The office also decreed that each vendor must either wear or display a sign while selling. Inspections also became routine in Moscow's market. Sanitation checks were regularly carried out, for example, in the Okhotnyi Riad meat market.[14]

Therefore, well into the nineteenth century, the tsarist state, along with municipal authorities, intervened in various aspects of commercial-industrial and corporate affairs. According to some scholars, this arrangement hindered Russia's economic development and the growth of the middle classes and civil society. Thomas Owen argues that the state's bureaucratic regulations and its overriding desire to protect its own economic interests inhibited the development of corporations and corporate law.[15] Acknowledging the obstacles presented by the Russian state's bureaucracy, monopolies, and competition with merchants, other historians suggest a "two-sided relationship" in which merchants and the state profited from each other, even if merchants relied on the state and "grew up under its shadow."[16] Some historians also suggest the existence of a "cozy relationship" of negotiation and accommodation wherein government officials and merchant elites were "more often in league than in conflict."[17]

The official attention given to various aspects of commerce and the retail trade and the institutionalization of their regulation indicates that the retail sphere was growing and diversifying. State and municipal officials viewed some of the consequences of growth and diversification as threatening to their own interests or to their subjects' well-being, and they thus restricted or regulated commerce. However, the relationship that developed between merchants and state authority was not entirely adversarial. Tsarist and local officials, along with members of the educated public and retail workers and consumers, frequently found areas of common concern and cooperation. The issues of Sunday and holiday commerce and of working conditions, for example, preoccupied authorities at both levels, as well as merchants and individuals as ideologically different as Konstantin Pobedonostsev and A. Gudvan, a labor organizer in Odessa. These various constituencies took different positions on these issues, but they all identified them as urgent and put forth measures to address them. By 1905, the gradonachal'nik's office in Odessa had issued a decree stipulating hours of operation for holiday and Sunday commerce.[18]

In the mid-nineteenth century, the state began to promote and sanction commerce in new ways. In 1828, in cooperation with merchant representatives, the state started to award manufacturers and merchants gold and silver medals and monetary awards for products deemed superior at periodic exhibitions of trade and industry. After 1848, these awards also gave the winners the privilege of displaying the imperial seal in advertisements and on places of business.[19] The tsar and his ministers also began to bestow on select firms the title "Purveyor to the Court of His Imperial Majesty," a coveted honor that also entitled recipients to display the imperial seal. In order to receive this title, merchants were required to submit a petition to the Ministry of the Imperial Court, which investigated the business to determine if the firm had consistently and favorably supplied the royal family for at least eight years. This title and others could also be granted at the special request of a member of the royal family.[20] Those merchants whose products found royal favor included Savva Morozov & Sons (textiles), confectioners Abrikosov & Sons as well as A. Siu & Company, perfume and cosmetics manufacturers A. Ralle & Company as well as A. M. Ostroumov, A. M. Mikhailov (furrier), Eliseev Brothers, Filippov Bakers, the St. Petersburg Factory-Produced Shoe Company, tea merchant V. Vysotskii & Company, Odessa textile merchant and haberdasher V. T. Ptashnikov, and an Odessa dressmaker who had created dresses for the empress. As these few examples indicate, Russian and non-Russian, Orthodox and non-Orthodox, and small and large businesses alike merited the honor.

Merchants eagerly sought the awards, no doubt hoping to profit from the association, as well as to bring their firm honor. Those who were successful readily incorporated the seal of the double-headed eagle and their conferred title into advertisements and prominently displayed them on their shops and shop signs. The tea emporium of V. Perlov & Sons on Moscow's Lubianka Square, for instance, featured a giant, three-dimensional imperial crest at one corner of the building. This lending of the imperial insignia extended to merchants and their firms a majestic aura of prestige and respect. Its conferral also served as a royal seal of approval, giving the impression that the tsar endorsed a firm's products or at least guaranteed their quality. One writer, recalling his childhood impression of the double-headed eagle perched atop a chemist's shop in Odessa, believed the symbol gave the chemist "a sort of official status," as if "higher authorities granted him power over the health and lives of everyone in the neighborhood coming to his shop for protection."[21]

Manufacturers and merchants also sought to affiliate their products with the symbols of the tsarist regime through the production and sale of items that commemorated epic, historic events or honored royal personages and the imperial ideal. The German confectioner Einem's product line included cookies dubbed Aleksandra, Imperial, and Rodina (a word meaning "homeland").[22] Siu

& Company produced a facial cream called Tsarina's Cream, a product that promised to soften skin and perhaps to imbue the consumer with a regal patina.[23] To mark the one-hundredth anniversary of the Patriotic War of 1812, Ralle & Company created an eau de cologne called Napoleon's Bouquet, distilled from essences of the emperor's favorite flowers, and the firm I. L. Ding packaged its caramels in a commemorative tin depicting the triumphal entrance of Tsar Aleksandr I into Moscow.[24] During the Russo-Turkish War, Brocard & Company had sold in its stores a soap branded Military and a pomade called Bouquet of Plevna, the latter recalling the site of an 1877 battle. The firm's regular offerings included soaps dubbed Empress, National, and Russian Coconut, the last carrying a label that mixed religious, national, and military motifs.[25]

At the same time that merchants were profiting from imperial product endorsements and royal associations, the court realized an advantage in adopting the tactics of mass marketers. The regime of Nicholas II was the first to authorize the production of various kinds of consumer goods bearing images of the royal family and imperial insignia. In celebration of the Romanov tercentenary in 1913, officials in the Ministry of the Court gave permission to several manufacturers to produce a variety of commemorative items, including calendars, trays, candy boxes, and scarves, embellished with portraits of Nicholas and his family. Einem introduced a tea cookie, Moscow, which was embossed with the double-headed eagle and "1896." More expensive items, including china and the regal fragrance Sunshine of Russia, created by Ralle & Company, were also produced in honor of the anniversary.[26] The Russian court's entry into the commercial market was part of a larger European trend. In Great Britain, the years between 1870 and 1914 saw a similar commodification of images of the monarchy. Queen Victoria's fiftieth-anniversary jubilee in 1887 and diamond jubilee in 1897 were defined by the participation of the media, manufacturers, advertisers, and theater producers, as well as by the court, civil servants, and politicians. Souvenirs, press coverage, and theatrical productions became as integral a part of the event as the official procession.[27] Likewise, the retailing of souvenirs bearing images of the Romanovs was not simply a sideline to the purveying of the state ceremonies. Imperial images endowed these items with worth beyond their production value. In turn, such goods helped to constitute state ceremonies, generating anticipation and enthusiasm for them and promoting them to Russians as momentous public occasions.

Retail merchants also contributed to the celebration of the coronation of Nicholas II in May 1896 by staging mini-spectacles at their places of business. Adorning their store façades, shop windows, and interiors with lavish, artistic displays and providing entertainment, merchants on the best streets set up their retail spaces as integral, "must-see" sites during the festivities. An Odessa newspaper reported that no other street was as magnificent and beautiful as "the street of luxury and fashion," DeRibas Street. Julius Vedde & Company, dealers in foreign merchandise, hung a twenty-eight-by-sixteen-foot banner featuring the tsarist eagle in the "Russian style" and life-size depictions of the emperor and empress with the words "God Save the Tsar" and "Reign in Glory" overhead.[28] The exquisite decorations at the popular Libman Café, the Popov and Perlov tea stores, and retail stores in the Wagner and Sinitsin commercial buildings were also described in detail. Everywhere on this street, spectators encountered multicolored lights, giant banners, garlands, flags, red fabric, banners with the royal regalia, portraits of Nicholas and Aleksandra, and their initials and "1896" rendered in flowers. Moscow's merchants mounted equally impressive "fantasies," the commercial streets of Tverskaia, Kuznetskii Most, Petrovka, and Miasnitskaia being the most elaborately decorated. Filippov Bakers and Abrikosov & Sons, among others, were singled out for special mention in the press. Filippov's festooned its balconies with gold fabric trimmed in ermine and affixed over the main entrance a giant, raspberry-colored velvet shield trimmed in gold tassels and braid and monogrammed with likenesses of the tsar and tsarina. Abrikosov covered its façade in red and pale blue fabric embroidered with the two-headed eagle and Romanov coat of arms.[29] Many individuals decorated their homes and most public buildings had their exteriors decorated for the august occasion, but the scale of merchants' decorations surpassed most others. Newspapers reported that crowds gathered at Vedde & Company, Filippov's, and other stores simply to admire the displays, making the owners of these commercial sites coproducers of the coronation festivities.

Retail merchants also helped to mythologize events important to the court. Following the rescue of Aleksandr III and his family from a train derailment on October 17, 1888, an act proclaimed in a tsarist manifesto to be a "miracle by the mercy of God," the public exhibited their thanks to God and reaffirmed their devotion to the tsar through special prayer services, devotional pamphlets, and church dedications.[30] Merchants played their part. The vendors of Okhotnyi Riad sponsored a liturgy and prayer service, followed by a religious procession to the Aleksandr Nevskii tower of the Kremlin. They also planned to donate money for an icon of the All Gracious Savior, embellished with a depiction of the events of October 17 and images of the tsar's family, which would be placed at the tower.[31] Some merchants directly capitalized on the event, parlaying the tsar's charisma and Orthodox sentiment into profit, even as they presented the event as a solemn moment. In 1889, Muir & Mirrielees displayed in its department store N. N. Karazin's painting, *The Wreck of the Emperor's Train,* and advertised for sale lithographs depicting the "miraculous deliverance" of the imperial family.[32]

The advent of consumer capitalism, with its tactics of publicity, advertising, and mass merchandising and retailing, transformed the way that state ceremonies and momentous events were presented and changed the role of the public in them. Grand state ceremonials were no longer witnessed only by court officials and dignitaries. The commodification of such events allowed a broader participation that included, but was not limited to, spectatorship and consumption. Subjects, urban and rural, wealthy and working class, male and female, could take some part in state ceremonies by buying a souvenir, reading an account of the event in popular newspapers, or strolling the streets and viewing the decorations and partaking of the entertainment provided by merchants. Court rituals and commemorative occasions had already become public events prior to the late nineteenth century, but in this period they became not only popular street celebrations underwritten in part by retail merchants but also opportunities for personal consumption. Whereas Russian subjects had been previously denied access to court ceremonies, except through reports in the press, now they could view the urban spectacle that accompanied them, could become part of the spectacle, and even claim a small piece of the event by purchasing a commemorative item.

Throughout their long association, the interests of Russian merchants and the state sometimes concurred and sometimes clashed. The state both promoted and restricted merchants and commercial activity. Members of the merchant elite turned their multifaceted relationship with the state to their best commercial advantage. These merchants learned to appeal to the public by using familiar and resonant imperial imagery and by promoting and commercializing their associations to the regime. They also promoted the court's royal image by selling imperial-themed merchandise and staging small-scale spectacles that popularized the celebration of important state events.

Consuming Subjects

By placing images of royalty in the homes of ordinary Russians and taking a public part in celebrating important state events, merchants began to play a mediating role in the relationship between the tsar's court and subjects. Of course, the merchants recognized the profit potential in products bearing imperial motifs and images of the emperor and his family; however, the sale of such items does not imply solely manipulative aims. These items were profitable because consumers wanted to buy them. Merchants' financial calculations and perhaps even their own belief systems and values surely influenced their decisions to market such goods, but a more immediate relationship between product and consumer also existed, one in which consumers were active participants. Representations of the empire, the tsarist regime, or the coronation ceremony were all marketable products, or, in today's parlance, "brands" that could be packaged and consumed. A consumer who nibbled one of Einem's "Moscow" cookies with tea, for instance, could consume the fantasy of the coronation prompted by the cookie. Even if a consumer had not attended the fabulous event, the daily ritual of tea and a biscuit allowed him or her to vicariously participate in the ceremony, in a small, private way, over and over again.

Certainly, there were no fixed, denotative ideas encoded on these material goods. Consumer fantasies were diverse and complex. Although the court initiated the marketing of the royal family and imperial imagery and merchants parlayed that decision into saleable goods, consumers did not necessarily passively accept messages from political and business elites without adapting, manipulating, or sometimes even subverting them. Nor did their consumption indicate primarily a process of social imitation or desire to display status.[33] In cities across Europe, mass-manufactured goods, popular entertainment, and mass-circulation publications were becoming increasingly available. Urban dwellers began to construct identities based on fantasies of fashion, beauty, upward mobility, independence, amusement, and adventure.[34] The literature on urban life and consumption in Russia demonstrates that a developing leisure and entertainment industry and emergent culture of consumption afforded city dwellers a multitude of opportunities for self-fashioning beyond state imperatives and socioeconomic status, gender, and profession.[35] Retailers tapped into popular aspirations, marketing products to abet their dreams. Abrikosov & Sons sold candies with names such as Snow Maiden, Fortune, and Blue Hen (a symbol of good luck), and Krakhmalnikov Brothers produced Chocolat Aviatique to commemorate the Wright brothers' experiments in flight. Brocard & Company, perhaps one of the most innovative marketers, offered soaps and perfumes called Bouquet and Divine and People's Pomade, the label of which included a short verse by the writer Ivan Krylov.[36]

Self-fashioning that occurs through the acquisition and display of consumer goods does not, however, preclude immersion in fantasies associated with ideas of tradition or authority. The most successful retailers in Russia kept in touch with customers' tastes and preferences and marketed products by tapping into their emotions, loyalties, and dreams. A market for products bearing imperial images clearly existed among consumers still devoted to or at least in awe of tsarist power and its trappings. In the process of investing cookies, perfume, and ordinary household items with such motifs, merchants transformed ideas of the nation and Russian royalty from intellectual concepts to tangible, material goods, a form that perhaps aided their internalization or subversion through display or consumption. Such concepts became increasingly identified with and represented through consumer goods and marketed and sold—in essence, com-modified—by innovative entrepreneurs eager to increase sales.

Merchants also marketed their retail firms to consumers. Through market-ing and advertising campaigns, they hoped, of course, to habituate consumers to shopping in their stores on a regular basis and to asking for specific brands and products. They also tried to create an air of occasion around their stores and to familiarize consumers with those stores to such an extent that consum-ers began to identify with the firm's name, its merchandise and activities, and the store itself. The store premises became an important part of this agenda. Merchants built large, opulent venues that resembled not so much places of business as theaters, museums, or palaces. Perlov & Sons built many of its tea emporiums in the style of Chinese pagodas. These extraordinary buildings featuring Chinese lanterns, parasols, dragons, vases, and other motifs became advertisements in themselves and prompts for fantasies of travel or of the de-lights of the city. The remodeling of the building that housed Eliseev's store supposedly elicited curiosity and expectancy among Muscovites. The building, originally constructed in the late eighteenth century, had been the palace of the Siberian gold mine heiress, E. I. Kozitska. In the 1820s, Kozitska's granddaugh-ter, Zinaida Volkonskaia, hosted a literary salon in the palace, which Pushkin and other writers attended. The building passed through other hands in the intervening years, and, in 1890, Eliseev acquired it. According to the journal-ist Giliarovskii, the reconstruction of this venerable edifice caused quite a stir, especially because Eliseev's architect, G. V. Baranovskii, did the work under a veil of mystery. Covering the entire mansion with boards, he turned it into "a big wooden box" for more than two years as he undertook renovations. Giliar-ovskii claims that some individuals sneaked inside to find out exactly what was being built. Reports ranged from an Indian pagoda, to a Moorish palace, to a pagan temple dedicated to Bacchus.[37] By his account, the unveiling of the store was an event itself.

Merchants also devised ingenious promotional stunts to attract customers and involve them in the life of their firms. Some of these were purely com-mercial events that combined frivolity and self-indulgence in the promotion of new items; others affected the solemnity and import of official state cer-emonies. When Brocard & Company opened a new store in Moscow in 1878, the firm advertised a special collector's set of toiletries to commemorate the event. On opening day, the store was inundated with visitors and two thousand sets sold. Brocard also called attention to itself at the 1882 All-Russian Indus-trial Arts Exhibition in Moscow with a fountain filled with its Floral eau de cologne and an invitation for everyone who visited the exhibit to sample the fragrance. Police allegedly had to intervene to restore order because so many people wanted to draw cologne from the fountain.[38] Perlov & Sons staged an event at its headquarters on Miasnitskaia Street on the occasion of the 1896 visit of the Chinese ambassador to Russia, Hongzhang Li. A crowd was reported to have gathered to view the elaborate decorations, which included Chinese and Russian flags, to listen to the orchestra's mingling of a Chinese hymn and the Russian national anthem, and to await the arrival of the ambassador.[39] Certainly, Perlov's receiving of the Chinese ambassador was predicated on business matters, but the firm made his visit a vehicle for urban entertainment and commercial self-promotion.

Merchants appealed to a broad urban consuming public by advertising in newspapers that reached a diverse readership, thus building a constituency that crossed class, occupational, and gender lines. Muir & Mirrielees advertised almost weekly in *Moskovskii listok,* one of Moscow's most popular boulevard newspapers. The gossipy, folksy newspaper reached approximately forty thousand readers, many of them from lower-middle and working-class groups, including clerks, shopkeepers, and servants—hardly the elite clientele one would expect the store to target. The store also sought an educated, well-to-do audience. Advertisements appeared periodically in the "thick" journal *Russkaia mysl',* in the national newspaper *Russkoe slovo,* the liberal *Russkie vedomosti,* and the more conservative *Moskovskie vedomosti*—all newspapers mostly concerned with political and social issues and aimed at a well-read, middle-class or professional readership. Petrokokino Brothers in Odessa, likewise appealed to a cross-section of the population, placing advertisements in *Odesskii listok, Odesskie novosti,* a popular and well-respected newspaper, and publications such as the *Iuzhno-Russkii al'manakh* (Southern Russian Almanac).[40]

The range of advertising placements suggests that retail merchants strived to cultivate an image of middle-class prosperity and sophisticated exclusivity at the same time that they advertised everyday value and universal appeal. Stores such as Muir & Mirrielees and Petrokokino's relied on clientele with enough disposable income to make steady purchases of clothing, shoes, fabrics, and luxury items like musical instruments, bicycles, and luggage. These two firms presented themselves as cosmopolitan purveyors of fine merchandise that brought a world of goods to their customers' doors. Muir & Mirrielees billed itself as the "Leading Department Store in Russia," while Petrokokino's advertised its store as a "Wholesale Store of Foreign Merchandise." Ads in the boulevard press, however, indicate that the two retailers were also targeting consumers with at least some disposable income and leisure time, two prerequisites that made such individuals potential customers, even if only for small, relatively inexpensive items. Advertisements tailored to suit their budgets featured more prosaic items such as school supplies, which were marketed as "the best value at very reasonable prices."[41] Other advertisements declared, "We will not be undersold," a statement that guaranteed moderate prices.[42] Petrokokino's official policy of equal treatment ensured that everyone could expect to be received politely, whether making a purchase for one hundred rubles or five kopeks or simply browsing.[43] Both stores conducted periodic sales and broadcast them to the general public, calling attention to the fact that prices were significantly reduced.[44] These retailers also pitched empire-wide appeals. Petrokokino's made its general and specialized consumer catalogs available free of charge. Muir & Mirrielees had even greater ambitions. Asserting that "every home needs our catalog as a reference book," the firm pledged to deliver anywhere within the Russian Empire, free of charge, an order valued at fifty rubles or more and accompanied by a deposit, a policy that essentially brought the far-flung corners of the empire together under one commercial roof.[45]

Retailers operated in the public eye, and those merchants with ample capital and influence cultivated the limelight, creating situations in which their stores would be set off to best advantage and potential customers would take note. Many consumers responded to their efforts, finding in the publicity, promotional stunts, and in-store events entertainment, excitement, and a sense of inclusion. While evidence suggests that the owners of large, prominent retail firms endeavored to create a broad-based audience, in reality, they were not entirely successful in uniting individuals across class lines. Varying income and educational levels and understandings of consumer goods surely precluded such unity. Instead, retailers sought to meld different constituencies into a public for their own ends. The merchant elite's efforts to attract a clientele created an urban-dwelling public that took an interest in their businesses and began to think of their stores and the entertainments on exhibit there as integral parts of the city landscape and an urban lifestyle.

Merchants and the Orthodox Faith

For generations, scholars have puzzled over the paradoxical relationship between commercial activity and religion, in particular between merchants' earthly preoccupation with money and profit and their spiritual obligation to renounce worldly goods and avoid avarice. In one of the key texts on the problem, Max Weber postulated that Protestantism and commerce were not actually at odds with each other. Instead, Protestant asceticism had facilitated the rise of capitalism in the West through its emphasis on the "calling," a devotion to one's occupation as a means of glorifying God and serving the community.[46] In the years since Weber published his theories, scholars have critiqued and revised his thesis, but the relationship between commerce and religion has remained a vital issue for those studying the merchant and middle classes, the rise of consumer capitalism, and civil society.[47] Taking a cue from Weber, William Leach has argued that John Wanamaker, founder of Wanamaker's Department Store in Philadelphia, did not believe commerce and Christianity were incompatible and that he turned to religious activity as a source of moral authority and out of a need to "sanctify his business."[48] Leach, however, concludes that retailing and religion were contradictory, noting that although Wanamaker tried to incorporate Christianity into the new culture of consumption, he ultimately "marginalize[d] religion and doom[ed] it to irrelevance."[49] Scholars of Russia have also examined the relationship of religion to the merchant community, some hewing closer to a semblance of Weber's thesis than others. Focusing attention on the number of successful merchant-industrialists from Old Believer communities, one scholar argues that religious subcultures encouraged enterprise and entrepreneurship.[50] Others argue that Russian Orthodoxy tended to preserve conservative, traditional outlooks among the majority of merchants.[51] The spiritual dilemma also engaged Russian contemporaries, some of whom adopted this latter view. One such observer, commenting on merchant life in early-twentieth-century Moscow, remarked that merchants loved to discuss religious issues (even carrying on such discussions at taverns), displayed an "almost hysterical" devotion to ritual, adhered stubbornly to traditions, and maintained a "pious outlook that perfectly coexisted with their shrewdness in daily life."[52] Other scholars have pointed out, however, that the merchant elite's devotion to their faith, in particular the admonition to care for the poor, resulted in their patronage of monasteries, orphanages, hospitals, and charities and thus contributed to the rise of civic activism and public life.[53]

The important issue here is not whether merchants' extension of their personal spiritual concerns to their commercial pursuits constituted a conservative or progressive agenda, however those terms may be deployed in explaining the emergence or obstruction of capitalism in Russia. What is foremost here is that the relationship between merchants' private motives and their public activities is an important dimension of the rise of the city and urban life and of the culture of mass retailing and consumption that became inseparable from them and indeed helped to define them. The advent of modern modes of retailing did not displace religion from retailing. Rather, new methods of merchandising and retailing seemed to make the link more explicit, even to publicize it. Retail merchants deployed the rites and imagery of the Orthodox Church to create their own distinctive rituals, which served to consecrate their firms and the act of consumption in public. Although the Russian Orthodox Church did not overtly endorse commercial activity, its symbols, liturgy, and rituals served to legitimate the rise of an urban lifestyle based on browsing, acquisition, and entertainment, a process that defies easy classification as either conservative or progressive, traditional or modern.

Religion did not merely guide the personal lives of many Orthodox merchants; it pervaded their daily business routines. At one time, the Orthodox Church had been an active retailer in its own right. As early as the sixteenth century and as late as the 1840s, the Orthodox Church operated lavkas in Kitai Gorod, where monks and priests sold books, icons, and other religious items and, according to one source, haberdashery and hardware items.[54] Even after the Church removed itself from Moscow's commercial center, religion continued to have a strong presence. Icons hung inside stores and shops and on the front of market stalls and booths; each business day customarily began with prayer. Recalling his job in a ready-to-wear store, one former shop assistant remarked that upon entering the store each morning, the owner "made the rounds," praying in all four corners and on all four floors.[55] Merchants also marked business time by the church calendar. They traditionally ended the commercial year during Easter Week and undertook business ventures on auspicious religious dates. The establishment of a new firm and the laying of the cornerstone of a new commercial building, for example, were ordinarily held on religious feast days in the hope that the enterprise would find divine favor.[56] Merchants customarily held special sales on St. Thomas Monday, the second Monday after Easter, following which they stopped at the Kremlin's Savior Gates to offer thanks for having unloaded old or outmoded merchandise. Many annual markets and fairs, including the Lenten-time Mushroom Market and Willow Bazaar in Moscow, coincided with religious holidays. Moscow's merchants also organized prayer services at the successful conclusion of the Nizhnii Novgorod Fair every year.[57]

Important days in the business calendar were not the only events that merchants honored. They also organized annual prayer services and processions of the cross to commemorate occasions important to the community, for example, the deliverance of the city from cholera and other epidemics in the years 1830, 1845, and 1848.[58] These rituals were frequently held in the German, Smolensk or other markets, or on commercial streets or squares, including Nikol'skaia, alongside the Upper Trading Rows. Merchants invited the public to these services, and, in reporting on them, the press often noted that "the square was full of people" or that "a great number of worshipers" attended. As late as 1913, such thanksgiving rituals were still being held in Moscow, one that year being organized by the Church of St. Paraskova on Okhotnyi Riad. This particular procession began at the church and proceeded to the Lapin Building, named after the grocer who operated a business there, where merchants had hung the icon of All Saints on the wall. There, the bishop led the public in prayer.[59] More elaborate rites took place in larger venues. Prior to the rebuilding of the Upper Trading Rows in 1888, Row merchants had held a prayer service there every fall. The merchant Slonov recalled that this service was a great celebratory event. In preparation, the merchants of each row designated a spot beneath their row's icon for the service and decorated it with other icons and sacred objects borrowed from parish churches, adding carpets, foliage, and red fabrics, festooning the windows and doors of their shops with juniper, and strewing aisles with branches. On the day of the service, a full choir, usually accompanied by famous soloists, performed. This service was open to the public, and, according to Slonov, a great many people always attended. Afterward, merchants repaired to a nearby restaurant or tavern to celebrate with much drinking.[60]

Icons, religious processions, and communal prayer services outside the church had been part of Orthodox religious culture since at least the Muscovite era. Icons were common objects in Russian Orthodox homes, and, given that believers prayed before icons, it is not surprising to find them also in places of business. Processions of the cross, prayer services, and the blessing of and sprinkling of holy water on people, houses, fields, cattle, and horses were believed to expel evil spirits and to relieve stricken individuals, animals, and locales. These rites and celebrations served to unite believers of a community and reaffirm their membership in and identification with it, and they also met the desire to sacralize all areas of life.[61] Traditional peasant belief also held that the well-being of a household could be ensured with the correct performance of customary rituals, including the blessing of the home.[62] *The Domostroi*, probably first published in the sixteenth century, instructed believers to invite priests into their homes on holy days to perform the appropriate ritual, which usually included prayers for the tsar, tsaritsa, and their children, as well as prayers "for all that is profitable for the man of the house, his wife, children, and servants."[63] This household manual further advised the host to pay the priest and provide some sort of repast. The origins of the commercial blessing are not completely clear, but because prayer and blessing rituals were so central to Orthodox religiosity and because seeking divine protection for a business and workplace was surely as important as seeking it for a household and home, merchants undoubtedly extended to the commercial realm the rituals that took place in the private domain. Furthermore, since merchants constituted a community within the city, in terms of proximity to each other and a shared profession, it is not surprising that they arranged for their own communal rites. Given the similarities between the blessing of homes and of commercial establishments, it seems safe to assume that commercial rituals were at least nearly as old as those held in the home and village spaces. This intermingling of the sacred and secular was not unusual. As Chris Chulos has pointed out, "the presence of the sacred in secular spheres of public life was viewed throughout Russia as natural and inseparable."[64] Churches had been traditionally located in village centers on the grounds where markets and fairs were held; therefore, religion and commerce were regularly juxtaposed.

What is perhaps more remarkable is that the rituals organized by merchants were neither exclusive nor organized solely to mark commercial events. Merchants belonged to a larger public that attended to local spiritual needs, and they used their skill of attracting customers to assemble worshipers. Their visibility and familiarity to urban residents, moreover, placed them in a position to sponsor public rituals, a role that had primarily been reserved for the church and court. Of course, merchants could not sponsor the rituals without having priests on hand to conduct the services, but they initiated and financed them, staged them on commercial premises, and defined their format and character. While they probably did not intend their initiatives to directly challenge established authorities, their arranging for the services meant that urban public rituals were no longer the exclusive domain of the church or court.[65]

As advertising and new modes of merchandising and retailing became more common in Russia in the late nineteenth century, they did not displace religion's central place in commerce. Instead, these methods seemed to make the link more explicit, even to publicize it. Popular forms of Russian Orthodoxy were becoming enmeshed in urban life and in its commercial entertainment and leisure industries. Merchants readily incorporated the familiar imagery and rituals of Orthodoxy into advertisements and promotions, making them a prominent feature of marketing campaigns. Special sales and store events were still timed to coincide with religious holidays, but merchants devised more innovative associations between commerce and religious holidays. The German confectioner Einem issued calendars with all holy days listed and marked in red, surrounded by pictures of its chocolates and cookies and a price list.[66] Merchants not only suggested items for gift-giving at Christmas and Easter but also prescribed candy, flowers, jewelry, and other items as the perfect accompaniments to religious feast days and saints' days. One typical advertisement recommended stationery items as appropriate gifts for St. Catherine's Day.[67] Downtown retail businesses also marketed specialty holiday items. During Lent, confectionery stores sold pink and blue "Lenten sugar." Abrikosov & Sons created special Christmas and Easter candies and confections, and perfumers created egg-shaped soaps and perfume bottles. Filippov's lined its display windows with "Lenten larks," bread baked in the shape of little birds. Christian holidays were not the only ones subject to commercialization either. Odessa merchants advertised wine, cognac, and other items for the Passover table and Rosh Hashanah.[68]

The Orthodox Church was not always comfortable with the incorporation of religious imagery in advertisements and merchandise displays or with the sale of religious-themed goods. At times, the Holy Synod intervened, in one instance, in 1910, objecting to advertisements that contained a cross and in another, in 1913, objecting to the incorporation of Nikolai Gay's painting *Christ at Golgotha* in an ad for cigarette papers.[69] Local police officers were enlisted to conduct periodic checks of retail stores, shops, and street vendors and instructed to seize merchandise deemed blasphemous or subversive. In one case, in 1901, police cited S. & A. Prostakov Brothers stationers, located in the Upper Trading Rows, for a window display of religious pictures arranged in the shape of a cross. The problem, according to a newspaper report, was that one of the pictures contained a "half-naked woman."[70] In Odessa, sweeps of stores selling jewelry, music, and books, even of rather sizable venues operated by second-guild merchants and located in the center of the city, were regularly conducted. During one, police searched twenty stores for crosses and other images of the Orthodox faith and for records that advocated the Baptist and other evangelical faiths.[71] A strict line between advertising and religion, however, was not drawn. Religious publications such as *Tserkovnye vedomosti* (Church News) ran advertisements for tea, watches, and other consumer goods in the back pages of their journals.

Shopping was becoming part of the holiday routine. In the days leading up to Easter, for example, consumers went to markets and shops to purchase gifts and ingredients for *kulich* (Easter cake) and *paskha* (a sweet cream cheese dish), both traditional holiday specialties. One Muscovite native, journalist and theater critic Il'ia Shneider (1891–1980), remembered that the Willow Bazaar, held on Red Square the week before Easter, elicited anticipation among residents: "Everyone waited for it, everyone went to it, and walked around there, shoving and pushing each other, and wore themselves out. After buying something that they did not need or something that they could buy any day at the store in their building next door, they finally became tired, managed to extricate themselves from the crowd, and hardly able to drag their feet along, returned home."[72] As his comments indicate, the bazaar was not simply a place to buy holiday items. Visiting it was considered a central part of the holiday, an event in itself.

The promotional tactics of large, prominent retailers took the concept of the retail store as holiday destination to a new level. These firms relied on a policy of browsing in order to attract customers to elaborate exhibits designed to satisfy the spectator's urge and stimulate sales. Each year, Muir & Mirrielees and Petrokokino Brothers constructed fantastic holiday landscapes inside their stores to display Christmas ornaments and toys and Easter eggs. Such firms strove to make holiday activities more than a simple matter of trimming the tree at home with homemade ornaments. Merchants sought to entice the public, especially the middle classes upon whom they relied for business, to include as part of their celebrations an outing to their stores to view the holiday decorations and offerings. For some, buying special items, even relatively inexpensive ones, from particular firms acquired the status of a holiday tradition. Commenting on the consumption habits of Muscovites at Easter time, Shneider recalled, "Those who didn't make paskha and didn't bake the kulich at home ordered them at Einem, Abrikosov, and Tramble and bought chocolate at Kraft. To order the paskha and kulich at Filippov's was tantamount to a well-dressed lady buying a ready-to-wear hat at Muir & Mirrielees. The 'simple public' [*publika poproshche*] bought paskha and kulich at Filippov's, but their 'betters' [*pochishche*] began to order only '*baby*' there."[73] For Moscow residents like Shneider, a trip to these stores was part of the holiday preparations and the consumption of their paskha and kulich, part of the celebration. Moreover, buying them at the "right" place carried a certain cachet. Einem, Abrikosov, Filippov's, and others had assumed a place in a hierarchy of retailing, the purchase of their products signaling the social position or sophistication of the consumer.

Religion entered the commercial sphere as a consequence of Orthodox merchants' private devotion to Orthodoxy. They assumed a visible position in the community by sponsoring public religious devotions, thus acquiring for themselves roles as patrons of the church, public benefactors, and organizers of public ceremonial events. They also capitalized on the connection between religion and their businesses, recognizing the profit potential in marketing specialty holiday items. While religious precepts warned against the dangers inherent in the retail trade, commerce and religion coexisted rather harmoniously.

Reinventing the Commercial Ritual

The ceremonial blessing of stores, shops, marketplaces, and fairs, as well as of other commercial-industrial enterprises such as factories, artisanal workshops, railroad stations, medical clinics, hospitals, and public utilities, was a ubiquitous ritual that marked a milestone in the life of a business firm. By the late nineteenth century, the commencement of construction on a new retail store and the laying of its cornerstone, a store opening or reopening after renovation, and the anniversary of a firm all occasioned the requisite blessing ritual. Certainly, the original purpose of the ceremonial blessings was to beseech divine protection for merchants and their businesses and to create ties among the merchant community, perhaps even to incorporate customers into that community. In late imperial Russia, however, large-scale modern retailers transformed the ritual blessing into something more than an act of faith. Differing in scale, opulence, and spectatorship, the ceremony became a grandiose public spectacle dedicated to the celebration of urban life based on Orthodoxy, tsarism, and modern retailing and consumption, elements that celebrated social stability, morality, beauty, rationality, abundance, and fashion, among other things.

The performance of distinctive commercial rituals does not appear to have played as important a role in the elaboration of consumer capitalism in western Europe or the United States. Of course, important state-sponsored commercial events were marked by state ceremonials. For example, in 1851, Queen Victoria opened the Great Exhibition of the Works of Industry of All Nations. As reported in the press, crowds cheered, cannonades sounded, and a band played "God Save the Queen" as Victoria made her way to the Crystal Palace with her children, ladies-in-waiting, and state officials to formally inaugurate the exhibit. The Great Exhibition, however, was organized at the initiative of the Crown and constituted a collaborative effort among state officials, merchants, and industrialists of the various participating countries. The queen's appearance befitted an event in which the state played a large, organizing role.[74] In contrast, although reliant on the state to a certain extent, Russian merchants initiated the rituals. These ceremonies incorporated state imagery, but they were commercial, not state, events.

Less majestic commercial events in Europe or the United States did not warrant solemn, high-profile ceremonies. When Aristide Boucicaut laid the cornerstone for his monumental new Bon Marché department store in Paris in 1869, only his wife and closest associates attended. The press apparently took no notice, perhaps considering the event a private affair.[75] In Chicago, the press deemed the opening of the Marshall Field & Company store on State Street in 1868 a newsworthy event. The *Chicago Tribune* dwelled on the store's palatial size, its opulent interior, and many fine departments. Its account of the formal opening, held in the evening, told of the splendid carriages that conveyed stylish men and women, who partook of the visual delights on offer inside.[76] The *Tribune*'s adulation of the handsome new store and its marvelous offerings and the detailing of distinguished guests indicate that the opening was an important and fashionable social event, but not a ritual occasion.

Unfortunately, neither members of the merchant community nor consumers committed to paper their reasons for staging or participating in these ceremonies. The theoretical literature on ritual and a consideration of the political, social, and cultural context, however, point to several interpretations. The blessing ceremony can be interpreted as part of a strategy to win some measure of public approval or respect. Increasingly in this period, social critics cited the department store and other new kinds of retailers for contributing to profligacy, idleness, and the breakdown of Russian customs and institutions, social and gender hierarchies, and traditional modes of doing business. Those members of Russia's merchantry who pioneered new forms of retailing may have revamped

the blessing ritual as a means of presenting themselves to the public as trustwor-
thy, reputable entrepreneurs loyal to Russian traditions and culture.[77] Paying
formal obeisance to the tsar and Orthodox faith demonstrated that they still
valued inherited authorities. Innovative and perhaps even calculating businessmen whose prime motive was to turn a profit, many nonetheless remained, or
at least hoped to be perceived as, sober, pious, faithful, and reverent.

State power and Orthodoxy, however, did not simply stand for stability and
morality, and modern retailing did not merely symbolize prosperity, style, and
rational business methods. The wealthy, prominent merchants who staged magnificent ceremonial blessings believed that the brand of retailing they practiced
was as important a part of a formula for constructing a modern, orderly, moral
society as were the state and the Orthodox Church. They trusted that their
firms exhibited progressive, transparent, efficient operating practices, service to
the community, and paternal relationships with their employees and endorsed
them as a way to ensure social progress, harmony, and principled, responsible
behavior in a rapidly changing world. It was not that these merchants were simply attaching themselves to established authorities and institutions and the rites
that conferred legitimacy on them. They offered themselves and their firms as
worthy partners to the state and the church in guiding and inspiring society.

Moreover, the task of a successful retailer was to create the impression that
a store or retail venue was what Clifford Geertz has called a "center" of social
activity, a place in a society "where its leading ideas come together with its leading institutions to create an arena in which the events that most vitally affect
its members' lives take place."[78] Geertz explicitly refers to monarchies and their
enactment of rituals that conferred charisma, but he points out that charisma
can arise in any realm that is sufficiently focused to seem vital. In its scope and
utility, the retail sphere was a constitutive sector of Russian society around
which daily life revolved. The intent of large-scale capitalist retailers was to
make their stores institutions, fixtures in the community, places where consumers not only purchased goods but also organized their daily activities and their
lives. Merchants hoped to instill loyalty in their patrons and to insinuate their
business premises as primary sites of identification. A middle-class lifestyle, for
example, was defined as much by the stores one patronized as by political affili-
ation, religion, or occupation. A customer who repeatedly returned to Muir &
Mirrielees might conceivably begin to think of himself or herself as a Muir &
Mirrielees customer, an association process that brought the firm revenues and
signaled the customer's appropriation of several available identities attached to
the department store, such as middle- or upper-middle class urbanite or fashion
sophisticate.[79] "True Russians" might define themselves, in part, as persons who
patronized only the stores of Russian merchants, while cosmopolitan aesthetes

might consider themselves so if they chose to shop only at stores operated by foreigners on Kuznetskii Most. Merchants tried to cultivate these associations with the aim of making their stores "centers," places that inspired devotion and to which consumers looked for guidance, entertainment, and self-fashioning. The most prominent retail merchants in the late empire period devised various strategies aimed at creating the impression that their stores were centers of urban life. For instance, some Muscovites, and probably even many individuals residing outside Moscow, began to think of Muir & Mirrielees and the Trading Rows as local and national institutions or landmarks. Certain stores were also looked to for expert advice in matters of fashion and manners.

The blessing ceremonies also exhibited an instructive purpose. Proprietors sponsoring them may have felt the need to acquaint and accustom consumers to such rituals. Press coverage was especially important in this regard, since it served to teach urban residents about the stores and their new business techniques and to make explicit the link between the new methods of buying and selling and values of beauty, prosperity, culture, rationalization, transparency, benevolent paternalism, and progress.[80] Enhanced by the symbols of the imperial regime and the Orthodox faith, the performance of the reinvented ritual blessing created an aura of authority, tradition, and grandeur around places of business. Despite the borrowing of imperial and religious imagery and symbols, however, the focus remained on commerce and consumption. Merchants provided the setting and the impetus for the rituals, and they orchestrated the elements to present a vision of a world based on social and political stewardship, morality, and a prosperous, cultured lifestyle. Commercial rituals conveyed the idea that the retail marketplace was a center around which society was organized, one inextricably linked to other consequential social centers and to fundamental, established values.

In this regard, the enactment of the ritual, bolstered by public participation, suggests that large retail enterprises provided spaces in which the city and the empire presented themselves to the public as a body of civic-minded business leaders, representatives of church and state, and consumers. Increasingly throughout the late nineteenth century, European royal ceremonies were becoming more elaborate, in part as a way to appeal to more of the population.[81] After the emancipation of the serfs in Russia, any effort to present the monarch as a figure who enjoyed popular support necessitated, for example, the mention of peasants and jubilant crowds in newspaper accounts of court ceremonies.[82] To say that Russian retailers took a cue from the court in their attempts to play to a large audience, however, ignores the democratizing impulse in many of the merchant innovators' business strategies. In staging these rituals, they carefully recreated them to appeal to a wide popular audience of ordinary individuals even as they incorporated long-standing traditions and customs.

Along with myths and other traditions that represented individual merchants' power to the larger merchant elite and to society, rituals also served to legitimate the power of the merchant elite.[83] Richard Wortman has demonstrated the significant role of "symbolic display" in elevating and sustaining the power of the Russian monarchy, arguing that court ceremonies, especially the coronation, served as an "essential mechanism of tsarist rule in Imperial Russia."[84] In effect, the Russian monarchy engaged in image-making and promotional strategies to justify its power. The pervasiveness and scale of commercial rituals, especially the ceremonial blessing, as it came to be practiced by high-profile retailers, indicates that the court was not the only institution that engaged in its own myth making and invention of traditions to legitimate itself in the eyes of society. Even though all merchants held rituals, not all, of course, had the means to project themselves into the spotlight. Still, those who were ambitious proprietors of large, prosperous firms sought to make a statement of their power and aspirations in a society that restricted their political initiative and activity. In this sense, the publicized performance of commercial rituals was as much about the self-presentation of the economic, social, and cultural aspirations of rising, successful business owners as it was about winning customers. Nonetheless, these merchants inserted themselves and their firms into existing power structures without seeming to threaten or displace them, surrounding themselves with the rites and imagery of the church and imperial court to reassure the merchant community and public of their trustworthiness.

Church and court rituals lent themselves rather easily to emulation in the retail sphere because, like Orthodox clergy and members of the court, retail merchants relied on scripted performative strategies. Ritual employs conventionalized language, action, and symbols in a social setting that encourages shared interpretation and integration into the existing order, or criticism of it.[85] The commercial ceremonial blessing followed a standard, scripted format, regardless of the merchant's wealth or the size of his or her business. Merchants' performances, like clerical and court performances, also required an adoring, consuming public. The divine liturgy, for example, needed faithful worshipers to witness the transubstantiation of the Eucharist; the coronation needed devoted subjects to witness the monarch's procession through the city. Similarly, a lucrative retail firm depended on the successful sales pitch to loyal, admiring patrons. The talents required to sell in Russia—the exhibition of merchandise, the practiced dialogue of flattery and intimidation, the scripted haggling over prices—gave to the retail trade a dramatic, if sometimes comedic, flair. In this sense, retail stores were not only places to buy and sell items but also every-day sites of theater, each sales transaction a short, one-act routine. As discussed earlier, certain markets, stores, and shops became known as urban attractions owing to the showmanship of merchants. Visitors went to these retail venues sometimes merely for the sake of becoming a part of the show. Even as department stores and self-avowed respectable retailers began to forgo what they viewed as corrupt and undignified methods of selling, preferring to institute more refined and restrained tactics, they nevertheless retained the theatricality of retailing. Making the ritual blessing a dramatic and spectacular pageant, therefore, may have seemed a logical application, given merchants' penchant for dramatics and their need for spectators. As advertising, promotional events, and publicity increasingly became part of a retail firm's marketing strategy, savvy Russian merchants, operating within a society dominated by church and state but seeking to carve out their own space, took cues from the Russian court and the Orthodox Church, infusing rituals with the methods and style of modern retailing and the mass entertainment industries more generally. The commercial rituals they staged satisfied commerce's proclivity for lavish, spectacular self-promotion and consumers' appetite for entertainment and spectatorship.

The discussion of these motives is not intended to discount the sincerity or the genuine spiritual impulse in the ritual blessing but to uncover other motivations in its transformation into a public and well-publicized spectacle. Merchants were surely not motivated exclusively by profit. Many were fervently devoted to the tsar and their faith and earnest in their patriotic and religious observances. Given what we know about religious devotion in the merchant community, there is no reason to suspect that they performed these rituals disingenuously. At the same time, their religiosity did not preclude integrating elaborate shows of faith and political affiliations into their commercial pursuits. Merchants' motives were not compartmentalized. Commerce, private life, religion, civic responsibility, and political beliefs influenced and intersected with each other.

The ritual blessing organized by Petrokokino Brothers in 1896 for the opening of its new showplace store on Greek Street in downtown Odessa encompassed these multiple, complex, and interrelated interests and motives and serves as a prime example of the phenomenon.[86] The owner, first-guild merchant Evstrati Petrokokino, embodied the empire's merchant elite. He had built a large, successful, and prominent retail business that employed modern methods of marketing, merchandising, and retailing; he played a role in municipal and merchant governing bodies; and he sought to cultivate public renown and regard for his firm through an extravagant version of the commercial blessing. Evstrati and Dmitrii Mikhailovich Petrokokino founded Petrokokino Broth-

ers in 1859. The business grew to become one of the largest and best retailers in
Odessa and also one of very few that registered its own trademark. Petrokokino
Brothers billed itself as a "Store of Foreign Goods," a slogan that in practice
meant the operation of twenty departments selling a wide assortment of fine
merchandise, much of it imported, including housewares, luggage, perfume,
stationery, toys, furniture, cigars, and Chinese and Japanese pieces of art. By
1914, the firm turned one million rubles a year.[87]

Newspaper journalists helped merchants like Evstrati Petrokokino attract
attention by building anticipation for the ceremonial blessing, informing readers of the preparations under way, and explicating the various elements of the
ritual in lengthy articles published after the event. The remarkable similarities
among post-event press reports suggest that newspapers framed the rituals in
a script of stock images and phrases meant to guide readers' perception and
interpretation.[88] The reports almost always began with an account of the background and rise of the owner-proprietor. Petrokokino's portrait, like those of
many others among the merchant elite, was a composite of merchant masculinity based on restraint, reason, individual initiative, and energy.[89] Reporters portrayed him as a worthy member of the community, one whose industriousness,
foresight, and rational cultivation and application of his abilities had resulted
in his personal success. Readers were informed that Evstrati Petrokokino, a
longtime Odessa resident from a Greek family, had worked his way up from a
position in his father's store to owning his own store with his brother Dmitrii.
This storyline suggested that Petrokokino, having been in business for more
than thirty years, was a stable influence in the community. Petrokokino was
also recognized as a collegial member of the merchant community, one who
was generally "well liked" and who held the post of deputy elder of the Odessa
Merchants' Soslovie.[90]

Journalists presented the store as the physical manifestation of Petrokokino's business ethic. In this narrative, a merchant's and firm's records of success
were not only feats of individual accomplishment but also achievements that
brought substantial, tangible advantages to the city. According to the writer
for *Odesskii listok,* through the investment of time, money, and energy, Petrokokino had endowed the city of Odessa with more than just a beautiful new
retail store. He noted that in the last few years "Industrial Odessa" had been
"enriched" (*obogashchaetsia*) with several handsome commercial buildings, but
Petrokokino's store, which he dubbed the "Odessa Louvre," was, in his opinion, a "store superior to anything we have accomplished . . . up to now." He
dwelled on the store's appearance, inside and out, describing the building as a
beautiful, modern structure worthy of veneration, and linked its physical appearance to its role as a symbol of beauty, culture, and progress. This writer

was clearly trying to send the message that such retailers brought honor and dignity to the city and that their fine stores provided evidence of the inherent superiority of their methods. The older merchant ethic, which had rested upon male sociability and a free-wheeling, unkempt disorder, was being challenged by a new ideal of individualism, order, and competition. Making this point explicit, the journalist contrasted the new, splendid magazin with the "squalid, drab" lavkas in which retailers formerly operated and noted further that merchants now competed with each other to build the finest store in the city. He asserted that such competition redounded to the benefit of residents because it resulted in magnificent buildings that not only served commercial interests but also beautified city streets and made visible the city's accomplishments. Paying tribute to the vigor of private initiative, the writer also noted that Petrokokino built his store in one year, while renovations to the municipal market remained uncompleted even after several years.[91]

Descriptions of the store's exterior and interior echoed the themes of beauty, culture, and progress in their precise attention to the building's design and state-of-the-art technology. Designed by Italian architect A. O. Bernardazzi, also responsible for the city's Stock Exchange (1889), the three-story structure referenced western European models of refinement and culture and in fact resembled the Louvre with its combination of French baroque and Italian elements and decorative motifs and reliefs, although its detailing differed and there were some modern and classical motifs.[92] The press reported that Petrokokino had traveled abroad to study the architecture of the best stores, most of which had been modeled on palaces and museums, and that he himself had chosen the design for the building. Overall, the effect of the entire façade, illuminated by electric lighting bright enough, according to the newspaper, to be seen from a great distance, was spectacular. Mention of the building's price tag of four million rubles also apparently attested to its monumental place in the city. The interior was also palatial. The main floor occupied a space 108 feet long and 59 feet wide, extending upward the entire height of the building. Elegant parquet flooring covered the main floor, and a fountain surrounded by sofas stood in its center. Arc lights "equivalent to 8,000 candles" set off the entire area. A double staircase led to a choir loft that received light from a giant three-paned window and the galleries, where merchandise was arranged into departments. The ceiling featured a mural with an image of Mercury, the god of commerce, an emblem of labor, and beehives, the symbol of industry. Gracing the four corners of the mural were female allegories of several nations and continents, among them India, Africa, and China, perhaps suggesting the global reach of the firm, and commerce more generally. The top floor featured sixty-four variously shaped windows between which were engravings and backlit busts created by the

sculptor Molinari. Besides aesthetics, Petrokokino's offered comforts and amenities, including a ladies' lavatory, trunks in which shoppers could store parcels
during the day, and services such as wrapping and delivery. Modern technology showed in the American cash registers that generated printed receipts for
customers, antifire measures that ensured their safety, and antitheft measures,
including alarms that guarded the store's interests.

In its eclectic mix of classical and modern design styles and motifs, artistic
tributes to internationalism and exoticism, craftsmanship, and use of modern
equipment, the store represented the pinnacle of the retail trade. Petrokokino
presented clients a handsome, refined, and contemporary, if ostentatious, space
where they could shop for fine merchandise while cultivating their aesthetic
sensibilities. The intent seemed to be to equate consumer goods with art and
shopping with more highbrow activities such as a visit to a museum. Significantly, the *Odesskii listok* journalist depreciated the commercial function of the
building in his opening paragraphs, focusing instead on the store's appearance.
To him, the store was a mark of distinction for Odessa, a source of pride, and
an indication of the city's level of culture and progress, which he measured in
terms of business ingenuity, technology, and a display of material wealth.[93]

The representation of merchants as active, cultivated business leaders who
afforded the public a new kind of urban experience was central to the narrative of the ceremonial blessing, but so too was showing them to be paternal
benefactors who kept traditions and customs and upheld the social order. An
important part of many blessings was the employees' presentation of gifts to the
proprietor, a show of devotion that recalled the customary rites that merchants,
shop assistants, and apprentices performed on religious holidays. On the occasion of Petrokokino's reopening, employees presented their employer with the
traditional gift of bread and salt on a silver platter, the icon of Saint Nicholas,
and a portfolio with a silver monogram in one of the corners that bore the
inscription: "I have children—my employees." On behalf of the entire staff, a
senior employee delivered a speech in which he humbly expressed the "feelings
of deep gratitude and devotion that had accumulated in the souls of each of us"
for Petrokokino's "humane—no—kind, paternal treatment and esteem" and
for his never-stinting material and moral support.[94]

This presentation of gifts and the employee's public address gave symbolic
reassurance that the modern retail firm had eliminated tyrannical merchants
who abused their employees and apprentices but retained the traditional symbolism of a paternalistic master who fostered well-being while ensuring order.
Many among the merchant elite attempted to promote a "moral community"
in the workplace in which employer and employees displayed mutual respect,
affection, and responsibility.[95] The proprietors of large, prominent enterprises

strove to provide a measure of protection for employees and to better their lives. These companies provided benefits such as medical care, credit unions, reading rooms, and free meals, as well as lodging, especially for young female employees. Through such actions, they hoped to present themselves as benevolent employers who cared for their employees and, to that end, strived to establish a familylike atmosphere. These paternalistic policies also benefited their bottom line, since they aimed to train employees to be loyal, productive, disciplined workers. Thus, employees' presentations to their employer prior to the ritual blessing recalled the respect and duty that had characterized the former relationship between master and apprentices and attempted to improve on it by highlighting a generous, compassionate proprietor and dutiful, respectful employees. Employee presentations may also have served as deferential reminders to employers to treat employees well, an interpretation that suggests that merchants were not entirely in control of the messages produced during the ritual. In this interpretation, employees formulated a part of the message and appropriated some portion of the ritual for themselves.[96]

Guests were also important participants in the rituals, constituting a chorus of approval for the exhibition of modern retail businesses. The tenor of a guest list denoted the importance of the occasion and typically included the political, social, and cultural elite of a city, such as the mayor and other municipal leaders and political dignitaries, police and military officials, museum curators, architects and artists, representatives from various professional, cultural, and charitable organizations, and members of the press. Invariably, the majority of guests were male, an indication that the commercial sphere, at least in its public, ceremonial, or symbolic aspect, was primarily a masculine province. Men assumed prominent roles in all aspects of the rituals, the owners serving as the architects of Russian commerce, the priests as executors of the blessing, and honored guests as bestowers of public acclaim.[97] Women lent their own symbolic credence to some ritual events. The festivities surrounding the opening of the Upper Trading Rows, for instance, included a charitable bazaar staged by the Christian Guardianship for the Poor, an organization that had as its patron the Grand Duchess Elizaveta Fedorovna and counted many elite women among its membership.[98] Odessa's Passazh hosted similar kinds of charitable events. The year after the opening of the arcade, the Odessa Society for the Physical Education and Protection of Children staged a grandiose bazaar there, and the organization's chairwoman, M. F. Kich, members of the board, and "lady-patronesses" in elegant dress presided.[99] Participation in such charitable organizations and events was considered an appropriate public activity for women, as it accorded with their perceived natural tendencies to nurture and serve others. At the same time, even if they were auxiliary to the main event of the ceremonial spectacle, women's display of their philanthropic roles amid the rows of the lavish arcades brought them visibility. The pairing of male-coded rituals and female-coded charitable events conveyed the idea that modern retailing was more than a method of business that allowed merchants to accumulate money. The merchantry had been known for its generosity to the poor, and such fundraising events in the arcades complemented a new conception of public philanthropy developing in the late nineteenth century, one that placed an emphasis on eliminating poverty through a central, coordinated collection of donations from a broad public, rather than individual almsgiving.[100] The merchant elite and modern retail firms played a role by providing the public space for male merchants to pursue rational modes of business, which, in turn, allowed their female counterparts to carry out rational acts of philanthropy.

Adorning a retail venue was another important element of the ceremonial blessing, and it typically included bedecking the interior with garlands and other kinds of greenery, the Russian flag, busts or portraits of the emperor and empress, colorful carpets, and/or red fabric. Icons and sacred objects brought from parish churches were also positioned inside wherever the service would be held. In the center of his store, Petrokokino assembled his guests around a podium flanked by busts of Nicholas and Aleksandra. Canopies and banners with religious inscriptions were also common. Decorations for the 1888 anniversary prayer service at the Postnikov arcade in Moscow, for example, included a canopy with the inscription "Lord, Save Your People." Beneath the canopy, organizers had assembled the icons of the Savior, and Iversk Mother of God, among others.[101]

The Orthodox liturgy and clergy, of course, provided the content for the prayer service and blessing. At Petrokokino's ceremony, Russian and Greek Orthodox clergy conducted the rite jointly, perhaps a tribute to Odessa's Ukrainian heritage or to the owner's own ethnic background. The priest Seletskii opened with a prayer, giving thanks to God, "without whom not one single building is created." He ended with a benediction that praised the firm and its contribution to the city and also asked for God's goodwill: "Our city is adorned with a new, splendid building and enriched with an extremely rare commercial establishment. Let us pray that God's blessing always be on this building and those who work in it!"[102] Priests ordinarily delivered a short homily during the service, addressing their comments to merchants to remind them of their moral obligations to the public. Although newspapers did not divulge the contents of the sermon delivered at Petrokokino's, accounts of the blessing of the Passazh reported that the same priest, Seletskii, appealed to the assembled merchants "to strive to conscientiously conduct their businesses and to furnish the public with good-quality merchandise and not let themselves be guided by the petty con-

cerns of profit and loss."[103] The priest's comments, especially the admonition not
to deceive customers or seek to gain an advantage by selling defective or poor-
quality merchandise, suggest that in the eyes of the Orthodox Church and the
community, the operation of a retail business was not merely a secular concern.
Retailing consumer goods carried with it a moral and spiritual obligation to the
community. At Perlov's one-hundred-year jubilee, the officiating priest made
similar remarks. Observing that the celebration of a century in business was not
only a momentous occasion for a merchant, his family, and the firm but also for
the public, he reminded attendees that a successful century could not have been
accomplished without the special blessing of God. He further connected God's
blessing to Perlov's industriousness and civic mindedness, asserting that the success of the business resulted from "earnest devotion to the business, of honest
service, united with the fulfillment of public duties and the commandments
of God."[104] The presence of sermonizing priests admonishing them to beware
the evils of business, bear in mind their responsibilities to the community, and
remember the golden rule when transacting sales allowed merchants, who were
mindful of their trade's reputation for dishonesty and underhanded methods, to
demonstrate their endeavor to conduct themselves and their businesses according to God's word and thereby reassure a doubting public.

In the final act of the religious service, priests walked the entire premises
of Petrokokino's, blessing it with holy water. This customary rite signified the
warding off of malevolent spirits and perhaps the ill effects of commerce. In this
public setting, the blessing may have also given the appearance of sanctioning
modern retailing and consumption, the consecration of a retail venue creating
the impression that these were legitimate activities, approved and blessed by
God's representatives on earth.

As noted, merchants paid clergy to perform these services, and there is little reason to suppose that most priests found the task objectionable. In fact, a
story penned by a journalist-priest and published in *Kormchii* (The Helmsman),
suggested that in the last years of the empire some clergy believed, or at least
promoted the idea, that ritual prayer services and ceremonial blessings could
serve as a stabilizing element and bulwark against rebellion. In the story, set in
1905, a pastor receives a request from three young workers, with intelligent-
looking, cheerful faces, to conduct a service at the large-scale enterprise where
they work. When the pastor asks the reason for the service, the three tell him
they and their fellow workers want to show their gratitude to their employer,
who, after being asked by workers not to make the customary winter-time
reduction in pay, not only did not reduce their pay but increased their work
hours. The pastor delightedly agrees, and upon arriving at the workplace, on
the very eve of general strikes in the capital, he is moved by a "touching show

of unity among employers and workers." To the pastor, this group of "prayerful people" embodied the "great, sober, and prudent part of the population, which steadfastly stands up to the outbreak of spontaneous outbursts of agitated passions."[105] At the end of the service, all kissed the cross and, at the request of the workers, sang the national hymn. Following the service, the pastor encounters on the street frightened-looking, sullen individuals gathered in groups discussing the possibility of clashes. The priest, however, warmed by the thanksgiving service, is calmed by the knowledge that many workers are grateful to their employers and do not share in the tense anxiety evident on the streets. Accepted at face value, the story suggests that some workers may well have had genuine confidence in their employers and have earnestly attempted to create a moral community in the workplace by, among other things, taking the initiative to organize a prayer service. With its setting in 1905, the story also reads as a moral tale in which employers reward trusting employees with kindness and generosity while religion unites them in a sacred bond that averts social conflict.

At the dinner that followed the prayer service and blessing at Petrokokino's, the customary round of toasts began with the city governor proposing the obligatory first toast to the health of the tsar, tsarina, and all of the royal family. Two newspapers reported that guests greeted this salute "with enthusiasm, and a rousing, unanimous 'Hurrah!' that reverberated for a long time throughout the store." Following this show of approval, a choir sang the hymn "God Save the Tsar," apparently only once, but it was not unusual for the hymn to be reprised several times. More toasts then followed: to the prosperity and success of the firm, to the health of the owner and his wife, to Bernardazzi, to the city governor, and to the employees, among others. Congratulatory speeches and additional proclamations of the new building as an "adornment" to the city were also common, especially in Odessa. Guests lifted their glasses once again for the last toast to the "precious health" of the tsar and royal family, a proposal that elicited another loud "Hurrah!" and a repeat performance of "God Save the Tsar."[106]

Descriptions of enthusiastic expressions of approval for the tsarist regime constituted a routine part of the reportage on the blessing of retail venues. The wording that journalists deployed, whether in Moscow or Odessa, was so similar as to resemble a boilerplate. Yet, since merchants' political opinions ranged widely, it is difficult to say exactly what was being acclaimed. Some merchants, Grigorii Eliseev, for example, apparently retained a faith in and dedication to the regime or at least paid public lip service to the idea. In a speech delivered in 1913 at the one-hundredth anniversary of his firm, Eliseev himself commented on the long-term success of his business, attributing it to his family's "selfless devotion to the Orthodox faith, the Russian tsar, and our homeland."[107] Es-

pecially after 1905, however, merchant-activists, including members of the
Riabushinskii Circle (an activist group of textile manufacturing magnates), the
Odessa merchant press, and some among the Moscow merchant press, were
either openly critical of or hostile to what they perceived as the government's
incompetent leadership and slack attitude toward commerce. Many merchants
no doubt stood between these two poles, displaying ambivalence about the tsarist regime and being attached to, but sometimes resentful of, state tutelage over
industry and commerce. However one interprets the sympathies and motives of
merchants who orchestrated these elaborate public commercial ceremonies—
as genuine shows of loyalty, disaffected affection, political conservatism, or
as merchants' attempts to ingratiate themselves with a political order that still
largely held commerce in contempt—such tributes, as presented to the urban
public, linked the merchant community to the tsarist regime.

Acclamations and public displays of devotion were not confined to Russian
Orthodox merchants. Foreign subjects also staged traditional blessing ceremonies that incorporated the customary displays of political fidelity. Given the
ambivalent attitude toward foreign investment and capitalism among landowners, some tsarist ministers and advisers, some Russian industrialists, and certain
conservative newspapers, foreign merchants may well have endeavored to ingratiate themselves with the government and the communities in which they
operated.[108] As noted earlier, the majority of merchants operating in Odessa's
Passazh were non-Russian and non-Orthodox. British citizens Walter Philip
and Archibald Merrilees, proprietors of Muir & Mirrielees department store
in Moscow, marked several stages of the construction of their Theater Square
flagship store, which opened in 1908, with Orthodox religious services and holy
water blessings.[109] The French-owned Brocard & Company inaugurated a celebration of the company's twenty-fifth anniversary in 1889 with an Orthodox
service in the factory courtyard.[110] Perlov's one-hundred-year anniversary was
celebrated with church services in its branch offices and in its retail stores in
Kiev and Warsaw.[111] As in the case of the Passazh, sometimes the ritual was
modified to reflect the ethnic or religious background of owners or workers,
although it does not appear that Catholic priests or Protestant ministers offici-
ated at ceremonial blessings. At the Jewish-run Second Men's Shoe Artel' in
Odessa, however, a local rabbi led prayers on behalf of masters, apprentices,
and shoe retailers. Although the service did not include a sprinkling of holy
water, other elements common to the traditional ritual were retained. The
rabbi ended the prayer service with a proclamation of long life to the tsar and
royal family. In his address, he called artisanal work a "blessing from God"
and praised the commercial undertaking as a worthy enterprise that is "hon-
orable in every respect."[112] Despite such efforts at acculturation, however, the

appropriation of Orthodox symbols and rituals by non-Orthodox merchants, particularly Jewish merchants, may not have gone unquestioned. A featured columnist for *Moskovskii listok* reported that readers had written to ask whether Jewish stores should be allowed to display Orthodox icons with lamps burning before them.[113]

The motives of non-Russian, non-Orthodox merchants living in the Russian Empire were complex, their actions suggesting that even though they were neither Russian nor Orthodox, they attempted to acculturate themselves and their firms. For example, although British citizens held the majority of shares in Muir & Mirrielees, the company billed itself as a "Russian-English" firm, a marketing strategy that linked the firm's foreign origins and its long-standing presence in Russia. Moreover, some foreign merchant-subjects had resided in Russia for generations and no doubt felt a kinship with Russia and its culture. Henri Brocard never accepted Russian citizenship or converted to Russian Orthodoxy, preferring to remain French and Catholic, yet he had lived in Russia for almost forty years prior his death. His wife, Charlotte Rave, daughter of a Belgian citizen who operated a commercial business in Moscow, spoke Russian and was socially well connected in the city. Despite his French origins, Brocard and his family were at home in Moscow. The celebration of his firm's anniversary with an Orthodox religious service suggests the affinities felt by some foreign merchants who had long-established businesses in Russia. Brocard may well have sponsored the traditional rite out of respect for his employees' or customers' faith and a perceived need to appeal to emotions and spiritual impulses familiar to them. In this interpretation, the incorporation of the ritual served to integrate the owner and firm into the larger community and to create affective ties between a French employer and his Russian employees. The degree to which Brocard was successful in integrating himself and his firm into Russian society may be seen in the commentary published upon his death in 1900. A writer for *Moskovskii listok,* reporting on the funeral, remarked that although Brocard was French by birth and a "foreign guest" in Moscow, he was without a doubt a "Muscovite."[114] The animosity toward foreign merchants, overt at the highest levels of the political structure and widespread among landowners and intellectuals, may not have resonated throughout all levels of society.

The degree to which consumers accepted foreign merchants and their firms may be judged in part by the success of their retail businesses. Consumers' interpretations of the ceremonial blessings, however, are difficult to gauge. Some indications of the appeal of these public spectacles and of consumers' enthusiasm for them exist in the reportage, albeit indirectly. The ceremonial blessings were usually by invitation only, but, as the opening vignette of this chapter suggests, some part of the urban populace was interested in these events and participated as spectators and shoppers. The blessing ceremony of the Upper Trading Rows in Moscow attracted a crowd of sixty thousand people, who presumably stood outside the Rows or in the upper galleries during the ceremony.[115] Several thousand people reportedly visited the stores in Odessa's Passazh on the day of its blessing.[116] Ceremonies held to mark the anniversaries of the opening of the Aleksandr and Lubianka retail arcades also reportedly drew large crowds.[117] Merchants, understanding the importance of public acclaim, played to the crowds, with owners of the largest retail venues hiring orchestras to entertain the people and thus generate goodwill and patronage. Their attempts to incorporate the local population into the activities indicate that blessing ceremonies were not only meant to be solemn occasions where merchants paid the requisite tributes to political and religious authorities, while their peers in municipal government and artistic and professional circles lent support. The scale of the ceremonies, as well as the prominent press coverage they received, suggests that they were also staged to appeal to a consuming public as a form of publicity and entertainment. The crowds and the reading public were essential participants, even if they did not witness the actual blessing. Their presence signified approval and/or spectatorship, both of which were necessary for endowing the event with public significance and providing acclaim for the vision of an urban society sponsored by merchants who believed they were advancing a progressive, ethical business credo, buttressed by moral authority and political fidelity.

The rise of modern retailing and the emergent culture of consumption in Russia did not constitute an exclusively secular process that necessarily undermined established authorities and hierarchies or threatened Russian culture and traditions. In addition to encouraging individualism, autonomy, and materialism—values commonly associated with modern mass retailing and consumption—the blessing ceremonies reinscribed communal and patriarchal values and reminded merchants of the conflicts and moral perils inherent in commerce. They also allowed merchants to defer to tsar and God. In short, they demonstrated stability, sobriety, and morality in a rapidly changing world. It may seem paradoxical that merchants incorporated familiar and established authorities, images, customs, and rites into their promotional strategies as they were laying the foundations for a capitalist economy predicated on consumer desires. However, Orthodox and tsarist imagery and rituals did not remain static in this process. They were drawn into the commercial sphere and became commodifiable objects. Moreover, as the state began to adopt some of the techniques and idioms of mass marketing, merchants relied on associations with tsarist power and religion to publicize their retail firms and its offerings and to advocate the merchant's role as civic patron and cultural arbiter. Finally, the associations exhibited in advertisements, product lines, and the blessing ceremonies also served to sanction modern retailing and to accustom a consuming public to a culture of acquisition and materialism and to promote a larger industry whose aim was to sell material goods, entertainment, and spectacle to urban audiences.

The merchant community did not remain quiescent in the midst of an increasingly volatile political atmosphere, however. The merchant elite's changing self-perceptions prompted the most activist among them to articulate new ideals more explicitly and widely and to challenge the political and social order that the ceremonial blessing appeared to endorse. However, the aspirations of the retail merchant elite and their new promotional strategies did not go unquestioned. Some members of educated society, along with urban observers, voiced concerns about the merits of modern retailing and values of a consumer-oriented society.

4

Visions of Modernity
Gender and the Retail Marketplace,
1905–1914

The merchant elite's orchestration of promotional events publicizing associations with tsarist power and the Orthodox faith clashed with self-perceptions some merchants had developed in the decade prior to World War I. As the Russian retail sector continued to grow, diversify, and serve a rapidly increasing population, the political situation in Russia became volatile. The Revolution of 1905, which brought limited political rights, relaxed censorship laws, and gave workers the right to organize, led to increased opportunities for public expression, as well as disillusionment in state-guided reform. Throughout this period, educated professionals began to organize, dedicating themselves to finding a solution to society's ills. A new generation of activist merchants, aided by allies in the educated classes, began to move away from symbolic alliance with the tsarist state and Orthodox Church. The activist merchants sought to self-consciously articulate a new ethic and vision of modernity in which a new kind of male merchant, supported by emergent sources of authority, including middle-class ideals of masculinity and a model of modern commerce, played a leading, progressive role. Conservative social critics, troubled by new forms of retailing and changes in urban life, advocated a society founded on patriarchy and native Russian structures and customs, free from the influence of Western business methods and unruly women and young men.

As one of the centers of public life that had helped to usher in enormous changes, the retail marketplace became a flashpoint for changing definitions of modern urban society. Gender was inextricably bound up in these definitions. Conceptualizations of modern urban society were based on the creation of new icons of merchants and consumers in which men figured either as rational leaders of a just and efficient retail marketplace or as obsequious manipulators and women, as either rational consumers or wayward, profligate shoppers. Activist merchant-journalists mounted a campaign to promote modern retailing and the businessman as emergent progressive forces in Russia. There emerged in Russia an economic conceptualization of modern retailing that advocated the department store as an efficient, democratizing institution for all citizens. Critiques and condemnations of the department store also arose, and some of these characterized modern retailing and the fashion industry as threats to male authority. Although a consensus on the value of modern retailing did not emerge, discourses about its merits and drawbacks reveal the tensions about social class and gender roles that characterized late imperial Russia.

The *Kupets* and the *Kommersant*

Decades and even centuries of accumulated resentment toward merchants and the retail trade had resulted in a stock of negative stereotypes, offset by romantic and idealized characterizations. Neither represented the complex social realities of early-twentieth-century Russia. By 1905, a new generation of merchants, born between the 1860s and 1880s to wealthy, socially prominent commercial-industrial families that were educated, culturally refined, and politically active, had emerged and established a solid presence. At the same time, a corps of merchant-journalists in cities throughout the empire had founded commercial publications dedicated to the joint goals of rehabilitating the image of merchants and reforming the retail sector and, more generally, the economy. The men who edited and wrote for these publications hoped they could bypass the obtuseness of the economic policies of Nicholas II and reeducate merchants. They hoped to use their expertise and training to resolve problems of politics and social relations. The most activist merchant-journalists launched a campaign to inspire merchants to model themselves after a new ideal founded on middle-class standards of masculine behavior and contemporary retailing practices, in essence, to remake the *kupets,* or small shopkeeper, into a *kommersant,* or professional businessman. Their agenda signaled a new social and political awareness on the part of a small group of men who sought to accomplish with such a campaign nothing less than a thorough transformation of Russian society.

A few journals and newspapers devoted to commerce and industry had been in circulation prior to 1905, the longest-running ones being *Torgovo-promyshlennaia gazeta* (The Commercial-Industrial Newspaper, St. Petersburg, 1901–1916) and

Torgovyi biulleten' (The Commercial Bulletin, Odessa, 1901–1916). After 1905, however, the number of such publications rose to more than twenty-five, as business leaders in Moscow, St. Petersburg, and Odessa and even in smaller commercial cities, including Tiflis, Samara, Khar'kov, and Irkutsk, founded their own journals. These publications appeared in part in response to the up-heavals and civil unrest of 1905, when Nicholas II granted and then gradually disavowed political reforms and civil liberties. Such turmoil left members of educated society frustrated but fearful of further instability. Many of these new journals and newspapers were short lived, and most concentrated solely on giving commercial advice. A few, however, lasted until 1914 and, in addition to advising their merchant-readers on business matters, pressed an overt political agenda that asserted the significance of a new breed of merchants to the establishment of a more productive, just, moral, and cultured Russia. The most activist and longest-running among them were *Torgovoe delo* (Commercial Business Affairs, 1907–1914) and *Torgovyi mir* (Commercial World, 1909–1912), both based in Odessa. Although they enjoyed a brief existence, *Torgovo-promyshlennaia Rossiia* (Commercial-Industrial Russia, 1906–1907) in Khar'kov and *Torgovlia, promyshlennost', i tekhnika* (Commerce, Industry, and Technology, 1909) in Moscow also contributed to this agenda and discourse. Mediating between what they viewed as a politically lethargic state unresponsive to the needs and demands of modern commerce and thousands of small-scale merchants and vendors mired in outmoded, unprincipled business practices, the editors of these journals sought to professionalize the retail trade and to groom merchants to lead Russia into a new age. The modern retail marketplace they envisioned was a beautiful, tidy realm where honest, disciplined, knowledgeable, and industrious merchants operated large-scale, rationalized, efficient businesses oriented toward raising the material and cultural standards of the population. Such a retail system, they believed, would eradicate merchants' worst instincts and help quell consumers' basest impulses.

The agenda the trade press articulated was part of a larger discourse about order and morality that developed in many professional circles after 1905.[1] The Riabushinskii Circle also championed commercial-industrial entrepreneurs as the only rising force in the empire possessing the vision, skill, and economic power to mobilize and revitalize Russia's productive forces. Pavel Riabushinskii exhorted fellow entrepreneurs to sobriety, individual initiative, industriousness, and a disavowal of predatory instincts and behaviors.[2] There were no direct ties between the activist trade press and the Riabushinskii group, even though they advanced similar ideas. Moreover, the editors of the trade press, especially those based in Odessa, distinguished themselves from Riabushinskii and other prominent merchant reformers, who displayed a passionate, nationalistic belief that only leaders from Moscow's merchant community, based in the historic capital in the heart of Russia, were capable of leading the country to renewed greatness. By contrast, the Jewish editors of Odessa's robust trade press adopted an international, cosmopolitan outlook, no doubt a consequence of their ethnicity and residence in a commercial city on the periphery of the empire. E. S. Gal'perin, who served as secretary-steward of the Odessa Exchange, edited the journal *Torgovoe delo* from 1907 to 1914, and P. I. Sigal-Meiler and M. Ia. Khaimovich guided *Torgovyi mir* from 1909 to 1912. These men assumed a less ethnocentric approach to Russia's political and economic problems. One of Sigal-Meiler's editorials even ridiculed Russocentrism and insularity among Russia's merchant-industrial classes. Mocking those who asserted that "it is time to give Russia back to the Russians," Sigal-Meiler interjected, "My God! Just who is taking Russia away from us?" He answered his own question, charging that Russians were undermining their own standing and had only themselves to blame for the "imaginary domination" of foreigners.[3] The editor ended his piece by exhorting merchants to stop overreacting and instead to develop positive work habits and attitudes. Only then would Russia be powerful enough to compete with foreign capital.

The men who advocated on behalf of the business community turned out to be no less critical of the merchant classes than most other Russians. Acknowledging the accuracy of the worst stereotypes of Russian merchants, many declared that, given their dishonest methods, merchants frequently deserved the insults slung at them. The editor of *Torgovyi mir* placed much of the blame for society's disdainful attitude toward merchants directly on merchants themselves. A lack of public conscientiousness, he believed, had resulted in the public's disapproval and distrust.[4] A journalist writing for *Torgovo-promyshlennaia Rossiia* (Commercial-Industrial Russia) under the pen name Agrikola similarly held Russian merchants accountable. Declaring that the outstanding characteristic of Russian commerce was its slovenliness (*neriashlivost'*), he faulted merchants for their chaotic and undisciplined style of management as well as their heavy reliance on the state. This writer went on to accuse merchants of routinely cheating their customers, something he considered not only dishonest but also uncultured and embarrassing. As he saw it, deceptive business practices discredited Russia in the eyes of the "civilized world," and he urged merchants to reform themselves, not only for the good of their firms but also for the good of the population and the good of Russia's international standing.[5]

The main purpose of these journals, however, was not to further denigrate merchants but to instill in them a sense of worth and purpose. As *Torgovyi mir*'s editor asserted, "It is finally time for merchants to say to themselves that they are not pariahs in their own country, but fully equal citizens."[6] To inspire and instruct readers, journalists reconceptualized the merchant as the kommersant, the energetic, decorous, middle-class professional and socially conscientious, rational organizer of the marketplace. The creation of the image of the kommersant coincided with the rise of a visible minority of successful urban merchants active in political and cultural life. These real-life merchants probably inspired the construction of the iconic kommersant in the pages of the trade press. Writers for the journals fleshed out the traits of the exemplary merchant, creating a didactic icon that also represented the goals, interests, and outlooks of the new merchant elite and those who aspired to it. Writing for a relatively small readership, numbering in the thousands, journalists pursued their cause earnestly, conveying confidence in a bright future.[7]

The kommersant symbolized the rejection of Russia's customary retail culture as exemplified by the kupets and also embodied dissatisfaction with Russia's authoritarian political system and static social structures. The creation of the kommersant signaled a struggle for economic and social change, providing activist merchants with the language with which to present their aspirations and challenge the authorities and conventions of the past. The dominant ideal of European masculinity throughout the eighteenth century had been that of the gentry, based in land ownership and kinship, allied with the state through service in the military, imperial bureaucracy, or provincial administration and opposed to the agricultural workforce.[8] In Russia, as late as the 1910s, the word meaning "noble" (blagorodno) suffused the ideals of Russian intellectuals, who scorned the "success ethos" as vulgar.[9] While the gentry ideal reigned supreme, subordinate models of masculinity, based on class, ethnicity, occupation, region, and sexual orientation, also emerged to represent masculine codes of behavior prevalent in other sectors of society. As Robert Connell, Michael Kimmel, and other historians of gender have pointed out, multiple, competing models of masculinity exist at any time, and all of them provide a field against which a dominant ideal of manhood is defined. Ideals, they remind us, change over time, and the prevailing model of manhood is always subject to challenge and displacement.[10] In late imperial Russia, the established model of the merchant, the kupets, represented a lower-class masculine model that, while subordinate to the gentry ideal, nonetheless dominated perceptions of the world of commerce.

The kommersant emerged in Russia during years of turmoil and great change, when other upwardly mobile groups were also formulating alternate models of masculine discipline and energy. Skilled urban workers, for instance, tried to distinguish themselves from the culture of drinking, physical aggression, and womanizing of their unskilled coworkers with a new model of masculinity stressing displays of education and refinement.[11] The so-called bourgeois rationalist, another version of middle-class masculinity, also appeared at this time in Russia, as well as in Europe and the United States, epitomizing competition in the workplace, individualism, rational behavior, discipline, and responsibility to home and family.[12] These constructions of model manhood were created at roughly the same time as self-help and advice manuals, which likewise sought to eradicate the backwardness, incivility, passivity, and other undesirable attitudes and behaviors assumed characteristic of the Russian male and to provide models with more productive qualities.[13] As proffered by the trade press, the Russian paragon of the middle-class merchant shared the bourgeois rationalist's set of individualist attitudes and disciplined habits. Yet, although writers for the trade press encouraged the development of responsible, refined behaviors and an energetic, competitive attitude, they did not see the acquisition of these traits as a personal goal or an end in itself. Their objective of inspiring their readers to pattern themselves after the kommersant was to encourage merchants to invest themselves in the larger goal of transforming society.

Constructed by men primarily in relation to other men, the kommersant and the kupets were both explicitly masculine models. That does not mean, however, that conceptualizations of femininity did not contribute to the creation of these models. The new ideal of merchant masculinity, like other masculine models, was defined not only in relation to other models of masculinity but also in opposition to femininity and, furthermore, was used to maintain authority over women.[14] As one feminist theorist of masculinity has observed, the focus on homosocial relations among men has helped us to understand the ways in which "patriarchal investments" are reproduced.[15] Men have conventionally been viewed as masters of the marketplace and women, as consumers. To some extent this situation reflected social realities. In late-nineteenth-century Russia, men outnumbered women in the retail trade ten to one.[16] Given that preponderance and the prevailing social and gender conventions about appropriate work for men and women, writers for the trade press assumed their audience to be male and tailored their publications accordingly, seldom portraying women as merchants or traders.[17] Such gender roles also fit within broader European cultural conventions, which conceptualized men as organizers of the marketplace and women as consumers. The kommersant of Russia's trade press, however, did not exhibit the deviousness of archetypal literary entrepreneurs such as Émile Zola's Octave Mouret, but the figure nonetheless conformed to a model of paternal benevolence in which females appeared as discerning, middle-class consumers in need of protection from the degraded kupets by forward-looking businessmen. The trade press also sometimes struck out in a different direction, eschewing the model of the woman as victim or wayward consumer and developing the image of the female consumer as an equal participant in an orderly, modern system of retailing.

Writers for the trade press sought to depose the dominant business norms and cultural ideals that devalued the entrepreneurship, knowledge, and leadership potential of middle-class merchants. The creation of the kommersant as an alternative to the widespread image of the obsolete, dishonest, backward kupets represented a new conception of the merchant that, while still subordinate to the gentry ideal, captured in language and imagery the multiple social tensions that accompanied the rise of modern retailing in Russia. In the minds of these writers, the gentry and the kupets represented the forces of reaction and underdevelopment, and they asserted the worth of the businessman, a model that derived legitimacy from new sources of authority, including emerging middle-class standards of behavior and the methods of modern retailing. They depicted the kommersant as a self-made, visionary man who espoused an ethic of energetic leadership, industry, integrity, and self-restraint in business and everyday life, traits fostered through professional organizations and channeled into political ambition. This ideal took physical shape in the masthead of *Torgovoe delo*. Portrayed in its pages as a master of commerce and industry, the kommersant appeared on the masthead as a man working at a big desk next to a window overlooking a panorama of commercial and industrial activity that included merchant ships, trains, a factory, warehouses, and a large retail store.

The positive icon of the kommersant communicated the embattled position in which many aspiring merchants believed they were caught by presenting merchants as potential leaders thwarted by what the trade press believed to be two out-of-date, ineffectual sectors of society. In the inaugural issue of *Torgovoe delo,* the editor, E. S. Gal'perin, made explicit this oppositional stance. He argued that "material prosperity" (*material'noe blagosostoianie*) for every individual person and for the *narod* (people) depended neither on a leveling of class differences nor political freedom but on the cultivation of "virtuous work habits" such as energy, enterprise, and independence.[18] Likewise, he proposed that a true freedom that results in human happiness derived not from a political but from a "moral freedom [*nravstvennaia svoboda*] and a moral self-discipline." Taking care to distance himself from the legions of small-scale traders and from political and social conservatives alike, Gal'perin defended himself against the idea that these were self-serving qualities, insisting that his ideas were not the tired platitudes of "bourgeois and petit-bourgeois ideology." Making clear his opposition to both of these groups, he asserted, "We are far from both the narrow and crude *meshchanstvo* and from reactionaries."[19]

Journalists contrasted the men who had dominated Russia in the past to the rising force of the new middle-class male merchant, repeatedly pointing out the failings of tsarist ministers and castigating the kupets's reliance on customary methods, while lauding the ideals and practices of the kommersant. The editor of *Torgovyi mir,* for instance, coupled a plea to the Ministry of Commerce and Industry to listen to the needs of merchants with the assertion that Russian commerce could no longer be guided by the "old methods inherited from our grandfathers."[20] With this statement, the editor paired men of the political elite with the tactics of old-fashioned merchants, asserting that both were past their prime. He went on to urge fundamental reforms that would give the kupets "a means of transforming himself from the Moscow Kit Kitych to a kommersant," in essence presenting the new generation of merchants as the alternative.[21] The editor of *Torgovlia, promyshlennost', i tekhnika,* likewise noting the ambiguous position of middle-class merchants, asked whether Russia "should move forward or languish under the conditions of the old regime?" Appealing to what he called the "progressive" and "capable" forces in Russian commerce and industry, he then urged his readers to assert their importance over Russia's "land-owning interests" and the "uncultured ways [*nekul'turnost'*] and helplessness [*bespomoshchnost'*] of the productive forces of the country."[22]

Many journalists acknowledged that the ideals of the kommersant were far removed from the realities of the lives of the majority engaged in the retail trade; most were from the lower or peasant classes and ascribed to a set of attitudes and masculine ideals that posed obstacles to reform. Reflecting on the social changes in the years since emancipation, a writer for *Torgovyi mir* asserted that the "kupets is beginning to look at himself not only as a small tradesman [*torgasha*] but as a kommersant," although he admitted that the transformation was still far from complete.[23] For *Torgovoe delo's* Novus, the difference between the kupets and kommersant primarily came down to differences in background and outlook. He discerned in the kupets a lack of self-assurance, pride, and any dream of raising himself higher. As he claimed, "Tomorrow does not exist for the *kuptsy,* who live only for today." As a consequence of such a demoralized mentality, he concluded that the kupets did not have the "ambition that moves mountains."[24] Yet Novus did not believe that the majority of Russia's merchants were intrinsically lazy or bad at heart. He felt that most were satisfied to have enough business to feed and clothe themselves, living on the modest hope that nothing worse would happen to them. Novus realized that the traits and habits of the kupets had been instilled over time by the harsh conditions of life in Russia. To overcome such deeply rooted counterproductive tendencies, he recommended that readers pattern themselves after the kommersant, a figure who could free himself from the constraints of his environment and limited purview, someone who, as he put it, "could never reconcile himself and will never accept the present situation" and thus would strive to expand and develop his business.[25]

The figure of the kommersant was clearly intended to model a set of personal work habits that would inspire merchants to build the trade press's version of an economically vital and socially just Russia. To that end, the journals published numerous morality tales, personal testimonies, and advice columns that contrasted successful (energetic, ambitious, innovative) merchants, who relied on fixed pricing, advertising, courtesy, and attentive service to attract and keep customers, with unsuccessful (lazy, complacent) merchants, who neglected their customers' needs and treated them disrespectfully.[26] Above all, the kommersant displayed a "conscientious attitude" (*dobrosovestnoe otnoshenie*) toward the management of his firm, consumers, and society, which amounted to the abandonment of old-fashioned, deceitful sales customs and the adoption of modern business practices. In pursuit of these two objectives, writers frequently inveighed against haggling, a time-honored custom they believed was the greatest cause of widespread ill will against merchants. In issue after issue, reform-minded writers portrayed haggling as outdated, dishonest, and ignoble and accused merchants who practiced it of tricking their customers into paying higher prices than they should. They urged readers instead to institute a policy of fixed prices (*bez zaprosa,* literally "without question"), asserting that assigning each item a firm price would ensure a fair exchange and preserve the mutual rights of merchant and consumer, as well as establish a transparent, rational, and honest style of transacting business that preserved the dignity (*dostoinstvo*) of merchants in the eyes of the public and protected them from censure.[27] Delving into the meanings behind conscientiousness and dignity, one writer contrasted the discord wrought by haggling with the harmony and lack of ill will he envisioned fixed pricing would make possible: "If a customer goes into a store with fixed prices, he or she knows that here they will not be deceived or have to argue with the merchant. He doesn't have to be on his guard against the merchant who, of course, wants to take from him as much as he can. . . . He doesn't have to regret when the deal is made and the item bought —'Why didn't I bargain even lower? Maybe I could have gotten another twenty kopeks out of him.'"[28] This writer believed that a customer could go "confidently" (*smelo*) and "freely" (*svobodno*) into a store with fixed prices without feeling as if he or she were going to do battle with an enemy. He imagined that once the potential for conflict was removed, a sales transaction would transpire thus: "'Here is an item; here is the price. Kindly pay the money and take it'—short, straightforward, and noble [*blagorodno*]."[29]

Concerns about haggling seemed to stem from the belief that dickering over money set merchant against customer, turning them into adversaries. Journalists perceived in the haggling exchange a range of destructive emotions—fear, anxiety, anger, aggression, deception, regret—a set of masculine attitudes and behaviors associated with a harsh, uncertain past based on arbitrariness, domination, and humiliation. These activist-writers sought to remove emotion from the marketplace or at least to allow only positive, affirming, and productive emotions. They hoped to imbue the sales transaction with straightforwardness, purposeful action, confidence, freedom, and dignity. Such an agenda reflected their optimistic belief that liberation from the reactionary forces of customary trading practices would create new men who, through restrained, rationalized action, brought cooperation, harmony, and a sense of fairness to the retail marketplace and removed suspicion and discord.

Journalists also endowed the kommersant with scrupulous shopkeeping habits and a keen appreciation for beauty, traits not traditionally associated with lower-class and peasant masculine cultures but that exemplified a well-appointed, clean, and orderly marketplace and signified cultured living. They repeatedly cautioned readers to pay attention to small details, revealing in their counsel a desire to help merchants enhance their image by exhibiting a respectable storefront appearance as well as a genuine concern to improve the physical conditions in which merchants and consumers transacted business. Clean floors, counters, and equipment, merchandise neatly stored and displayed in its proper place, and comfortable store temperatures became standards of the kommersant's credo. Habits that had become accepted—for example, employees or dogs lolling about in doorways—were discouraged as signs of slothfulness and as intimidating or distasteful to customers.[30] Tidiness alone, however, would not attract customers. Writers also advised merchants to spruce up their stores by installing sufficient light, decorating them inside and out, and dressing the windows.[31] This concern with cleanliness, light, and attractiveness not only reflected a desire to decorate for decoration's sake. To these men, brightly lit stores symbolized a merchant's willingness to conduct business openly, which meant giving customers a good look at merchandise for sale, unprotected by shadowy corners. Attractive stores with appealing displays and tasteful decors indicated progress, the achievement of a certain level of material well-being, and an appreciation for the finer things in life.

The beautification imperative also suggests that the trade press journalists recognized consumers as feeling individuals sensitive to comfort and aesthetics. In their opinion, a conscientious merchant would create a pleasant exterior and interior environment in order to attract and not repel customers, an effort that would be rewarded with increased sales. Some went further, implying that merchants had a kind of moral obligation to provide an aesthetically pleasing environment and to make a customer feel welcome and comfortable. One writer

made precisely this point, venturing that such efforts acknowledged customers'
dignity and their desire for beauty, traits that individuals at all levels of society
shared. As he argued, merchants should make a good impression by, above all,
keeping clean and tidy premises, but they should also recognize that a "poor
man [*bedniak*] likes elegance and beauty just as much as a wealthy one."[32] According to this writer, a dirty, bleak store made an unfavorable impression on
the lower and working classes just as readily as on the upper and middle classes.
He maintained that residents who lived in outlying districts frequently shopped
for expensive items on the city's main streets, even though similar stores operated in their own neighborhoods, because stores that presented a dreary, dirty
appearance induced a kind of "melancholy" (*toska*) in shoppers. This advice
shows a concern for the material and even psychological well-being of consumers, as well as a belief that consumers of all classes should be respected as human
beings endowed with needs, emotions, and desires.

The new code also stressed integrity, dignity, and honesty—traits thought
to distance the kommersant from the obsequious, deceptive flattery associated
with the kupets. Writers urged civil, dignified relations between merchants and
customers, confident that respectful interaction would bring a refined, principled order to the retail marketplace, as well as profits to merchants. Highlighting the negative impact of the customary practice of calling, Novus remarked
that when merchants or their apprentices went out on the streets to attract customers or called to them from the doors of their shops, the customer frequently
got "caught on the line."[33] For Novus, calling placed a passerby in a compromising position, leaving him or her vulnerable to the wiles of the trade. But it
also debased the merchant or shop assistant who practiced it, compromising his
business reputation and degrading his personal character. Novus suggested as
much when he then optimistically asserted that, in contemporary Russia, the
merchant had acquired a sense of "dignity" (*dostoinstvo*) and no longer wants to
"humble himself" (*unizhat'sia*) before customers. The writer also believed that
customers had changed, and he argued that "the modern shopper [*sovremennyi
pokupatel'*] demands courtesy" but does not like "abasement, which grates on
him [*sic*]."[34] His comments imply his belief that society had evolved, or at least
that it should be evolving, and that social relationships should no longer operate
on principles of domination/subordination or through the tactics of superficial
flattery. Rather, members of society should meet each other on equal ground,
conducting themselves with self-respect, treating each other respectfully, and
contracting sales in straightforward terms without evasions or subterfuges. Novus advised that merchants who wanted to attract customers should, above all,
be polite but maintain their self-respect. Others echoed this advice, cautioning
merchants, for example, against treating customers with "disdainful careless-

ness" and urging them to make customers feel "free and relaxed" by greeting them and treating them with courtesy.[35]

Writers also advised merchants not to boast extravagantly about an item or press a customer to buy it; they deemed such practices part of the vulgar tactics practiced by the kupets. They promised success to merchants who matched the customer's needs with appropriate merchandise, who discoursed in even, polite tones, and who paid tactful, patient, and knowledgeable attention to each transaction.[36] Some writers even presented the practice of gauging customers' needs as a responsibility, arguing that the merchant should be on the side of customers and not simply wanting to make a sale. As they saw it, merchants had a duty to try to provide customers with the most suitable products by genuinely trying to ascertain their tastes, wants, and character.[37] This advice indicates an earnest desire for merchants to adopt what the writers considered clear, transparent procedures that would not only help them boost sales but also end some of the resentment toward merchants and bring a tone of sincerity and mutual respect to public life.

Lessons in decorum filled the pages of trade publications. The express purpose of such lessons was to model a new code of solicitous, polite, and well-mannered behaviors and to point out those to avoid. In his columns, Novus frequently contrasted the behaviors of the old-fashioned kupets and the modern kommersant. One such article offered a profile of two grocery shop owners. One behaved rudely and indifferently to his customers, made them wait while he chatted unnecessarily, and, in selling to them, acted as if he were doing them a favor. The other merchant treated his customers politely, anticipated their needs, and tried to make their shopping experience pleasant.[38] Sometimes lessons in civility took the form of reportage. One publication reported the case of a female shopper named Chernina who brought two St. Petersburg merchants before a justice of the peace for rudely throwing her out of their store in the Gostinyi Dvor arcade.[39] The publication presented the behavior of the two merchants as disgraceful and warned that those who disregarded the new rules of commercial etiquette could be held accountable in court for their actions.

Beneath the pleas for fixed prices, cleanliness, and courtesy lay, of course, an attempt to reeducate the merchant into a middle-class model of masculine behaviors and thereby reform the culture of the retail marketplace. The urgency with which trade journalists pressed their cause, however, stemmed from a belief that, in reconfiguring the merchant ideal, in transforming the Russian kupets into a kommersant, merchants could spearhead wider political and social reforms and, ultimately, bring about a complete revitalization of Russian society. To effect such a change, members of the trade press believed it necessary to instill in merchants a sense of personal responsibility, not only for the sake of the economy but also for the moral climate. In essence, men had to behave differently. Attention to the restructuring of relations between merchants and consumers through the maintenance of clean, tidy, organized, attractive places of business, the adoption of nonconfrontational, transparent methods of buying and selling, and the institution of civil, dignified relations with customers reflected a desire to establish a just, harmonious social order and infuse daily behaviors and practices with virtue.

Consuming Citizens and the Democratic Department Store

Activist journalists found allies among some members of the educated classes, who found much to admire in the methods of modern retailing. Mikhail Nikolaevich Sobolev, professor of political economy and statistics at Tomsk University, regarded the department store as a marker of freedom, progress, and virtue.[40] Downplaying the economic hardships that the rise of such retail enterprises might bring to small-scale traders and the value some merchants and consumers may have placed on customary practices, Sobolev emphasized what he believed was the department store's superior format, economies of scale, and potential benefit to consumers. Although he was not a proponent of unbridled capitalism, he advocated competition in the economic sphere as a healthy means of working out the problems of Russian trade and industry. In his view, competition exposed the shortcomings and weaknesses in the economy and provoked interested parties—the state, workers, and owners—to remedy them. To Sobolev, a liberal economic theorist, the abstract forces of the market and rational motives of those who participated in it ensured efficient and proper functioning of the economy.[41] His conceptualization relied less on a model of male merchantry. Moreover, the consumer market he envisioned was not composed of overwrought, preening females who vied to outdress each other and fought over scraps of ribbon and lace at sales counters. He portrayed consumers as serious, sober individuals, men and women of all classes, who relied on accurate information and fair pricing to make judicious purchases of everyday, necessary items. Such consumers, he argued, required a new kind of retailer, one schooled in cost-effective business methods and honest sales practices. While he relied less on gendered constructs and explicitly masculine and feminine models of consumption, his vision nonetheless depended on women's traditional roles as wives and mothers and represented female consumption as directed toward ends traditionally construed as appropriate for women, in particular, the maintenance of their homes and families.

Citing Muir & Mirrielees as the Russian exemplar, Sobolev lauded the many advantages of the department store. He argued foremost that because of its larger size and greater working capital, the department store operated more profit-

ably than small shops and, therefore, served consumers more effectively and efficiently in terms of quality and price. As his logic went, big stores commanded
more resources, which enabled them to send buyers to different parts of the world
to acquire a more varied inventory of better-quality items. Because of their economic clout and ability to buy in volume, buyers for department stores received
discounts from manufacturers; therefore, the cost of goods was less, making the
markup smaller, a savings that was passed on to customers. He asserted that department stores also put their capital to more productive use, always keeping
it in motion, investing and re-investing it in an ever-changing assortment of
merchandise. Besides pointing out their competitive edge, Sobolev argued that
department stores offered services to consumers that smaller shops could not,
including delivery and return and exchange privileges. He also believed that the
employees whom department stores recruited were another asset. Contending
that better employees, meaning, presumably, men and women who were at least
literate and had developed the manners of the urban middle classes or could be
trained in them, worked at department stores, he reasoned that customers would
receive attentive, knowledgeable, and courteous service. Sobolev further praised
department stores for acting as good citizens within a community by informing
the public through advertisements and catalogs of their merchandise offerings
and prices. These things, the professor argued, served a strictly functional purpose, furnishing consumers with valuable information and saving them time
by making it unnecessary to go from shop to shop in search of items. Finally,
Sobolev pointed out that the big stores enriched a community with their reading rooms and the concerts, literary readings, and artistic exhibitions held in the
store, providing appropriately middle-class, cultured activities.[42]

Sobolev conceived of the department store as a modernizing, democratizing institution and a cornerstone of a new, egalitarian economic and moral
order. In constructing this icon of economic liberalism, he brushed aside complaints that department stores forced smaller-sized shops out of business and
impoverished their proprietors.[43] He also largely disregarded concerns about
social stability, traditional Russian culture, and custom, issues that several critics raised. He likewise gave no consideration to charges of immorality, viewing competitiveness as a moral force in itself. Sobolev proposed an alternative
system in which economically efficient enterprises delivered commercial justice
through the principles of modern management. Expanding this point, he explained that stores that managed their resources effectively were less likely to
resort to deception to sell products to the consumer. Like the writers for the
trade press, Sobolev discerned in modern retailing transparency and rational
calculations based on liberal economic principles, which equaled moral scru-
pulousness. By contrast, the customary practices of small shopkeepers, rooted

in improvisational sales techniques and independent deal making, amounted to deceit and disorder.

Consuming Women and Wayward Men

The rational, principled, dignified, and beneficial system of modern commerce presented in the pages of the trade press and Professor Sobolev's essays did not correspond with the views of all members of society, some of whom conceptualized Russian society as under siege by the fashion industry and its auxiliary retail agents. For critics, the fashion and modern retailing industries were ravaging, foreign, and feminized institutions that vaunted individualism at the expense of Russian traditions and culture and upset established social and gender hierarchies. Some urban chroniclers experienced a less vehement resistance, more akin to regret and ambivalence. As the paragon of modern retailing, the department store served as a visibly powerful symbol to critics and social commentators, who deployed it to critique modern, urban life and the perceived liberties that it extended, especially to women and young men. New notions of gender, fabricated from the perceived dangers of the fashion industry and methods of modern retailing, structured their arguments and gave them potency.

The arrival of the department store elicited loathing in one Iulii Lukianovich Elets. A self-ordained social commentator, Elets had served in the military in eastern Mongolia in the early 1900s, defending the Catholic mission there, before becoming a correspondent for the conservative newspaper *Novoe vremia* (New Times) during the Russo-Japanese War. He was evidently a rather important figure in the military, as evidenced by his inclusion in the military encyclopedia published in St. Petersburg in 1912. His interests extended beyond military affairs to include social and cultural issues and literature, including poetry.[44] It is unclear how Elets became interested in the subjects of fashion and commerce, but his histrionic tirade against the fashion industry and the department store, *Poval'noe bezumie (k sverzheniiu iga mod)* (Widespread Madness [Toward the Overthrow of the Yoke of Fashion]), published in 1914, delivered an unequivocal message: fashion and its auxiliary agents, particularly the department store, were immoral, their followers depraved.[45]

Employing an essentialist notion of femininity that equated women with irrationality and the libido and bolstered by patriarchal confidence and nationalistic appeals, *Poval'noe bezumie* distilled complaints about fashion's sway over women and the evils posed by the appearance of consumer capitalism in Russia. In Elets's view, the department store was a foreign, urban, capitalist institution that promoted idleness, rampant individualism, social turmoil, and unbridled consumption, primarily among women. Whether Elets had read Zola's novel of a Parisian department store, *Au bonheur des dames* (1883), or Theodore Dreiser's novel of a young American woman's obsession with fashion and finery, *Sister Carrie* (1900), his use of the language of passion and desire mirrored the devices these male authors used to depict women's supposedly inherent vulnerability to fashion and its potential to lead them into wayward liaisons and dubious career choices. As has been well established in the literature on consumer culture, critics in Europe, Russia, and the United States linked modern retail establishments to illicit female desires to produce a potent discourse that portrayed the department store as a feminine domain where women turned upside down the societal expectations of female subordination. Like his contemporaries, Elets portrayed the department store as a feminine domain, where women inverted society's rules.[46]

In Elets's scenario, female shoppers resembled throngs of frenzied, self-absorbed, weak-willed voluptuaries seduced by the panoply of finery, and their excursions to department stores were tantamount to a revolt against domesticity and male authority. Lured by the temptations of free and easy access to fashion and frivolity, women purportedly escaped their domestic confines and, liberated by the wide, open spaces of the sales floor, thwarted the authority of their fathers and husbands and bent male proprietors, managers, and shop assistants to their will with capricious demands. Amid so much luxury, women forgot their domestic responsibilities, entering into liaisons with shop clerks and idling men and picking up vices and bad habits. Making his case against the baneful influence of the department store, Elets claimed that, in their passion for making purchases, women sometimes forgot their children in the stores, only noticing their absence upon arriving home. He scorned the perpetual shopper, the woman who refused to stay home, slipping away every day from her wifely and motherly duties in order to wander from counter to counter tormenting store clerks with petty demands and requests to see piece after piece, only to pronounce each one more awful. Elets also derided women who created "scandals" in the stores, abusing store personnel and managers for perceived defects in the merchandise and demanding special treatment or privileges. He reserved his harshest criticism for women who recklessly spent a husband's or father's earnings on clothes or who reneged on their debts.[47]

In Elets's view, women by nature could not resist the allures of the department store. "Just as it is in a bird's nature to sing," Elets chirped, "so it is in a woman's nature to waste money."[48] According to this line of thinking, women were physically and mentally incapable of resisting the assault on their senses that department stores devised to sell them merchandise. They were especially vulnerable during sales, which to Elets were simply "bait" that most women swallowed. In one scene, Elets pictured the chaos that broke out when women ventured out to shop a sale: "On the first day of a sale, at one, even two hours before the opening of the store, a long line of ladies forms at the doors. . . . As soon as the doors open, the ladies squeeze themselves through, jostling each other so that they can make their way to the sale items more quickly. This hypnotic effect of low prices compels them to buy all kinds of rubbish, which they later don't know what to do with. . . . Sometimes at these sales ladies, worn out [from shopping], faint and a doctor almost has to be called to render aid."[49] Fears about female aggressiveness and women's loss of control over their bodies disturbed Elets just as much as the waste of money on frippery. In the above passage, the female shoppers' unladylike, competitive rush and physical (hence, masculine) jockeying for position alternated with their all-too-feminine susceptibility to spells and physical exhaustion. Women seemed to Elets to be at the mercy of merchants' sales tactics and their own bodies, both of which rendered them senseless and vulnerable to dangerous impulses and subconscious desires.

The writer G. Vasilich also believed that the tactics employed by the magazin produced disturbing effects on shoppers, although he did not indicate that women were more prone to them than men. Remarking that the lavka of yesterday did not try to "dazzle" (oslepit') or intoxicate the customer with a brilliant array of merchandise, he complained that the stratagems of the magazin "cloud the shopper's mind."[50] Vasilich interpreted the "cold splendor" and merchandising tactics of the magazin as "intelligent, psychological calculation," a manipulative strategy designed to seduce customers by rendering them incapable of resisting the temptations presented to them. Like Elets, he worried about such tactics and longed for an imagined past when merchants honestly presented goods and did not try to manipulate customers. Also like Elets, Vasilich distrusted new merchandising and sales strategies as tricks that acted on a subconscious level to undermine reason. Although neither the lavka nor its customary practices had disappeared—indeed, they still held sway in most quarters of the city—Vasilich nonetheless perceived in the machinations of the magazin larger processes at work, including urbanization, industrialization, and the rationalizing and commodifying impulses inherent in mass retailing, which he found disorienting and deceptive.

In Elets's scenario, no male consumer freely entered the doors of a department store; they might appear in that feminized realm, but only as emasculated characters, victims of their wives' or daughters' unrestrained spending habits or harassed store clerks and managers, who obsequiously catered to feminine whims. To Elets, the department store was no place for real men. In one particularly misogynistic passage, he claimed that only men under the age of forty could stand to work in a department store, and, given that these young men constantly spent time with women and saw their "unattractive side," he predicted that they would eventually develop a "deep scorn for women."[51] This veiled comment implied that male shop assistants were, or would turn out to be, homosexual. Clearly, Elets believed that the department store could only appeal to simple-minded women and men who had not or would never attain full heterosexual manhood. Neither of these types of person could be relied upon to use good judgment. The lone male character who retained his masculinity in Elets's vision was the manipulative merchant, who preyed upon women's weaknesses, forcing them into submission for his own financial gain.

The power of the department store to promote materialism and individualism to a mass audience also distressed Elets. Unlike some French social critics, who thought that department stores imposed anonymity and uniformity, Elets worried that department stores promoted individualism, which undermined established social norms and roles. He also seemed to fear that, in appealing to a wide audience, modern retailers contributed to a blurring of class distinctions. The problem was not only that women of the middling and lower classes might be able to purchase sale-priced goods that they would otherwise not have been able to afford and might thus assume social pretensions. It was also that department stores encouraged a possessive instinct that unified individuals of all classes in a common language of pleasure and acquisition. Elets charged that a woman of the working classes was just as vulnerable to the allure of lace, silk, and feather-trimmed hats as her middle- and upper-class sisters. "A poor, fashionable woman," he wrote, "will eat stale bread and drink water in order to save money to buy a hat or a ribbon."[52] Such striving for fashionable clothing, he believed, led to egoism, jealousy, and a constant preoccupation with buying new things, impulses he viewed as dangerously self-absorbed and destructive both to the individual and society. Paradoxically, Elets, like Professor Sobolev, pictured an egalitarian world made possible by mass retailing and consumption, but whereas Elets perceived such a world as dangerous, Sobolev perceived it as salutary.

In order to end women's obsessive spending habits and thwart the power of the department store over Russia, Elets urged women to refuse to follow the whimsical dictates of fashion and to adopt instead a national costume modeled after the native tastes of the people, by which he meant traditional peasant culture. As an alternative to Russia's submission to foreign designers and taste makers and to the individualistic tendencies promoted by the department store, his solution reveals an aversion not just to Western trends but also to urban influences. Peasant-inspired clothing, which he lauded as more pleasant than urban fashions, would proudly display Russia's native, communal spirit. His proposal aimed to turn women back toward traditional cultural referents, while simultaneously asserting that Russia did not need European tutelage or want its interference. Elets ended his tract by calling on "serious women" to unite and revolt against fashion instead of being slaves to its dictates and to appear on the streets and theaters in national dress.[53]

This view of modern retailing and mass consumption as corrupting, destructive forces was not confined to men like Elets, who considered themselves above the commercial fray. Even one among the Moscow merchantry found much to disapprove of in the nascent world of modern retailing, although his criticisms were not as ferocious. The merchant Ivan Slonov began his career in the 1860s as an errand boy in the three-story lavka of the merchant Zaborov in the Upper Trading Rows. He later became an apprentice to a shoemaker and bought out his master's business upon his death. Slonov then ventured into the trade of gold, silver, and bronze, and after fifteen years in that business received the title of Honored Citizen. He does not appear to have been either an intransigent social reactionary of Elets's ilk or an old-school merchant who stubbornly resisted change or the methods of modern retailing.[54] He was not one of Moscow's merchant elite either. He seems to have been moderately successful and to have largely devoted himself to his retail business and to serving in various posts in his parish. His profile suggests that he was representative of those Russian merchants who, as they became more successful, accepted some of the changes and ventured to experiment with new ways of doing business. In his memoirs, Slonov revealed that his objection to modern retailing was the "shift in psychology" it had occasioned, along with the abandonment of traditions and established roles and relationships that had accompanied the new psychology. Specifically, he drew a direct connection between the debut of the magazin and other new retail structures and the dissolution of patriarchal authority. The merchant remarked that in the years between the mid-nineteenth century and the present (1914), life seemed to have headed in a "new and unprincipled direction, especially noticeable in the commercial world."[55] Despite the less than favorable portrayal he drew of his previous master, Zaborov, Slonov lamented that masters no longer took an interest in the everyday life of their charges or concerned themselves with safeguarding the honor and respectability of their shop assistants. Freed from their masters' supervision and the obligatory performance of annual rites such as the Shrovetide ritual of reconciliation, which, according to Slonov, gave to each the opportunity to begin anew, shop assistants and apprentices lived the fast life, seeking diversion in public inns and cabarets and sometimes joining gangs of hooligans.[56] Perhaps a result of his experience as a shopkeeper in the refurbished Upper Rows retail arcade, Slonov targeted shopping arcades as places that invited shoppers to indulge not only in purchases but also in idleness and vice. He claimed as evidence his observation that merchants in the fashionable district complained about ladies' men and stylish women loitering about, using stores as rendezvous spots: "Today's fashion plates and lovers gallivant [*galantoniat'*] about Kuznetskii Most and Petrovka, where daily from two to six o'clock one can see many idling playboys for whom *passazhi,* luxurious *magaziny,* and chic confectioneries serve as places for flirtation."[57] Despite his disapproval, Slonov may not have been far off the mark. The upper galleries of the Passazh arcade in St. Petersburg were notorious as a cruising ground for men seeking same-sex liaisons.[58]

Despite their different social backgrounds and perspectives, Slonov and Elets shared some concerns. Although Elets unreservedly hated and feared the world of modern commerce and Slonov made a living within it, both worried that modern forms of retailing offered freedom from traditional patriarchal relationships and structures that governed women and young men. Both of their books were published in the same year, 1914, a year in which modern retailing had reached its culmination in Russia, with palpable impact. These men clearly felt threatened by the disappearance of a world they had known, and its values, too, and they undoubtedly also believed that their place in upholding those values was in jeopardy. Slonov and Elets bemoaned the breakdown of norms and customs that kept women and young men under the watchful eye of an authoritative male figure. Both explicitly blamed that development on modern retail venues, which they believed provided physical spaces cut off from the supervision of husbands, fathers, and masters and encouraged autonomous behaviors. The ascendance of a culture in which women and young men were free to some extent to set their own standards of behavior could only be viewed by them with apprehension. Elets identified women simultaneously as perpetrators and victims of the new urban commercial order. He believed that women, with the help of the department store, were transforming themselves from dutiful, house-bound wives and mothers to unruly, independent decision makers, adulteresses, and spendthrifts who thwarted male authority in the home and in public places. To a certain extent, Elets was correct. Women, especially young women, were entering the public realm to attend universities and take up jobs as teachers, nurses, and office workers. They were also more visible in public life, some of them devoting themselves to the cause of female emancipation. For his part, Slonov worried primarily about young men who pursued wayward, reckless lives instead of devoting themselves to learning a trade under the guardianship of an older, experienced male benefactor who initiated them, through established rituals, into a shared code of behaviors. Even though, by many accounts, an apprentice's training in the retail trade meant exposure to drinking, long hours in harsh conditions, and corporal punishment, Slonov believed that this male-dominated world of hierarchy stood for order and stability.[59] Advertising an aesthetic of consumption, leisure, and pleasure, the department store and arcade threatened to upset this customary world.

Elets and Slonov overlooked or misinterpreted the entertainment value that many women and men found in retail stores and downtown commercial districts. Prior to 1914, an increase in the kinds and number of urban entertainments resulted from the increase in leisure time and the growth of industries to fill that time. Along with visits to the circus, amusement parks, and movie theaters, shopping became recreation.[60] Yet neither Elets nor Slonov viewed window shopping, strolling the arcades, or browsing in a department store as pastimes. To them, those activities were the equivalent of loafing or abandoning one's responsibilities. To Elets, shopping for personal enjoyment was even immoral. Slonov viewed retailing from the perspective of a merchant, not a consumer. In his mind, buying and selling was a business, not a leisure-time activity. According to several accounts, however, the merchants of the Trading Rows, Slonov included, carried on a lively social life amid their lavkas.[61] Their interaction was part of a larger homosocial merchant culture that did not include female customers and that opened itself to young men only upon acceptance of a lengthy and difficult period of apprenticeship. Even if the business routine did include a certain amount of pleasure, that pleasure derived from inclusion in a male culture centered on the trade, not from indulgence in consumer goods and mass entertainment.

New retail venues gave individuals more freedom, offering them the space to improvise and to publicly engage in new behaviors or behaviors that previously either went unnoticed or were carried on elsewhere. Elets, Slonov, and others who interpreted the department stores and arcades as spaces that afforded opportunities to idle or flirt were correct. These new urban centers did offer young people places to gather and meet friends, as well as strangers, and to amuse themselves. However, these activities that had such a disgraceful meaning in the eyes of critics held other meaning for the men and women who engaged in them. Elets's and Slonov's protests indicate the anxieties that such men, whose social status and influence depended on established institutions, may have felt as an urban culture devoted to consumption and entertainment challenged familiar mores and customs. To be sure, a shift in gender and generational roles was taking place. Those shifts elicited anxieties on the part of some members of society, who worried, or at least wondered, about the impact of modern retailers, advertisers, and other purveyors of the urban mass market, which so visibly promoted a materialistic, individualistic lifestyle. Stories that could have been lifted from Elets's book had appeared in the mass-circulation press for years. Odessans, for example, read sensational stories in the boulevard press about young women who sued their fathers in the headstrong pursuit for a new dress or about wives who ruined their husbands with their passion for fashion.[62] Such stories raised questions about the limits of patriarchal power in an urbanizing, increasingly commercialized world and raised the specter of women empowered by access to new institutions, the department store, and the courts.

Together, the commentaries of Elets, Slonov, and Vasilich indicate that the rise of modern retailing prompted concerns not only about new economic systems of exchange but also about gender roles, morals and values, sources of authority, the nature of urban life, and standards of public comportment. These men believed that modern mass retailers were usurping the authority formerly wielded by husbands, fathers, and merchant-patriarchs and that, under retailers' powerful influence, women and young men were escaping traditional roles and forming new identities, as well as attachments to pleasure, leisure, and luxury goods.

Educated Russians did not reach a consensus on the value of modern methods of retailing and a culture of mass consumption. Advocates evoked an image of the department store as a democratic, progressive establishment that promised equality, just and civil relations, and general prosperity, embodied by a new "man of commerce," to rational consumer-citizens of both sexes. Critics and other observers, by contrast, viewed the rise of new kinds of retailers suspiciously. They often coupled their criticisms with critiques of women's and young men's increased visibility in urban spaces and expanding opportunities, conjuring images of depraved, domineering female shoppers and meek and emasculated or dissolute shop assistants and urban idlers. Some observers even expressed disenchantment with the changes that modern retailing had wrought. Despite their opposing interpretations, admirers and detractors both believed that the future of Russia was at stake in the rise of modern retailing, and they connected its significance to new conceptions of masculinity and femininity.

Activist-journalists and educated professionals circulated their interpretations with the intent to persuade the reading public that the retail sector either should or should not figure as a primary site of social organization and source of cultural values. As important as these analyses and impassioned treatises were to intellectual discourse and debate about Russia's future, they did not necessarily resonate with consumers or comport with their perceptions, everyday experiences, and understandings of shopping and consumption.

5

Consuming the City
The Culture of the Retail Marketplace

As much as the merchant elite's promotional strategies and campaign to recreate the retail trade orchestrated urban mass culture, consumers' daily actions and interactions in stores, shops, and markets contributed to the definition of an urban lifestyle, constructing what it meant to be a consumer, to belong to a certain social class and gender, and to live in a modern city. Buying and selling were ordinary aspects of daily life for most people, and consumers construed their experiences in the retail marketplace variously as part of a routine, a leisure-time activity, and a personal aesthetic experience. Their experiences were based on daily practice and differed qualitatively from those who had a vested economic or political interest in the retail sector or who debated the role and merits of modern retailing through an ideological perspective. The narratives consumers wrote about their shopping experiences convey the emotions and private motives at play and the personal attachments they formed in the course of browsing or transacting a sale. Looking at the retail sphere from their perspective emphasizes the point that, in entering stores and shops to exchange money for goods, consumers also created social relationships and a cultural framework, shaped self-identities, and constructed narratives of the city and their place in it.[1]

The ways in which mass-manufactured consumer goods transformed the lives of urban and rural populations are well known. In the decades between the 1860s and 1914, the growing middle classes based in the cities increasingly

sought opportunities to spend the money and leisure hours they were accumulating, and they found an array of stores, theaters, movie houses, restaurants
and cafés, museums, parks, and publications to satisfy their demands. The urban
working classes, although with less discretionary income at their disposal, also
partook of the city's offerings through purchases of consumer goods and visits
to markets, fairs, and pleasure gardens; men also regularly went to taverns to
drink with friends, neighbors, and coworkers. Even rural dwellers, especially
those who spent at least part of the year earning wages in manufacturing jobs in
nearby cities or who had a family member who did so, began to invest in basic
mass-manufactured goods and to learn the latest popular songs and dances. In
the years following emancipation, ready-to-wear clothing, fashion accessories
such as rings, earrings, shoes, handbags, and hats and manufactured furniture
and household items became status symbols in many centrally located villages
and transformed the appearance of peasants and their homes.[2] Watches and
clocks were highly desirable items among all classes of consumers, who viewed
the timepieces as marks of prestige. One journalist, remarking on the popularity that watches had attained among Russian consumers in the early twentieth
century, submitted that those who could not afford an expensive watch preferred to buy an inexpensive one, even if it ran slow or fast by a few minutes,
rather than have no watch at all.[3] Bicycles and roller skates also became popular. Costing approximately one hundred rubles, bicycles were affordable for the
middle classes, including skilled and clerical workers, and used ones could be
purchased for less.[4] Top-of-the-line roller skates made from nickel were available to upper-middle-class families, while those of the middle and working
classes could afford cheaper ones, which sported wheels made of compressed
cardboard.[5] Besides these newly mass-manufactured products, small luxuries
such as tea, coffee, candy, soap, and cigarettes were advertised regularly in the
back pages of daily newspapers and were popular items among consumers of
all classes.

The ways in which consumers procured these goods also transformed their
lives. The arrival of magazins, arcades, and department stores and the institution
of new kinds of retail practices in city centers meant that consumers who visited
them had to learn and perform new, standardized behaviors. Some consumers
enthusiastically embraced the new protocols and, in executing them, began to
think of themselves as consumers in a wider world of urban mass consumption
and entertainment. Others rejected contemporary retail procedures as personally alienating and continued to identify with older customs. In exploring the
various roles that consumers played in retail transactions and the frameworks
and identities they formed in the process, scholars are finding shopping narratives particularly helpful. Shopping narratives, as found in memoirs, consist of

an account of an experience in a store, shop, market, or other retail venue written by an individual as a consumer not intent on advancing a political or economic agenda or hoping to institute reform. Fictional stories published in the boulevard press and the observations of chroniclers of city life are also relevant, since they attempted to reflect the experiences of urban consumers rather than to guide or reform them. In these kinds of sources, analyzed separately from the works of Elets, Sobolev, and members of the trade press, the perceptions and experiences of consumers, instead of intellectuals or activist journalists, are highlighted. Although consumers might well have been influenced by the opinions, ideological perspectives, and agendas of these men and their campaigns for or against modern retailing, consumers nevertheless constructed for themselves the world of the retail marketplace, embedding it with their own meanings. More importantly, they created those impressions based on their own personal criteria and agendas, albeit situated within the context of current discourses. The picture that writers of shopping narratives presented of the retail marketplace, its customs, and their role in it was, of course, constructed in part to present the self or the city in a particular light. The presentation of the self as a consumer, however, is an entirely different process than the advancement of a political or ideological position.

Personal narratives do not necessarily ring more true than other kinds of writings on the merchantry, the retail trade, or consumers, but they reveal different intellectual and imaginative processes at work. Many reflect on childhood experiences and, as Richard Coe has stated, are more like "the poet's truth rather than the historian's accuracy" in their nostalgic expression of emotions and adult disillusionment with the present.[6] Even in narratives that were not written to recall childhood, nostalgia for a lost past frequently appears. Indeed, shopping narratives, since they are usually found within memoirs, are necessarily impressionistic, yet their emotional intensity gives texture to their interpretations of the retail marketplace and to their place within it and within the city. We know, of course, that memory may delete or at least mute unpleasant aspects of the past or, alternatively, cast it in a golden light. The propensity of writers to idealize the memory of trips to beloved stores and cafés or to romanticize cheerful shop assistants or haggling merchants may be attributed partially to the nostalgia of Russians who wrote during later, more tumultuous years. Their yearning for what was perceived as a happier, less complicated time is an integral and fascinating aspect of shopping narratives, which merits a study in itself, but it does not negate their value.

The shopping narratives examined here were penned by a diverse group of individuals, ranging from members of the upper-middle and middling classes to the working and artisanal classes, although men wrote the majority of them.

The prevalence of male voices presents an interesting interpretive challenge. As discussed earlier, much of the literature on consumer culture has identified shopping as a primary site of middle-class femininity and the woman, as the archetypal consumer. Men have been conceptualized as shoppers or consumers much less frequently. In Europe, most discourses on masculine consumption represented the male consumer as the dandy or rational collector or, alternatively, the dispassionate, black-suited, middle-class man who rejected an aristocratic, frivolous, effeminate pattern of consumption.[7] This latter image suggests willful resistance to the wiles of the marketplace.[8] Part of the lack of images and discourses of male consumers and consumption may be due to the kinds of sources scholars have relied upon to conceptualize the relationship between gender and consumption. The works consulted have been primarily those of social commentators and critics who deployed essentialist ideas about men and women as a rhetorical device to critique modern, urban life. The use of memoirs brings to light other models of masculine consumption that, while still firmly attached to gendered norms and values, were in fact more commonplace and widespread than the collector or the dandy.[9] The narratives demonstrate that the construction of gender in relationship to consumption was more situational and fluid.

The key conclusion drawn from the following interpretation of shopping narratives is that stores, shops, and markets played a central role in the lives of men and women who lived in Russian cities at the turn of the century. Besides serving as places for the acquisition of goods, they functioned as familiar anchors in a large city, served as sites of social interaction that initiated residents into the ways of urban life and mass culture, and defined private life and self-identities. The city was diverse and offered a variety of sites and experiences, both so-called modern and customary ones; neither one nor the other served as the essence of urban life. The seemingly insignificant details of shopping districts—the smell wafting from a baker's window, the fantastic sight of a tea shop fashioned after a Chinese pagoda, the startling array of goods artfully arranged in department store windows, the sounds of street peddlers hawking their wares, the fear and excitement of being jostled in a crowd of market shoppers or drawn into a haggling match with a shopkeeper—constituted for many urban residents the essence of living in a city and being a participant in a larger world of mass consumption and entertainment.

Romance and Routine in the Retail Marketplace

In conjuring up their pasts, many memoirists began with a description of the city landscape, invariably portraying favorite stores and markets and idealizing the look, smell, people, and products inside. For such writers, shopping districts were constitutive of their milieu. Il'ia Ehrenburg recreated Moscow by describing, among other sights, Smolensk Market, Okhotnyi Riad, and the foreign-owned stores on Kuznetskii Most.[10] Isaak Babel' recalled a childhood romance with certain shops in his native Odessa: "If you talk to me about a lavka, I recall the signboard, the washed-out golden letters scratched in the left corner, the female cashier with the piled-up hairdo, and I recall the air, which stirs in this lavka and doesn't live in any other. And from the lavka, the people, the air, theater posters—this is how I conceive of my native city."[11] The physical characteristics of a small, insignificant shop signified to Babel' the familiar or, even more importantly, as he put it, the "essence of things" (*sushchnost' veshchei*). The lavka formed an integral part of the city, one as important to Babel' as Odessa's monumental opera house or the sea air that residents breathed. Indeed, the author described every shop as offering a nearly transcendent experience, generating its own unique "air" that people took in as they entered.

Writers also frequently remembered a favorite store or shop as a local landmark, which they depended on to orient themselves in the city. Ekaterina Andreeva-Bal'mont (1867–1950), the daughter of A. V. Andreev, who owned a successful food store in Moscow, detailed her family's annual journey from their home in Moscow to their dacha, recalling that she registered various businesses along the route as signposts to pace the trip. She noted, for instance, that they drove "past the Siu confectionery building, from whose windows always wafts a divine aroma of chocolate." Then there was Filippov's, the bakery where, "over the entrance[,] there hung a great golden loaf of bread, which always swayed in the wind, and the marvelous smell of warm bread poured from the always-open doors."[12] For this woman, part of the excitement of the trip seemed to be the anticipation of taking in the sights and smells of her favorite places as she and her family drove away from the city. Mikhail Segal, an Odessan who later became a worker at the Odessa Film Studio and earned the title of Honored Cultural Worker, remembered the Staryi Bazaar (Old Market) as a point of orientation for the city's residents, who would check their watches against the old clock tower in the market, since they knew that it kept precise time. Segal also remembered a circle of retail businesses that he passed on his daily circuit. Among his favorites, the Hotel Spartak's chocolate store ranked highly. This store, he recalled, showed off amazingly beautiful cakes and sweets in the shop window, and it had once displayed a cake made in the shape of the Kremlin. Along with Hotel Spartak, Segal rattled off the names of other memorable retail shops and their specialties: A. K. Dubinin store, which sold canned goods, crabs, and other groceries; Chichkin dairy stores located throughout the city, all identical, all faced with white tiles, and, he claimed, with the best dairy products in town; and Vysotskii's tea and coffee store, a place where, he remembered, the aroma of a blend of teas greeted shoppers.[13]

Besides making up the physical landscape of the city, certain shops and stores became part of the routine or at least the imagined routine of everyday life in the city. Il'ia Shneider recalled the regular round of stops on his family's shopping itinerary in Moscow:

> You bought flour, groats, and oil at Egorov on Okhotnyi Riad. Meat, game, and greens at Lapin. Fish and caviar at Barakov. . . . You bought snacks, fruits, and groceries on Tverskaia at Eliseev, Belov, and Generalov. You bought tea and sugar at Perlov and Popov Brothers stores. . . . They sold bread, bagels, wheatmeal bread, and biscuits at Filippov and Chuev bakers. Dairy products at Chichkin and Blandov.
>
> There were two department stores, both belonging to English firms—Muir & Mirrielees and Shanks. The sale of ready-to-wear clothing was firmly in the hands of the Austrian firm Mandl'. . . . You bought hats and gloves only at Lemers'e and Vandrag. . . . Linens at Al'shvang. . . . Books at Vol'f. Sheet music at Jurgenson. . . . You shopped for toiletries at Brocard and Ralle. . . . Candy from Einem, Siu, Tramble, Flei, and Inai.[14]

Interestingly, Shneider's list included a mix of both Russian businesses and firms owned by foreign subjects, and he distinguished between those that sold goods prix fixe and those whose shop girls addressed customers as "Monsieur" and "Madame," indicating his awareness of differing protocols. In his memory, both Russian- and foreign-owned businesses were known to Muscovites, no doubt middle-class Muscovites, and patronizing those businesses had become part of the urban routine. Although not all of the retail sites he mentioned connoted middle-class prosperity (Okhotnyi Riad, for example, was the local meat and fowl market), these places had earned a reputation among Muscovites as urban landmarks. Whether or not Shneider and his family went on a regular basis to all of the places on his list of obligatory stops is beside the point. To him, they were integral to the urban experience, a vital part of living in and knowing the city.

Similarly, the memoirs of Vera Kharuzina, written circa 1912, revealed her middle-class family's shopping circuit, which was made up of trips to Russian- and foreign-owned stores in downtown Moscow. Kharuzina recalled going with her mother to Generalov to buy sausage, Swiss cheese, fudge, and special treats and then stopping for candy at Al'bert or Siu confectioners, where the shop girls spoke French. The last mandatory stop was Filippov's, which Kharuzina remembered as the best baker in Moscow. There, she recalled, her mother bought fresh, delicious-smelling French bread, soft rolls, and loaves of bread flavored with rose oil and saffron.[15]

Judging from these narratives, living in the city had become intertwined with consumption. Certain retail businesses had distinguished themselves in the minds of urban dwellers as purveyors of desirable products and as landmark institutions, places to see and be seen. Consumers had also formed deep attachments to them. Filippov's, the bakery located on Tverskaia Street in Moscow, was one such landmark retail firm that inspired customer loyalty and fantasies of consumption among a broad array of Muscovites.[16] The bakery's Easter cakes, fried pies (*pirozhki*), white and black bread, and other baked goods became favorites in the city and beyond and merited a place in recollections of life in the city. The writer Ivan Shmelev remembered that baked goods from Filippov's and the confectioner Abrikosov & Sons were highly anticipated treats at the family's annual celebration of his father's name day. Shmelev recalled that one year the family ordered from Filippov's a pretzel so large that it took eight men to carry it from the bakery to the Shmelev residence.[17] The royal family and court, avid consumers in their own right, even numbered among Filippov's fans. The baker made daily deliveries of dark and white bread and sweet rolls to the palace in St. Petersburg. Such was Filippov's fame that when the firm's founder died, a local poet penned a quatrain in his honor, calling him "one of a kind" who was "famous and familiar to Muscovites" and jesting that even the flies stopped swarming to mourn.[18]

Other retail stores attracted the enthusiastic admiration of many consumers and earned the public's affection for their size, novelty, beauty, and vast array of goods on display. Nikolai Teleshov wrote that, when Muir & Mirrielees opened its new store in Theater Square, people were so astounded by the abundance and range of goods that they forsook the Upper Rows on Red Square.[19] Although Teleshov's claim may be an exaggeration, according to Anastasiia Tsvetaeva, a writer and sister of the poet Marina, the construction of Muir & Mirrielees's new store in 1908 did arouse excitement and anticipation among city residents. She recalled that in the years prior to the reopening, many residents became intrigued by the building of the monumental art moderne style edifice and took walks past the store to survey the progress or gathered at the site simply to pass the time.[20] Visits to such monumental venues became unforgettable events. Tsvetaeva recalled her uninhibited joy at stepping into the store for the first time, finding there a beguiling fantasy land: "So many floors! Glitter! Delirious abundance! The fantastic sweep of the stairs! The brilliance of crystal and china! Pictures! Stuffed teddy bears! Ornaments! Toys!"[21] Consumers like Tsvetaeva expressed amazement at the store's décor, range of choices, and fantastical displays. Muir & Mirrielees presented a façade of beauty and prosperity, the fantasy of consumption accessible to everyone who walked through the doors, and Tsvetaeva indulged the fantasy even years later. Besides magnificent displays of merchandise, Tsvetaeva recollected her astonishment upon encountering a feat of modern technology in the store. She described the store's elevator as a "bright, little room that glided airily up and down . . . disappearing into the space between the floors and coming back to the surface from the abyss, like magic."[22] Vera Broido, born in 1907 in St. Petersburg to Russian Jewish parents, likewise recalled childhood visits to the "famous patisserie" on Bolshoi Prospekt as trips to "wonderland," where there were tall engraved mirrors, gleaming chandeliers, and awe-inspiring displays of cakes and pastries.[23]

Narratives also described visits to older, less majestic, but no less colorful retail landmarks that gave consumers the sensation of being transported to another realm. Of all the retail venues in Moscow, the Upper Trading Rows on Red Square garnered the most tributes. After the reconstruction of the Rows in 1893, the building that had previously stood in its spot began to be referred to as the Old Rows, which acquired a legendary reputation among Muscovites old enough to remember it. Narratives describing this venue are valuable not only for the detail they give about the exchange culture of the Old Rows but also for what they relate about the sentiments Russians experienced as they saw the city's landscape transformed. Although Kharuzina did not pen an entirely positive assessment of the interior of the Old Rows (she found it rather dirty and decrepit), she did pay homage to its environs, remembering it as a bustling, buzzing place where vendors of *shiten* (a hot drink made with honey and spices) walked around with giant copper tea kettles and bunches of white wheatmeal bread slung from their waists and where pirozhki vendors carried giant wooden trays that hung from their shoulders by leather straps. She was also impressed by the clever, provocative ditties of the vendors, characterizing them as exemplary of coarse folk humor. But the scene just outside the front entrance to the Rows particularly struck her fancy. There, women wrapped in big shawls sold baskets decorated with gold and silver threads and pale blue glass beads. Kharuzina particularly enjoyed the candles that the women burned because they gave off a "spicy, heady fragrance, which in our home was just not tolerated."[24] Her visit to the Rows brought her a mix of wonder and pleasure, even a vicarious thrill at breaking free from some of the confines of her life at home. For this young woman, such a trip meant an escape from the ordinary, an opportunity to experience a free-wheeling, even exotic, urban setting.

Not all Russians reported delight and pleasure in their shopping narratives. A visit to a rickety, grubby, noisy, wooden-walled, glass-roofed arcade on Odessa's Malaya Arnautskaia Street made writer Valentin Kataev aware of the poverty and social injustice in the world and induced in him dread, as well as pity for the Jewish shopkeepers, tailors, shoemakers, and dressmakers who maintained businesses there.[25] Other writers revealed confusion and the awkwardness and anxiety associated with acquiring new kinds of knowledge and experiencing unfamiliar desires. Experiencing new sensations, both thrilling and frightening, however, was part of the allure of the city and the retail marketplace. Judith Walkowitz has written that London was "an oasis of personal freedom, a place of floating possibilities as well as dangers."[26] That appears to be how many Russians viewed the city and its retail offerings. Intellectuals and conservative journalists and social commentators warned of the dangers of kleptomania and reckless overspending, both believed to have been occasioned by feelings of anxiety brought on by women's supposedly frail nature and exposure to too many sensory temptations in department stores. Some consumers apparently were overcome by anxiety and confusion, especially when confronted with the spectacle they encountered in some retail venues, although not necessarily only modern retail stores. Vera Kharuzina described the "torture" that immediately seized her upon entering the side entrance to the Old Rows. There, she knew she would encounter candy stores displaying giant glass jars full of fat, spiral sticks of malt sugar, jellied nuts, big white mint pastilles, fruit drops of various flavors and colors, and sticks of khalva. She expressed the feeling that gripped her upon feasting her eyes as "something extremely alien to me," by which she may have meant greed, unbridled delight, or apprehension about choosing wisely from among so many enticing choices. Vera Broido related similar feelings of confusion and discomfort, reporting that it was "just torture" to have to choose from among the many tempting offerings at her favorite patisserie and that she usually ended up just plunging in and taking anything on the nearest tray.[27] The feelings that Kharuzina and Broido reported do not exactly suggest a neurosis or complete loss of control. They do, however, suggest the power of retail venues—both those that favored customary sales methods and those that opted for modern retailing techniques—to encourage new and potentially risky behaviors.

Narratives also reveal other kinds of anxieties. For example, despite the attraction stores and shops held for Babel', he confessed that on one occasion his fascination left him feeling confused and humiliated. He remembered that one time, while perusing the shop windows in downtown Odessa, he became transfixed by the pale pink corsets and garters in Madame Rozali's store, which caught the attention of a tall, mustachioed student who happened to be passing by. The student clapped Babel' on the shoulder and asked condescendingly, "Are you studying them? Keep up that spirit, my friend. I compliment you," then laughed and walked away.[28] Babel' reported feeling deeply embarrassed and claimed that he never again glanced into Madame Rozali's windows. Possibilities for sexual fantasy were part of the urban landscape. Gazing at the pink corsets—items intended to attract the attention of passersby—Babel' indulged his fantasies. The public nature of the display that prompted his musings and his own position on the street, however, left him feeling ashamed when his private desires were exposed.

Consumers who entered stores clearly faced various pressures and, moreover, had to be prepared to operate within a store's parameters. Urban mass culture required new codes of behavior, and authors of shopping narratives often recalled excursions into the retail marketplace as a kind of initiation into urban life. Familiarity with a city's stores, markets, and arcades, especially those that had acquired the status of urban legends, became, if not in fact then in memory, a way of laying claim to being an authentic urbanite and of learning the rules of public comportment. A certain protocol reigned in and around a retail venue, and the required protocol at Muir & Mirrielees, for instance, differed from that at the Okhotnyi Riad market. A trip to a department store, magazin, lavka, or open-air market gave one the opportunity to observe and imitate the appropriate behaviors; in effect, visiting the retail venue enabled a person to learn how to shop and live in the city. Learning the appropriate behaviors for different public settings was a prerequisite to participating in urban mass culture. Successfully performing the correct act at the right time in the right context conveyed the information that one had mastered the skills necessary for urban living and partaking of the city's offerings. Individuals could thus demonstrate that they knew their way around. Knowing one's way around did not simply mean being able to find the way to Kuznetskii Most, the Gostinyi Dvor, or Odessa's Passazh. Besting a trader in a haggling match at Sukharev Market could be just as important as conversing with a shop assistant at Muir & Mirrielees in a courteous, undemonstrative manner. Being familiar with the range of retail sites and knowing when to haggle and when to moderate one's actions were essential to being an urban dweller. The popular writer Vladimir Giliarovskii implicitly made this point in his chronicle of the city's streets, *Moskva i Moskvichi* (Moscow and Muscovites). Consisting of chapters devoted to depictions of local landmarks, Giliarovskii's book imparted the urban lore and legends of Moscow, thereby helping Russians to discover the most renowned and most notorious sights around the city: Theater and Lubianka squares, Sukharev and Okhotnyi Riad markets, the Khitrov quarter, various notable stores, bakeries, restaurants, taverns, and bath houses. His vivid descriptions of these places and of the characters who frequented them suggested that to be a true Muscovite meant having a firsthand knowledge of such sites and experience in successfully navigating them. His description of Sukharev Market's "aristocracy" of secondhand booksellers and antique dealers and the book collector who haggled so fiercely that even the booksellers dreaded his weekly appearance is rich in detail.[29] His description of Okhotnyi Riad market as a mix of "burlap bags alongside the sable furs of millionaires," as a place where cooks of the finest traktirs and restaurants, servants of nobles and merchants, merchant housewives, and lowly cooks "all jostled each other and argued over a kopek" conjured up the diversity of the retail sphere.[30] Such illuminating portraits suggest that those who had not seen such sights had missed out on the real Moscow. Similarly, for some Odessans, frequenting the two most prominent cafés, Robina and Fankoni, was considered tantamount to being an insider. For one local columnist, they were part of the city's attractions. As he put it, "To live in Odessa and not go to the Robina is like being in Rome and not going to see the Pope."[31]

Ekaterina Andreeva-Bal'mont expressed the excitement that came from immersing oneself in the urban throng and the satisfaction in knowing and performing the code of compulsory behaviors expected at Filippov's. Noting that there were always many people at the popular bakery, she recalled that "it was a lot of fun to push through [the crowd] to the front of the counter," where mounds of *baranki* (ring-shaped rolls) and towers of rusk reached almost to the ceiling. She described the routine that ensued once it was her turn:

> You thrust forward your 15-kopek piece to the *prikazchik* [shop assistant] and loudly declared: "A pound of gingerbread." Without fail, the prikazchik joked with you as he quickly-quickly raked up the gingerbread with a scoop from a giant drawer under the counter and poured it into a paper bag, deftly smoothed out. He never made a mistake: it weighed exactly a pound when he put it on the scale. He gave it to you and took your 15-kopek piece, throwing it into the cash drawer. . . . You had to immediately move away [from the counter] and surrender your place to the next customer.[32]

She also noted the poor people, who usually stood at the door with submissively outstretched hands, remarking that no one gave bread to them but instead put change in their hands.

Andreeva-Bal'mont's retelling of a seemingly ordinary trip to the bakery captured the aesthetic experience of urban mass culture and conveyed an awareness of herself as a consumer in a downtown retail store. The press of the crowd, the overwhelming array of baked goods and their fanciful presentation, her declaration of intent, the shop assistant's prattle, the sure sounds of his scoop and the ring of the coin as it hit the till, and the contingent of beggars distilled the sounds and sights of life in the city into one discrete mini-event. What is perhaps most remarkable in her account is that she revels not only in the sensory aspects of the transaction and the excitement of being part of the scene at a local landmark but also in executing standardized behaviors. She reconstructed the routine as a pleasant, reassuring performance, one that she expected would be repeated over and over again in just the same way every time she visited the bakery. In her memory, the routine at Filippov's was not tedious; it was fun and novel. Andreeva-Bal'mont expected to play the role of consumer, and she expected the man behind the counter to play the part of shop assistant; both knew the dialogue to recite and the gestures to make, and both expected a certain outcome. The novelty of the modern sales transaction was that it was simple and prescripted. To this woman, the predictable, almost ritualistic execution of routinized acts on the public stage of a downtown bakery seemed a splendid performance. Standardized routines, of course, regularly went awry. Shop assistants were not consistently cheerful or accurate. Customers were not always patient or enthusiastic about the offerings. Either could easily subvert the routine or the anticipated result. What is interesting, however, is that while Andreeva-Bal'mont's story may seem ordinary to those of us long accustomed to and made weary by the monotony of such retail routines, their execution seemed thrilling to her. Further, we should not discount the importance of learning to stand in line, requesting a specific quantity of an item, and then paying for it. This may seem a straightforward enough series of acts, but as the next section demonstrates, their performance departed significantly from the way in which retail transactions had customarily been conducted.

Haggling as Public Performance in the Marketplace

Despite the new protocols that urban residents were learning at the turn of the century, haggling remained the single most important skill that a Russian consumer had to master. In order to buy anything in the majority of stores, shops, and markets, a customer had to engage in a haggling or bargaining match with the proprietor or vendor to arrive at an agreed-upon price. Haggling had existed in Russia for centuries. The advent of stores that strived to cultivate a refined atmosphere by advertising fixed prices had not eradicated haggling, which persisted as a characteristic feature of the retail marketplace until after the Bolshevik revolution and civil war and probably even thereafter on the black market. Some may be tempted to explain the endurance of the custom by labeling Russia's economy a pre- or protocapitalist one that had not yet sufficiently developed the necessary structures and systems that would allow it to operate solely on a goods-for-money basis. However, such assessments are bound up in a modernization paradigm that privileges the path of western European economies. True, Russia had relatively few large-scale retail outfits operating on the principles of contemporary mass retailing, and, therefore, most sales were conducted in the customary way. A purely economic explanation, however, overlooks both the personal investment that merchants and consumers made in haggling and the relationships that it engendered. As seen in the trade press's unrelenting crusade to eradicate haggling, many Russian merchants and consumers were still deeply invested in the custom. Activist-journalists, however, expended little energy trying to understand the population's attachment to haggling in terms other than the rhetoric of economic rationalization. As a result, we know relatively little about the sociocultural meanings of haggling and its role in the commercial realm. Consumers' shopping narratives, however, frequently included accounts of haggling, revealing a description of the steps by which haggling matches proceeded and outlining the strategies and roles that merchants and consumers adopted to bargain. Fictional tales and feuilletons published in the popular daily newspapers, as well as chronicles of city life, corroborate what these narratives reveal. Understanding the process and the meanings of haggling from an over-the-counter perspective tells us of the value that some consumers placed on personal interaction in the retail marketplace and conveys the mixture of regret and relief that some Russians felt as customary practices began to be challenged by the appearance of modern mass retailers that forbade them.

Buying and selling were profoundly social and public transactions. Russia's retail sector had historically operated on a set of sociocultural norms and business practices that encouraged cooperation but that also sparked conflict. The sales transaction entailed contention, even disagreement, but merchants and consumers also recognized that both parties had an interest in ultimately coming to an agreement. If this were not the case, as one scholar, commenting on sales practices more widely, recently put it, "the bargaining and haggling would never commence."[33] One mid-nineteenth-century account of haggling vividly illustrates this point. G. T. Lowth, an Englishman who traveled to Moscow in the 1860s, got a kick out of visiting the Upper Rows and matching wits with the merchants. In his travelogue, he related the routine of haggling as it usually played out in the Rows. As he came to learn,

> you always met the price asked with a shake of the head—a mild objection; and this being the first blow, others followed; until perhaps after ten minutes of conflict, you holding steadily to your offer, and the man abating and hesitating till he had reached the point below which he would not descend, another man, perhaps the shop owner, would come forward from somewhere, put on a hard look, and carry the article away. . . . The matter was finished, the struggle over. . . . Then you would put on a hard look too, and walk away. But as you went with one ear listening backwards, you would hear a call, "You shall have it"; and then all the assumed sullenness was fled, and smiles were in its place, and you secured your prize.[34]

Lowth's description, although perhaps colored by the smug attitudes of the foreigner, captures the mix of aggressive flattery and self-interest inherent in haggling. Yet it also illustrates that distrust of merchants was tempered by the anticipation of bargaining and the expectation that a deal would be concluded.

Haggling, however, was not simply a method whereby two parties negotiated a price. Some Russians considered it a "custom" (*obychai*) that had been
around since time immemorial. The Moscow chronicler Vasilich, for instance,
regarded haggling as one aspect of the "manners" (*nravy*) of the old merchant
community.[35] Another Muscovite, recalling the practices of the retail trade in
the mid-nineteenth century, stated emphatically that Moscow shopkeepers
tried to deceive their customers, whom they mostly perceived as victims, and
he advised consumers to keep a sharp eye out when dealing with shop owners.[36]
Even as these writers suggested that haggling was an old-school practice, they
also recognized its persistence. The author of an illustrated reference book on
Russia remarked, "If a thing costs one ruble, a merchant asks ten for it."[37] Writing in 1912, Vasilich himself remarked that commercial relations in Russia were
premised on the adage that "if you don't cheat [the customer], you won't sell
[anything]."[38] These writers implied that haggling was dishonest or that it put
the consumer at a disadvantage, but other comments suggest a more complex
interpretation.

As described by contemporaries in the decades prior to 1914, haggling was
a ritualistic, physical, and combative custom that required a great deal of determination and patience, as well as skill in sizing up one's opponent and judging his or her limits. As described by native Muscovite Nikolai Davydov, both
merchant and consumer invested their bodies, intellects, and persuasive skills
in attempting to gain the upper hand during the transaction: "The shopper and
clerk grappled with each other, one praised, the other denigrated the item. Both
shouted, swore, and lied. The shopper offered half the asking price; if the clerk
did not make concessions willingly, the customer would pretend that he was
leaving. This was repeated several times."[39]

Vasilich similarly portrayed haggling as a confrontational exchange between a seller, who, without fail, began by asking a very high price, and a customer, who named an impossibly low price. Once the haggling commenced, he
wrote, the two tried to persuade each other, "flying off the handle, and finally
agreeing upon a price, at times reveling in the very process of the struggle over
five kopeks."[40] In contemporary retellings, such commercial confrontations
were very often highly theatrical. They took place with the buyer and seller
standing in close proximity to each other, either over a counter or simply standing facing one another, sometimes outdoors. It is easy to imagine the expansive
gestures, facial contortions, and shouts, perhaps even the merchant or the customer laying hands on the other in an effort to clinch the deal.

Mindful of the conflict of interests at play but driven by the necessity of
making a purchase, Russian consumers had been socialized to try to dominate

the sales transaction or at least to hold their own against a practiced merchant and get a tolerably good deal. This awareness required consumers to develop an effective bargaining strategy, since success or failure depended in part on being an "informed" or "uninformed" consumer.[41] Being an informed, skillful consumer required accumulating sufficient experience in order to learn which merchants could be relied upon to yield to a fairly equitable agreement and which could not. Given Russian merchants' reputation for being crafty and deceitful, such knowledge was considered invaluable. Being skilled also involved having a general sense of the value of goods. Otherwise, one could not initiate price negotiations or know when one reached the point at which it was time to agree that the best possible deal had been reached. Noting the penchant of merchants at Moscow's Sukharev Market to ask an "impossibly high price" and then to make "endless reductions," Vasilich claimed that experienced shoppers knew how to compel the seller to reduce the original asking price by 300 to 400 percent.[42]

There were rules of comportment, and, to succeed at haggling, both merchants and consumers had to master them, which meant affecting winning personas and devising a persuasive patter. Bargaining personas and routines were no doubt individualized and depended on the temperament of the individual and on experimentation with certain guises, phrases, and tactics, but there were also bargaining "types." Haggling tales frequently depicted a merchant in the role of the put-upon, reluctant compromiser or chatty glad-hander, while a customer usually appeared as the knowledgeable, no-nonsense bargainer, carping critic, or flattered but wary shopper. For example, just prior to Christmas one year, *Moskovskii listok* ran a "one-act play" called "The Christmas Tree Bazaar," which depicted various buying and selling personas. When one "young gentleman" pronounced a seller's price too expensive, the seller responded, "Oh, my dear Sir, if you only knew what it cost me to get this tree, you would not bargain with me." The young man countered with, "How hard can it be? You just go to the forest and cut one!" His challenge prompted the seller's long-winded explanation of his exploits cutting down the tree on the private property of a count, which entailed hiring his friends as guards and buying them drinks afterward. Another tree vendor in this vignette engaged an "old rich businessman" with familiarity and humor. His approach inspired the buyer to tell the vendor about his "modern" young daughter-in-law and his wish to spoil her with a nice tree. This confidence elicited a sales pitch laced with respectful smooth talk, one surely tailored to the buyer's age and status, but also to his motive for buying a tree. When the buyer asked the price, the seller replied, "One old lady offered me three rubles for it, but I refused to sell it to her for that price. I did not like her personality—she was too ignorant! But for you, dear Sir, I would sell it for this price."[43] The buyer knew better than to immediately agree and so counter-offered one and a half rubles.

Whatever role buyer and seller assumed, each knew there was a script to follow and routinized behaviors to perform. A haggling match usually began with a prelude to price negotiations, wherein the seller flattered or insulted the buyer or, alternatively, the buyer flattered or insulted the seller. Either the seller or the buyer could begin the actual negotiations by naming a price, to which the other feigned alarm and surprise. Next, the other issued a counteroffer, to which the first usually expressed shock and offense. A back-and-forth give-and-take ensued, and both merchant and consumer had to gauge the point at which patience had been exhausted and agreement was in both of their best interests.

In recreating the purchase of a coat at Odessa's flea market, the reputed haunt of cunning vendors and con artists on the make, Leonid Utesov, the famous actor/singer/comedian of the 1930s, revealed the retail routine that prevailed when he was a young man—the language, gestures, tones of voice, reactions, and timing—necessary to bring a deal to a satisfactory conclusion. Once he had selected a coat, Utesov opened with a bid:

> —Thirty.
> —Thirty what?!
> —Rubles.
> —I thought you meant kopeks.
> —Well, twenty.
> —Twenty what?!
> —Rubles.
> —That's unreasonable. I wish you all the best.
> —Fifteen more.
> —Fifteen what?!
> —Kopeks?
> —May I see the sun at night, I cannot go less than fifteen.
> —Five more.
> —Give me your hand and we'll shake on five.
> —Five what?
> —Rubles.
> —Knock off two and it's a deal.
> —I will knock off one.
> —One and a half.
> —You're killing me. Rothschild himself would love to have this coat, yet we can't agree on a price.[44]

The two eventually came to an agreement. Utesov obviously had a knack for comedic timing and banter, and while we cannot take his dialogue literally, it is clear that he and the merchant both knew the customary stances and stratagems necessary to conduct business. In adopting his haggling persona, Utesov comes across as a confident adventurer and a man not only out to purchase a coat but also to have a little fun and to acquire material for a good story. Utesov's representation of himself resembles the flaneur—the male spectator who roams the urban landscape and, due to his middle-class status, establishes, as Judith Walkowitz puts it, a "right to the city."[45] Just as the flaneur felt self-assured as he traversed the city, so the haggler exhibited not only a sense of belonging and poise that issued from his social position but also confidence in his knowledge and skill. Further, just as the flaneur was always "scanning the gritty street scene for good copy and anecdote," so the haggler seemed to be engaged in a bargaining match not only to strike a good deal but also to be able to tell a good story later.[46] Yet, unlike the flaneur or the dandy (the two most commonly recognized masculine consumer roles for prosperous and privileged men), the haggler represents a masculine consumer role that involved sober, rational calculation, as well as emotion and theatrics. Further, the haggler was a role that most men, as well as women, found themselves in on a regular basis, although certainly there were differences between the social realities of haggling and its representations in memoirs and other literature. Finally, the haggler represented a consumer who was fully engaged in the transaction and social relations of the marketplace and not simply a voyeur or extraordinary consumer.

A more elaborate, if exaggerated, routine of haggling can be found in a feuilleton published in one of Odessa's popular newspapers. Unlike Utesov, the character depicted in this tale was an uninformed consumer, naïve in the ways of transacting business, who, as a result, is manipulated into making an unfavorable deal. Still, the story follows a similar script and points up the importance of social interaction. As the tale opens, a young man enters a shop and approaches the owner, who immediately attempts to size up his opponent with conversation and slightly barbed social pleasantries:

> —Well?
> —I need a tailcoat.
> —What quality?
> —Cheap.
> —Um. . . . Are you going to a ball?
> —A wedding.
> —How many people are invited?
> —About thirty.
> —How much vodka, wine, and beer did you buy?
> —Sixty rubles worth.
> —What is your occupation?
> —I sell meat at the market.

—Do you like to drink? (asked in a friendly manner)

—I do consume [alcohol]. (trying to be official and maintain his dignity)[47]

After gauging the young man's acumen, the merchant talks him into renting a tailcoat made of tarpaulinlike cloth, completely unsuitable for such a garment. As the conversation continues, the haggling begins when the young man ventures,

—How much?

—Three rubles.

—For one tailcoat?

—Such are the times.

—A wedding doesn't cost that much.

—And a funeral? . . . Take it or leave it! You don't have to. I'm not holding you here.

—I'll take it.[48]

The hapless customer does not bargain effectively and, as a result, loses the upper hand to the merchant, whose acerbic queries catch him off guard. To conclude the transaction, the merchant asks the young man for a deposit, but he has none. As a guarantee, the merchant demands the young man's passport and his signature on a release detailing an absurd list of requirements, including that the young man swears to roll up the sleeves of the tailcoat before eating and drinking, not to commit suicide while wearing the coat, not to spill beer on it, and not to go near a fire. The release also absolved the merchant from any responsibility should the young man contract typhus, smallpox, cholera, or any other infectious diseases while wearing the coat.

The veiled pleasantries, conflict, and final, in this case dubious, agreement reported in this tale, as well as in other narratives, support the idea that buying and selling were based on social relationships, even if they were not always pleasant or civil. The retail trade, as it had evolved in Russia, required a verbal exchange between seller and buyer, as well as attempts to assess the buyer's needs and ability and willingness to pay. This particular tale, designed to entertain working- and middle-class urban readers, and, therefore, exaggerated for comic effect, must at least have been authentic enough in its tone to resonate with readers, many of whom had at some time likely fallen prey to the machinations of a clever merchant.

Despite the pervasiveness of haggling, it did not always bring the desired result. With its bellicose, physical style, haggling sometimes fostered contention between merchant and customer. The Row proprietor Ivan Slonov confirmed that conflict, anger, and even conspiracy against the consumer sometimes held sway on the sales floor. In his description of a deal gone awry, he recalled how one of his customers became angry when he overheard Slonov's fellow prika-zchik tell Slonov to "stick it to him [the customer]!"[49] Slonov reported that the man became angry and began to shout at him, threatening to call the police, although in the end he merely left the shop without buying a thing and called everyone in the shop fools.

For the most part, though, consumers did not seem to regard haggling as a necessarily disagreeable or undesirable activity. After all, the goal was agreement, and that entailed acquiescence in the performance. Further, there was more than economic gain at stake. Some narratives suggest that victory in a haggling match brought other kinds of personal rewards. Merchants and consumers alike boasted of haggling as a skill that set them apart, many relishing the chance to try to outwit the other. Consider the judgment made by the writer Vasilich on the ethics of haggling: "In the end it was not considered disgraceful for the seller to palm off rotten merchandise or to shortchange the customer by half when weighing the goods. The unfortunate customer felt disconcerted in such instances, but in the depths of his soul admired the adroitness and cunning of the seller."[50] Emerging the victor was a matter of personal pride. There was, of course, no glory in losing, but, curiously, there does not seem to have been much of a sense of having been wronged either. Winning the "game" entailed honing one's skills and outmaneuvering the opponent, in a sense, fair and square. The unfortunate loser, whether merchant or customer, might feel disappointment but could still admire the other's aptitude and flair and secretly respect his besting him.

Unlike the men who wrote for the trade press, those who wrote shopping narratives regarded haggling as a valuable skill, even as a part of a sophisticated urban identity—all indications that the custom held more than practical significance and had become part of the way they constructed their identity. Utesov, for example, referred to his ability to haggle as an "art" (iskusstvo), a word that connotes the perfecting of an individual talent rather than a common ability. The merchant-industrialist Nikolai Aleksandrovich Varentsov (1862–1947) remembered his grandfather's gift of eloquence and skill at bargaining as central features of his personality. The grandfather loved to make purchases for the household, and because of his ability to carry on a conversation, he frequently succeeded in obtaining reductions by haggling, a skill of which he was very proud. Varentsov maintained that his grandfather was so good at "smooth-talking" that once his son-in-law, Ivan, challenged him to try to get a discount at a fashionable store on Kuznetskii Most that sold objets d'art on a firm prix fixe policy. Ivan had visited the store and tried to wangle a discount on a desired object, and he warned his father-in-law that, "despite all of [his] know-how," he would not succeed in obtaining a price reduction. Much to Ivan's dismay, however, Varentsov returned from his venture proudly relating how he had talked the owner into knocking something off the price of the item that Ivan had coveted.[51]

The writer Valentin Kataev recalled with similar fondness and pride his annual visit to Ptashnikov's store in Odessa to purchase his school uniform and supplies: "Ah, what bliss it was—to shop for my school cap. First, you tried it on for a long time. Then haggled over the price. Then picked out a coat of arms."[52] Kataev regarded haggling as a memorable part of the autumn ritual of returning to school, perhaps even an activity that, along with his cadet status, conferred manhood on him as he himself negotiated the price with the shop assistant.

The tendency of these men to memorialize themselves as accomplished bargainers tells us that the custom of haggling was coded as an appropriately masculine consuming behavior, at least in certain circumstances. With its tactics of intimidation and verbal punches delivered in the form of offers and counteroffers, haggling can be understood as a metaphoric boxing match or duel. The men who wrote of their skill at haggling took pride in showing off their physical and intellectual prowess and delighted in the ego-boosting pleasure of the tussle over a few kopeks. All of them spoke of their commercial conquests as feats of accomplishment that conferred a semblance of daring and a confidence in their ability to dominate business transactions. In contrast to the activist-journalists who considered haggling an old-fashioned, lower-class or peasant practice, the chronicler Giliarovskii suggested that haggling contributed to a sense of class identity when he observed that middle-class Moscow natives felt at ease with haggling and sought opportunities to assert their skill. In "departing for the Rows," he remarked, he left "almost with the same sort of feeling that possesses a hunter departing for a snipe bog."[53] Masculine privilege and urban adventure and the confidence in an easy conquest that came from being a man of a certain class in the city also suggest themselves in Giliarovskii's comment. Along with tales and narratives of haggling, this observation shows that men with some disposable income considered haggling a diversion, an amusement that brought the thrill of a struggle, a contest of bodies and minds, and the satisfaction and esteem derived from making the best deal and prevailing over a less-skilled male opponent, often of a lower class.

Judging from the narratives, however, women, or at least women of the middle and upper classes, neither delighted in the close, interpersonal contact that went with haggling nor regarded it as central to their social and gender identities. In fact, although evidence is limited, the opposite seems true. Women and even men who wrote about women in the marketplace did not represent the relationship between women and haggling in the same ways. As a matter of fact, it appears that during this period, middle-class femininity became associated with the rejection of customary behaviors such as haggling. In going about their everyday procurement routines, women, or their female cooks and servants, had to haggle in order to buy things. Such was the nature of buying and selling in Russia, and being of the "delicate sex" did not exclude one from the necessity of fighting for a good price. As mentioned previously, Giliarovskii noted that the female cooks and merchant housewives who frequented Okhotnyi Riad haggled furiously with vendors.[54] Some women's magazines, for example, *Damskii mir* (Ladies' World), which catered to a middle-class female audience, even advised its readers to bargain with shop assistants since fixed pricing was not a universal policy and failing to haggle would result in their finding in a neighboring store something better at a lower price.[55] Such sources affirm that, in practice, women did engage in haggling.

Consumer narratives and tales of haggling, however, usually failed to represent women as bargainers, or at least successful bargainers. Vera Kharuzina touched upon the custom in her recollections of mid-nineteenth-century Moscow but did so in an oblique manner that indicated her disapproval. Instead of paying tribute to boisterous, quibbling merchants, she dwelled on a polite, quiet shop owner, whom she recalled as having conducted himself with dignity.[56] Vera Broido wrote about her trips to local markets with her mother, recalling the colorful atmosphere and recounting the "ritual" of buying melons, choosing between shapes and colors and sampling them, but she never mentioned haggling.[57] Utesov recreated in his memoirs an exchange between a female fish dealer in an Odessa market and a potential female customer:

—Little lady, buy some fish. Take a look at this mackerel. It's a nice piece of fish. Take it, beautiful.
—How much for your mackerel?
—Ten kopeks.
—That's expensive.
—You think it's expensive. Then, go change your clothes, throw yourself in the sea, and catch one yourself. Then you'll get it free.[58]

Accomplished in obsequious flattery and the stinging insult, Utesov's female vendor conforms to the customs of the trade. His depiction of the female shopper, by contrast, is curious. Utesov had described himself overcoming a coat seller but depicted a female shopper as disarmed by the fishmonger's challenge, unable to muster a quick retort. The abrupt ending and lack of a conclusive deal places the female shopper in the role of an unskilled bargainer. Likewise, in *Moskovskii listok*'s tale of the Christmas tree bazaar, a "poor-looking, elderly woman" fails to strike a deal with a seller. Her objections to his "sweet talk" and unwillingness to engage in the banter necessary to successfully negotiate a price end in his dismissal of her and her angry departure.[59]

Clearly, consumers' interpretations of shopping were gendered, situational, and coded with multiple meanings. The ways that men represented themselves as consumers differed from the ways that women did. Moreover, the representations they created to talk about their experiences as consumers did not always match reality. Women of the working and middling classes, those who did their own shopping at markets and lavkas, of course, had to haggle in order to obtain a good price, given their limited incomes. But middle- and upper-class women usually sent cooks or servants to the markets to do the shopping, at least for basic necessities such as food, and so they may not have joined the throngs of hagglers. Such women might, as the *Damskii mir* article implies, negotiate prices in certain kinds of stores. Alternatively, they may have patronized stores where haggling was disallowed. In any case, neither women of the working and middling classes nor women of the middle and upper classes represented themselves as hagglers or told stories about haggling as part of a strategy of representing themselves. Some women wrote about consumption, but they usually focused on material goods that held meaning or special memories for them rather than describing the process of or struggle associated with acquiring them.[60]

The conflicting images of male and female consumers found in these various tales and narratives of haggling indicate that the meaning of the custom was in flux and had become a symbol of changing definitions of social class and gender in the early twentieth century. The writers' works examined here presented haggling as a normative behavior for middle- and upper-class men and for women of the lower classes or servants. The realities of the retail marketplace, of course, demanded that women, as well as men, be skilled at haggling. Yet women were seldom portrayed as individuated bargainers. When they appeared in accounts of haggling, they were represented either as a gaggle of unruly shoppers or shown to fall mute when met with a challenge. The lack of literary representations of female hagglers can be partially explained by the changes taking place in the retail marketplace. At the same time that writers for the trade press were trying to reshape Russia's retail culture by eliminating haggling, some taste and opinion makers were promoting a new, middle-class code of behavior prescribing that men and women refrain from engaging in loud, boisterous, aggressive behaviors.[61] One etiquette book published in 1911, for example, introduced readers to the subject of good manners by informing them that knowing how to conduct oneself in public without reproach was essential for everyone.[62] The book meticulously described prescribed behaviors, and, generally speaking, such prescriptions reflected the goal of restrained propriety. The writer advised readers, for example, to dress tastefully and appropriately for each occasion and time of day, to eat soup slowly and quietly without smacking the lips, and to cut food without obvious forceful effort. The book counseled men, when in society, to smoke only if someone offered a cigar or cigarette.[63] With such advice set beside the discourses of haggling as found in the trade, fashion, and advice presses, it appears that the newly prescribed middle-class code of restraint and decorum was not firmly established. There still existed spaces within which middle-class men could perform behaviors that in some circles were being deemed improper among polite society.

Some evidence suggests that certain consumers, especially women of the middle and upper social classes, disliked haggling and other customary methods of sale. Kharuzina's narrative, although silent on the subject of haggling, contains an account of calling, another pervasive practice, and may help to partially explain the reasons for objections to customary practices more generally. She remembered that, in the Old Rows, shop assistants walked back and forth in front of their lavkas all day, pausing now and then to shout, "Ribbons, needles, pins!" When an approaching shopper ignored the call and walked past, a shop assistant then tried to catch the next passerby with the question, "Would you like [to buy] some lace?"[64] Kharuzina found this practice not only disagreeable but disconcerting as well. In her telling, the outwardly benign figure of the prikazchik more closely resembled a degraded, menacing presence whose pressing invitation shades into an indecent proposal: "This calling, this intrusive pestering to which all passersby in the Rows were subjected, embarrassed me more than anything. And to this day, I recall the common type of such a shop assistant's face: impudent underneath an appearance of refined courtesy . . . giving a gesture with his right hand and inclining his head to one side. There was something humiliating in this device of calling and when finally the new ways of commerce banished the older ways, I was for some reason sincerely happy."[65] According to Kharuzina, calling turned shopping into a tribulation that tried her patience and placed her in the uncomfortable position of feeling solicited. In her narrative, merchants and their assistants represented an intimidating masculinity set on sexual conquest, not the worthy opponents in a rough, familiar game, as depicted in men's accounts.

All passersby, both men and women, had to endure these sidewalk harangues. Recounting a characteristic piece of street theater, a former prikazchik recalled that he and his fellow store clerks stood in a row outside their shop, shouting to customers about the merits of their wares and trying to drag them inside to have a look. Passersby reacted to such tactics with scorn and a torrent of abuse; many of them, he recalled, treated them as if they were a mob of hooligans and called them dogs.[66] Giliarovskii also considered the practice harass-

ment and described how, when he would be walking past a shop, a merchant
or shop assistant would grab hold of him, imploring, "Please come shop at our
lavka." Whether you wanted to or not, he wrote, they pulled and dragged you
toward the shop, and suddenly, gathered all around you, were the shop assistants, each delivering his memorized spiel. As he wrote, "They forced you to
have a look and to try on everything: a fur coat, an overcoat, and a light coat,
even if you don't need anything at all."[67]

Giliarovskii may have disliked calling and the annoying tactics of sellers,
but as a man he did not feel compromised by them. He realized, however, that
women faced an especially difficult trial when confronted by such forceful
salesmanship. His description of an encounter between a group of shop assistants and an approaching, "respectable-looking" woman illustrates this point:

> "Madam! Shop at our lavka. An overcoat for your husband, coats for the
> children."
>
> The tone of the calls changes, however, as the lady proudly walks on by.
>
> "Madam, madam! Isn't there something here in my trousers that you
> want?!"—he yells, rushing after her, to the amusement of the other prika-
> zchiki.[68]

Women like Kharuzina may have felt embarrassed and even assaulted by such
unwanted attention and might have preferred to patronize stores in which
salespeople were not allowed to aggressively pursue customers or to make
insulting comments. For such consumers, the advent of fixed price policies
and courteous service may have brought some relief by creating an exchange
culture less threatening to them. Some scholars have suggested that the rise
of the magazin, arcade, and department store was connected to middle- and
upper-class women's need for a safe, respectable place in cities, away from the
marketplace and the streets, where unfamiliar men and "loose" women were
believed to roam.[69] As Kharuzina's and Giliarovskii's comments indicate, the
threats may have come, in part, from merchants and their customary practices.

To those who fondly memorialized haggling in their memoirs, however,
the practice represented a way of life that was vanishing in a rapidly changing
world. Even though Vasilich wrote in 1912, when haggling remained prevalent, he believed that the rise of the magazin and principles of modern retailing
had succeeded in instituting a strict regimen of aloof, calculating efficiency.
He particularly disliked the imposition of what he saw as methods of sale that
precluded a personal, verbal exchange between seller and buyer: "Lavka owners
enter into personal relationships with customers, haggling with them, shower-
ing praise on their goods, arguing, talking the shopper's head off. The magazin operates like a machine. The shop assistant is the gallant robot [*galantnye
avtomaty*] and transactions are concluded with heartless precision." Vasilich's

comments reveal a nostalgic longing for the past, for a time when, as he put it, the "tempo of life" was not "disciplined, shackled to the iron framework of the pace of the machine."[70] He perceived that the mechanization and commercialization of the magazin had markedly changed the manner and tenor of urban life. He obviously found these trends disorienting and threatening to previously familiar ways of living and thinking. The rise of the magazin conjured up for him isolation, anonymity, and even the dullness of modern urban life. He missed those merchants who verbally engaged their customers, even if they pestered them, and he lamented the appearance of large, impersonal stores staffed by trained automatons, who executed sterile sales transactions without granting him an active role in the process. To Vasilich, contemporary retail practices had created a world of uniformity. Fixed prices and courteous service amounted to detachment and a lifeless mode of interaction. Like the authors of haggling narratives, Vasilich celebrated customary practices as part of an exchange culture built on active participation and some degree of improvisation in the sales transaction. As he put it, with the advent of the magazin, all "good-natured sociability, lovable disorder, and freedom have gone out of life."[71] For this commentator, modern retailing threatened personal autonomy, subverted inventiveness and spontaneity, and engulfed one's identity in a standardized world of mass culture.

In contrast to Andreeva-Bal'mont, the woman who found the prescribed routine at Filippov's bakery delightful and enticing, Russians like Vasilich thought the courteously scripted transaction to be intolerable. Whether consumers performed long-established or new routines, they found meaning in the practices and protocols of the retail marketplace. Neither new practices and ways of conceiving of the self nor customs and traditional identities dominated, but instead persistence and change in cultural patterns defined the era. In going about their everyday procurement routines, consumers engaged in activities that, while seemingly ordinary, transformed buying and selling. Their public performances in stores and shops helped residents develop an identity associated with living in the city and being an urban dweller and also contributed to new middle-class conceptualizations of appropriately masculine and feminine behaviors. By learning to queue up to buy something or by perfecting a haggling strategy, urban residents defined the outlines of urban life and created a sense of self and one's place in society.

FIGURE 1. The Upper Trading Rows in 1886, just prior to that structure's demolition. *Source:* A. S. Razmadze, *Torgovye riady na Krasnoi ploshchadi v Moskve* (Kiev, 1893).

FIGURE 2. View of the Upper Trading Rows from above, 1886. *Source:* A. S. Razmadze, *Torgovye riady na Krasnoi ploshchadi v Moskve* (Kiev, 1893).

FIGURE 3. *(above)* View of the Upper Trading Rows from Il'inka Street, 1886. *Source:* A. S. Razmadze, *Torgovye riady na Krasnoi ploshchadi v Moskve* (Kiev, 1893).

FIGURE 4. *(opposite, top)* Interior view of Big Cloth Row in the Upper Trading Rows, 1880s. *Source:* A. S. Razmadze, *Torgovye riady na Krasnoi ploshchadi v Moskve* (Kiev, 1893).

FIGURE 5. *(opposite, bottom)* Little Secondhand Clothing Row, Upper Trading Rows, 1886. *Source:* from the collection of Mikhail Zolotarev.

FIGURE 6. Ceremony celebrating the laying of the cornerstone for the new Upper Trading Rows, May 21, 1890. *Source:* A. S. Razmadze, *Torgovye riady na Krasnoi ploshchadi v Moskve* (Kiev, 1893).

FIGURE 7. Construction on the new Rows structure. *Source:* A. S. Razmadze, *Torgovye riady na Krasnoi ploshchadi v Moskve* (Kiev, 1893).

FIGURE 8. Construction work on the interior of the Middle passage. *Source:* A. S. Razmadze, *Torgovye riady na Krasnoi ploshchadi v Moskve* (Kiev, 1893).

FIGURE 9. The Upper Trading Rows, circa early twentieth century. "Moscow: Souvenir de Moscou."

FIGURE 10. View of the newly constructed Upper Rows down Il'inka Street. *Source:* A. S. Razmadze, *Torgovye riady na Krasnoi ploshchadi v Moskve* (Kiev, 1893).

FIGURE 11. Interior view of the completed structure of the new Upper Trading Rows. *Source:* A. S. Razmadze, *Torgovye riady na Krasnoi ploshchadi v Moskve* (Kiev, 1893).

FIGURE 12. Interior view of one of the cross-passages. *Source:* A. S. Razmadze, *Torgovye riady na Krasnoi ploshchadi v Moskve* (Kiev, 1893).

FIGURE 13. Interior of the Sapozhnikov Brothers store. *Source:* A. S. Razmadze, *Torgovye riady na Krasnoi ploshchadi v Moskve* (Kiev, 1893).

FIGURE 14. Cover of A. S. Razmadze's *Torgovye riady na Krasnoi ploshchadi v Moskve* (Kiev, 1893), the publication of which coincided with the opening of the new Upper Trading Rows, 1893.

No. 45. Одесса - Гостинница „Пассажъ".
Odessa - Hotel du Passage.

Одесса. Внутренній видъ Пассажа.
Odessa. Vue intérieure du Passage.

FIGURE 15. *(above)* Passazh Hotel and retail arcade, Odessa. *Source:* from the collection of Mikhail Zolotarev.

FIGURE 16. *(left)* Interior view of Passazh retail arcade, Odessa. *Source:* from the collection of Mikhail Zolotarev.

FIGURE 17. *(opposite, top)* Interior of Perlov tea store on Miasnitskaia Street, Moscow. *Source:* from the collection of Mikhail Zolotarev.

FIGURE 18. *(opposite, bottom)* Muir & Mirrielees department store on Theater Square, Moscow. *Source:* from the collection of Mikhail Zolotarev.

FIGURE 19. *(above)* Interior view of Eliseev's store on Tverskaia Street, Moscow. *Source:* from the collection of Mikhail Zolotarev.

FIGURE 20. *(opposite, top)* Okhotnyi Riad (Hunters' Row) meat and fowl market, Moscow. *Source:* from the collection of Mikhail Zolotarev.

FIGURE 21. *(opposite, bottom)* Okhotnyi Riad market, Moscow. *Source:* from the collection of Mikhail Zolotarev.

Москва.
Moscou.

Охотный рядъ.
Okhotny riad.

Изд. А. А. Горожанкина. Москва. 1911 г.

169

FIGURE 22. *(left)*
"GUM—Everything for Everybody!" / "Grab onto this Life Preserver! High Quality, Inexpensive Goods, Direct From Manufacturers!" (text by V. Maiakovskii, design by A. Rodchenko, 1923).

FIGURE 23. *(left, below)*
"A Man Must Have a Watch. / Only a Mozer. / Mozer Watches Only at GUM" (text by V. Maiakovskii, design by A. Rodchenko, 1923).

FIGURE 24. *(opposite, top)*
"Trade the Dark for Light! Where Will You Find It? Buy It at GUM! Dazzlingly Bright and Cheap" (text by V. Maiakovskii, design by A. Rodchenko).

FIGURE 25. *(opposite, middle)*
Addvertisement for Mossel'prom's Dining Rooms No. 20 and 34 at the former Praga Restaurant and at 24 Arbat Street. The addvertisement states, "Everyone Needs to Eat Lunch and Dinner. But Where? Nowhere Else but Mossel'prom. Open until 2 A.M. With Orchestra and Variety Show" (text by V. Maiakovskii, design by A. Rodchenko, 1924).

FIGURE 26. *(opposite, bottom)*
Advertisement for Era Cigarettes with the caption, "Era Cigarettes Are All That Are Left to Us of the Old World. Nowhere Else but Mossel'prom!" (text by V. Maiakovskii, design by A. Rodchenko, 1924).

FIGURES 22–26: © Estate of Alexander Rodchenko/RAO, Moscow/VAGA, New York.

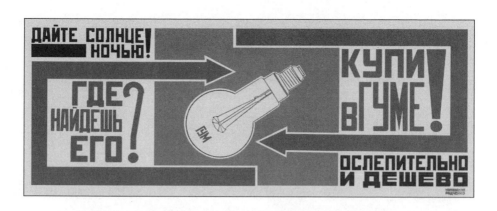

FIGURE 27. *(above)* Agitational candy wrappers, from a series for Red October's Our Industry caramels. Each wrapper features a piece of machinery with a short verse about its virtues and exhortations to adopt it for use. The verse on the tractor wrapper, for example, states, "It is time for the peasant character to accustom itself to the tractor. Do not turn the earth with a prehistoric plow" (text by V. Maiakovskii, design by A. Rodchenko, 1924). The red-and-white wrapper is for Freedom, a Mossel'prom candy, and it features the monument to the first Soviet constitution and a hammer and sickle (anonymous, not dated).

FIGURE 28. *(left)* Candy wrappers for Red October's Proletarian caramels featuring images of Mikhail Kalinin, chairman of the Central Executive Committee, and Georgii Chicherin, commissar of Foreign Affairs (design by A. Rodchenko, not dated).

FIGURES 27–28: © Estate of Alexander Rodchenko/RAO, Moscow/VAGA, New York.

6

War and Revolution
in the Marketplace,
1914–1921

Russia's entry into World War I, the two revolutions in 1917, and the civil war that followed interrupted the campaign of activist-journalists and debates about the nature and value of modern retailing, as well as consumers' daily shopping routines. The hardships of war and implementation of revolutionary imperatives led to state interventions into the retail economy and the politicization of the retail trade and consumption, along with new ways of buying and selling goods and interpreting consuming behaviors. During these years, the retail marketplace and its culture were transformed, although not in the ways that members of the trade press or liberal and conservative commentators had hoped.

The war and civil war shaped the environment within which the Bolsheviks took power in October 1917. Thus, in order to gain a full understanding of the retail trade and patterns of consumption in the early Soviet era, one must first have an understanding of this wartime era. It is often assumed that the new communist state set into motion the campaigns of expropriation and nationalization that transformed the retail economy. Scholars who have assessed the relationship of World War I to the 1917 revolutions, however, have shown that a remarkable degree of continuity existed between the economic policies of the wartime tsarist government and the policies of both the provisional and the early Soviet governments. Nicholas II and his ministers initiated policies that, over the next seven years, had enormous consequences for merchants, the retail trade, and consumers, as well as for the culture of the retail marketplace. Lars Lih has characterized the entire period from 1914 to 1921 as one united by a "food supply crisis that was both symptom and breakdown of national economic and social life."[1] More recent scholarship concurs with Lih's characterization. Peter Holquist argues that a "continuum of crisis" marked the period.[2] Peter Gatrell considers the Great War "a stepping stone on the path to revolution," while Eric Lohr, in his study of the campaign against enemy-subject participation in the economy, contends that the war was a "nationalizing event."[3] Julie Hessler identifies the economic crisis of 1916–1922 as the "crucible of Soviet socialism" and argues that policies during these years not only conditioned the Soviet state's policies but actually "helped to create the possibility of socialist revolution."[4]

Thus, despite the different ideological perspectives of the three regimes that governed Russia from 1914 to 1921, their economic policies showed a great deal of continuity. The tsarist government intervened in the wartime economy in ways that were unprecedented; it centralized production, confiscated and nationalized private enterprises, and enacted discriminatory policies. During the nine-month tenure of the Provisional Government, officials continued these policies and tactics, and when the Bolsheviks came to power, they significantly expanded them. Of course, the inspiration and political goals of the Bolsheviks differed from those of the other two governing bodies. Marxist ideology provided the Bolsheviks with a framework and a rationale for centralized planning and class-discriminatory policies, and they carried out these measures in order to enact class struggle and redistribute wealth. The tsarist regime, and to a large extent the Provisional Government, did not seek wholesale transformation of social and economic structures and institutions. Nevertheless, despite widely varying ideological positions, the three regimes heralded an increasingly interventionist state that orchestrated economic activity, transgressed Russia's fledgling ideals of private property, and, as Lohr puts it, "embraced a radical program to nationalize the economy by transferring ownership and jobs from enemy aliens to Russians, other 'reliable' individuals, and the state."[5]

Beginning in 1914 and continuing through the civil war, there were dramatic changes in the structure and culture of the retail marketplace and in the behavior of merchants and consumers. As the documentary evidence suggests, the reorganization of the retail sector and redistribution of consumer goods were central to waging war and making revolution; moreover, the imperatives profoundly altered the ways in which goods were bought and sold and the meanings attached to the retail trade and consumption. Merchants and consumers contributed to these changes by initiating their own campaigns, organizing alternative means of obtaining goods, and adapting and subverting state policies. The regimes in power expropriated goods from and launched liquidation campaigns against enemy subjects during World War I, and consumers had to craft their own responses to the hardships of war. The Bolsheviks undertook municipalization and nationalization campaigns and made early attempts to publicize those campaigns as part of a masculine, working-class mandate. During the civil war, Russians began to buy and sell goods in different ways, as the value of material goods changed and consumers struggled to adapt to a deteriorating economic environment. At issue are the role of the retail sector in the transition from tsarist, to liberal, to communist economy and society, and the impact of war and revolution on the retail trade and consumers. Some prewar ideas, institutions, and practices persisted into the post-1914 years, although many were uprooted or revised. Moreover, the roots of many characteristically Soviet marketplace behaviors can be traced to this era of war and civil war.

War and the Retail Marketplace

The outbreak of hostilities in August 1914 and the need to supply the army with grain and to transport large numbers of troops across long distances disrupted Russia's commercial networks. The war also cut Russia off from some of its most important trade partners, Germany among them. Waves of shortages and inflation ensued immediately, and the retail sphere began to contract. As Russian industry struggled to supply the military with weapons, ammunition, clothing, and equipment, the production of consumer goods was relegated to secondary status. Shortages of labor (due to conscription), raw materials, and fuel further hampered the industrial sector's ability to produce goods for consumers. In the first few months after the war began, approximately one out of four firms that manufactured cotton goods and textiles closed, and those that survived shortened their workweek. Even when popular manufactured goods such as textiles continued to be produced in large quantities, supplying the army took priority. Consumers increasingly found fewer places to buy goods, and those stores and shops that remained open had fewer goods to sell. Later, as supplies of food and especially flour, butter, and other basic items, such as shoes, dwindled in the winter of 1916–1917, all kinds of stores and shops throughout the country began to close. Consumers tried to adapt through various strategies, including panic buying, speculation, and queuing. Those who lived in rural areas sometimes found themselves at a comparative disadvantage; even prior to the war, there had been fewer stores in the countryside. With the shortages and closures, many rural dwellers had to travel to the city to try to purchase manufactured goods.[6]

Even in the earliest stage of the war, the state implemented extraordinary measures to supply the military, and these measures brought fundamental changes to the structure of the retail sector and trade, and to habits and norms of consumption. Although the tsarist government had a long history of regulating commerce and industry, the number, range, and scope of policies pursued during wartime established a pattern of broad and far-reaching intervention. In late 1916, when shortages and inflation reached crisis proportions, tsarist officials instituted fixed prices for cotton yarn and fabrics. That same year, they also instituted sugar rationing and a system for rationing fuel that ranked consumers according to their importance to the war effort and attached a certain quantity of fuel to each rank. These were precedent-setting steps. Even if the state's attempts to fix prices were largely unsuccessful and its rationing schemes did not match the Soviet regime's plan to institute social inequity, as Gatrell argues, such actions nonetheless "paved the way for a more systematic assessment of production and consumption."[7] In this uncertain economic atmosphere, however, peasants did relatively well. The war put more money in their pockets. In fact, peasant consumption increased approximately 10 percent in 1915. Urban workers, however, struggled to maintain their standard of living, as higher prices on food, fuel, and clothing consumed a higher percentage of their wages. Even those workers who had lived relatively comfortable lives prior to the war struggled against escalating rates of inflation, which, in 1914, pushed prices upward by about 27 percent and, in 1915, by a further 20 percent. In 1916, prices rose by 94 percent and, in the first half of the following year, another 125 percent.[8] As manufactured goods became less available and their prices rose faster than those of most agricultural products, many grain-producing peasant farmers chose not to market their grain. In response, the state introduced a quota system intended to correct for an imbalance between the price of agricultural and manufactured goods but that also imposed delivery targets. Mandated delivery did not solve the grain supply problem, but the establishment of quotas indicates an expansion of the state's purview of power and an attempt to coerce producers into selling their goods.

Another series of measures, devised to dispossess enemy subjects of their commercial and industrial enterprises, was more thorough and successful in accomplishing its goals. The measures that tsarist officials undertook amounted to a categorization of the population and, according to Lohr, a "sorting [of] them into friend from foe."[9] Within a few months, officials had implemented measures that exceeded in "severity and permanence" those taken by other warring countries.[10] Even one contemporary, Baron Boris Nolde, an official in the Foreign Ministry, believed that the war had become not just a military struggle but an "economic war" that attempted to "injure the economic interests of enemy nationals."[11] Popular pressure urged the dispossession campaign, initiated by government officials in 1914, to move forward. Shortly after war began, the Council of Ministers took under consideration the issue of enemy subjects' capital and investments in Russia, but that body came to the conclusion that trespassing upon their rights would be contrary to law and would also put an enormous strain on the Russian economy since foreign capital played a significant role in industry and commerce.[12] In August, the minister of internal affairs announced that only the firms of those who had entered enemy military service or displayed hostility toward Russia would be seized or sequestered. At that time, the ministry also ordered the deportation of enemy subjects of military service age, an order that resulted in the abandonment of hundreds of small businesses. Some Russians did not believe these measures went far enough and pressured the government to take further steps. Calls for a boycott of German and Austrian firms issued from the military, as well as from some members of the Moscow duma and Moscow Merchant Society, the Progressist Party, nationalist groups such as Petrograd's Society of 1914 and the Union of Russian People, and the editorial boards of several newspapers. Some Russian-owned firms and organizations also petitioned to assume stewardship of competing firms belonging to enemy subjects.[13] That fall, in response to calls to free Russians from German economic influence, government officials changed course and enacted a series of laws that infringed on and eventually revoked the economic rights of enemy subjects. In September, the Ministry of Internal Affairs ordered the confiscation of property belonging to anyone suspected of holding membership in a pan-German organization.[14] Another law prohibited enemy nationals from buying property in Russia or managing such property.[15]

In January 1915, the state enacted the first major, far-reaching law. One of its clauses mandated the liquidation of firms entirely owned by German and Austrian nationals, who were deemed "enemy subjects."[16] Several days of rioting and looting in Moscow heralded the approach of the highly publicized June 1 liquidation deadline. Armed with national flags and portraits of Nicholas II, a group of workers attacked the Emil Tsindel' and Shrader factories and the Einem and Tsindel' stores in the Upper Trading Rows. At the Rows, rioting spread and crowds began to attack and loot stores with any kind of foreign name and also even some Russian-owned stores. Despite these disturbances and a plea for calm from Moscow's supreme commander, the state's campaign proceeded. In all, more than one thousand businesses, primarily small- and medium-scale firms engaged in commerce, voluntarily closed, changed ownership, or were forcibly liquidated.[17]

In December 1915, an additional decree expanded the state's liquidation campaign to large-scale industrial enterprises, amounting in all to 460 corporations. One such targeted firm, Straus & Company, a German-owned wholesale-retail business, had operated in Odessa since 1842, and although anti-German sentiment inspired its liquidation, religious prejudice also accompanied the procedure. In documents relating to the case, officials identified the firm not only as a foreign firm but as a "foreign Jewish firm."[18] In April 1916, the tsar appointed an official from the Ministry of Agriculture to act as liquidator. The official, in turn, asked the Odessa Merchants' Board and the Craftsmen's Board to appoint two of its members to assist him. The trio took a detailed inventory of Straus & Company, measuring and appraising all fabrics in stock and detailing the contents of the firm's office and warehouse, including everything from furniture and clocks to postage stamps. Ironically, among the items duly noted by the assessors were a portrait of the tsar, an icon, and an icon lamp. These objects, along with the rest of the firm's property, were sold at auction that November.[19] Other prominent German-owned corporations, including Siemens and several firms that built railroads and provided electricity and electric trams to various cities in the Russian Empire, were also liquidated, their shares divided among the state treasury, Russian financiers, and municipalities. In this state of heightened tension, a few firms were erroneously identified as German-owned or the agents of Germans and thus subjected to extraordinary measures. These included Kunst & Al'bers, a large retail enterprise owned by Adolf Dattan and Alfred Kunst, two Germans who had become Russian subjects in the 1880s, and Singer Company, an American firm and one of the largest corporations in the empire.[20] As the liquidation campaign further shrank production and retail networks, consumers and local officials, suspicious of shopkeepers and frustrated by the state's inability to ensure supplies, began to organize alternative supply and distribution systems. Some urban working-class consumers organized consumer cooperatives, sparking the rapid growth of a movement, which had begun in the 1860s. By late 1917, Russia had about twenty thousand co-ops, which served approximately seven million to eight million members. Members paid fees, or dues, to own shares in the co-op, which used these funds to buy provisions and sell them to members, or sometimes to the public, on credit. The rising strength of the cooperative movement was reflected in its capture of total retail sales, which in 1915 amounted to 14 percent, a figure that rose to 28–35 percent in 1918–1919. Some municipalities and zemstvos took it upon themselves to organize distribution, either by delivering meat, sugar, salt, and other foodstuffs to co-ops or by selling them directly to consumers at wholesale prices. Consumers also found other ways to supply themselves, including buying goods on the black market.[21]

Shortages and inflation fueled rumors about war profiteering and "speculation" and led to scapegoating and criticism of industrialists, merchants, bankers, middlemen, and petty traders in the press and in popular entertainment. The term *speculation,* which in the Soviet era came to stand for a variety of market behaviors, became a rhetorical device that tsarist authorities invoked to explain high prices and the absence of goods from store shelves, as well as to justify grain requisitions.[22] Officials also deployed the word to blame middlemen for price increases, thereby shifting responsibility away from land-owning and peasant producers.[23] It is notoriously difficult, of course, to separate rumors and frustration with shortages from actual speculation, whatever that activity may entail, but it is clear that wartime hardships further entrenched the negative image of merchants and the view that retail trade was deceitful.

In such dire conditions, consumers' pre-existing wariness of merchants, which anxiety and desperation enhanced, turned into the conviction that merchants exploited ordinary people. As scarcity and long queues became daily realities and inflation escalated, the potentially adversarial aspects of the retail transaction took on new intensity. Stores and shops, especially in urban areas, often became sites of open conflict. Accepted protocols of exchange fell by the wayside. Militaristic tactics, in the form of subsistence riots, often led by lower-class women, became regular occurrences. Reports of wartime subsistence riots from various provinces, amassed by Barbara Alpern Engel, tell of crowds of rioters who protested high prices and shortages by destroying shops and market stalls, demanding inspections of storerooms, seizing goods and distributing them among themselves, and forcibly closing shops.[24] One rioting crowd directly accused merchants of treachery and exploitation with their shouts of "The traders themselves rob the buyers!"[25] Garrison soldiers and sailors, who saw their rations decline in mid-1916, also blamed merchants, whom they accused of withholding grain in order to speculate in it.[26] Of course, prosperous individuals, police, and local officials also found themselves the target of rioters, but merchants and traders may have been easier, more accessible targets.

Such direct, militant action indicates, according to Engel, "the degree to which ordinary acts of buying and selling had become infused with a potential for conflict."[27] In essence, the war politicized the retail trade and consumption to an unprecedented degree, escalating hostility between the state and merchants and between merchants and consumers. Shopping, while never simply a leisure pursuit, especially for lower-class consumers, became a fierce struggle to obtain access to goods at a fair price. Wartime riots demonstrated the degree to which many consumers were willing to engage in extralegal measures in order to preserve their right to consume.

Revolution and Class Struggle in the Retail Marketplace

The abdication of Nicholas II in February 1917 did not put an end to extraordinary measures or to consumers' agitation. Indeed, under the Provisional Government, the state's liquidation campaign increased apace. In the roughly eight months between the establishment of the Provisional Government and the Bolsheviks' October revolution, 59 of the 460 firms affected by the December 1915 law had been completely liquidated and 75 were in the midst of the process. Another 1,839 commercial firms and 59 large industrial firms had either changed owners or been liquidated, while dozens more had been sequestered and transferred to state or social institutions. The Bolsheviks did not abandon the laws against enemy subjects either. In their first few months in power, they continued the campaign, liquidating another 191 of the firms that the tsarist regime had targeted for liquidation.[28] Thereafter, they broadened the campaign by identifying new targets and then carried out a far more thorough and radical reorganization of the economy than the tsar's ministers or the Provisional Government had intended. Instead of defining enemies in terms of ethnicity or national origin, they identified adversaries in terms of class, although xenophobia and ethnic and religious prejudices did not entirely disappear.

The destruction of the capitalist commercial sector and the creation of a network of state and cooperative stores were obligatory steps in the Bolsheviks' project of revolutionizing the economy and society. Building such a network, however, was fraught with ideological and practical complexities. Karl Marx had commented on the alienation that he believed resulted from commodification. And visions of material abundance had animated many socialist dreams of the future. The socialist economy and society had been predicated on industrialization, however, and the distribution of consumer goods had received relatively little attention from Marxist theorists. Yet, since the ultimate aims of Soviet socialism were the redistribution of wealth via the reorganization of property and resources and the institution of a centrally directed economy, the retailing of consumer goods could not remain in private hands. Merchants, especially those who had owned the largest and most profitable firms prior to 1917, were considered members of the exploiting classes. On the other end of the socioeconomic scale, small-time shopkeepers and vendors were dismissively regarded as petit bourgeois. Despite the vast disparities in wealth between these two groups, the Bolsheviks intended to appropriate the retail properties of all of them to benefit the working classes, who would no longer support the lavish lifestyle of capitalist merchants or tolerate the thieving of small-time traders but would themselves enjoy a higher material standard of living with assistance from the state.

In order to achieve these long-range goals, state and local officials had to restructure the retail economy along class lines and recast buying and selling as productive socialist endeavors. The latter would prove to be a very difficult task because, over the previous decades, retailing and consumerism had become intertwined with values of acquisition, pleasure, and leisure and connected to the adventures of urban life, the social aspirations of a rising merchant elite, and

Orthodox religious practice. Most of these associations were no longer appropriate. Party theorists and state officials hoped to detach retailing and consumption from those meanings and identities they no longer found ideologically consistent or constructive, while retaining those that still held value for a socialist society. First, however, state and local officials had to take physical control of existing retail premises, equipment, and merchandise stocks and determine the business formats that would constitute the new socialist retail sector. They also had to regulate supplies, prices, and consumption and to recreate methods of buying and selling. Motivated, therefore, by ideological imperatives and the pressures of mounting political opposition, the new communist government issued a series of decrees within the first year that communicated its intention to take control of all small- and medium-sized private industrial and commercial enterprises and place them at the disposal of state and municipal authorities, in other words, to municipalize them. On October 28, just three days after the revolution, state officials gave municipal governing boards the authority to confiscate, requisition, and sequester all privately owned buildings, warehouses, equipment, machines, materials, and transportation vehicles and to set prices on all food products. Officials also decreed that all personnel employed at sequestered enterprises remain in their positions, and they gave municipalities the right to conscript students in higher educational institutions and upper-level students at secondary schools to work in provisioning organizations.[29] Soon thereafter, the state declared monopolies on various goods, including some food products, matches, and candles. At the same time, all wholesale warehouses became subject to strict merchandise inventory controls, with goods being released only on special order. In December 1917, the state nationalized banks and formed one public bank, the People's Bank of the Russian Republic. Foreign commerce was nationalized and placed under the jurisdiction of the Commissariat of Commerce and Industry in April 1918. Additional decrees established special commissions to police prices and general activities in the marketplace. In June 1918, the state issued a decree on nationalization that brought large factories and joint stock companies officially under its control. The nationalization process then began, starting with large wholesale businesses that dealt in important commodities such as tea, coffee, rice, and spices.[30]

The nationalization and municipalization campaigns focused on retail operations in Moscow, Petrograd, and other cities and towns, including those in the central provinces of Riazan', Simbirsk, and Tula.[31] Most retail enterprises, being relatively small in size and scope, were subject to municipalization. The Supreme Council of the Economy (VSNKh) drew up plans and guidelines for municipalization, deputizing city entities to carry out the process. In July 1918, a commission on municipalization attached to the Moscow soviet, chaired by a Comrade Grosberg, began with the largest commercial and retail firms in the city, including the department store Muir & Mirrielees, Pavel Sorokoumovskii & Sons furriers, and Chichkin dairy stores. The largest perfume and cosmetics enterprises in Moscow, among them Brocard, Ralle, Siu, and A. M. Ostroumov, as well as shoe manufacturer Skorokhod, the grocery store of I. I. Lapin, and other large enterprises with valuable inventories were also slated to be municipalized that year. Mid- and small-scale retailers would follow later. By 1919, even toy stores and shops that sold fishing equipment were being municipalized. As this process continued, the state also moved on other fronts, declaring a monopoly on textiles and ordering all inventories transferred to the state. On November 21, 1918, the Council of People's Commissars (Sovnarkom) formally declared the elimination of private trade and its replacement with cooperative and state retail stores, which would be supervised by local soviets. By that time, the state had expanded its monopoly over many other consumer goods, including paper, salt, tea, coffee, cocoa, galoshes, and most manufactured goods.[32]

Municipalization was supposed to follow the standardized process set out by VSNKh and to take place only after the local soviet or other body had received approval. VSNKh's guidelines stipulated that a warehouse or store must first be sealed and the keys requested from the proprietor. The owner was then obliged to make an inventory of merchandise in the presence of an authorized individual and have it verified by a representative of the municipalization commission. This representative would declare the merchandise confiscated and dismiss the owner without compensation, although exceptions were to be made for small-scale traders who would otherwise be left without any means for survival. Property, employees, and merchandise were to be transferred to the city soviet, although in many instances, much of the inventory was diverted to central entities of the state.[33]

In practice, the municipalization campaign, at least as carried out in Moscow, faced various difficulties and obstacles that complicated the process. Controlling the pace and ensuring that procedures conformed to guidelines proved difficult. Unauthorized seizures took place regularly, despite the repeated issuance of decrees forbidding expropriations without VSNKh's approval. The municipalization of retail firms had actually begun spontaneously as early as April or May 1918, when, in the absence of central instructions and motivated by the fight against speculation, city and regional soviet deputies began to seize commercial enterprises to prevent the concealment of food and provisions and their resale at inflated prices.[34] All kinds of practical and logistical problems also dogged the process. Many merchants and traders refused to cooperate. Some Moscow furriers reportedly failed to show up at their stores with the keys on the day designated to begin the municipalization process.[35] The vendors of Smolensk and Tolkuchok markets in Moscow were warned that if they did not show up with keys, their stalls and booths would be opened in their absence.[36] Retail employees also often failed to oblige authorities. *Izvestiia* reported, for example, that a "sector of politically unconscious retail employees" was sabotaging the inventory process. The Union of Commercial-Industrial Employees tried to send responsible workers to help, but few volunteers could be found.[37] The refusal of merchants and employees to assist in the municipalization process meant that inventories had to be conducted by representatives deputized by the Moscow soviet, without the assistance of specialists. More prosaic kinds of problems, including a lack of heating inside stores and extreme shortages of office supplies, also slowed the process.[38]

More troubling problems, including corruption and illicit activity, turned up in a report on the shortcomings of municipalization prepared in April 1919 for VSNKh. The report noted that, in March, several hundred workers from the Moscow division of the Extraordinary Commission for Combating Counter-Revolution and Sabotage (commonly known at this time as the Cheka) received orders to go to the Kitai Gorod area to open dozens of warehouses that were either unaccounted for and had not been inventoried or that had thus far been concealed from the municipal authorities. Besides remarking on the obvious— the discovery of so many undetected and/or underutilized warehouses of valuable stores of goods—the report also detailed illegal trade activities. Ushakov & Sokolov, a store that had already been inventoried but not yet municipalized, was still doing business freely, although, according to the owner, it was following the order of Central Textile (Tsentrotekstil') in doing so. The warehouse belonging to the cosmetics firm Ralle was reportedly operating as a kind of secret warehouse, where people could buy as much soap as they wanted. Problems having to do with the sealing of closed businesses were also noted. Many stores and warehouses, including several in the Upper Rows, had apparently been carelessly sealed; many other seals were found broken. Investigators also came upon one warehouse with its door still sealed but with a window beneath the staircase that allowed access. Other warehouses remained sealed, but no one could find the keys. Finally, the report faulted some members of liquidation committees for their unreliability, charging that a number of them had taken valuable goods from stores and warehouses they were assigned to appraise and even that they returned a few times a week to get more merchandise. No doubt they were selling these items on the black market.[39]

Despite all of its flaws, municipalization succeeded in altering the retail landscape, turning some former palaces of consumer capitalism into monuments to a workers' state and closing others down. In November 1918, the Moscow Consumers' Cooperative of the Moscow Union of Consumer Societies (MSPO) took over operation of Muir & Mirrielees. The privately owned department store with the distinctive foreign name became a collective venture with the stark, though superior, designation of Store No. 1.[40] The board of the Upper Trading Rows continued to negotiate and renew rental agreements with tenants until at least the fall of 1918, after which all of the stores were closed and the arcade was used to house government offices, including those of the People's Commissariat of Provisioning (Narkomprod).[41] Some retail stores, among them the former Shanks & Company, a well-known fine haberdashery on Kuznetskii Most that had been owned by British subjects, served as places for the distribution of rations. Others were appropriated to serve as cooperative stores.

In this early phase of revolutionary euphoria, the conquest and occupation of prominent, luxurious retail stores and venues were depicted enthusiastically in the press as events that subverted the old order and claimed the retail marketplace for the working classes. In an article on the decoration of Moscow's downtown streets for the first anniversary of the October revolution, which recalled reportage on decorations for the coronation of Nicholas II, a journalist for *Izvestiia* alluded to the physical and ideological makeover that the city's central retailers had received. At the First Moscow Bakery, the former Filippov's, an exhibition titled "One Year of the Dictatorship of the Proletariat" had been erected. As part of the display, a large red poster proclaimed, "The Bright New World of Labor Has Come to Replace the Old World."[42] The mounting of an exhibit that communicated a message of working-class conquest in the highly visible, centrally located retail space of a formerly successful and popular downtown baker served to show that the retail sector had been assigned a new role and purpose. Filippov's was no longer just a bakery owned by capitalist entrepreneurs and patronized by well-heeled Muscovites. It had become the province of the working classes, a locus of the revolution where workers could learn about their place in building a socialist society.

Images of working-class triumph on the revolution's first anniversary are not surprising. A December 1918 *Izvestiia* feature article on the municipalization of several prominent retail landmarks in Moscow, however, interpreted the appropriation of stores and shops as a working-class masculine prerogative. In this article, municipalization was construed as an element of the transformation of a trivial, profit-making, bourgeois, feminized retail sphere into a practical, equitable, masculine realm. The journalist opened with a description of some of the extraordinary scenes taking place on Moscow's streets, noting that workers, with the help of police, carried off faded signboards from sealed stores, while onlookers whooped their approval. The writer contrasted the dismantling of these fancy stores with the appearance of new, presumably more democratic businesses displaying simple, white, makeshift canvas signs with black letter-ing that spelled out a store's name: "Ready-to-Wear Store No. . . . of the Mos-cow Soviet of Workers and Soldiers' Deputies."[43] Turning to happenings at the Golofteev and Aleksandr arcades, the writer inverted the conventional image of women as shoppers and men as merchants and retail workers, to portray the exclusion of middle- and upper-class women from these elegant retail premises and the incursion of working-class men as integral parts of the revolution. As the writer remarked, before the revolution, ladies (damy) had passed time in the arcades, shopping and trying on clothing, but now the municipalization com-mission had taken over and set up its headquarters there, amid the scattered debris of middle-class female frivolousness. Setting the scene, he described how boxes that once held gloves, ribbons, and other expensive fashion goods now lay empty, littering the floors, while typists sat hammering away and reckon-ing accounts on tables piled high with papers. Female laborers rushed around laughing, carrying under their arms mustachioed, ruddy-faced mannequins. In concluding, the writer noted the disorientation of third- and fourth-ration category consumers, who, standing in queues in front of shops, found it difficult to reconcile themselves to the idea that the "new shopper [novyi pokupatel'] at Al'shvang's stylish store is the muzhich'e, that is, the working population of the proletarian capital."[44]

Reports of joyful attacks on leading retail businesses represented the over-throw of the old commercial regime and constituted symbolic and practical acts of revolution that were part of a larger, popular movement to destroy the symbols of the past. Following the February revolution, Russians had begun vandalizing and stripping monuments to privilege and wealth and putting in place their own. Such acts amounted to the destruction of the past and its recon-struction.[45] Just as statues of Nicholas II were monuments to the tsarist regime, so the Al'shvang Brothers store and the Golofteev and Aleksandr arcades sym-bolized the old socioeconomic order that had catered to the middle and upper classes, especially women. The occupation and devastation of the stores and arcades—the display boxes emptied of their luxurious contents and thrown carelessly on the floor, the giddy removal of mannequins, and the appearance of government employees with their messy stacks of paper, noisy typewriters, and abacuses—signaled the overthrow of the exclusive, leisure-oriented bourgeois commercial realm and the inauguration of a democratic, purposeful socialist sphere that favored workers and peasants. Moreover, these former retail palaces were being converted from places where shoppers, primarily women, indulged in idle pastimes to sites where the important business of rebuilding the economy consumed female workers.

The vision of a shopping experience that privileged working-class male consumers would become a stock image in the campaign to recreate the retail sector and reinterpret the meanings attached to consumption in the 1920s. Even though consumption had not been represented as a solely middle-class or feminine pursuit prior to the revolution, the scenario represented in *Izvestiia* constituted a departure from past rhetorical conventions. Symbolically, it conveyed the idea that Moscow's best retail venues were being cleared of middle- and upper-class women, and it asserted that the right to occupy them was being secured for male laborers. Women participated in the events of municipalization as auxiliary laborers and white-collar workers but not explicitly as consumer-beneficiaries of the revolution in the retail sphere. Certainly, such images did not reflect social realities. They speak more to the masculine political culture of the early Soviet era.[46] The author's claim that the working class dominated these prominent, fashionable spaces is especially provocative, since the Russian word *muzhich'e* unambiguously denotes a man, possibly a peasant, and a loutish, uncultured one at that. The term *muzhich'e* drew a sharp distinction between privileged, refined ladies of leisure, who formerly assumed the right to shop at Al'shvang Brothers, and disenfranchised, simple laboring men, who now claimed the right of consumption through acts of municipalization. As the piece implies, the retail sphere was no longer to be associated with images of feminine entitlement but with democratic masculinity, as represented by the male peasant. This representation might seem curious, given the prior discursive connections between femininity and consumption, yet that was precisely the point. The symbolism employed in this report, however, does not exactly conform to the revolution's standard iconography either. Most literary and visual propaganda depicted the male worker as the victor or the guarantor of the revolution, often with the male peasant as a helpmate.[47] In this feature story, the male peasant alone represents the triumphant working classes. Perhaps given prior associations between women and consumption, this journalist was not completely comfortable depicting the male worker, the hero of the revolution, as the archetype of consumption. Instead, he delegated the symbolic right to consume to the peasant, the figure in Soviet iconography that represented the less educated and politically conscious of the masculine heroes. In other words, as much as many state and party officials wanted the working classes to have access to and enjoy material goods, many remained a little suspicious of the implications of the democratization of consumption or had not yet worked out a consistent iconographical representation of it.

Surviving the Civil War

By the end of 1918, the state's nationalization and municipalization campaigns augured an economic, social, and cultural realignment that promised to either subsume or eradicate private enterprise. Although the start of the civil war had interrupted the plan to establish a state-run retail sector, the state's struggle against private enterprise continued. One of the most significant and symbolic acts in the civil war period was the closing of Sukharev Market, the city's most popular market, by order of a Sovnarkom directive, on December 13, 1920. Commenting on the rationale for and significance of the closure, V. I. Lenin declared that Sukharev formed the "basis of capitalism," which "lives in the souls and actions of every small-time proprietor."[48] The implication here was that Sukharev was both a physical manifestation of capitalist practices and a breeding ground for capitalist impulses. The Moscow soviet's presidium charged the Cheka with closing Sukharev, and the event was well publicized. According to merchants who had conducted business there, an exultant crowd responded to the tearing down of the stalls with a whoop.[49] The Okhotnyi Riad market was also officially closed in March 1920, and its stalls were removed from the premises.

The outbreak of civil war brought more disruptions to production and transportation and more business closures. Images of jubilant workers seizing opulent retail venues were replaced by images of broken-down, abandoned stores, haunted by desperation and want. British journalist Walter Duranty recalled Moscow's forlorn landscape: "Of all that I saw in Moscow, I think what struck me most was the fact that no shops were open. . . . Some of them were boarded up, but in most cases the boards had been torn away for fuel and you saw empty windows or no windows at all, just holes, like missing teeth."[50] A similarly dismal sight met the residents of Odessa, a city that in 1919 came under the control of White Army general Anton Denikin. The writer Konstantin Paustovskii surveyed the scene: "The wind blew piles of half-burnt papers and soiled Denikin currency into heaps alongside the drain pipes. The bills were worthless—they wouldn't buy even one olive. Stores were closed. Through the windows you could see packs of red rats searching in vain for food on the dusty counters. The busy market squares—Privoz, the flea market—looked like a cobblestone wilderness."[51] The desolation that Duranty and Paustovskii described reflected the straitened economic conditions under which the population lived throughout the civil war. As the number of retailers rapidly shrank, Moscow, St. Petersburg, and Odessa—the empire's commercial centers—were left with very few retail outlets. *Izvestiia* reported in January 1919 that out of a total of 3,409 retail stores in Moscow that had been sealed by the municipal soviet, only 133 had been reopened.[52] In March, only 215 nonfood stores were operating in Moscow, a mere 4 percent of the number prior to the revolution. And although 879 stores that sold food products were operating, not all of them were open to the general public. Some factories, housing committees, and soviets operated stores to supply their workers and members.[53] These numbers declined further as the civil war dragged on. By June 1920, the number of food stores in Moscow had decreased to 540. Shoe retailers went from twenty-three to eleven, haberdashers from eleven to eight, and toy and furniture dealers completely disappeared.[54] The decline reflected not only the breakdown of commercial distribution networks, the emigration of many wealthy, successful merchants, and the dispersal of small-scale traders but also the overall deterioration of the economy and a sharp decline in urban population that was occurring throughout the former Russian Empire. Large-scale industry virtually collapsed between 1918 and 1920, with production plummeting to less than 20 percent of its 1913 level. Agricultural output fell by approximately three-fourths. As a result, less than one-fifth of the total amount of consumer goods produced in 1912 was available in 1920.[55] Moreover, Moscow and St. Petersburg both lost nearly half of their inhabitants, and, on average, the population of Russia's twenty-three largest cities declined by 25 percent.[56]

The state instituted ration plans that simultaneously reflected the economic crisis and the Bolsheviks' commitment to class struggle. The new ration system, established in September 1918, was a class-based plan that allocated different amounts of food on the basis of an individual's social class and type of employment. The plan initially divided the public into four categories. Those employed in heavy physical labor received the largest rations, followed by workers engaged in light physical labor and those involved in nonphysical "mental" labor. The nonlaboring classes received the smallest rations. Later, workers employed in heavy and light manual labor were combined into one category, and, in 1919, an addendum to the program provided extra rations to privileged groups that performed useful labor. A 1920 Sovnarkom decree then put all individuals employed by Soviet institutions in Moscow and St. Petersburg into the first-tier, large-ration category.[57] The rationing system never functioned effectively or efficiently enough to satisfy the populace. Some workers felt resentment toward privileged groups of workers and toward workers paid at their places of employment in, for example, textiles, which were highly prized goods that could be resold. Rations, as well as ration cards, were also easily resold, thus undermining the system. Rations were not always completely fulfilled either, and even when they were filled, they rarely met an individual's nutritional requirements.[58] Of course, those with the means could shop at markets, where goods were abundant at very high prices, although, as with Sukharev, some of these eventually closed. Most consumers had to resort to other means to obtain goods.

During these years, trade primarily operated through episodic and illicit forms of exchange involving novel kinds of sellers who sold or bargained for their wares in temporary or unconventional sites. Although relatives, friends, or servants visiting the countryside sometimes brought back provisions for city dwellers, most trade was conducted through thousands of ambulatory traders or "bag men," many of whom had no prior experience. Bag men (or women) made trips to the countryside and brought back sacks of food to sell to friends, neighbors, and acquaintances or, furtively, to strangers on city streets and in former marketplaces. Individuals, including many from the dispossessed classes, also gathered along certain streets and in markets to sell off their personal possessions and thereby supplement their meager incomes and rations.[59] Despite the Cheka's frequent raids, arrests, and confiscation of goods, this kind of errant trade continued unabated. State authorities had not foreseen these developments, and although the Petrograd and Moscow soviets had in 1919 authorized men over fifty, women over forty, and the disabled (essentially those who were not subject to compulsory labor laws) to engage in trade, the state could not control the number and types of individuals who made a living or supplemented their income by selling or exchanging goods at their disposal. Central authorities could not always control the actions of local officials either. Alexis Babine, a resident of Saratov, reported that eight carloads of wheat flour intended for Moscow had been intercepted by local Bolsheviks and sold to residents. Incidents like these were surely not uncommon. These occasional vendors and improvised networks—the so-called black market—became the public's primary source for bread and other staple foods, as well as manufactured goods, many of which were either stolen from state stocks or provided by peasants or workers in cottage industries.[60]

Russians adapted and improvised, relearning not so much how to shop but how to obtain basic foodstuffs through unconventional means and from unlikely, sometimes dubious, kinds of sellers. The process of obtaining goods this way frequently involved traveling great distances, relying on information, tips, and favors, and breaking the law. Iurii Got'e, professor of history at Moscow University and one-time associate director of the Rumiantsev Museum, recorded in his diary that on one occasion he walked across town to obtain milk and then headed to another section of the city to buy eggs and rice. On another occasion, he went to four different areas of the city in order to purchase flour, cabbage, eggs, and meat, as well as a small stove to heat the family's apartment.[61] Got'e must have known exactly where to go to find such items before setting out on these long, time-consuming excursions. In the absence of permanent, established shops and vendors with stable, steady supplies, such information was essential to obtaining the goods one sought. Alexis Babine's diary makes precisely this point. As early as December 1917, Babine seems to have developed a network of merchants, traders, and individuals upon whom he relied for information and favors. He recorded in his diary that month that he stopped by a Jewish refugee family's shop, where he learned that white bread would be issued later in the day. As he wrote, "It was an unexpected piece of good luck," which resulted in the acquisition of ten pounds of white bread "by special favor," which meant that he was able to purchase the bread using ration tickets designated for other days.[62] Babine later reported his good luck at obtaining "by chance" the address of a peasant woman from whom he bought twenty pounds of millet and his good fortune of getting the address of a peasant woman who sold him ten pounds of onions.[63] Even armed with such precious information, Babine still had to walk approximately five miles to a village to purchase the millet and three to procure the onions, and then he had to carry the heavy bundles back home, risking robbery and, in the case of the millet, confiscation by Soviet officials. Not all of his excursions were so successful, though. In May 1919, after his bread ration had been reduced, Babine and a few friends organized a "bread hunt." Their scavenging expedition took them about four miles from Saratov to a village where they failed to find bread. From there, the party went to another village not far away, where they inquired at every house they passed, but they came away empty handed.[64] Diary entries from later that year and the next reveal that on several occasions, he had no bread whatsoever. As his academic-class ration was further reduced and famine threatened the Volga region, the amount of bread he received was often insufficient or the bread so full of chaff and other fillers that it made him sick.[65]

As consumers struggled to supply themselves with food and basic provisions, the meanings and functions of all kinds of material goods fluctuated, and patterns of consumption changed. More often than not, consumers found themselves improvising, transforming items previously used for one purpose into substitutes for a deficit good. Odd juxtapositions of objects or substitutions of one item for another, symbolizing the upside-down, fluid nature of the material world, often showed up in newspaper reports and literature, as well as in memoirs. In essence, in conditions of shortage, objects did not have stable meanings.[66] Tea and coffee, chronically in short supply, were replaced by or fortified with various surrogates. According to one report, in Moscow only state institutions received rations of "pure coffee." The population was to make do with a mixture that was only 25 percent coffee, the remaining ingredients consisting of grains such wheat, barley, and rye.[67] People often brewed tea from carrots and sweetened it with raisins, and they made cakes from potato peelings or black bread crusts. Several contemporaries declared that bread contained all kinds of things, many of them indigestible, including husk straws, dust, and even old soldiers' coats, or it might be filled with a bitter liquid.[68]

People also improvised clothing, furniture, and other nonfood items. Walter Duranty reported seeing a girl wearing a skirt made from a Persian prayer rug and "hundreds" of homemade garments fashioned from blankets and curtains.[69] The State Rubber Factory, tasked with developing a substitute for leather soles, was reportedly experimenting with a new type of sole made from a mixture of ground-up rubber and leather scraps.[70]

Konstantin Paustovskii's 1921 short story about the existence of a former director of *Russkoe slovo* during the civil war reflected the new relationships among people, spaces, and things. Paustovskii's narrator lives in three rooms on the second floor of Al'shvang Brothers, the formerly elegant store, an arrangement that perhaps alludes to the evictions of the well-to-do from their residences and their improvisation of living quarters in formerly nonresidential buildings.[71] During the daytime, he drinks tea made from dried-up carrots and beets. At night, he sleeps on a door that had come off its hinges and that he had placed across two chests, all property of the former retailer. One of his rooms is still adorned with elegant Bohemian glass mirrors, which he tries to remove from the walls in order to take them to Novyi Bazaar to barter for food.

In the absurdist material world that diarists, writers, and journalists described, expensive luxury goods no longer carried the status they once had; indeed, they also lost their former monetary value, their only currency being as a means of obtaining food or doubling as ordinary, more prosaic items. As Duranty remarked, the Persian-prayer-rug-turned-skirt would have sold on Park Avenue any day for five hundred dollars. But in civil war–era Russia, its value had depreciated; it served a more immediate, fundamental purpose. Alluding to the fluidity of the value of material goods, Vladimir Galitskii recalled accompanying his father to an Odessa market, where lively bartering was going on. As he watched, his "sister's little boots turned into corn flour, a child's dressing gown into pieces of lard."[72] Galitskii also remembered that his father traded a treasured personal possession (his watch, given to him in recognition of a tour of duty in Tashkent) for a bag of salt. Others recalled selling a father's neckties in order to buy two small white buns and the exchange of silk stockings and a small piece of chocolate for a pound of butter.[73] In the words of one Muscovite who witnessed residents of the Arbat, mostly women, selling off silverware, candlesticks, books, and hats with ostrich feathers, "All of these things had no value. Who in hungry Moscow needed these remnants of former luxury?"[74]

Some consumers bought goods at legal, state-run stores, although buying things in these retail establishments did not resemble shopping so much as navigating a bureaucracy. Those who bought from state stores had to learn a new, convoluted protocol and, according to American journalist Marguerite Harrison, be persistent. Harrison reported that in order to apply for a permit to buy a saucepan, she first had to present her papers to an official in the local food administration, whereupon she received an order signed by three officials that entitled her to buy the item. The next day, she took the order to the state store, where she chose a saucepan from the samples on display and received a coupon, which she took to the cooperative in her residential district. After that, she had to figure out which days saucepans would be sold, a comment suggesting that even a foreigner with credentials had to be informed in order to get the goods. She went to the store early in the morning on that day to stand in line hours before its opening, thus ensuring that the saucepans would not be sold before her turn. Harrison eventually obtained the desired object for three rubles, cheap, in her opinion, although she acknowledged that the entire process took up a large part of an entire week.[75]

Harrison's tale of Soviet-style shopping left out one important element, namely, that access to a state store required membership in a certain ration category, something that Babine, whose third-grade ration status was connected with his post as an English instructor and librarian at Saratov University, knew only too well. However, Babine discovered that one could sometimes circumvent the rationing system. Ruminating about his chances of acquiring pots in which to cook his food, Babine realized that his ration category did not include the privilege of buying them at a state store nor did he have the "fortune" it would have taken to purchase them at a market. Passing the state store one day, he noticed the daughter of friend working inside. Babine later stopped off at the home of this friend, a Mr. Maizul, and went into the store the following day to deliver to the store manager Mr. Maizul's greetings. "In less than five minutes," he wrote, "I chose three cast-iron pots . . . saw them charged to a fictitious purchaser on the books, paid my 29 rubles and 66 kopecks, and went home absolutely happy."[76] On this occasion, knowing someone, and someone who was willing to collude with him, was enough. In another instance, when he needed to buy two water pails, Babine found that he had to bend to prevailing political winds. Even then, however, he was not completely successful in obtaining all of the goods he needed. Having previously refused to join a union, he gave in and then prevailed upon union officials in late 1919 to provide him with a "paper," which he presented to the Consumers' Association, where he received an order issued on a state store. When workers at the state store informed him that no pails or washbasins were available, he went back to the Consumers' Association to ask for a tea kettle instead, a request that necessitated an application to the manager. His request approved, Babine went back to the store, where he found two iron horse pails and a coffeepot, not exactly the items he sought, but close enough to serve as substitutes.[77] The following day, Babine, feeling "encouraged" by his recent successes, returned to the union to appeal to the president to authorize his application for a longer list of goods. The president approved the entire list, although the manager of the Consumers' Association only endorsed about one-third of the items. Nevertheless, Babine was content that he managed to buy a frying pan, oil can, iron dipper, and whetstone. All told, however, this shopping excursion took two mornings and "plenty of walking."[78]

War and the struggle to recreate the commercial realm forced Russian consumers like Babine to be frugal and learn to be inventive, even devious. Such adaptation and survival mechanisms, born of years of war, would prove necessary throughout the Soviet era.

The retail trade and the practices and meanings attached to consumption underwent enormous change between 1914 and 1921. Conflict erupted as the tsarist state, then the Provisional Government, and finally the communist state deemed certain groups of merchants to be enemies and former exploiters. The world war followed by the civil war further disrupted production and distribution networks, and the three regimes instituted their various rationing measures, with the result that certain social groups were deemed less useful or deserving and so received less than others. Some consumers took out their frustrations on merchants, as well as local officials, charging them with fraud and criminal activity. In essence, as war raged, the retail marketplace seethed with hostility and even violence. By the end of the period, various ethnic and social groups among the merchantry and population at large had seen their property expropriated or had been formally disenfranchised and prevented from obtaining a sufficient amount of goods or from obtaining those goods through official channels. Even those favored by the state, however, often found it difficult to obtain adequate amounts of necessary goods.

The economic breakdown and sociocultural dislocations that defined this era destroyed the majority of established businesses and rendered ineffective many established practices of the trade, both customary and modern. Consumers had to adopt new tactics: queuing, relying on relatives and friends for goods, sourcing tips on where, when, and how to obtain things, and, for those allowed access to state stores, following new, intricate protocols. Many also had to figure out how to outsmart the new protocols. More than ever, consumers had to be informed, wary, persistent, and prepared to travel long distances and sometimes engage in unconventional or illicit activities in order to obtain necessary goods.

As the civil war wound down in late 1920 and early 1921 and production and distribution and retail networks slowly revived, the state moved to reinvent the retail trade with a network of state-run and cooperative stores and a new code of socialist consumption. Consumers, conditioned by seven years of economic hardship and faced with continued shortages in the 1920s, however, entered stores prepared to do battle with merchants and those employed behind the counter.

7

Retailing the Revolution

A 1926 newspaper article headlined "Under GUM's Glass Heaven" presented a vision of socialist retailing that depicted Soviet citizens indulging in the pleasures of shopping in the fabulous Red Square premises of the State Department Store (Gosudarstvennyi universal'nyi magazin, or GUM).[1] The article opened with a description of GUM's giant display windows, exhibiting "everything needed to clothe and feed a person," from suspenders to forks, starched shirts, shiny patent-leather shoes, stockings in all colors of the rainbow, and "proud, brilliant" Primus paraffin stoves, in short, hundreds of wonderful things to draw the attention of passersby. Inside, shoppers bustled and browsed, treating themselves to purchases made possible by the workers' credit program.[2] The journalist noted among the clientele a "thick-set peasant," who stood for a long time longingly stroking a sheepskin coat. Turning the purchase over and over in his mind, the peasant tried on the coat five times and even smelled it before finally deciding to buy it. Women who were laborers or office workers excitedly thronged the women's ready-to-wear department, trying on clothes for hours in front of mirrors. Publicizing GUM's commitment to democratizing consumption, this lighthearted scenario suggests the importance of a Soviet-style consumer culture in the building of socialism. As discussed previously, nationalizing or municipalizing private enterprises and redistributing wealth were central to the revolution. But revolution meant more than simply taking the means of production and distribution out of the hands of private entrepreneurs. In cultural terms, the revolution meant bringing the comfort and delights of life to those previously denied them and turning them into modern, socially conscious consumers. Indeed, the goals of eliminating private enterprise, social leveling, and retraining the population in conscientious, rational, cultured modes of living and working intersected. In order to build a socialist society in which workers and peasants enjoyed the benefits of an urban, industrial society, the state was obliged to create places where workers and peasants not only obtained coats, shoes, and other material goods but even dreamed about and shopped for them.

The conversion of the Upper Trading Rows, once the centerpiece of Moscow's retail marketplace and a bastion of merchant culture, into the State Department Store epitomized the state's liberation of society from capitalism and its plan to create a socialist retail economy and working-class culture of exchange. Founded as a model retailer, GUM dedicated itself to "retailing the revolution," a phrase used here to suggest several interrelated activities, which can be broadly grouped as either instrumental or symbolic. The instrumental activities include GUM's participation in achieving the regime's socioeconomic goals in the commercial sphere, including the struggle against private enterprise, the democratization of consumption, and the establishment of efficient, dignified norms of buying/selling and patterns of consumption compatible with socialist values. Symbolic activities included GUM's utilization of the tools of mass marketing, especially advertising, to publicize the regime's achievements and goals and to retrain the population. GUM integrated these instrumental and symbolic activities into its operations and thus served as both agent for the creation of a Soviet-style mass consumer society and vehicle for communicating with and educating the public. The state established GUM as a model retail venue where the revolution would be enacted, a place where the state would remake the population into model Soviet citizen-consumers who supported state enterprises and learned ethical and courteous behaviors while making their daily procurement rounds. In essence, GUM was intended to achieve nothing less than economic, social, and cultural transformation.

GUM was thus not simply a department store but a diversified commercial-political venture slated to deliver consumerism through socialism, and vice versa. According to the image the retailer cultivated, working-class men and women could indulge in fantasies of consumption and shop for clothing and other desirable goods in a luxurious environment made possible by a benevolent socialist regime. In this brand of socialism, access to and acquisition of consumer goods was a primary right, an integral part of the agenda of eradicating socioeconomic privilege. Conversely, the simple act of buying goods from a state retailer constituted a purposeful revolutionary act, fundamental to the installation of new norms and values and, ultimately, the transformation of the economy and society. The retailer's role in constructing and implementing the revolution points out the mutual influence of mass politics and mass culture in the twentieth century.[3] With its establishment, the business of mass marketing and retailing became intertwined with politics and economic theory, each supporting and transforming the other. Revolutionary politics infused the retail trade with new principles and operating practices aimed at creating a just, egalitarian economy, while methods of mass marketing and retailing gave state and party officials ways to access and appeal to a broad population.

Despite the affinities between the political and commercial worlds, however, socialist retailing was not always an easy sell. The state's model retailers did not set the terms of the retail trade or influence consumer habits. During the NEP period from 1921 to 1928, state, cooperative, and private retail enterprises competed in a mixed economy. Although state commercial officials benefited from the eclectic nature of the market, drawing inspiration from various available business models, state retailing did not always peacefully coexist with private enterprise. State stores such as GUM often found themselves outflanked and outmaneuvered by more adept, resourceful private retailers and vendors. Indeed, the NEP era is typically conceptualized as one dominated by the attractions of private retail stores, restaurants, cafés, nightclubs, and other private businesses.[4] In drawing out the important roles that private entrepreneurs and merchants played in the 1920s, scholars have revealed the unofficial economy and the urban high life that became indelibly intertwined with the decade's image. The figure of the "NEPman" certainly loomed large in both official rhetoric and popular imagination. However, state retailers and cooperative ventures also played a defining role in inaugurating new ideals, values, and practices. Acting as primary merchant, GUM, along with other state enterprises, infused the culture of buying and selling with concepts of political struggle, social justice, and rational consumption and institutionalized concepts of consumer entitlement and complaint. At the same time, the retailer could not completely divest itself of the legacy of the pre-1917 retail marketplace. Many Soviet officials identified with the methods and practices of modern retailing and, in seeking to implement them, furthered in part the vision that the merchant elite had endorsed. For their part, consumers remained attached to goods and attitudes that many party members and state officials found frivolous or detrimental to state goals.

Model retail enterprises such as GUM reflected the Soviet regime's impulse during the NEP years to gradually transform society through education and modeling, although the state was also prone to coercion and force when it came to private enterprise.[5] The campaign to create a socialist retail sector and promote new norms of consumption and the institution of a procedure to handle consumer complaints demonstrate dual impulses of persuasion and compulsion.

The Campaign for a Socialist Retail Economy and Culture

In late 1920, the Bolsheviks faced unrest among sectors of the population, some of which began to rebel against the strict "war communism" policies the state had enforced during the civil war. Facing a political crisis, the state adopted in piecemeal fashion a set of measures, which became known collectively as the NEP, throughout the spring and summer of 1921. These measures attempted to make concessions to an exhausted population and to revive a failing economy by permitting a mixed economy of private, cooperative, and state-owned enterprises. Nikolai Bukharin championed the NEP, arguing that it would revitalize agriculture, industry, and commerce, placate a rebellious peasantry, and gradually guide Russia to socialism via economic competition between the public and private sectors. Advocates like Bukharin believed that state enterprises would eventually outperform private ones by better supplying the population, their victory in the marketplace ensuring a centralized, socialist economy. In March, the Tenth Party Congress signaled its intent by ending grain requisitions and replacing them with an in-kind tax. That same month, a decree permitted peasants to sell surplus produce at designated markets after first paying a tax. The state also authorized private trade and manufacturing on a limited basis, although it retained control over heavy industry, banks, transport, communications, and foreign commerce. In May, Sovnarkom allowed small, private manufacturers to sell products in permanent premises and from stalls, booths, and vending trays. State trusts could also sell their products to private merchants if cooperatives were unable to buy them. In July, decrees gave anyone over sixteen years of age the right to engage in the retail trade, provided he or she acquired a license and paid the required taxes. Finally, NEP reopened Russia to foreign investment.[6]

Private merchants were initially reluctant to open businesses, but Sovnarkom began to provide more encouragement. Restrictions were lifted on private manufacturers and artisans, who were urged to increase production and assured that they could sell their products freely. Sovnarkom also repealed laws that had nationalized small factories not already operated by the state and declared that anyone eighteen or older could establish a small-scale manufacturing business, employing no more than ten to twenty workers, and then sell products on the market. These initial decrees helped launch a flurry of industrial and commercial activity. Beginning in 1922, the number of permanent private retail stores in Moscow rose by 83 percent, from twenty-nine hundred to fifty-three hundred. Many of these first businesses were opened by individuals who had previously been merchants or shop assistants.[7]

A vibrant street life and images of abundance began to replace the wartime specter of hunger and desolation. Mikhail Bulgakov, making a living as a writer for various publications, declared a "commercial renaissance" in Moscow and the city "open for business":

> On Kuznetskii Most, the painted faces of toy figures made by artel craftsmen smile. In the former Shanks store, ladies' hats, stockings, boots, and furs gaze out at the clouds. . . . On Petrovka, windows sparkle with ready-to-wear clothing. . . . Waves of fabric, lace, rows of boxes of face powder. . . . There is a confectioner's shop at every step. And all day until closing, they are full of people [narod]. The shelves are full of white bread, wheatmeal loaves, French rolls. Countless rows of pirozhki cover the counters. . . . The luxurious displays at the gastronomes are startling. Mounds of crates with canned goods, black caviar, salmon, smoked fish, oranges.[8]

Markets that had been closed reopened. Officials first allowed trade to be conducted at Sukharev for a couple of weeks prior to Easter in 1922 and then extended the term. In February 1925, Sukharev moved to a new, permanent location, with new stalls and booths, a tea house, and a three-story building to house the market committee and packaging and shipping operations.[9]

Russians privately registered the changes that NEP occasioned by remarking on the reappearance of small luxuries in their lives. Iurii Got'e, who had subsisted on an academic-class ration during the civil war, felt his spirits lift when the family was able to mark his son's name day in July 1921 with all the customary pre-war treats, including pies and candies, and again in January 1922, when he was able to purchase a fir tree and goose to celebrate the New Year.[10]

The reopening of shops selling caviar and holiday provisions failed to delight some party members and communist supporters, however. To them, the potentially deleterious effects of the retail trade and the temptations of consumer goods outweighed the benefits of restoring distribution and retail networks. On one hand, many party members viewed merchants with contempt and suspicion and conceived of the retail trade as an occupation that produced no value and exploited individuals for a profit. Party members opposed to NEP were especially skeptical, arguing that NEP stood for the "New Exploitation of the Proletariat" and the "NEPman" for bourgeois luxury.[11] As Aleksandr Barmine, an ardent young Bolshevik, remembered, in 1921, he and his like-minded comrades were astonished at Lenin's announcement of NEP. While he acknowledged that food became more plentiful and its quality better under NEP, he worried that "money was once more becoming the touchstone of social life" and that the "old inequality" they had fought so hard against had returned.[12] He anxiously reported the reappearance in Moscow of elegant sleighs drawn by thoroughbreds and the opening of several new restaurants, all of which, he complained, were beyond the reach of the men of the revolution. For Barmine, NEP was a "slippery slope" that led right back to capitalism and left him and his friends wondering whether they had fought the civil war in vain.[13] On the other hand, a number of party members and state functionaries justified the revival of private enterprise. In their view, the toleration of a private market would encourage peasants to produce enough grain for export, a primary source of state revenue, and to feed the urban population, two requirements for industrialization. The disagreement between party members who perceived in the NEP's gradualist approach to socialism a "retreat" that hindered the building of socialism and those who believed it would be only a temporary phase of "recovery" resulted in the state's vacillating policies toward private merchants and the retail trade throughout much of the decade.[14] Even though the state tolerated private enterprise on a limited scale, it did not entirely abandon coercive policies. In its drive to bring "class warfare" to the retail sector, the state instituted discriminatory policies, including the tightening of credit, the levying of crippling taxes and fees, and disenfranchisement, all devised to give the state sector a competitive edge and ultimately drive private entrepreneurs out of business.[15]

Another conflict arose between many party members' desire to enable the working classes to have more comfortable lives and competing concerns about the corrupting influence of a preoccupation with material goods. The consumption of "nonessential" or "luxury" goods worried those communists who had adopted a revolutionary asceticism and believed conspicuous consumption promoted frivolous, even dangerous pursuits, rather than political resolve. Not all party members considered issues of consumption incompatible with revolutionary politics, though. Many prominent communists realized that, without a transformation of daily life, and indeed material life, the political revolution would fail. Leon Trotsky wrote several essays on the urgent need to revolutionize daily habits and customs.[16] Aleksandra Kollontai, the first commissar of social welfare and head of the party's Zhenotdel (Women's Bureau) from 1920 to 1922, as well as one of the most stylish dressers among the Bolsheviks, also understood that in order to appeal to women and ultimately reform and emancipate them, the party would have to coordinate their organizational efforts around issues of *byt* (everyday life).[17] Kollontai and other Zhenotdel leaders and workers discovered that the best way to persuade women of the benefits of socialism was to speak to them about the issues that most immediately concerned them and constrained their lives.[18] Zhenotdel organizers, therefore, routinely addressed motherhood, housekeeping, drinking, literacy, religion, habits of speech, and polite behavior. Indeed, they reported that these topics seemed to interest most women, particularly in the villages, and to attract the greatest number of them to Zhenotdel meetings.[19]

In support of the agenda to reform everyday behaviors and attitudes, state agencies created thousands of posters instructing the population on the basics of health, sanitation, propriety, and safety. Posters admonished the population not to swear, beat their children, smoke, eat from a communal bowl, or smudge books and cautioned them against stepping in front of a tram. They urged them to learn to read, wash their hands before eating, brush their teeth, exercise regularly, and look both ways before crossing a street.[20] Reforming the population's shopping habits was part of this campaign. One series of posters, for example, instructed consumers, "Don't Touch Goods with Your Hands" and "Having Tasted a Product, Don't Give the Remains Back."[21] Party theorists and commercial officials, therefore, tried to detach buying and selling from practices and meanings they considered vulgar, backward, or unhealthy and to recast them as deliberate acts that assisted state goals. They sought to erect a centralized system of state retailing, supported by rural cooperatives that could rationalize distribution, equalize acquisition of consumer goods, and school the population in what they considered modern, dignified, and politically conscious behaviors. They hoped to appeal to consumers and convince them of the superiority of state retailing, ultimately leading them to forsake private retailers, thereby supporting collectivist economic institutions and ideals of social justice and civility.

Beginning in late 1921, state and municipal authorities began to organize manufacturing and retailing ventures, combining them into trusts that went by such names as Mossel'prom, Mossukhno, Rezinotrust, and Moskvoshvei (the Moscow food, textile, rubber, and clothing trusts, respectively), all under the supervision of economic councils attached to the Moscow soviet. Created in January 1922 for the production and distribution of food products, candy, alcohol, and other consumer perishables, Mossel'prom was one of the largest trusts. Maintaining its own retail stores, kiosks, and street vendors, Mossel'prom also operated a mail-order division and maintained vending machines in factories, trams, buses, and theaters.[22] Moskvoshvei established a network of stores to sell ready-to-wear clothing, hats, and notions throughout the Soviet Union. By 1925, the trust operated twenty-four divisions, which oversaw fifteen stores in Moscow, including the Fashion Atelier at 12 Petrovka Street, and shops at Sukharev, Smolensk, and Central markets, as well as outlets in Ukraine, Samara, the Urals, Irkutsk, and Omsk.[23]

The state also resumed its nationalization and municipalization campaigns and began to reorganize, rename, and operate several of the largest, most successful prerevolutionary retail enterprises. In December 1921, Sovnarkom approved the statutes of GUM, which took up residence in the enormous, ornate retail arcade formerly known as the Upper Trading Rows. Mostorg (Moscow State Joint Stock Company), created under the Moscow soviet's Board of Commerce, opened a department store in March 1922 in the building on Petrovka that formerly housed Muir & Mirrielees and its civil war incarnation, Store No. 1. Mostorg's published aims were to supply Moscow industrial enterprises with goods and materials for production and to serve the "mass consumer" (*massovoi potrebitel'*) of the working classes. A similar process was occurring in other parts of the Soviet Union. Komvnutorg of Ukraine formed the joint stock company, Larek (literally "stall"), in November 1922. The outfit opened its first retail outlet in Khar'kov in December 1922, and within four months it also operated divisions in Kiev, Poltava, Ekaterinoslav, and Odessa. By 1923, Larek had 23 divisions and 1,046 commercial outlets throughout Ukraine.[24]

As part of the process of claiming these businesses for the workers' state, officials rechristened them with names that evoked revolutionary myths, personalities, and imagery. The confectioner Abrikosov & Sons was nationalized in 1922 and renamed P. A. Babaev State Confectioner after a prominent Moscow Bolshevik. One of its rivals, A. Siu & Company, was resurrected in 1924 as Bolshevik Confectioners. Einem became Red October Confectioners, and Odessa-based Krakhmalnikov Brothers, the Rosa Luxemburg Company. Filippov's became known as the First Moscow Bakery. Perfume and cosmetics manufacturers Brocard & Company and A. Ralle & Company were recast as New Dawn and Freedom, respectively. Some large cooperative ventures were also appointed prime retail spaces. Eliseev's lavish wine and food emporium was reopened as Store No. 1, the Kommunar co-op's retail store that served the Moscow soviet, the Moscow party, and the Comintern. Municipal officials in other parts of the nation also renamed and reopened formerly successful firms and enterprises. In Odessa in 1926, a group of local businesses founded the Odessa State Department Store, locating it in the luxurious Petrokokino Brothers premises.[25] The Odessa branch of Abrikosov & Sons became the Khalva Candy-Chocolate Factory, and Promsoiuz (Union of Manufacturers) Confectionery opened a retail store in the formerly popular Fankoni café. The centrally located Passazh continued to operate as a retail arcade, retaining its original name and leasing individual spaces to both state and private retailers. Although the state forged ahead in bestowing new, revolutionary-themed names for previously private enterprises, the revolutionary imagination did not always trump prior associations. The acronym of the new state soap and cosmetics trust, TEZhE, of which Ralle and Brocard were a part, when pronounced, sounded French and refined.[26]

State enterprises also appropriated the products that had issued from these firms and gave them politically symbolic names and packages. Babaev Confections produced many of the same candies that had won Abrikosov & Sons fame but retailed them under names such as Red Moscow and Internationale, the latter clad in a brightly colored wrapper featuring Red Army soldiers marching under banners with the slogan "Proletarians Unite." The product line of Bolshevik Confectioners featured Cooperative Caramels, and Hammer and Sickle, Red Navy, and Pioneer candies.[27] Advertisements for these products often featured both the new and old names of the factories or products. Red October ads, for example, included the tagline "Formerly Einem."[28] This tactic doubtless served the dual purposes of ensuring consumers that products were the same high-quality ones they had previously enjoyed and letting them know that state enterprises had seized the products that capitalist entrepreneurs had once produced and had now endowed them with a revolutionary spirit and purpose. A 1923 ad for Soviet-brand cigarettes explicitly made this point. Showing a worker with a pack of Soviet-brand cigarettes under one arm and holding by the scruff of the neck an official from the old regime clutching a pack of Senator-brand cigarettes, the copy read, "We Don't Smoke Senator [Cigarettes]. For Us It's Soviet [Cigarettes]."[29]

Despite the creation of bold images that communicated a revolutionary break with the former merchant elite and their capitalist methods, Soviet commercial officials continued the campaign to establish modern, mass retailing via the same advertising, marketing, and merchandising strategies that successful Russian entrepreneurs had espoused in the decades prior to 1917. Rather than vaunting the virtues of private entrepreneurship and middle-class values, of course, Soviet officials promoted collectivism and unity among members of the working class. Nevertheless, official efforts to remake the retail sector and reform its methods and practices owed much to the legacy of the prerevolutionary merchant elite, especially the campaign launched after 1905. The most important conviction the two campaigns shared was the idea that large-scale, centralized, rationalized retail outfits that stocked an array of desirable, affordable goods in attractive, comfortable settings, that trained employees to courteously assist customers instead of haranguing them, and that aimed to educate customers and sponsor cultural events would help generate a moral economy, civil social relations, and an informed, cultured population. Several of the Soviet state's strategies and policies bear out this assertion. First, state and local officials reserved the most capacious, elegant, well-appointed, and well-known commercial venues in urban centers, including Muir & Mirrielees, the Upper Trading Rows, Eliseev's, Odessa's Petrokokino's, and St. Petersburg's Gostinyi Dvor, as sites for the foundation of model retail enterprises. Several factors explain this course of action. All of these retail venues had widely recognized names and were located in prime retail space that was familiar and accessible to urban residents. The Rows and Gostinyi Dvor stood on spots that had served as the city's central retail district for centuries. These premises also offered facilities, equipment, and, in some cases, personnel. Locating state and cooperative retail stores in these places, therefore, was the most practical route to quickly setting up operations with the least amount of investment and attracting customers. Rather than having to start completely anew, state business leaders could build on pre-existing advantages by appropriating established sites. Instead of entirely erasing memories of former merchants and their firms, the state capitalized on their names and reputations, using the familiar locations to orient consumers trying to adjust to a plethora of new street names, acronyms, and monikers. Many of GUM's advertisements referred to the retailer as "GUM in the Upper Trading Rows," and the words "Former Muir & Mirrielees" frequently appeared in larger print than the word "Mostorg" in ads for that retailer.[30]

Theoretically speaking, Soviet commercial officials, like the prerevolutionary merchant elite, believed that large, centralized, rationalized retail enterprises, especially the department store, were best for delivering consumers high quality and savings. Iakov Gal'pershtein, a member of GUM's board, revealed this conviction when he argued that by virtue of its size and financial capital, GUM wielded enormous leverage when contracting with state manufacturing trusts, a position that would translate into lower prices for consumers. This position, moreover, lent itself to the goal of creating a socialist retail economy. Only such consolidated, wide-ranging retailers, in his opinion, could wage a competitive battle to win the market for the state.[31] This preference for large-scale enterprises accorded with the general modernizing and centralizing impulses in Bolshevik ideology. It also reflected the state of the field in contemporary retailing. Business leaders throughout Europe and the United States regarded the department store as the most efficient and advanced retail format, in fact, the only one capable of coping with distribution on a mass scale. Given the concurrence of these two trends, it is not surprising that officials like Gal'pershtein advocated the department store as the prototype for state retail stores.

The strategy of locating state retailers in prominent, formerly capitalist retail venues also reflected the regime's desire to engender a marketplace culture based on values of sophistication, beauty, quality, selection, service, cleanliness, civility, and cultured leisure. Their goal was, in essence, to give the working classes entrée to spaces that previously had been inaccessible and to accustom them to a commercial culture that offered more than simply supplying their material needs. Presenting a range of proposals on the "art of commerce" to the Presidium of the Moscow soviet, Comrade Leonidov, assistant manager of

Mostorgotdel, recommended making stores spacious and convenient, creating attractive, brightly lit window displays, coordinating merchandise (for example, showing socks, stockings, and garters with shoes), and employing a staff of information officers to answer customers' questions.[32] Commercial officials like Leonidov also believed that socialist merchants should aspire to high aesthetic standards in order to maintain the health of the operation and appeal to consumers. To that end, the state sent a team to conduct routine inspections of GUM's branch stores, tasking them to detail success or failure at keeping clean, tidy stores with organized stock and attractive displays of a variety of popular merchandise. Even though most inspections reported dismal conditions, the state nevertheless held up the department store as the ideal.

These capitalist strategies might seem incompatible with a socialist network of stores, but they complemented the regime's goal of lifting the material and cultural level of the population, and, therefore, they were not considered antithetical to the task of building a socialist retail economy. The department store model and methods of modern retailing were also preferable to the lavka and its customary practices, which, pervasive in prerevolutionary Russia, state commercial officials viewed as representative of a coarse, underdeveloped kind of petty trade.

Customary commercial practices believed to encourage artifice, swindling, and conflict were prohibited. In order to ensure that all shoppers paid the same amount, store managers had to clearly mark or display prices for all items. Haggling and the practice of posting workers outside to cajole or coerce customers to enter a store were banned.[33] Commercial officials intended citizens of a socialist state to have access to the best retail outlets in the city, managed using the latest methods, and to offer a world of consumer goods and convenient services. Moreover, the state commercial officials intended to romance the customers. Creating a state-run retail economy and Soviet consumer did not mean downgrading standards and offerings; it meant upgrading consumer expectations.

It is worth noting, furthermore, that many among the corps of Soviet commercial officials had been merchants or shop assistants prior to the revolution, and their knowledge and prior training conditioned the state's philosophies and approaches. Just as Lenin recruited scientists, engineers, and other technical specialists to help reconstruct industry, so, he argued, must the state embrace erstwhile private merchants because their expertise was needed to help restore the retail economy and teach communists how to run a business.[34] Most of the prerevolutionary merchant elite had lost their property and emigrated, however; others were imprisoned or executed or died during the revolution or civil war.[35] Some, however, remained in Russia and worked for their own former companies.[36] Others took up administrative positions within the state bureaucracy, served as procurement agents for state enterprises or co-ops, or opened their own businesses to supply state trusts. One Solomon Burshtein, for example, who prior to 1917 had been a first-guild merchant, worked during the 1920s as a procurement agent for state enterprises, including GUM.[37] Burshtein's experience was not typical, however. The prerevolutionary merchant elite had mostly been eradicated, leaving primarily small-scale operators and shop assistants to take up positions in commercial state enterprises or to become procurement agents for enterprises such as GUM and Petrotorg.[38]

Despite admiration for the efficiencies of the department store, state commercial officials, as well as some writers for the economic press, believed that the department store model had to be purged of its pernicious aims and predatory tactics before it could serve as a suitable socialist retail format. Acknowledging the financial advantages of the department store and the competitive edge it wielded against the ranks of petty traders, one writer for *Ekonomicheskaia zhizn'* warned that in order for state department stores to be successful, they had to reject the goals of "purely capitalist enterprises" by abandoning the sole pursuit of profit and the satisfaction of all of the "whims of the shopper." This writer continued that state department stores had to refrain from turning into "weak, trivial" enterprises by waging a struggle against small enterprises through a strategy of price reduction and fighting speculation and embezzlement.[39] Another article made similar demands, arguing that state department stores should not engage in commerce in the manner of the middling social ranks and philistines. As he put it, the department store had to exhibit a "state character," a quality he defined as pursuing the restoration of large-scale industry and uprooting from its ranks employees motivated by personal gain.[40] Thus, even though Soviet commercial officials took the department store as a template, they hoped to adapt it in order to bring it into line with the party's ideology of class struggle, the state's modernization drive, principles of egalitarianism and collectivism, and vision of a cultured *byt* (everyday life).

Experimental artists and architects, who hoped to use their designs to reorder everyday life and thought, provided inspiration for the project of creating state-run retail stores. Some of the most prominent constructivists of the day found employment in various state agencies and enterprises producing advertisements, consumer goods, and commercial buildings with a bold, industrial, revolutionary look.[41] In 1919, the Fine Arts section of Narkompros (Commissariat of Enlightenment) organized a competition to find a new design for newspaper and propaganda kiosks. Aleksandr Rodchenko won first prize for his visionary plan that rejected traditional architectural forms and featured exposed structures instead of flat surfaces. The most ingenious feature of his design was a mechanism that transformed a part of the kiosk into a speaker's platform, which could be used for political speeches and educational purposes.[42] Mossel'prom's new seven-story headquarters in Moscow on Kislovka Street, designed by Rodchenko with Vladimir Maiakovskii and completed in 1924, likewise exemplified an innovative trend in commercial architecture toward rational, functional design that also served the practical purpose of advertising. Mossel'prom's name and products appeared down the building's side in brightly colored block letters and motifs, spelling out the trust's name and its slogan— "Nowhere else but Mossel'prom"—on alternating floors.[43] Mossel'prom's small, portable kiosks, stationed throughout Moscow, also received a constructivist treatment. Attached signboards audaciously queried passersby about where to buy macaroni, candy, and other products, and supplied the answer: "Nowhere else but Mossel'prom." Mossel'prom's kiosks and peddlers wearing caps embroidered with the name became such familiar sights around the city that a 1924 film, *The Cigarette Girl from Mossel'prom,* featured a heroine who worked as a street-corner vendor for the trust. Sukharev Market was also slated for revamping. Konstantin Mel'nikov, one of the best-known Soviet avant-garde architects, updated the market concept with spare, functional rows of stalls and a brightly hued color-coding scheme that identified the items sold in each row.[44] Although such distinct commercial structures were relatively few in number in Moscow, they provided a clear, visual departure from the ornate neoclassical, Russian revivalist, and moderne style structures that merchants had favored before 1917.

Later in the decade, the utopian movement to rationalize labor also inspired the redesign of retail stores and reconfiguration of work and shopping routines. Motivated by the ideas of Alexei Gastev, as well as Taylorism and Fordism, the movement dubbed the "scientific organization of labor" (*nauchnaia organizatsiia truda,* or NOT) strove to create more productive, skilled industrial workers by gearing their movements to the tempos and rhythms of the machine.[45] The idea of applying efficient movements to the routines of retail workers, as well as customers, emerged as a part of the rationalization campaign of 1927 to make industry more efficient. In that year, the co-op Kommunar, which operated about one hundred stores in Moscow, planned to celebrate the tenth anniversary of the revolution by opening several new stores and remaking Store No. 54 in the Krasnaia Presnia neighborhood into a model store. After more than two months spent observing the store's operations, experts from Orgstroi, a body that worked to organize and rationalize buildings, concluded that the store was equipped "as if doing business three hundred years ago." They recommended the standardization of equipment, fixtures, and procedures, the redesign of the floor plan, and the installation of new cupboards and counters shaped like the Greek capital letter π, so that workers could use both hands and customers could buy items without any additional, unnecessary movements.[46]

Another inspiration for the state's retail system was the cooperative model. Frequently used throughout Europe and Russia as an alternative way to distribute goods and a way to encourage collectivist impulses, cooperative organizations offered an antidote to the individualist culture of capitalist consumerism.[47] Some cooperative movements were reformist and sought to inculcate in their members a sense of duty to undertake collective action and self-help, while more radical movements aimed to mobilize the working classes through strikes and the distribution of propaganda. Cooperatives differed from private retail businesses in that individuals paid a membership fee and bought shares in the venture, with the funds from the sale of shares being used as operating capital. Members were then entitled to a portion of the profits earned each year. Cooperative retail ventures also set as their mission to sell basic goods to members without reaping excessive profits or pressuring them with intense sales pitches. Sometimes, however, in order to compete, they adopted the practices of capitalist retailers, for example, advertising, and abandoned their reformist or radical political agendas. The number of memberships in cooperative enterprises had increased rapidly in Russia after 1914, and members numbered about 30 million by the end of the civil war.[48] Sovnarkom's 1919 decree on consumer cooperatives provided another impetus for expansion. In the 1920s, the number of co-ops expanded at a faster rate than that of state-run retail outlets, although there were still fewer of them than private operations. According to one report, in European Russia in 1925, there were three co-op stores for every 27 licensed private trade operations. In the countryside, the figure was three co-ops for every 10,000 residents. Still, co-ops outnumbered state retail enterprises, which maintained only 0.6 outlets for every 10,000 persons.[49]

Co-ops were natural allies in the war against private commerce, and as often as state and party leaders promoted the virtues of model retail stores, they also extolled the virtues of cooperative networks, especially in the villages, where the state had yet to fully extend its reach. Still, according to one historian of Soviet trade, even as the state relied on co-ops to organize distribution and inculcate new attitudes and retail methods, many officials distrusted their independence and the pre-1917 "cooperators" who largely staffed them. As a result of this hostility and the consolidation and reorganization of self-standing cooperatives into a state-directed bureaucracy, the cooperative movement ultimately did not expand widely enough to form an extensive retail network, and it emerged as both a "cornerstone of socialist distribution" and "gray area of the socialist economy."[50]

Finally, the defense of and advocacy for workers guided the invention of the socialist state retail store. Safeguarding workers' health and welfare was a priority. To that end, GUM officials mandated that state stores be well ventilated and equipped with lavatories stocked with washstands, soap, and clean towels and that they provide potable water. Female workers and breast-feeding mothers were allowed a thirty-minute break during their shifts.[51] In a revolutionary workers' state, however, officials also set out to reenact class struggle on the sales floor by overturning the old commercial axiom that the consumer was king/queen and by exalting the retail worker to a position of dominance. In order to effect this revolution, union officials and journalists acknowledged the need to reeducate retail employees and consumers, instilling a new consciousness and training them for new roles. The reinterpretation of the retail exchange cast the sales worker as a knowledgeable and objective adviser who fully and honestly gauged consumers' needs, rather than a self-interested lackey who pressured customers to buy things they did not need. State retail workers would be patient when helping inexperienced, working-class shoppers and judiciously advise them how to spend their workers' credit. Consumers would be patient, courteous, and observe the protocols of the store. Shades of the prerevolutionary campaign for a dignified, civil retail culture can be seen in these critiques, although, of course, the attempt to hold consumers partially responsible was novel. Moreover, a sense of revolutionary discipline pervaded this campaign. These and other writers argued that any kind of rudeness or negligence should be mercilessly eradicated through comradely censure and punishment by the trade unions.[52]

In sum, Soviet commercial officials took the department store as the model for a state-run retail sector, although they adapted it by following the trends and philosophies of modernist architecture and the cooperative and the rationalization of labor movements. The principle of class struggle provided the necessary inspiration for making the state stores revolutionary working-class institutions.

"Everything for Everybody" at GUM

GUM opened the doors of its Red Square store for business in March 1922. Full-page advertisements announced the fifteen departments, including grocery, confectionery, wine, perfume, books, haberdashery, sporting goods, and toys, that stood ready to receive customers. The merchandise on sale had been obtained from a variety of sources, including state and industrial concerns, cooperatives, and artels. GUM's Sovnarkom-mandated mission was to supply state, cooperative, and private enterprises with materials and manufactured products and to retail popular goods to consumers. Sovnarkom pledged to lend GUM five million rubles in start-up funds. At that time, GUM also maintained a New York office to purchase goods and handle the sale of raw materials. It also had nonretail divisions, including a printing house, textile mill, and meat processing plant, as well as cigar, cigarette, and shoe and ready-to-wear manufacturing enterprises. Created as a showcase of the state's aspiration to bring a world of style, quality, and beauty to working-class citizens at an affordable price, GUM was intended to exemplify the philosophical and operational principles of socialist retailing in its network of stores and to reeducate the population through advertising and promotional campaigns.[53]

At the time of its debut, GUM was a state institution under the jurisdiction of VSNKh, governed by a board of representatives from the Moscow soviet, the Commissariat of Finance, VSNKh, and the State Publishing Trust (Gosizdat) that coordinated store operations and maintained communications with government organs. Gosstrakh, the State Insurance Trust, became a shareholder shortly thereafter and contributed additional funds that amounted to 20 percent of the enterprise's operating capital. Half of the firm's profits were to go toward paying off the government's loan and the other half to expanding the business. At the end of 1922, due to a reportedly "dismal" financial position and failure to sufficiently develop the network of stores, Sovnarkom detached GUM from VSNKh and reorganized it as a joint-stock company, with the stipulation that the majority of shares be sold to state institutions. One of the reasons for the retailer's poor performance was the state's failure to deliver the promised start-up funds. As late as January 1924, the retailer had received less than one million rubles.[54]

GUM remained chronically short of funds throughout its nearly decade-long initial existence (1921–1931). The board constantly struggled to stabilize the retailer's financial position and set its stores on a firm basis. As a consequence, the number of stores in its network fluctuated from year to year. At the end of 1923, GUM maintained a fairly large retail network comprising twenty-five branch stores, at least five of which were located in the Moscow area and six in Petrograd. Other stores were operating in Tambov-Voronezh, Nizhegorod, Saratov, Orel, Elets, Kursk, Tula, Krasnodar, Samara, Perm', Tiumen, Ekaterinburg, and Khar'kov. Many stores, however, especially those in the provinces, led a precarious existence. A 1923 inspection characterized business in the three units in the Urals-Siberia division as "depressing," noting that the staff was "not completely apt" and that money was squandered on purchases of inappropriate and unpopular merchandise.[55] In 1925, another inspection concluded that stores in the Moscow division "most closely resemble a European-type department store," while stores in other cities "still have to transform themselves into true department stores."[56] In fact, the Red Square location was the only store that was large enough to resemble a department store, although the venue was technically an arcade.

In 1924, the enterprise abandoned its wholesale and import operations in order to focus on developing its retail network.[57] Beginning in July and continuing through 1926, GUM closed several of its branch stores, including those in Leningrad, Khar'kov, Krasnodar, Perm', and Tiumen, citing operational problems, disappointing profits, mismanagement, and executive corruption. The company also divested itself of its manufacturing enterprises, as well as its artisanal workshops, garage, and company steamship, in order to concentrate exclusively on its commercial functions and to pursue retail expansion on a sounder basis.[58] These measures did not bring improvement. Provincial stores continued to suffer from serious defects, including a lack of variety in merchandise and ordering irregularities. Although a few of the provincial stores, that of Saratov, for instance, did a fair business and showed steady sales increases, most reported uneven sales growth and regularly achieved only about 35 to 40 percent of their plan target.[59] As the provincial network shrank during these years, GUM expanded its network in and around Moscow, opening stores in the neighborhoods of Egorev and Sretenka, as well as in the nearby towns of Kaluga, Kolomna, and Vladimir. By 1927, GUM operated the Red Square location and ten branch stores in Moscow, along with seventeen tea stores, fifteen wine stores, and a shoe stall in Sukharev Market, employing a total of more than seven hundred persons.[60] The strategy of scaling back operations allowed the firm's management to more closely supervise the remaining outlets and made distribution easier, but it resulted in an exclusive focus on urban centers and a marginalization of the provinces.

Despite financial and operational difficulties, GUM presented itself as the Soviet Union's preeminent merchant and universal provider, designations that symbolically united all citizens in one, big imagined department store. To communicate those roles to a consuming audience, the firm employed all of the marketing strategies of modern, mass retailing. The advertising staff developed a distinctive logo and slogan: a circle topped by "GUM Moscow," the inscription "The State Department Store" below, and a slogan in the center: "Everything for Everybody." Advertising catchphrases revealed the scope of GUM's pretensions: "We Have Everything You Need at GUM!" and "The Latest Styles Only at GUM!" as well as "Colossal Assortment of High-Quality Merchandise at Prices the Competition Can't Beat!" GUM also proudly trumpeted its status as a large, important, and contemporary purveyor, billing itself as "The Only True State Department Store."[61] Advertisements for myriad items appeared in many and diverse kinds of urban and provincial newspapers and journals, including *Izvestiia,* the state's newspaper, *Ekonomicheskaia zhizn',* a journal devoted to economic issues and read mainly by specialists, and mass-circulation dailies such as *Vecherniaia Moskva* (Evening Moscow), *Rabochaia Moskva* (Workers' Moscow), *Rabochii put'* (Workers' Path), *Prozhektor* (Searchlight), *Rabotnitsa* (Working Woman), and *Krest'ianskaia gazeta* (The Peasants' Newspaper). Ads appearing in places as far away as Kazan', Rostov-on-Don, Riazan', Chernigov, and Vyshnii Volochek extended GUM's reach, linking distant consumers to the urban center with a pledge to send merchandise COD to all of the corners of the Soviet Union.

Combining bold graphics and commercial slogans with political rhetoric, GUM's ads politicized the seemingly inconsequential acts of buying and selling by drawing a correlation between individual acts of consumption and the transformation of the economy and society. In essence, ads became agitational and educational media. The state's ad agency, Dvigatel', unabashedly expressed this understanding of advertising, deeming it the "best means of economic propaganda."[62] Articles in *Zhurnalist,* a journal devoted to writers' issues and literature, likewise equated social-political work and the methods of modern industry and commerce. The journalists argued that the development of newspaper advertising, given the correct orientation, was the most powerful means for creating a "new [kind of] consumption, new consumers, and new markets."[63] To realize this concept of advertising, GUM employed some of the most prominent avant-garde writers and artists, including Vladimir Maiakovskii and Aleksandr Rodchenko. Both had worked for the Soviet government during the civil war, producing posters, sketches, and political cartoons, and they easily channeled their experience into "agit-advertising."[64] Maiakovskii considered most advertisements boring and ineffective, and he hoped to recreate the genre, an objective that complemented the Soviet state's desire to mobilize the population. In his words, advertisements should be so compelling that "a paralyzed person is immediately healed and runs out to shop, to buy, to look."[65] Maiakovskii and Rodchenko collaborated on advertisements, product packages, sign boards, and illustrations, creating a style and idiom that suited the commercial end of attracting customers and the political imperatives of advancing state enterprises and beating private entrepreneurs. Experimenting with "word-novelties," unconventional syntax, the "posterishness of a word," and "slogan-y lyrics," Maiakovskii penned texts that were as innovative poetically as they were politically.[66] Rodchenko illustrated Maiakovskii's texts, using vivid colors, simple, clear typefaces, and geometric shapes. One of their collaborative agit-ads captured in a few short, simple phrases GUM's ambitious mission of supplying all Soviet citizens' needs:

Clothe the body,
    Feed the stomach,
        Fill the mind—
Everything that a person needs
    at GUM he will find.[67]

This sales pitch declared that GUM satisfied all material, intellectual, and psychological needs, a claim reflecting the state's desire to consolidate the distribution of consumer goods through one central point and its expectation that state institutions would eventually organize all aspects of life. Centralizing buying and selling would help bring the socialist economy nearer, since, theoretically, if consumers turned to GUM for all of their purchases, then GUM could expand its network. Eventually, all consumers would buy everything they needed from GUM. In this way, ordinary acts of consumption would culminate in the establishment of a state-centered economy. Another agit-ad represented GUM as a life raft, an image that conveyed the impression that the state would "save" its citizen-consumers:

Grab onto this life preserver!
    High-quality, inexpensive goods, direct from manufacturers![68]

In this ad, GUM appeared as a lifesaver in the midst of an ocean of private entrepreneurs, offering to rescue consumers from the high prices of NEPmen and petty traders.

Although Maiakovskii's signature slogan for Mostorg ran simply, "Shop at Mostorg—You'll be delighted!" many of that retailer's ads also blended commercial and political aims.[69] An opening announcement listed the store's departments and informed consumers of the personal and political advantages of shopping at Mostorg. A three-quarters-page ad in *Rabochaia Moskva* ran the commercial slogan, "Mostorg Department Store Sells Direct to the Consumer Everything That One Needs," accompanied by political slogans like "The Middle Man Raises the Price of Merchandise" and "Mostorg Is Not a Profit-making Business. We Must Force Out the Middle Man."[70] Dual-themed advertisements like these communicated to consumers that shopping at Mostorg would be a pleasant experience that would also eliminate the middleman, which in turn, would bring lower prices for consumers and an end to private business owners who unjustly took a cut.

Imparting to consumers an awareness of class struggle was not the only objective that state retail enterprises strived to achieve with agit-ads. Endorsing the purchase of certain consumer goods supported the state's long-range goal of creating a modern, sophisticated, cultured populace. One of Maiakovskii's ads for GUM promoted the idea of wearing a watch and being on time, behaviors considered essential to a modern, industrialized society. Featuring a mechanical human figure constructed largely of clocks and watches, the text proclaimed, "A Man Must Have a Watch. Only a Mozer. Mozer Watches Only at GUM."[71] Lightbulbs were also promoted to complement the regime's electrification campaign: "Trade the Dark for Light. Buy Dazzlingly Bright and Inexpensive [lightbulbs] at GUM!"[72] Ads like these informed consumers that watches and lightbulbs were indispensable items for contemporary life and that GUM offered the best available. Even cigarettes were reimagined as modern accessories. One of Mossel'prom's ads, for example, reminded consumers, "Era Cigarettes Are All That Are Left to Us of the Old World." Other ads ordered consumers to change their shopping habits and become more discerning by purchasing goods at state stores: "Stop Your Street Habit. Remember That the Best Cookies Are at Mossel'prom!"[73] These ads reflected state enterprises' multiple roles as merchants, educators, and cultural authorities dedicated to bringing consumers quality, inexpensive products and to encouraging discriminating behaviors and attitudes that complemented the state's drive to transform the economy and population.

Ukraine's Larek also fashioned itself as a paragon of retailing that could deliver all things to all people. Its trademark slogan reflected a consumerist appeal to value and quality: "Buy Things at Larek—Cheaper and Better Than Anywhere Else!" But Larek also ran agitational ads, which combined praise of the firm's business acumen with political propaganda. One such agit-ad inveighed against the private trader:

> The petty private trader is seized with fear.
> Now he is shedding a stream of bitter tears:
> Alas, the end of his happy days has arrived.
> The Ukrainian Larek has met him in heated battle.
> The lavka stands empty. Its products rotting on the shelf.
> And an excruciating anguish gnaws at the trader.
> He calls out to everyone to come to his lavka—but in vain:
> Everyone hurries to get in line at Larek.[74]

In this excerpt, the image of a cowering, weeping private trader engaged in battle against a powerfully attractive Larek avowed that state enterprises would destroy the remnants of capitalism as they wooed customers away with their superior products and services. According to another of Larek's agit-ads, however, consumers also had a responsibility to act conscientiously:

> Consumer!
> You commit a crime against yourself,
> Against your family,

Against the state,
When you shop at a private lavka.

Shopping at Larek
Preserves your material interests,
and the interests of your family—
You don't strengthen private capital,
You don't help to establish the new bourgeoisie.[75]

This ad informed consumers that it was their duty to help starve out NEPmen. Patronizing private businesses constituted an offense that would delay the achievement of socialism. By shopping at Larek, consumers would undermine counterrevolutionary elements and help attain a historical goal that would benefit them, their families, and society.

While class struggle figured prominently in many ads, state retailers most often promoted their stores as welcoming, accommodating spaces for all social classes. GUM's signature slogan, "Everything for Everybody," represented this ideal of universal inclusion, though the message of universality was often undercut in ads by a textual or visual hierarchy of consumer types. One series of advertisements published in provincial organs prioritized peasants and workers with calls to "Workers, Peasants, and Other Citizens."[76] In the same way, a 1922 ad printed in *Rabochaia Moskva* informed "Worker-organizers, Red Army participants, and employees of state institutions" that GUM sold merchandise at special, wholesale prices.[77] Another ad accomplished social ordering visually. In its depiction of a line of people walking through a larger-than-life GUM logo, a Red Army soldier took the lead, a symbolic expression of his position as a privileged consumer.[78] Other state enterprises also employed this tactic. A 1925 advertisement for *Nasha Marka* (Our Brand) cigarettes showed clearly identifiable social types standing behind a box of the cigarettes, ordered in a line that reflected their social value. Led by a Red Army soldier, a factory worker, member of the intelligentsia, and peasant followed the soldier, while a man in top hat and tails and his fur-clad female companion brought up the rear.[79] As these ads suggest, although all social groups, even some who in reality were disenfranchised or discriminated against in some ways, were participants in a Soviet-style consumer society, male workers and soldiers took the leading positions.

Many of GUM's advertisements took this approach a step further by representing state retailing as one of the achievements of a masculine revolution. In this scenario, the male worker symbolized the heroic builder of the state retail sector, while the male peasant most often stood for its prime beneficiary. Building on the concept of the *smychka,* the economic and cultural union between city and village, these ads relied on semiotic tactics that represented the socialist state as a union of male workers and peasants.[80] One such ad portrayed a male worker and male peasant gazing at GUM's logo, the presumably more politically conscious worker pointing out to the peasant the store's logo and its pledge to provide everything to everybody.[81] Female figures did not appear in this ad at all, an omission that suggests that GUM did not conceive of or market itself as a "woman's paradise" but as a legitimately masculine arena where men were enjoined to partake of the material bounty proffered by the revolution. Other ads affirmed the privileged position of the male worker, albeit sometimes with symbolically incongruous images. In one, a male worker sits with the Roman god Mercury upholding the torch of commerce; in another, the male figure is promoting GUM's October bazaar at the branch in Orlov. In another, a male worker presides over a cornucopia of goods.[82] A series of ads created on behalf of a group of state enterprises portrayed men as providers and guides who enlightened the population and bestowed the comforts and conveniences of modern life. In one, two pilots fly an airplane over a village, dropping ads from GUM, Tsentrosoiuz, and other state enterprises. Male and female peasants run out of their huts to catch the leaflets as they float down through the air. In another, two men shine a searchlight on the night sky, revealing ads from Mossukhno, Rezinotrust, and other state enterprises.[83] In these ads, peasants, male and female, joyfully and gratefully receive knowledge about state-run enterprises and consume the goods.

The figure of the male consumer, embodied by the male peasant, also appeared in ads aimed specifically at rural dwellers. These ads typically depicted the peasant as a novice consumer learning to procure things in new ways that supported state enterprises. A collaborative ad sponsored by *Krest'ianskaia gazeta* contained a three-panel illustrated ad for GUM showing a male peasant writing a letter to the retailer and then receiving a box full of goods at his village home.[84] This ad symbolically linked the village consumer to Moscow's retail center and served to acquaint all consumer-newcomers, peasant or otherwise, with innovations such as mail order and to encourage them to support state firms. In truth, GUM was not making great progress in reaching the village. Two stores in the Tambov-Voronezh area, one characterized as a store for "peasant merchandise," were faulted for failure to carry hardware and items for peasant use.[85] Sales figures confirm that the firm primarily served an urban clientele.[86] Responding to charges that GUM had forgotten about the peasant, one official backpedaled on the vow to provide everything to everybody. He explained that GUM did not consider it an obligation to stock items for farming or agriculture, or even basic necessities, since co-ops were responsible for supplying them. He insisted, therefore, that GUM had not violated its slogan.[87] Ads nonetheless continued to feature the icon of the peasant consumer.

In ads targeting an urban audience, the male consumer sometimes took the form of a white-collar worker. Less likely to be portrayed as a neophyte consumer, the white-collar male consumer resembled the middle-class male consumer who had appeared in advertisements prior to 1917. Dressed in a suit and tie, and immersed in a world of goods, this figure exhibited the means and the know-how to shop. He needed only to be encouraged to patronize state stores. "All That the Heart, Body, and Mind Require," ran one such ad featuring a man, who, looking upward as he juggles a pocketwatch, baseball mitt, easy chair, shirt, socks, boots, books, fountain pen, and phonograph record, seems to be indulging his many consumer fantasies while confident in the knowledge that GUM can satisfy them all.[88]

This kind of ad also had a feminine counterpart, one in which a well-dressed woman in a fashionable hat considers the many items available at GUM.[89] Curiously, however, the female worker did not play the same prominent role in commercial iconography that the male worker did. In fact, none of the ads that have been preserved show the working woman as the builder of the state retail sector or even as the male worker's helpmeet in bringing state-manufactured goods to the village. This omission seems odd, given the inclusion of women in political posters that represented the triumph of socialism as a union of the male and female worker, or female peasant, or that depicted the working woman as a guide and bearer of new organizations intended to enlighten and benefit women. To be sure, the figure of the working woman sometimes embodied female consumption and showed the benefits available to women who purchased items at GUM, Mossukhno, MSPO, and the State Sewing Machine Trust with the help of workers' credit.[90] But the deployment of the figure of the consuming working woman appears to have been less common than might be expected. The state did create ads showing the peasant woman as consumer. One, for example, shows a smiling *krest'ianka* admiring a pair of galoshes manufactured by the state's rubber trust. However, it appears that there were even fewer ads depicting the peasant woman as a beneficiary of the state's retail sector.[91]

The figures of the female worker and the peasant woman dominated political posters that encouraged the founding and patronage of cooperatives. In two typical posters, created in 1925, one for urban and one for rural audiences, the working and peasant woman appear at the center, overlooking bright, clean, newly built cooperative stores.[92] The ways that the two women were depicted and the tone of the slogans, however, drew a sharp contrast. One poster commanded, "*Rabotnitsa*, Build Cooperation," and showed the woman worker confidently towering over the cooperative, directing consumers inside. The other poster seems to have been created to try to overcome the resistance of rural-dwelling women with its slogan, "*Krest'ianka*! Cooperation Is Your Friend!"

In this poster, the peasant woman stands with folded arms gazing at the co-op from a distance, a sickle thrown over her shoulder and a skeptical look on her face. Another poster for co-ops depicted a woman worker standing atop a platform and holding a child, while stretching out her arm to help a peasant woman clamber up to the top.[93] This set of posters suggests that, like the male worker, the female worker was judged the stronger, more capable and conscientious, ready to take on the tasks of building collective institutions, while the peasant woman still had to be convinced of the cause and persuaded to join. The state also assembled images of the female worker and peasant woman as cooperative shoppers.[94] Very often these posters included side panels contrasting old and new ways of life, implying that, for example, forsaking the shops of petty private traders would help transform daily life.[95]

Although state enterprises were reconceptualizing consumption as a universal right, the lack of an iconic working-class male consumer may reflect ambivalence on the part of state officials about fully endorsing personal consumption or perhaps reluctance to associate working-class men with an activity that had so often been connected to middle-class women. The apparent absence of efforts to fashion an icon of the female worker as a symbol of the revolutionary vanguard in the realm of state commerce also suggests that women's assumed role in rebuilding the economy was in the cooperative movement, not in the state retail network. While these various depictions of male and female consumers do not necessarily overturn conventional conceptualizations of men as the organizers of the economy and women as their assistants or consumers, or even indicate a symbolic reconfiguration of power dynamics, they call into question conventional conceptualizations of the female form as prime signifier of the material world and archetypal consumer. In the 1920s, organizers of the Soviet economy and consumers, whether in the state or cooperative sector, were embodied by both masculine and feminine figures; in fact, male figures, whether workers or peasants, occupied positions of prominence.

Commercial officials found other ingenious ways to convey messages through the medium of consumer goods, including issuing revolutionary-themed products bearing the symbols of state power and images of Lenin, Mikhail Kalinin, and other political leaders. While commodifying the emblems and personalities of the revolution, these products seemed intended to familiarize consumers with the new government and its achievements and to animate the world around them with images of a new society and life. Brightly colored "propaganda textiles," patterned with geometric shapes or agitational motifs of tractors, the new countryside, airplanes, cogs, wheels, levers, and the hammer and sickle, were designed to be made into mass-produced clothing.[96] The Precision Mechanics Trust produced wall clocks, grandfather clocks, and alarm clocks, primarily for rural consumption, with revolutionary designs and illustrations on their faces.[97] In honor of the revolution's tenth anniversary, the State Mail-Order Company and Bureau of Parcel Post created special commemorative items, including pencils embossed with Lenin's image, a mug with a relief of the state seal in gold, and agitational lanterns, fashioned in the shape of a five-point star and decorated with pictures of Kalinin, a Red Army soldier, and important moments in the history of the Soviet Union.[98] Items intended for a more prosperous, even foreign, clientele, were also produced. The Lomonosov Porcelain Factory, formerly the Imperial Porcelain Factory, enlisted artists to design plates, statues, and other porcelain items. Many of these fine objects rendered in cubist style the hammer and sickle, red star, Lenin's head, and even ration cards, and they incorporated slogans such as "He Who Does Not Work Does Not Eat" and "Long Live the 8th Congress of Soviets."[99]

Agitational-packaging, which distilled complex concepts of socialism into rudimentary slogans or imparted knowledge about new, practical concepts and technologies, encased some of the products that issued from state enterprises. Common, inexpensive items like candy often came in revolutionary-themed wrappers patterned with, for instance, workers and peasants or a red sun rising on Moscow in 1917. Maiakovskii developed more novel wrappers, including a series of eleven sequentially numbered candy wrappers for Mossel'prom's Red Army Star caramels that depicted the victory of the Red Army over the Whites, with accompanying verse. For Red October Confectioners' Our Industry caramels, Maiakovskii and Rodchenko collaborated on wrappers designed with illustrations of locomotives, airplanes, trams, tractors, trucks, and bridges accompanied by rhyming verses intended to acquaint consumers with modern forms of transportation and urge their use. The tractor wrapper, for example, enjoined, "It is time for the peasant character to accustom itself to the tractor. Do not turn the earth with a dry plow." Another sought to teach consumers the fundamentals of the metric system through illustrations and a rhyming verse that went, "The conversion is easy and straightforward [priam]. A quarter of a funt is 100 grams [gramm]." One ingenious candy wrapper incorporated moving figures. The wrapper depicted a worker and a peasant standing facing each other with a capitalist in the middle, as if preventing their union. When the consumer pulled an attached tab to open the wrapper, the hands of the worker and peasant met in a show of solidarity and crushed the capitalist between them.[100]

State retail enterprises also took up the role of community patron, sponsoring exhibitions and fairs, devised as much to educate consumers as to entertain them and win their patronage. Seeking to position itself as a firm that brought Muscovites new, unparalleled opportunities, GUM staged an exposition of fifteen hundred birds and another of more than one thousand dogs, billing the latter as "something never seen prior to the revolution."[101] Every year at the Red Square location, GUM also staged its "traditional" spring and fall bazaars, organized with the objectives of introducing Russians to new, modern products and, of course, getting people to shop at the department store. At the 1926 fall bazaar, GUM announced that it would hold a drawing for ten thousand prizes, among them bicycles, shoes, coats, musical instruments, gramophones, cosmetics, and samovars. For each five rubles spent, a shopper would receive one lottery ticket.[102] Newspapers reported on the bazaars enthusiastically, if briefly, noting that great crowds attended them. Other state retailers organized similar public events. Gosizdat sponsored Dni pechati (Book Days), a three-day book fair on Tverskaia Street in Moscow. While its main purpose was to promote reading and sales of the state publisher's overrun books, the fair was also advertised as a *gulian'e* (outdoor party) for the populace, who could enjoy the two orchestras or visit the many booths set up to provide games and other amusements.[103] Similarly, Mossel'prom promoted its model cafeteria, Praga, as a place where one could find physical, mental, and political nourishment in its clean, bright dining room and delicious meals, reading room, and political stage.[104]

State retailers also organized promotions to encourage consumers to celebrate new Soviet holidays or support worthy causes. GUM, Larek, Mostorg, and other state retailers routinely held sales to mark the anniversary of the October revolution, which they advertised in popular newspapers. In honor of the seventh annual commemoration, Larek organized a "Larek Octobering," offering fabric, soap, cookies, sugar, cigarettes, and other "prizes" to parents who bestowed a revolutionary name on a child born on the anniversary date. That same year, Mossel'prom launched a campaign to introduce its new Treasure cigarettes. Packs of the cigarettes contained lottery tickets and chances to win cows, horses, tractors, and furniture. Proceeds from sales went to support homeless children and orphans from World War I and the civil war.[105] Exhibiting both agitational and commercial purposes, such promotions sent the message that the attainment of socialism was connected to the personal acquisition of consumer goods. GUM's bazaars acquainted shoppers with new merchandise and highlighted recently lowered prices at a time when consumers were more able to afford purchases.[106] Obviously, a commercial tactic to get shoppers into its store, the promotion was also created to generate excitement about bicycles, coats, and gramophones, which suggests that ownership of basic and leisure-time goods was part of a larger agenda of raising the material and cultural level of the population. Larek's Octobering promotion implied that Soviet children should be born into homes supplied with all of the material things necessary for their care, and it simultaneously encouraged new communist rituals with the promise of small luxuries for those who adopted them. In short, the state rewarded citizen-consumers with material things, and citizen-consumers aided the state by purchasing items produced by state enterprises. The benefits were mutual, although perhaps not equal.

Such advertising campaigns, product tie-ins, and promotions recalled the marketing strategies of the prerevolutionary merchant elite, who had conferred on their tea cookies the names of empresses, staged sales to coincide with religious holidays, promoted important state events in advertisements and in their stores, and staged rituals that incorporated the imagery of state power. Given the integration of the images of tsarist power into retailing and consumption prior to 1917, it is not entirely surprising that Soviet commercial officials marketed Lenin's likeness and marked new Soviet holidays with contests and in-store events. Revolution had certainly brought momentous changes to the retail sector, transforming the nature of property ownership and methods through which goods were sold. However, modern marketing and retailing strategies continued to be employed, the primary difference being the political content of the ideas marketed and commodified.

Defining Socialist Norms of Consumption

Images of revolutionary retailing and ad campaigns urging productive consumption could not ensure that consumers would reject desires and norms that thwarted the revolution's goals. Two issues that proved particularly vexing to commercial officials and consumers alike centered on the role of fashion in socialist society and the production and sale of religious-themed items.

In theory, a socialist society was supposed to lift the worker's standard of living, which in practice meant an increase in personal consumption. Throughout much of the 1920s, however, personal consumption was tied to the shifting fortunes of state industry, agriculture, and the NEPman. As a consequence, consumers faced inflation, deflation, unemployment, and an unrelenting shortage of basic goods, which made achieving a higher standard of living difficult. Economic recovery in both agricultural and industrial sectors following the end of civil war was slow, and state policy in the 1920s toward merchants and the retail trade was erratic. As a result, consumers often found little to consume. The decade began with a famine in 1921, a catastrophe that led to millions of deaths and a decline in grain harvests, which, to consumers, meant continued shortages of bread and other agricultural produce. In the industrial sector, shortages of capital, labor, materials, fuel, and experienced management persisted, leading to shortages of manufactured goods, especially consumer goods. Furthermore, the NEP mandated that state enterprises shift to commercial accounting and pay for materials and wages out of their profits. Initially, few enterprises

could afford to maintain large workforces, and in order to comply with regulations, they had to lay off workers. The year 1923 brought a "scissors crisis," an
economic predicament in which agricultural production began to recover and
grain prices fell, while industry failed to regain its pre-war capacity and prices
of manufactured goods continued to rise. In 1922, industrial production had
recovered only 26 percent of its pre-war capacity, but agricultural production
reached 75 percent of pre-war levels. By the fall of 1923, industrial prices were
three times higher relative to agricultural prices than prior to the war. To force
prices down, the state decreed maximum prices and other measures aimed at
assisting industrial recovery; by the following year, the price of manufactured
goods had fallen by almost 25 percent and agricultural prices had risen. With
the closing of the price gap, the national currency began to stabilize, and, by
mid-decade, the economy had started to recover.[107]

As conditions began to improve generally, average wages began to slowly
rise. The general rise in well-being can be partially attributed to the state's
authorization of private trade in agricultural goods, which created favorable
conditions for those relatively well-off peasants who could provide food for
their families and sell the surplus in markets in cities and towns. The consumer
goods industries also began to slowly recover and more goods became available.
The years 1925 and 1926 are generally acknowledged to have been relatively
propitious years for the socialist state. Still, even near the end of the decade,
in 1928, national income was approximately 10 percent below, or at best equal
to, the 1913 level, and the production of food, drink, and tobacco in 1926–1927
remained below the 1913 level. Economic historians interpret such data to mean
that average workers and peasants did not see any real rise in their standard of
living. At the same time, scholars generally acknowledge that the mid-1920s
were relatively prosperous compared to the years after 1927, when the rationing
of bread and other essential goods was reinstituted, due to a decline in agricultural cultivation following the repression of grain-producing peasants, the
arrest of thousands of private traders, and the subsequent breakdown of production and distribution networks.[108]

Despite the chronic dearth of goods, images of consumption were published
and discussions about the role of consumers and the proper meaning of consumption in a socialist society occupied party members, commercial officials,
journalists, and consumers. Many commentators sympathized with consumers and their needs and argued that state enterprises and co-ops should supply
consumers with basic kinds of goods. Some went so far as to defend consumers'
desire to buy high-quality, fashionable items that they really wanted, instead
of poor-quality, indistinguishable ones that state enterprises found most expedient and cost-effective to produce. Indicative of this pro-consumer stance,

one journalist for a workers' newspaper remarked that many consumers wanted to buy "something a little better" (*polushche*) for the winter season and would rather invest more money in a coat of fine, thick wool than to spend less for one made from a coarse grade.[109] Another writer, discerning a shift in expectations, contrasted the consumer of the civil war years with the consumer of 1925. He asserted that consumers would no longer buy just anything stores managed to have on hand. Instead, he claimed, they were looking for certain requirements and would buy an item only after thoroughly inspecting it.[110] Such advocates defended the consumer against the imperious attitudes of "commercial organizations" whose officials complained that the consumer had become too exacting. They demanded that officials take seriously the needs and tastes of consumers.[111]

Many party members and state officials, however, believed that the personal preferences of consumers clashed with the goal of channeling consumption to constructive, socially correct ends. To provide guidance, VSNKh, Narkomfin (Commissariat of Finance), and Narkomvnutorg (Commissariat of Domestic Trade) collaborated on lists of "basic necessities" (*predmety pervoi neobkhodimosti*) and "luxury items" (*predmety roskoshi*), the former signifying those things essential for life in Soviet society and the latter, those judged imprudent. Although the lists were compiled for purposes of taxation and administering the workers' credit program, they nonetheless were clear attempts to try to distinguish suitable needs and tastes from unnecessary extravagances. Luxury goods included those made from silk and velvet fabrics, suede, or kidskin, patent-leather shoes, ladies' hats with feathers or egret plumes, imported lace, bedsheets, tablecloths, napkins, and lingerie made from linen or batiste, and items made from furs other than wolf, rabbit, deer, seal, elk, or gopher. Photographic equipment, fireworks, caviar, foreign cheeses, out-of-season vegetables, art objects, cars, perfume, and cosmetics also made the list.[112] Mostorg, the Moscow Union of Consumers' Societies (MSPO), and other state and co-op retailers that sponsored workers' credit programs generated their own lists. They deemed fabric, ready-to-wear clothing, coats, shoes, furniture, and linens as basic necessities, which workers could purchase on credit in their stores. The credit program excluded things like sports equipment and alcohol.[113] Glavpolitprosvet (Central Committee for Political Education under Narkompros) provided some guidelines in household manuals written to instruct workers and peasants on how to set up a comfortable, well-appointed dwelling. In one guide, the author recommended two changes of clothing for everyone in the family, shoes for each family member, a cupboard for dishes, separate bowls and towels for each person, lamps, curtains for the windows, and a tablecloth.[114] Literature written by prominent communists also contained clues to those items judged inappropriate to a conscientious working-class lifestyle. These included chandeliers, silver cutlery, linen cloth, and wine.[115] There was general agreement about the essentiality of certain kinds of goods, although official lists and prescriptive and literary advice did not end debate or confusion. Narkomfin's tax board sent a memo to Moskvoshvei to clarify the status of goods containing fur. The memo explained that only items made entirely or predominantly from more expensive furs were considered luxury items. A man's coat made from Russian wool and trimmed with an Astrakhan collar, for example, would not be classified as a luxury item because the collar constituted only a small part of the coat.[116]

Politically committed consumers were also trying to define for themselves which things were practical, politically constructive purchases and which were frivolous extravagances. Depending on the degree of their ideological commitment and conception of the role of material goods in socialist society, they came up with different answers. One male worker, for example, reported to *Rabochaia Moskva* that he was doing away with the old custom of buying his child a toy for his birthday. He advised readers to follow his example of buying a *razumnyi* (rational) gift for children and recommended what he had chosen: registration in the organization ODVF (Obshchestvo druzei vozdushnogo flota or Society of Friends of the Air Fleet).[117] For this consumer, political enthusiasm took the place of personally indulgent, nonproductive activities such as playing.

Discussions about legitimate versus illegitimate modes of consumption often centered on fashion goods and female consumers. Given the associations made between women and consumption prior to 1917, such discourses reflected not only the persistence of essentialist assumptions about women but also the interests of many young female activists. One group of female factory workers in St. Petersburg wrote to tell *Rabotnitsa* that as a sign of their commitment to political and social issues, rather than personal ones, they had decided not to powder their faces or wear makeup.[118] In a later issue, a lengthy discussion about the meaning of beauty and the role of cosmetics and fashion in a socialist society ensued when the journal received a letter signed "Komsomolka G," who challenged the editorial board's belief that women must struggle against beauty: "Why do you hold in contempt women who wear makeup? After all, aren't red lips much more pleasing than chapped, yellowish-green ones? Moreover, claiming that cosmetics are harmful to my face seems more like scorn and ridicule."[119] According to the columnist who responded to the letter, Komsomolka G had misunderstood the party's line on fashion and cosmetics. In fact, the journalist argued, the Communist Party had not taken any position. "Whoever said anywhere," she parried, "that communists have been ordered to wear long skirts and to wear such-and-such a style of blouse?" In the analysis she proceeded to lay out, however, the columnist condemned both the power that the fashion industry wielded over women who blindly followed its dictates and the competition that trend setting had created among wealthy women. "Have you ever been to the Bolshoi Theater, G?" she asked. There, she explained, one would find ladies sitting in the front row wearing expensive furs and comparing their silver earrings and chinchilla to their neighbor's blue fox and gold necklaces and bracelets. The result of such competition, she concluded, was that wealth had come to signify a person's worth, an idea that she argued had been overturned by revolution. Moreover, such rivalries obscured the material needs of the average person. She also linked an interest in certain kinds of fashion with immorality by questioning the motivations of women who wear skirts with slits and open-work stockings, items she considered provocative and favored by bourgeois women looking to attract men.[120] As interpreted by the party's leading women's political journal, women who followed the latest fashions and aspired to or wore luxurious or daring items exhibited a lack of serious purpose and personal morality, as well as a dehumanizing subjection to the values of the bourgeoisie. Interestingly, the editor's argument that fashion threatened women's personal integrity and moral certitude echoed the complaints of pre-1917 critics like Iulii Elets, despite their vastly different political views, suggesting that political radicalism was no guarantee of less conventional views of women. Ending her column with the claim that *Rabotnitsa*'s editors were not against fashion per se, the writer recommended that readers wear "beautiful, cultured clothes that are neat, graceful, and becoming" and, in lieu of applying lipstick, get physical exercise so as to give the lips a healthy tint of red.[121]

This exchange purportedly elicited a flood of responses from readers. Published in a later issue, the responses reveal a wide range of opinions and solutions. In seeking to define beauty, one Comrade Poplevina, a factory worker from Penza, paraphrased Lenin: "Beauty is that which meets the interests of the proletariat in their struggle for socialism. Beauty is everything that is consonant with our struggle for a new life." Comrade Genia from Nikopol' concurred and argued that *komsomolki* (female members of the Young Communist League), who were builders of a new life (*novyi byt*), should eliminate makeup, this "rotten stuff, which philistines and people with old worldviews find pleasing."[122] This reader expressed the hope that women would adopt a new understanding of beauty and turn away from a sole preoccupation with physical appearance and begin to find beauty in a woman's knowledge, strong will and character, healthy body, and hands skillful at building a proletarian society. However, many readers wrote to object to the persistent emphasis on a woman's body as the site of beauty, even if a body was healthy, fit, and strong. As one put it, "What's the difference between an athlete wearing shorts that expose her arms and legs and some petit bourgeois woman trying to arouse men's attention with her short skirt and open-work stockings?"[123] Several other readers, however, defended short skirts as practical. In their opinion, long skirts inhibited women's movement, whereas shorter hemlines made it easier to move around and, thus, were more practical. On the matter of wearing jewelry, all of the writers whose letters were published agreed that, as one woman phrased it, "it's time to throw off the tinsel of gold." Finally, a few readers defended fashion and cosmetics for their own sake. Admonishing those who rejected traditional ideals of femininity, one wrote, "Everyone is not born beautiful, and might want to try to make themselves [sic] look like it. Wearing makeup in such instances," she argued, "is not a crime." Another explained that "a humdrum existence eats at a young woman's heart, and if she goes around with colorless, chapped lips—what then? Wearing makeup is more fun."[124]

As evidenced by the responses, a range of views existed on issues of beauty and fashion. But in this case, *Rabotnitsa* had the final word and chided the last two contributors for reducing all of life to outer, physical beauty, as well as for striving for a "deceitful beauty" and complaining of a humdrum existence at a time of unparalleled equality and opportunity for women. Although the party did not issue any decrees on fashion or makeup, this discussion communicated the message that expending too much thought and time or money on these things was not in the best interests of the individual or society. At best, clothing and cosmetics were trivial distractions or delusions and, at worst, a surrender of class principles and the class struggle. Beauty, as the writers and editors of *Rabotnitsa* conceived of it, consisted of simplicity and naturalness. Red was the color of the revolution, not of cheeks and lips. Only in dedicating themselves to the party, the organization of co-ops, the literacy drive, or other political movements would women brighten up the colorless life of the past.

These kinds of debates would continue throughout the decade. And even though *Rabotnitsa* adopted a utilitarian view of fashion and downplayed the importance of material goods, the manufacture and retailing of clothing, while complicated by issues of whether certain styles or items were appropriate, did not necessarily transgress any of socialism's major tenets. The production and sale of religious-themed goods by state and cooperative enterprises was less easy to defend.

Disentangling religious holidays from the retail sector was fraught with complexity. Continued adherence to religious practices, especially the celebration of religious holidays, compounded the problem. Throughout the decade, new Soviet holidays and festivals were introduced as substitutes for the customs and rituals that had previously accompanied religious holidays and feast days, and these new celebrations served as harbingers of a new world. The "experts of cultural production" who played a role in defining a new "Soviet style" hoped that the new "Red calendar" would eventually come to mark time in people's lives, just as the Orthodox calendar had in the past.[125] In the meantime, however, commercial officials faced a dilemma: state enterprises could either try to shape consumer wants and preferences or simply allow consumers to decide for themselves what they wanted and then provide them with it, no matter the ideological cost. Private retailers did not face this dilemma. They continued to sell Christmas tree ornaments, candles, and religious images in markets and in their shops, even those on prominent city streets.[126] State enterprises and cooperative ventures, however, found themselves caught in the midst of the cardinal commercial tenet to provide the goods that customers wanted, the practical and political necessity of turning a profit and besting private traders, and the party's ideological commitment to uprooting religious beliefs and practices.

In 1924, *Vecherniaia Moskva* exposed the difficulties that state and cooperative retailers faced in sorting out the relationships among state commerce, consumers, and religion. One of the newspaper's reporters objected to the fact that Mossel'prom was advertising made-to-order paskha and kulich holiday desserts decorated with religious messages and that MSPO was selling Passover wine labeled as having been produced under the supervision of a rabbi. In response, Comrade Karasev, managing director of Mossel'prom, flatly denied the trust was selling paskha or Passover wine at its stores, since, he stated, those items were associated with religious practices. He then proceeded to admit that Mossel'prom was selling the kulich cakes, although not in connection with Easter. As he explained, Mossel'prom regularly baked these cakes for a "certain circle of consumers." The cakes' presence in the stores that month, therefore, was nothing special. Karasev added a political justification, noting that there were a great number of unemployed pastry cooks in Moscow and that Mossel'prom only began to accept orders for the kulich cakes in order to put people back to work and prevent NEPmen from getting rich off of the sale of these "luxury items."[127] Comrade Epshtein, vice-president of MSPO, likewise denied the sale of Passover wine but acknowledged the sale of the kulich and paskha desserts, albeit without decorations like crosses or the initials "Kh. V." (meaning "Christ has risen"). Like Karasev, Epshtein rationalized the sale of these items, pointing out that since "religious prejudices" persisted, the refusal to sell goods associated with religious holidays meant surrendering profits to private merchants, something that would only delay their defeat.[128] Caught in a contradiction, Karasev and Epshtein revealed that although state enterprises did not refuse to manufacture or sell holiday items, they found it necessary to justify their sale with legitimate social or political objectives, in these instances, the desire to assist unemployed workers and to beat NEPmen.

The public airing of this issue did not prevent state and cooperative enterprises from producing items for religious holidays, although some ads omitted an explicit mention of the holiday. During the pre-Christmas shopping season, Larek advertised that its shelves were stocked with wine, fruits, and sweets and that the deli was preparing patés, aspics, and other traditional dishes for celebrating "the holidays."[129] The next spring, GUM's ads declared that the Food Department was accepting orders for kulich and paskha desserts and that a large assortment of chocolate, candy, and cookies from the best makers would be available for "the holiday."[130] A December 1926 article titled "The State Understands the Importance of Having Merchandise for Holiday Shopping" summed up the official attitude, acknowledging acquiescence in supplying the "essential products" that consumers wanted for celebrating the "upcoming days of rest."[131] State manufacturers and retailers, in fact, turned out items for many religious holidays. Babaev made special cakes, candy, and cookies for St. Catherine's Day. The State Factory of Chocolate and Cocoa and the Leningrad Union of Consumers' Societies made chocolate Easter eggs and candy. Red October Confectioners produced an assortment of Christmas chocolates, figurines, and gift boxes.[132] Crosses and icons were also reportedly on sale at one of the stores run by Moskopromsoiuz (Moscow Manufacturers' Union), as well as at Sukharev Market. Even though Sukharev was not a state enterprise, a consumer lodged a complaint in the market's complaint book. An inspector assigned to investigate the complaint concluded that the sale of icons and other church accessories was not against the law.[133] In spite of pressure from consumers, however, state enterprises did not completely surrender the push to acclimate the population to new holidays. Mossel'prom marked its 1925 calendars with red-letter days, including December 25 and every Sunday, as well as November 7 and May 1.[134]

As much as state enterprises sought to model exemplary consuming behaviors, they could not entirely dictate customs and norms, and in order to generate revenues and compete with private retailers, state enterprises and their officials had to compromise certain goals in order to pursue economic ones. Allowing the sale of religious items in state stores was consonant with the party's relatively tolerant stance on religion and reflected the composite nature of the NEP. Following the party's decision to end the violent campaigns against the Orthodox clergy and the Komsomol's counterreligious parades and mock pageants, which had alienated and angered believers, Lenin, Trotsky, Emelian Iaroslavskii, and other party leaders recommended trying to convert believers to atheism through persuasion rather than coercion.[135] The pluralism of NEP allowed the postponement of long-range goals such as the eradication of religious practice in favor of peaceful economic recovery and social conciliation.

Private celebrations of religious holidays may have been tolerated, but public commercial devotions, which had been so pervasive prior to 1917, were il-

legal and disappeared from public life.[136] Certainly, some merchants continued
to hold ritual blessing services quietly and in private, but newspapers no longer
reported the details. Some evidence suggests that devotional alternatives were
created, connected not with any established church, of course, but with the
state. Upon the anniversary of the founding of the Red Army, the GUM branch
in Tula reportedly installed a Lenin corner. Set up in its own separate room
was an exhibit to the deceased leader and literature on socialist topics.[137] One
inspector's report casually noted the presence of a Lenin corner in the Tverskaia Street GUM.[138] Lenin corners drew on the tradition of the icon corner
in private homes and were an attempt to borrow a familiar religious form to
evoke new political reverence and devotion among the population.[139] Their
presence in state stores suggests that state retailers may have adopted corners as
a substitute for the icons, prayer services, and rituals that had previously been
part of the daily business routine, although there is only limited evidence for
such a development. Furthermore, Lenin corners were not unique to the commercial sphere but appeared in factories, schools, workers' clubs, and a broad
range of organizations and institutions. As distinctive rituals disappeared from
all sectors of public life, the state inserted its own.[140] In the commercial sector,
however, celebrations of store openings resembled those the merchant elite had
pioneered, albeit without the blessing. The opening of the Passazh Department
Store in Leningrad, for example, served as a "focus of civic pride" and was celebrated with festive decorations, speeches from municipal officials, and a performance by a chamber orchestra.[141]

Retail firms were no longer independent organizers of community rituals
but vehicles of the state. Although the ritual celebrations and product associations of the late empire had blended commercial objectives with the symbols
of religion and state power, merchants or important dates on the commercial
or religious calendar had usually supplied the impetus. In the 1920s, model Soviet retailers became synonymous with the state and its imperatives. Retailing
provided a platform through which state enterprises like GUM affirmed state
power and supplemented the regime's efforts to mobilize the population in support of eliminating private enterprise and inculcating socialist values.

Like the prerevolutionary merchant elite, Soviet state commercial officials
advocated the methods of modern retailing as the way to an egalitarian, efficient, rational, and cultured society, although they did not adopt wholesale
the philosophies, business models, and practices of modern retailers. Through
networks of state stores, product associations, advertisements, and promotional
campaigns, state retailers attempted to encode the retail trade and consumption with new meanings and functions, particularly practical consumption in

support of state objectives. In practice, however, the state could not direct consumers' desires, and in order to retain a place in the market, officials acquiesced in selling "luxury" items and religious-themed goods. Divergent ideological positions within the party and the lack of a consensus on norms of socialist consumption permitted state and commercial officials to conciliate consumers while they simultaneously hoped consumers would become more disciplined and responsible by adopting modern, secular attitudes and behaviors.

By mid-decade, the campaign to establish a network of model retail firms had brought the state closer to one of its goals: driving private entrepreneurs out of the market. In 1922–1923, private commerce had accounted for 78 percent of all retail trade. That share fell to 42 percent in 1924–1925 and to 37 percent in 1926–1927.[142] The state's accomplishment was not achieved primarily through the merits of its retail network or promotional campaigns, however, but largely through coercive measures and discriminatory tax policies intended to create hardships for private merchants and traders. Furthermore, despite the optimistic face of ads and promotional campaigns, criticisms about the retailer's efforts to reach a broad customer base persisted. Even those customers served by GUM accused the firm of failing to deliver on its promises.

8

The Customer Is
Aways Wrong
Consumer Complaint in
Late NEP-Era Russia

Creating advertising and promotional campaigns that reflected revolutionary ideals and endorsed visions of a modern working-class consumer society were relatively easy tasks. Commercial officials faced more intractable problems, however, in implementing egalitarian operational policies and procedures and creating a working and shopping environment that inculcated conscientious attitudes and restrained, purposeful behaviors. Although advertisements promoted state stores as spaces where the customer's every desire would be fulfilled, trade union activists argued that in both state stores and cooperatives, workers, not consumers, should be prized. As a result, state stores like GUM became places where consumers asserted their rights to goods and courteous, efficient service and where workers declared that living in a workers' state meant a modicum of respect, as well as freedom from consumers' personal demands. By the late 1920s, the ambitious marketing campaigns of state and cooperative enterprises had stalled while their sales floors turned into arenas of struggle in which consumers and retail employees locked horns in a battle of wits and words. In the complaints they penned, consumers protested the shortages, lack of selection, shoddy merchandise, pricing irregularities, rude service, and arbitrary, inefficient, and bureaucratic procedures they encountered in their daily pursuit of bread, shoes, clothing, and other essential goods. In turn, retail employees charged that complainants were temperamental, self-centered shoppers who abused the employees, expected special treatment, and tried to circumvent Soviet laws and regulations.

The culture of complaint that developed in the NEP era became institutionalized in the retail sector after 1926, when the state established a formal system for receiving and handling complaints. The tide of complaints gained momentum at the end of the decade, when economic conditions worsened. Evidence of the situation may be found in the grievances that consumers registered in mass-circulation newspapers and in GUM's complaint books, as well as in the responses of state and cooperative retail employees. Although consumers did register complaints about private retailers and market vendors, especially about their murderously high prices, state and cooperative retailers—institutions founded to serve the working classes—came in for the most abuse. In fact, nearly half of the complaints in the sample used for this study were directed against cooperative stores, and about one-third targeted state stores.[1] Only 10 percent of complaints involved private retailers, although editorial commentary and other kinds of reportage in the press offset this imbalance.[2] Together, letters to the editor and complaint entries relay the conflicts that arose in the seemingly routine activities of buying and selling. They also demonstrate recognition by both the state and society that consumers had the right to complain about the material and sociocultural conditions of life, such as the price of butter or a sales clerk's insulting rebuff, and that workers also had the right to counter that a customer's request for help amounted to intolerable or unlawful behavior. Moreover, the designation of public forums that accepted complaints indicates the existence of public spaces, albeit circumscribed to some degree by state and party organs, established to call attention to and, in the case of newspapers, circulate criticisms.[3] In registering complaints and responding to them, consumers and retail employees, along with activist journalists, worked their way toward outlining the behaviors, attitudes, and practices they believed consistent with a socialist society.

Consumer complaints fit into a narrative genre dating to Muscovite Russia.[4] Throughout Russia's history, but particularly in times of economic trouble, political upheaval, and social unrest, Russian subjects attempted to come to terms with change by writing various types of narratives to those in positions of power. In the late imperial period, writers composed letters, poems, petitions, and other narratives in an attempt, for example, to comprehend changes to the law or to express their experiences of revolution. In the process, they reflected on widely accepted understandings of social identities, values, and relationships by mixing older images, ideals, and forms of address with new concepts of citizenship, freedom, and justice.[5] In the 1920s and 1930s, citizens who penned petitions, denunciations, and other narratives likewise tended to

rethink older concepts by combining previously resonant language with revolutionary terms and ideas.[6] These various narrative genres gave individuals
ways to call attention to corruption and abuse, appeal for relief or clemency, or
obtain retribution against neighbors and rivals while simultaneously reshaping
social identities and defining abstract ideals and values.

Consumer complaints from the late NEP period constitute a related, albeit
unique narrative genre that reflects the concerns of consumers struggling to
reinterpret routine interactions in stores and shops within a new political system and precarious economy. As commercial officials optimistically established
model retailers that endeavored to conduct business in revolutionary ways, previous conventions and understandings of the retail relationship persisted, clash-
ing with the goals of building a socialist retail economy and culture and creating
tension and conflict on the sales floor. The consumers and retail employees who
participated in the complaint process filtered past experiences and expectations
through the discourse of working-class revolution, while coping with scarcity,
in an attempt to define civil rights and appropriate norms of socialist retailing
and consumption. The complaints also demonstrate a link between the NEP
and early Stalinist political culture. As Elena Osokina and Julie Hessler have
pointed out, NEP-era policies in the retail sector wrought a dearth of choice,
material deprivation, and, especially after nationwide bread rationing was rein-
stated in early 1929 and norms of essential food items set, high levels of anxiety
and conflict. The political agenda adopted in the 1920s continued into the early
1930s, fulfilling goals of centralization, social differentiation, and the liquidation of private enterprise and thus laying the foundations for a restructuring of
the economy and society.[7] The analysis of consumer complaints presented here
stresses that the shape the Soviet retail sector eventually assumed owed at least
as much to the struggles that grew out of the NEP-era campaign to revamp the
emergent, consumer-driven, capitalist retail economy of the late empire as it did
to the "campaign for cultured trade" of the 1930s.[8]

To explore the conflicts that resulted from lingering sociocultural legacies
in an atmosphere of transformational enthusiasm and economic uncertainty, the
complaint process is treated as a narrative struggle among consumers, retail employees, and activist journalists. Each group attempted to control the meaning
of interactions on the sales floor by representing their interpretations of them
as consonant with revolutionary terms and principles. As shown, in the 1920s,
retail stores became sites where consumers and retail employees debated the nature of civil/uncivil and licit/illicit public behaviors and disputed the practices
and relationships that should make up public transactions. The complaint process reveals anxiety-ridden consumers and retail employees trying to reckon the
practical meaning of the ideals advanced by the regime. By expressing in their

own words objections to preferential treatment and disorderly, rude behavior and attaching these offenses to the discourses of social justice and equality, consumers and workers began to define what socialism meant in their daily lives.[9]

Retail Workers, Consumers, and the Late Imperial Legacy

One of the cornerstones of the capitalist retailing ethos was enshrined in Philadelphia retailer John Wanamaker's slogan, "The Customer Is Always Right." Coined to earn the public's trust and publicize his firm's commitment to provide customers attentive and courteous assistance, Wanamaker's slogan nonetheless brought no end of trouble to many proprietors and retail employees. As Susan Porter Benson has noted in her study of the development of the American department store, "Once services had become accepted features of department stores, certain customers demanded special individual attention. To some women of the upper and middle classes, the emphasis on amenity and luxury was not just an invitation to consume in style, but also a blank check for the exercise of their class prerogatives."[10] While the image of the customer as queen—or king—continued to reign supreme in the West, even as trade journals filled with stories of ill-tempered customers who defied the noble ideal, the establishment of state-run and cooperative stores in a newly socialist society called into question the privileging of the consumer. As Benson's remark suggests, serving the customer connoted an unquestioning deference on the part of sales workers, who were expected to fulfill the personal requests of middle- and upper-class female shoppers and indulge their whims. In a society founded to uphold the rights of the working class, this unequal relationship symbolized the reenactment of class struggle on the sales floor and, therefore, would have to be reversed. The process by which the Soviet state tried to recreate the retail sector and alter the relationship between retail workers and consumers, however, was by no means as straightforward as simply inverting class and gender dynamics. Consumers were not always middle or upper class. Neither were workers and consumers always female. Moreover, socioeconomic struggle became only one factor at play on the sales floor. Equally important, the customs and relationships that had structured the sales transaction prior to 1917 continued to influence the retail transaction.

Judging from the scorn emanating from both sides of the counter, retail workers and consumers perceived each other as adversaries, not allies, in the project of remaking the retail economy. As already demonstrated, this adversarial relationship was not born of the Soviet era. The potential for conflict was inherent in some of the customary practices, like haggling, that merchants and consumers had relied on to conduct business prior to 1917 and had intensified during World War I, when shortages and inflation prompted some consumers to engage in direct action in order to obtain necessary goods. In the 1920s, the customs and traditions of the pre-Soviet retail exchange and the hardships of wartime still influenced the behaviors and attitudes of Soviet consumers, and the acts of buying and selling continued to mimic a struggle.

Prior to 1917, shop assistants had labored under difficult working conditions.[11] Their work was regulated by the Torgovyi Ustav (Commercial Statute) of 1732, which was revised several times, the last time in 1903. The provisions of the statute gave proprietors the right to punish and fine employees for, among other things, leading a dissolute life and selling items below a pre-arranged price. Proprietors were able to strictly supervise their assistants because many lived with the owner and spent their spare time working around the shop or its yard. Work as a shop assistant meant low pay and long hours; most shops opened at six o'clock in the morning and closed at midnight, and assistants had very short or no breaks at all. In the 1880s and 1890s, municipal authorities and labor activists tried to remedy some of the worst conditions by decreeing the closing of stores on Sundays and holidays. These attempts were not very successful because most merchants still compelled their employees to do other work, such as stocking the shelves, or they completely disregarded the decrees. The bans also did not extend to shops and stores selling food and provisions, which engaged a majority of retail employees. Moscow's shop assistants were the first to organize, doing so in 1861, followed by those in Odessa, Kursk, Nizhnii Novgorod, and other cities. These associations tried to protect retail workers from exploitative working conditions and to improve their cultural level, although their primary functions became charity and mutual aid.[12]

The fledgling trade union press portrayed the life of a shop assistant as one of long workdays and a joyless, austere lifestyle. A feuilleton in a 1907 issue of *Vestnik torgovykh sluzhashchikh* (Bulletin of Commercial Employees) portrayed the sales transaction from the point of view of workers, showing the fatigue and indignity they faced each day at their posts. From this perspective, consumers appeared as "hundreds of hands—greedy, fearless, haughty, timid"—who overwhelmed the shop assistant with hundreds of despotic demands. The shop assistant was required to "Be attentive!" and to make the merchandise sparkle with deft words and tempting promises. If customers tormented sales clerks, got on their nerves, or accused them of lying, the assistants were required to smile, soothe cranky customers with a gentle phrase or two, and attentively and humbly look into an unruly customer's impudent face. According to the story, female shoppers brought their own peculiar demands: one wanted to flirt, another lost a lover and so wanted something in a dark, sorrowful color. And if one of these capricious customers did not buy anything, then the shop assistant suffered the wrath of the proprietor. After a day spent indulging the whims of shoppers, assistants returned to their small, squalid, dark dwellings. The feuil-leton ended with the query, "And this is life?"[13]

The revolution's goals of eradicating the exploitation of the propertied classes and ameliorating the miseries of the working classes extended to the struggle that the Bolsheviks perceived in the relationships between owner/worker and consumer/worker. Soviet commercial officials and trade union leaders both pledged to upgrade the position of retail workers by creating bet-ter working conditions for them and redefining their responsibilities and rela-tionship to consumers. Linguistic changes signaled this shift. After 1917, the term *prikazchik* (shop assistant), which had previously been routinely used, fell out of use. Retail workers were thereafter dubbed "workers of the counter" (*rabotniki prilavki*), "sales workers," or simply "sellers." These new titles divested sales workers of associations with the age-old term *prikazchik,* which in Mus-covy had referred to a government official, and disassociated them from notions of servility to customers. The titles also signified recognition of retail workers as part of the larger corps of the proletariat.[14] The term *consumer* (*potrebitel'*) also became common. Prior to that, consumers had been called "customers" or "shoppers" (*pokupateli*). This change in terminology denoted a de-emphasis on individualism and choice and an emphasis on collectivity and the mass market.

New terms also reflected the changed conditions under which goods were bought and sold, signifying that shopping was no longer a leisurely pastime but a straightforward matter of meeting material needs. Retail employees no longer romanced shoppers over the counter with affable chitchat or drew them into heated haggling matches. Instead of selling goods, they issued (*otpuskat'*) them. Workers no longer served or waited on consumers, either; they supplied or satisfied (*udovletvoriatsia*) their requests. At GUM and other state stores, a new protocol—the three-queue system—redefined shopping. In order to buy some-thing, a customer first approached the counter and asked a worker for items in the quantities he or she wished to buy. The worker calculated the cost of the items, wrote an order, and gave it to the customer, who proceeded to the cashier, presented the order, and paid for it. The customer then returned to the counter and presented the order and receipt to the sales worker or, at GUM, to a worker in the Control Department, who issued the merchandise.[15] The establishment of the three-queue system transformed the nature and mean-ing of buying and selling. If sales workers no longer sold, customers no longer shopped. The three-queue system, as well as long lines and a lack of selection, made lingering over merchandise and mulling choices difficult. Persisting until the end of the Soviet Union, this retail regimen represented a departure from the tenets of modern mass retailing, which relied on looking, browsing, touch-ing, and talking to generate sales and customer loyalty. The three-queue design instead inaugurated a system that came to symbolize the inefficiency and unresponsiveness of the state's bureaucracy.

Commercial officials and trade union activists hoped to staff state and cooperative stores with workers who fit the new titles, but discussions in the press reveal that they believed that Russia lacked such individuals. According to the officials and activists, the existing corps of retail workers had internalized deferential, adulatory attitudes that degraded them and jeopardized consumers. As one official remarked in *Pravada* in 1925, "The old commercial specialists, the former masters' shop assistants, do not correspond to the new demands."[16] These workers were often good and honest, he argued, but "old habits" (*privychki*) still held sway among them. Because they had been brought up in the "old merchant milieu," they acted in the interests of the owner, not the consumer, and would sell the poorest-quality merchandise to a worker or peasant "with a clear conscience."[17] Pointing out the ignominy of these old attitudes and habits, one journalist for *Golos rabotnika* (Voice of the Worker) asked, "Do we really want the groveling shop assistant of old? The type who called out to customers: 'What may I do for you?' and upon their departure rang out: 'Good luck!' Or do we want courteousness and attentiveness of a different sort?"[18] Union activists like these hoped to give sales workers some dignity by training them to act in the interests of the consumer without trading their self-respect in the process.

According to this view, the retail transaction should not resemble a social encounter. Parties to it should not play the roles of master and servant, the customer lording over the retail worker and the worker exhibiting a sly, cloying submissiveness. Instead, an exchange should be transparent and professional, with both parties exhibiting a restrained, sober manner and no pretense of superiority or debasement. Being an obliging, courteous, and attentive retail worker meant issuing the correct merchandise in an efficient and decorous manner, not serving, entertaining, cajoling, or even pleasing an individual shopper. However, the state's commercial officials did not completely abandon modern retailing's tenets of customer service. GUM outlined in its employee handbook the fundamentals of courteous customer service, which combined previous norms of well-mannered, helpful behavior with revolutionary ideals. Workers were exhorted to treat shoppers politely, to assist them in selecting items, to observe the established order for issuing them, and to ensure that customers were not delayed in lines. Workers were also instructed not to show a preference for one customer over another and not to read, hold personal conversations, wander around the store, show up to work drunk, or drink on the job.[19]

Given that the corps of state retail employees included individuals from widely different social backgrounds who had varying levels of experience, the prescription for a new kind of retail worker was not easy to fill. Many workers were new to the trade and lacked the skills necessary to courteously and efficiently assist consumers.[20] Still, experience did not necessarily guarantee the right attitude, skills, or manner. Late in the imperial period, the rule of attentive, polite customer service had been observed primarily at large, fashionable urban stores that cultivated reputations as trendsetters and respectable community leaders. Most merchants had relied on customary sales tactics that did not involve assisting customers so much as humoring and pressuring them into buying. Thus, even experienced shop assistants, whether they had been trained to assiduously attend to customers or to banter with and press them, found that many of their skills were outdated.

Reformers also recognized the need to reeducate consumers to understand that living in a socialist society meant showing respect for workers, being less demanding, and having more patience and trust. The trade union of commercial workers, which often found itself in the position of defending retail workers against the charges of consumers, became one of the most vocal critics of sales customs and practices that seemed to require deference from sales workers and to grant customers a license to abuse them. As one Volzhanin, a writer for *Golos rabotnika,* saw it, "lavka misunderstandings" in co-op stores were as often the result of the consumer's lack of understanding about the rights and responsibilities of workers as they were a worker's inattentive attitude.[21] In order to preserve the dignity of both, Volzhanin advocated a new exchange relationship based on educating consumers in a cooperative consciousness. Explaining the onerous demands placed on the sales worker during a workday—issuing merchandise to more than one hundred customers and dealing with their outbursts at the busiest hours—he argued that, although consumers tended to blame inattentiveness on a worker's "insufficient social training," consumers themselves were largely at fault. He chided them for their assumption that membership in a co-op gave them the right to receive merchandise out of turn, make remarks to sales workers, ask the price of things they did not intend to buy, comment on a store's deficiencies, or make small talk. All of these bad behaviors, he asserted, came from the old attitude of "I am the master of the worker." In conclusion, he offered the following solution: "We not only have to breed cultured *torgovtsy* [sellers] and *prikazchiki*, but a conscientious cooperative mass." Consumers had to realize that the worker was no longer a servant but master of a cooperative store, a position that required their respect, not "a cold shower of mistrust."[22]

The new job description for sales workers did not always sit well with some former shop assistants. Many who had taken pride in their positions, as well as in their trade union movement, experienced the new guidelines as "deskilling," a decline in their status from shop assistants to bureaucrats who merely issued products. Some sales workers also objected to what they perceived as the state's neglect of the consumer. They understood that, although retail workers played a different role on the sales floor, they were not completely at odds with their customers. After all, workers were also consumers, who, while trying to maintain their professional dignity, understood the plight of consumers. One self-declared group of "red sales workers" employed at Moskvoshvei's retail outlets, acknowledging the common cause of workers and consumers, argued that the problem with Soviet retailing was not the fault of either retail staff or shoppers but the sorry condition of state commerce.[23] Taking offense at the *Pravda* article cited above, this group of "politically conscious comrades," who rejected the idea that they were "the pupils of the old merchantry," drafted a letter to Moskvoshvei's board to express dedication to the task of reviving commerce and to demand respect for their profession and more concern for consumers. They argued that the way to win over customers was to satisfy the smallest of their caprices, to stock the greatest possible assortment of merchandise at all prices, and to introduce an endless array of new styles. The Moskvoshvei workers recognized that, through no fault of their own, their stores lacked all of these things but that they directly felt the wrath of the consumer, who ridiculed them and demanded explanations for deficiencies. Interestingly, this group of retail workers did not blame problems on consumers' misdeeds. Instead, they endorsed the tenets of modern retailing as the means to a strong socialist retail sector and blamed the state for the problems. Despite their critiques of retail workers and consumers, union journalists also recognized that blame lay primarily with the state. They admitted that a lack of experienced, capable commercial officials and the resultant mismanagement, deficits of popular merchandise, and high prices were larger problems that the reform of sales workers and consumers alone could not remedy.[24]

These discussions took place within the context of a series of highly publicized show trials that targeted the retail sector. In 1923, the state tried GUM's chairman of the board, Aleksei Belov, his assistant, Aleksei Mishukov, and other executives on charges of failing to accomplish GUM's mission of supplying the population with consumer goods and conquering the market for the state, as well negligence and unscrupulousness in discharging their duties. Because of a series of disastrously unprofitable agreements contracted the year before, these executives stood accused of incurring losses for GUM that amounted to hundreds of thousands of gold rubles.[25] In 1925, in another high-profile trial, the manager of GUM's Leningrad division and other executives faced charges of taking part in a money-making scheme with Solomon Burshtein, former first-guild merchant and a GUM procurement agent, to sell Oriental carpets from GUM's warehouses. Although Burshtein had disappeared by the time of the trial, the others were charged with counterrevolution and sentenced to prison.[26] It is difficult to know the extent to which the trial uncovered illegal activities and the extent to which the trial stemmed from the state's desire to stage a political spectacle that identified scapegoats. Illegal activity, however, was apparently rampant in all levels of GUM. Investigators routinely discovered price and merchandise switching, accounting irregularities, bribe giving and taking, the sending of merchandise without an order for it, and cash and merchandise shortages, as well as employees independently contracting purchases with GUM's funds.[27]

Commercial officials understandably had a difficult time balancing consumers' expectations of helpful assistance and considerate treatment with efforts to assert the class prerogative of the workers. The problem of redefining the retail transaction came down to determining the degree to which retail workers should subordinate their interests to consumers in the service of building a functioning retail network and the extent to which consumers should readjust their expectations in the interests of working-class well-being.

The Institution of Soviet Complaint

Throughout the economically erratic decade of the 1920s, consumers railed against the dysfunction that afflicted their daily shopping routines in letters to popular newspapers and in complaint books. The kinds of complaints that appeared in these two media were similar, although their formats and the procedures for registering the complaints differed. Drawing on the legacy of such popular prerevolutionary newspapers as *Moskovskii listok, Odesskii listok,* and *St. Peterburgskii listok,* NEP-era mass-circulation newspapers provided a public forum for readers to vent their frustrations. Required to pay expenses out of their profits, publishers needed to appeal to a broad audience, but they also had to support the goals of the state and the party organs that often subsidized publication.[28] Emulating proven formulas and turning them to political ends helped newspapers like *Rabochaia Moskva* and *Vecherniaia Moskva* turn a profit and satisfy their political sponsors at the same time. Ideally, features that exposed the transgressions of private retailers served as a type of propaganda that could help persuade readers of the wisdom of a state-dominated economy. *Rabochaia Moskva*'s recurring column "Gde nazhivaetsia chastnik" (Where the Private Businessman Gets Rich), for example, which chronicled the unprincipled pursuit of profit, seemed designed to disclose the self-interested and unethical practices of private businesses and thereby justify their gradual elimination. Just as often as they castigated private merchants and traders, however, these newspapers revealed the shortcomings of state and cooperative enterprises. Contests such as *Rabochaia Moskva*'s 1926 "Who Is the Worst Retailer?" invited readers to expose the deficiencies, abuses, and unscrupulous practices of state, cooperative, and private retailers that were "particularly dangerous to the interests of the mass consumer."[29] This contest, whose sponsors vowed to conduct an investigation of the incidents reported in each entry, was only the most pointed of features in a newspaper that regularly ran complaints, and it seems to have been devised to educate as much as to entertain readers.

Published complaints in the mass media took several forms, ranging from brief, reportage-type items, to anecdotes punctuated with sarcastic asides or a punch line, to mini-epics of frustrated consumption. Of those who penned letters to newspapers, most were men and part of the *aktiv,* worker or peasant correspondents (*rabkor or sel'kor*) who often had literary, artistic, or journalistic aspirations and contributed to newspapers on a regular basis. Other contributors most likely fit the profile of the "middling" worker or employee, who participated in the new Soviet public culture by reading and sometimes writing to newspapers. These writers may not have reflected the voice of the masses, but they showed relatively high interest in politics and in having a voice in state media. By expressing themselves publicly, therefore, they became the individuals who helped shape socialist norms, values, and behaviors.[30]

The complaint book appears to have originated in late-nineteenth-century Russia in the railroad industry and from there spread to other sectors of the service economy.[31] In the Soviet period, the complaint book became a symbolic guarantee of popular control of state institutions and open, equal access, as well as an instrument for achieving the regime's objectives of social leveling, economic centralization, and cultural training. In 1926, Narkomtorg (the People's Commissariat of Commerce) mandated that all state, cooperative, joint-stock, and private commercial enterprises, as well as markets, keep in a visible, accessible place a complaint book (*kniga zhalob*) and post its rules and the name of the individual responsible for maintaining it. Unlike a newspaper, which required a complainant to have some literary skill and win approval from the editor, the complaint book was ostensibly open to all, although some degree of literacy was necessary. According to Narkomtorg's guidelines, all a customer had to do to register a complaint was request the book from the manager or other designated employee, give an account of the offending incident(s) in the column provided, and then sign the complaint and supply an address for follow-up purposes. The complaint book also provided a column next to the customer's entry for the manager or employee against whom the complaint was lodged to respond. Within two weeks an inspector attached to the retailer would investigate the case, record the findings in a third column, and send a reply to the complainant.[32]

Narkomtorg officials apparently foresaw that disputes might ensue and took precautions to try to guarantee customers the right to lodge a complaint without infringing on the rights of workers. Realizing that employees might not easily surrender the complaint book, they stipulated that customers denied the book could ask a police officer to file a charge on their behalf or file a complaint at the commissariat's local branch office. They also tried to protect workers from false allegations by requiring complainants to give their names and addresses. Narkomtorg took seriously the right of consumers to complain, but it also held them responsible for their statements, declaring that an individual who misused the book or used abusive language in expressing a complaint would be reprimanded.

In theory, this prescribed, written procedure routed each complaint through the same avenues, eliminating the inequities presumed to be inherent in the retail exchange by granting workers and consumers the same rights of recourse. The establishment of specific procedures suggests a desire to wean workers and consumers from tactics of persuasion, intimidation, and bargaining and to accustom them to a legalistic system that documented grievances, allowed a defense, and mandated evidence gathering and resolution. In essence, the complaint book was intended to remove the emotion and personal idiosyncrasies associated with customary practices and install a standardized scheme with the state as the ultimate, supposedly objective, mediator. In practice, the process often broke down. Although the book was theoretically freely available, store managers sometimes guarded it and did not always willingly surrender it. One reporter, who surveyed the contents and procedures of complaint books in Moscow's cooperative stores, found that in most, the book resided in the manager's office and was not so easy to get. In other stores, managers did not relinquish the book unless customers first told them what they intended to write.[33] Sometimes managers also reportedly asked for personal documents from customers before handing over the book, a request that presumably intimidated them.[34]

The rules established to govern the complaint process imply that the public act of writing in a complaint book was rife with potential volatility. Unlike sending a letter to a newspaper, writing in a complaint book required a consumer to publicly declare his or her intent to criticize a store and/or its workers, to ask for the book from possibly unsympathetic or even hostile employees, and then write an indictment in full view of those accused. Choosing this mode of complaint also meant that no intermediary or more educated or savvy family member or adviser was present to help polish the complaint with rhetorical flourishes or official language, nor would an editor refine the prose. A complainant had to rely on his or her own instincts as a storyteller, awareness of revolutionary principles, and skill in attaching his or her social identity and experience to those principles in order to write an effective complaint. Since complaints could be easily construed as the expression of discontent by "former people" (i.e., former landowners, industrialists, and merchants) or speculators, a consumer needed to construct a legitimate complaining persona. Claiming membership in one of the "right" social classes allowed individuals privileges denied those who belonged to the "wrong" ones.[35] Many consumers relied on the persona of the worker-consumer or citizen-consumer, an individual legally entitled to access, respectful treatment, and a means of recourse.

Complaints published in newspapers differed from complaint book entries in their tone and in the devices writers used to compose them. While letters to newspapers often relied on humor, complaint book entries brimmed with hostility and personal resentment and more closely resembled personal denunciations, complete with accusations that often identified employees with telltale characteristics. Complaint books also gave retail employees a chance to respond. Many took the opportunity to discredit complaining shoppers by signaling their political unreliability and attempts to undermine ideals of egalitarianism. Some of the bitterness captured in complaint books reflects the fact that complaints were written on the fly, in the heat of conflict, and thus reproduced the emotions and urgency of a conflict in process. The differing purposes of mass newspapers and complaint books also accounted for differences in tone. While newspapers did not shy away from controversial topics or refrain from mercilessly ridiculing undesirable social types or offensive behaviors, they seldom singled out a retail worker by name, although private traders were fair game. Also, editors may have deleted or rewritten especially virulent passages to make them more palatable for a broad reading audience or to ward off state and party critics who might accuse the newspaper of undermining state enterprises. Alternatively, editors may have embellished the letters to entertain readers. Furthermore, unlike the aktiv, who contributed to the popular dailies, GUM's complainants did not constitute an organized group or contribute in a systematic way to public media; most described themselves as workers, employees, housewives and mothers, or trade union and party members. They were not writing for a reading audience and most likely wanted to express what they viewed as a legitimate grievance or hoped to gain a personal advantage or to retaliate against a worker they perceived as rude or uncooperative. Thus, they had no motivation to tone down a complaint. Indeed, knowing the complaint would be forwarded to a higher authority, the impulse may have been to ratchet up the rhetoric. Finally, there is one similarity worth mentioning. Like the aktiv, GUM's complainants were primarily men. Although evidence indicates that women bore the daily burden of procuring food and other goods, many men apparently also endured the frustrations of the Soviet retail system. Men enjoyed certain advantages, including higher literacy rates, which may have given them more confidence in their ability to make public declarations.[36] More men also joined the Communist Party.[37] Both the revolutionary call to wage class struggle in the commercial-industrial sectors and chronic shortages made retailing and consumption highly charged issues. Under those conditions, policing the state stores may have been viewed as a suitable political activity, even a duty, for men who belonged to the party or were at all politically inclined.

Extraordinary Misadventures in the Land of Soviet Consumption

Rabochaia Moskva's contest to identify the worst retailer sparked a creative impulse in many disgruntled consumers. Some ambitious entrants constructed fantastic tales of frustrated consumption, which distilled the flaws in the state and cooperative retail sectors into mini-epics of a maddening pursuit to obtain consumer goods. In such tales, a hapless consumer, who initially exudes faith in the system, suffers one humiliating ordeal after another in an absurd world of systemic dysfunction, complete with impertinent, ignorant, and negligent workers and bureaucratic bungling, all of which ultimately foil the goal of acquisition. Tales of frustrated consumption contained elements of folk and fairy tales, including a heroic quest, a feature that Nancy Ries has also identified in perestroika-era "tales of heroic shopping," a genre she likens to a lament.[38] However, whereas the tales of Ries's subjects most often concluded with triumph over obstacles and the procurement of some item, the stories that NEP-era consumers told ended unhappily, without success. The world reproduced in these complaints more closely resembles that portrayed in the popular short stories of Mikhail Zoshchenko and novels of Il'ia Il'f and Evgenii Petrov, a darkly humorous world of outlandish, shady characters and ridiculously trying situations. In spite of this difference between perestroika- and NEP-era tales, Ries's idea of a ritual lament is a helpful way to analyze consumer complaints, since they exhibit a particular set of literary and rhetorical devices that served to express frustration and despair.

Tales of frustrated consumption were particularly effective at challenging the state's guarantee to make consumer goods available to everyone. The significance of the state's glaring failure to keep that promise was made all too clear in these stories, as writers related how an activity as seemingly innocuous as shopping could quickly devolve into political capitulation. One such tale opened with the author introducing himself as "a principled person, someone who shops only in state stores," who went to Mostorg and asked "in a quiet voice" for a chisel.[39] The writer's self-introduction, explanation of his purpose, and representation of his manner are important elements of the consumer complaint. Identifying himself as principled, the writer conspicuously aligned himself with the regime's campaign to conquer the private market. His stated intention of purchasing an item used in productive work and not, for instance, a necktie perhaps conveyed his status as a laborer or his purposeful mode of consumption. He also signaled his civility. Noting that he asked for a chisel quietly, he implied that he did not transgress rules of propriety; he went to the store to make a legitimate request, not to pester workers or waste their time. On closer examination, however, his proclamation of himself as a principled person is complicated. It is not entirely clear whether his assumption of the role of a conscientious, loyal Soviet citizen was a genuine assertion of faith or an ironical device used to mock the state's campaign against private retailers. The principled shopper's story continued with his revelation that, after a sales worker showed him a chisel, the worker told him that it was not for sale because no one had yet put a price on it. The shopper then related that he proceeded to another department, where he successfully obtained a hammock but was sent to another floor to buy hooks for it. In this department, sales workers informed him that hooks could not be sold because the accountant had not yet processed the invoices for them. Presenting himself next in the sporting goods department, the persistent consumer found that employees there were too busy taking inventory to assist him. Frustrated at every turn, he headed for the elevator to go to the store manager's office to lodge a complaint, only to be met by an "Out of Order" sign on the elevator, a symbol of the broken-down state of retail facilities. Running up four flights of stairs, he reached the office on the fifth floor but, once there, found no remedy. The manager rebuffed him, deeming his complaints unreasonable: "Why are you so dissatisfied?" he demanded. "We have to take inventory. Prices are necessary! So there!" In the end, the once-ethical, now-beaten consumer reported that he "quietly" headed to a private store and bought everything he needed in three minutes. He concluded his tale of woe with an exclamation that contained more than a touch of offended sarcasm: "To think that I, a principled person, am shopping in a private store! And yet they ask me why I am dissatisfied!"[40]

This story of a bizarre ordeal in a state department store resembles a political morality tale, with the moral revealed in the principled consumer's admission of defeat and his repairing to a private store. Well-intentioned consumers were being driven to the brink by the short-sighted apathy of retail employees and bureaucrats and an inefficient, unresponsive system, and they ended up surrendering their principles by buying from private merchants. While each individual offense at Mostorg may have been relatively minor, together they added up to the conclusion that the store's failures were creating disaffection among potential customers and, ultimately, would undermine the fight against private enterprise and the promise to raise Soviet citizens' standard of living.

In another cleverly devastating mini-epic of frustrated consumption, published in *Rabochaia gazeta* in 1927, one Zvonov (probably a pseudonym derived from the Russian word *zvon,* meaning banter or gossip), mocked GUM's pretensions to being the universal provider. Zvonov began his letter with a recollection of the rumination that led to his decision to order a shotgun: "I wanted to buy a 16-gauge Berdan shotgun and decided to order one. But from where? From GUM, of course, since they have good-quality merchandise and will promptly send anything that you could desire. After all, GUM is a state enterprise and cares about [its customers]."[41] As in the tale of the principled person, the reader of this shotgun story cannot be quite sure whether, with this profession of faith, Zvonov was feigning credulity or accurately representing his initially well-disposed attitude. Either way, this prelude sets Zvonov up as a loyal supporter destined for disenchantment. The tale continued, Zvonov recalling that he mailed a thirty-ruble deposit for the gun to GUM in August, but after one month, he still had not received it. Indicating his continued optimism, Zvonov explained that he thought the delay was due to GUM's attempt to find for him the highest-quality gun, "one capable of hitting targets better than any other gun," a declaration that exposed the worthlessness of another of the retailer's vaunted advertising claims. He waited, but when no package arrived, he sent another letter inquiring about the status of his order, to which GUM replied that no guns were available and that as soon as the firm received 16-gauge shotguns it would send one to him. Zvonov wrote back asking instead for a 20-gauge. "No luck," he wrote. "Still no gun. Again GUM fell silent." The image of a large, powerful state enterprise losing its voice is particularly evocative, emblematic of the retailer's and, by extension, the state's bureaucratic indifference. Zvonov reported that after another month, he sent a third letter to request either the gun or his money back. At the end of November, he received a refund of twenty-nine rubles, eighty-four kopeks, in other words, sixteen kopeks short of the sum he had sent three months earlier, an offense he regarded as "hitting the customer's pocket twice." Conveying a sense of having been ignored and cheated, he ended his story with a sarcastic swipe at GUM's self-proclaimed preeminence: "Anyone who wants to order a shotgun should absolutely order one from GUM, at its address in the Trading Rows on Red Square in Moscow. GUM will send a high-quality gun . . . without delay. Isn't that delightful? Well done GUM! You really pulled it together."[42]

This last remark about the Red Square location further amplified the retailer's deficiencies. Obviously, GUM could not live up to the reputation that its presence in Red Square should warrant. By pointing out its proximity to the seat of state power, Zvonov implied a connection between GUM's failure and the shortcomings of the Soviet government.

Despite its creative flair and blatant contradiction of GUM's mission, Zvonov's letter failed to persuade GUM's administrators to make amends. The inspector assigned to investigate the incident concluded that Zvonov's order had fallen victim to "bureaucratic entanglements" among GUM, the Arms Trust, and the Hunters' Union.[43] Instead of trying to resolve the problem, however, the investigator quibbled over the date of receipt of Zvonov's order, essentially assigning him the blame, and exonerated GUM's employees, claiming they had committed no wrongdoing. Backing up the inspector, GUM's chairman of the board and the manager of the Inspection Department penned a joint letter to *Rabochaia gazeta* affirming the firm's innocence, a judgment that perforce rendered the facts of the case, as they put it, "irrelevant." The two ended their letter by declaring that since it was not GUM's fault that the order was delayed, Citizen Zvonov's remarks "do not correspond to reality."[44] What is most significant about Zvonov's and the retailer's communiqués is not that GUM failed but that administrators expressed no regret and seemed to resist trying to appease the customer in any way. There is no reason to doubt that the firm's managers and board members wanted to provide customers with quality merchandise and good service. Their denial of the veracity of Zvonov's experience and assertion of an alternate version of reality, however, exposed a gap between an official narrative and consumers' daily experiences.

More often than penning long tales like these, complainants who sent letters to newspapers wrote brief accounts of their experiences that pinpointed one flaw. Complaints of pricing irregularities were very common and usually consisted of very short, straightforward statements of, for example, a difference in the price of Chlorodent toothpaste at Store No. 11 of the Baumanskii cooperative and at Kommunar's Store No. 25, a one-ruble difference in the price of Red October cocoa at the Tanners' Co-op and a nearby MSPO co-op, or a disparity between the marked price of tea and the price asked by the seller at the Doprosoiuz cooperative.[45]

Despite the brevity of the majority of published complaints, however, many exhibited a sense of humor and flair for storytelling and resembled anecdotes more than statements of complaint. Several of the complaints about poor-quality goods published as part of *Rabochaia Moskva*'s contest ended with a punch line of sorts. One reader lamented the purchase of an extraordinary "ten-minute ham" from a cooperative on Maroseika Street in Moscow that spoiled on his eleven-minute walk home. According to him, when he tried to exchange the ham for a fresh one, the manager refused, declaring, "We are only responsible for the quality of our products ten minutes from the moment of purchase!"

The flabbergasted consumer reported that he left, wondering, "If I live eleven minutes from the store, does that mean that I will always have rotten food?"[46] "Citizeness Lukanina" complained that she found a rat in a loaf of black bread purchased at the Podbel'skii co-op in Moscow. She asserted that she would have gladly taken a fly instead.[47] The co-op responded to her charge in print, acknowledging that a rat can end up baked in bread if a bakery uses unprocessed flour, but denied that the Podbel'skii co-op used such flour.[48] A Comrade Suchkov claimed that four times he had found "big, whiskered roaches" in the black bread purchased at the MOGES co-op. Accepting his fate, Suchkov concluded that "all the time I thought that I was buying bread with roaches, but now I see that I bought roaches with bread." MOGES flatly denied Suchkov's allegation.[49] Another unlucky consumer wrote that despite being "a strong *narod* with iron-clad constitutions," they could not stomach the bread produced by Bakery No. 5, part of the Proletarian Might co-op, which, he charged, was charred, crumpled, and sometimes adorned on the bottom with bits of charcoal and all kinds of things baked into it. In this instance, the co-op board admitted that bread from this bakery was sometimes burnt and crumpled, and it reported that it had instructed the bakery's administration to institute stricter monitoring procedures.[50] Even complaints unconnected to *Rabochaia Moskva*'s contest resembled anecdotes, although their writers did not usually use humor in describing their experiences. One woman found neither sympathy nor justice when she discovered that one leg of the pair of stockings she had just bought was longer than the other. She reported that she returned to the store to make an exchange twenty minutes after purchasing them but met opposition. The sales worker agreed that the stockings were defective but reacted with indifference. When the consumer demanded another pair, he retorted, "We aren't money changers. You yourself ruined the stockings." Shocked, she asked, "Just for fun?" to which he replied, "Who knows? We don't know you." An argument reportedly broke out, but in the end the woman left with the same pair of ruined stockings.[51]

Consumers who registered complaints about poor-quality and defective products in GUM's complaint books tended to treat the sale of such goods as a personal injustice. Unhappy over a manager's refusal to exchange a defective lamp, someone named Minakov asked the board to attend to this problem and, in his closing statement, pleaded that GUM not make buyers its "victims."[52] One man who returned a pair of kidskin gloves two months after purchasing them from GUM's Haberdashery Store No. 2 because they had torn claimed they were defective. Adding that he would not have knowingly bought such a poor-quality pair of gloves, he insinuated that shoddy merchandise had been foisted upon him.[53] The inspector cast doubt on his accusations, denying that GUM sold defective gloves and advising him to return them to the store where he had purchased them. The customer Kireev found himself left in the lurch when a bed he ordered by mail from GUM arrived broken. GUM's inspector concluded that the bed had been damaged en route to Kireev's residence, and, therefore, the railroad, not GUM, was responsible for the damage.[54]

Consumers also objected to behaviors they perceived as dishonest, unsanitary, or inefficient and, therefore, obsolete. Referring to what he called the "outdated" methods in a Moscow Larek store, a male student wrote to *Rabochaia Moskva* to protest a sales clerk's ploy of pressing his fingers on the scale when weighing butter, thus giving him less than he paid for. He also deplored the sales clerk's unsanitary habit of using his fingers to add more butter to the order.[55] "Pokupatel'nitsa" (a female shopper) likewise found repulsive the habit that shop clerks had of licking their fingers before taking a piece of paper to wrap food products.[56] "Prickly" faulted Moscow's Smychka co-op for selling stale bread, not cleaning dirty counters, and failing to organize a lavka commission.[57] Deploring such offensive behaviors and the neglect and mistreatment of customers, one contest entrant in the *Rabochaia Moskva* contest wondered why "workers don't try to win over the shopper."[58] As evidence, he cited the example of two stalls that sat side by side, one private, the other a co-op. At the co-op, he charged, there was usually only one shop assistant and one could not ask him questions; he also complained that the co-op frequently posted announcements such as "Closed for vacation." Next door, he countered, the private vendor was "doing all kinds of business." Another agreed with this assessment, questioning the state's ability to beat private retailers at their own game. Expressing disappointment that Larek did not have a business regimen worthy of its size and stature, he wrote that if one asked for cigarettes, stamps, or anything else, they did not have it. "This," he deduced, "is not a business."[59] The chronically inefficient protocol at the Red Presnia cooperative store got on the nerves of another consumer, prompting him to nominate the co-op as worst retailer. He reported that every morning a long line of despondent customers formed at the cashier's desk, waiting as the cashier sat totaling their bills. Meanwhile, the sales clerks idled about, passing the time in friendly conversation. Why, this frustrated consumer asked, couldn't the sales workers figure bills so that the cashier could attend to her immediate task of taking money?[60] To these and other complainants such practices were not only unacceptable but unworthy of state and cooperative stores.

Retail workers' domineering attitudes, inflexibility, and bureaucratic attitudes and behaviors inspired many other complaints. Criticisms of ill-mannered and abusive shop assistants were not new, of course, but appearing in media established for the working classes, they showed the conflict between elevating the status of the worker in society and democratizing consumption. One

Rabochaia Moskva reader submitted a story about a despotic sales worker at the state's main tea store whose exacting ways exasperated him. According to his complaint, when he asked the worker for four hundred grams of sugar, the worker evenly replied, "Two kilograms."[61] The consumer protested that he needed only four hundred grams, to which the worker responded as he weighed out two kilos, "Take two kilograms and you will have your four hundred grams." This suggestion caught him off guard, and he stopped to consider it. The delay irritated the worker, who barked, "Don't hold up the line. Take it or leave it. This is not a pharmacy!"[62] This rebuke let the patron know that he should not expect any kind of special treatment or inconvenience others waiting in line.

GUM's complaint books contain descriptions of many such trivial incidents. One occurred when a male consumer approached the worker Smirnov in the main GUM store's food department to buy some sugar. Noticing that on the right side of the bin there were dirty pieces of sugar, he asked Smirnov to give him sugar from the left side. Smirnov refused, maintaining that he was "not supposed to pick out [*vybirat'*] sugar, only issue it."[63] When an inspector questioned him, Smirnov explained that he was only following instructions that forbade him to choose between lumps of sugar, adding that, anyway, the sugar was not dirty, except for two pieces, on which a few specks of dust had accidentally settled. In this instance, the inspector judged the complainant's version "true," and Smirnov "completely wrong," although the victory was a small one, given that no concrete action was taken. The customer Temichev, also finding himself caught up in a frustratingly annoying circumstance, objected to the bureaucratic indifference that reigned at GUM's store in the Sretenka neighborhood. He wrote in the complaint book that, upon entering the men's shoe department, he asked a seller whether or not size 6 men's galoshes were available. When his question went unanswered, Temichev went to stand in line. When he finally made it to the front of the line, the seller informed him that there were no size 6 galoshes. The manager's version deflected Temichev's criticism of workers' "bureaucratic, formal attitude toward their duties" by denying the incident was motivated by spite and calling it bad luck.[64] He explained that the sales worker told Temichev to wait in line because there was a big crowd of shoppers, and it just so happened that when he reached the front, all size 6 galoshes had already been sold. According to the accused worker, his reply to Temichev was not bureaucratic but a way to ensure a rational, equal treatment of a large crowd of customers.

The complaint process, especially as captured in GUM's complaint books, shows the conflicts of interest at play on sales floors. Registered alongside each other, consumers' complaints, employees' responses, and the findings of inspectors suggest that workers interpreted any request that deviated from a narrowly defined set of standardized procedures as proceeding from a manipulative self-interest or peevish personal whim, neither of which was worth indulging. This interpretation was in line with the agenda of respecting a worker's dignity and treating all shoppers equally, even if pettiness also played a role. To the fastidious Smirnov, a customer's request for special handling violated his understanding of egalitarianism. His refusal to sift through sugar cubes demonstrated his adherence to egalitarianism and a refusal to discriminate among customers, or at least that is how Smirnov framed it. After all, as he might have asserted, someone has to take the dirty sugar. Why not this customer?

Of all the charges lodged against retail workers, rudeness was the most common. Of approximately 285 complaints registered at several GUM stores between fall 1927 and early 1928 and summarized in reports for management, one-third concerned employees' rudeness and inattentiveness.[65] Like charges of bureaucratism, complaints of rudeness gave vent to frustrations on both sides. In their complaint entries, customers commonly depicted retail workers as petty tyrants of the counter who wielded undue power in obstructing their rightful access to goods and who verbally abused or ignored them. Moreover, they considered these behaviors intolerable in a state enterprise dedicated to serving the laboring classes. GUM employees disputed the accuracy of these accusations and tried to turn the tables on customers by discrediting their complaints with assertions that workers had been mistreated by self-centered, demanding shoppers who disrespected them and disregarded the rules of state stores. In one case, the shopper Vasil'ev protested a female sales worker's lack of tactfulness (*taktichnost'*) when, after making him wait ten minutes to show him a pair of gloves, she allegedly turned to him with the sullen remark, "Here, have a look."[66] An inspector saw it differently, determining that the worker was not guilty of any wrongdoing, given that she was busy with another customer.[67] As he explained it, having to wait on more than one customer at a time was taxing, and Vasil'ev had no right to expect her attention. According to this reasoning, helping one customer and replying to another's question were mutually exclusive activities. Workers were not to be burdened by multiple, simultaneous requests.

Another male shopper, Sevriugin, called a young female sales worker's inattention "completely intolerable."[68] According to his account, the worker, Bespalova, informed him she could not show him a shirt because she was helping two other shoppers, but he got the impression that she was "leaning on" a decree of the Moscow soviet that provided for retail workers to wait on only one customer at a time. The inspector dispatched to investigate reported that he went into the store incognito three times to observe Bespalova at work, and not once did he witness any mistreatment or neglect of customers. He instead speculated about Sevriugin's character, pointing out a "series of motifs" in his complaint that he believed showed Sevriugin as a customer "completely lacking in conscientiousness toward the sales worker." Sevriugin's "inappropriate language" and "illegal" demands and his insistence that Bespalova leave the counter to show him to the manager's office struck the inspector as not only unreasonable but criminal. To make matters worse, Bespalova was a young, female apprentice, making Sevriugin's behavior particularly inappropriate. The inspector, therefore, deemed the complaint "groundless."[69] Finally, a customer named Gorbachev complained that sales workers at the Vindavskii GUM treated customers rudely and disrespectfully. He cited the worker, Bazhenov, who, he stated, told him that there was no cheesecloth in stock. When Gorbachev pointed out the cheesecloth to him, Bazhenov allegedly replied angrily, "You don't have to teach me," but he made no move to get it for Gorbachev. Instead, he informed the customer that he could not issue the item since it was not in his section.[70] The store manager defended Bazhenov, pointing out that the sales worker treated customers very politely and that no other complaints had been made against him. He furthermore denied the customer's version of events, claiming that Gorbachev had asked for calico, not cheesecloth, and that Bazhenov had informed him that calico was located in the textiles section. He further claimed that Gorbachev wanted to be issued merchandise out of turn, an accusation that cast suspicion on him.[71] The inspector, however, disagreed with the manager, ordering him to pay attention to this "extremely intolerable occurrence" and immediately eliminate such incidents from the store. He then warned him that, if another similar complaint about Bazhenov was registered, his rudeness would then be an "established fact."[72] The inspector's attempt to establish evidentiary benchmarks is noteworthy. One complaint was apparently insufficient evidence. Certainly, the inspector meant to suggest a reasonable policy toward employees whose behavior brought them censure, but his decision asserted that he, as a representative of the state, would decide how much evidence constituted an authentication of events.

Some complainants understood that inattentive, rude behaviors had greater consequences than their own offended sensibilities. Two male customers, both members of trade unions, wrote that they held GUM accountable for the worker Shefer's "completely intolerable rudeness and inattentiveness."[73] The men protested that Shefer refused to answer their question about the price of linens because he was showing them to another customer. They reported that, after their third query, Shefer tersely answered, "I can't talk to you. I am busy." The men warned that failure to correct such problems would lead to the widespread repudiation of state commerce. The inspector was unmoved. He claimed that he had written statements from witnesses that Shefer had not treated the

two rudely. In addition, he stated that since Shefer was busy with other customers, he could not be held accountable for being rude.[74]

The bitter accusations and counter-accusations reflected a clash between the
desire to provide consumers with a pleasant shopping environment and knowledgeable, capable assistance and to ensure workers a workplace free from abuse
and gratuitous demands. What consumers depicted as a worker's blunt reply
or obstruction of their right to goods, retail employees represented as a customer's presumptuous expectation of personalized service or an infraction of
regulations established to ensure workers' rights. This contestation of rights
was clearly detailed in the case of a Comrade Zhivotovskii, who portrayed
himself as a customer oppressed by bureaucratic, arbitrary worker-despots who
obstructed his attempts to purchase goods at GUM's egg and poultry store; in
short, he charged that they were ultimately serving their own, personal interests instead of meeting consumers' material needs. Zhivotovskii expressed
anger at what he perceived as the violation of his civil rights when, in protesting
a GUM store manager's brusque refusal to issue him products fifteen minutes
prior to the store's posted lunch break, he asked, "Is it right to refuse to issue
products to me . . . and to deny me the complaint book?"[75] In the next sentence,
he answered his own question: "I think it is not only improper but even illegal
[bezzakonno]." Zhivotovskii also expressed frustration with bureaucratic obfus-
cation. He reported that, when he asked the manager why the policy of closing
earlier than the scheduled lunch break was not posted on the door or window,
the manager reportedly answered that the public is notified about the "order
of business" through general announcements, not in individual stores. The inspector, however, argued that it was Zhivotovskii who violated the principle of
civil rights and legal decrees, citing Zhivotovskii's failure to comply with the
Moscow soviet's decree permitting retail stores to close ten or fifteen minutes
prior to the posted closing time in order to allow workers to issue products to
buyers already in the store and still receive their entire lunch break.[76] Likewise,
when a male party member named Chamov termed "intolerable" GUM's underhanded practice of admitting friends and acquaintances of employees into
the store after the close of business to make special deals with them, a manager
claimed that Chamov had simply failed to observe the store's operating hours,
and, therefore, deemed his complaint "unfounded."[77]

Part of the hostility evinced in the complaint process can also be attributed to the reinstitution of rationing for basic goods in the late 1920s. At that
time, state retailers set up an identification procedure to verify that those who
received scarce goods were legally entitled to them and that those consumers
defined as most important to the state's industrialization drive, for example,
factory workers, received priority. Attempts to authenticate customers, how-

ever, did not prevent some from feeling as if they had been wrongfully denied access. Indeed, the new procedure only seems to have heightened tensions and conflict. To one woman, for instance, the verification process more resembled an interrogation than a sales transaction. She complained that in refusing to sell her six meters of calico, which she said she wanted to buy to make two dresses for herself, the manager informed her that the Soviet constitution prohibited acquiring more than one dress. Labeling this manager's behavior "autocratic" and accusing him of "overstepping the limits of the duties assigned to him," she hinted that his tactics resembled those of the police and that he had treated her like a criminal suspect: "Does the manager have to conduct an investigation of every customer who is issued merchandise?"[78] The investigator assigned to her case responded in the affirmative, rejecting her complaint because of the need to prevent merchandise from falling into the hands of speculators. A worker by the name of Chuvilov similarly charged that in being rudely denied two and three-quarters meters of calico, he was wrongfully excluded. Others, he maintained, were given fabric, despite the fact that they did not present ration books.[79] The inspector rejected his version, countering that Chuvilov was not buying the fabric for himself but intended to resell it at a higher price.

As these last two cases indicate, customers were sometimes suspected of disguising their true identities and intentions. The task of distinguishing between consumers buying for their own and their families' needs and consumers buying to resell was extremely difficult, especially as nearly everybody resorted to reselling goods in order to make ends meet. In these tense conditions, retail employees often connected a customer's failure to observe store procedures (for example, cutting in line or requesting to be served out of turn) with speculation. Certainly, behaviors that were merely irritating, such as a customer's pressing a demand too persistently, also may have led workers to retaliate against a customer. Too, customers' desperation and expectation that persistence might lead to gratification contributed to confusion and tensions. The woman who deemed the verification process an interrogation, for example, readily admitted in her complaint that, "at her insistence," she received more fabric than the manager was at first willing to issue her.[80] Such assertive behaviors sometimes got customers what they wanted but also angered workers and other customers. Workers' depiction of disobedient or annoying consumers as speculators discursively marked them as individuals opposed to new social norms and retail protocols sanctioned by state and municipal authorities, thus casting doubt on their credibility. Additionally, anxiety about "former people" who were "masking" their pasts was common in the 1920s, creating additional pressure to try to establish identity. At risk of disenfranchisement, stigmatized individuals sometimes went to great lengths to disguise their social backgrounds.[81] In these circumstances, even those with impeccable credentials might garner suspicion. Such was the case with a trade union member named Narshtein, who, given his membership status, would seem to have been a preferred customer. But employees at GUM's Haberdashery Store No. 3 in Moscow declined his request for a kerchief, even though he showed them his union card, because they found suspicious his visit to the store with a woman who had just purchased one. When the woman then reappeared with a different man to try once again to purchase a second kerchief, the employees dispatched someone to follow the pair to find out whether or not they were Narshtein's accomplices. An investigator, however, revealed that Narshtein was indeed a trade union member and cautioned the manager not to make hasty decisions.[82]

The factory worker Vasin wrote a lengthy narrative about preferential treatment at the Briansk GUM store that laid bare contestations over social identities and behaviors. Vasin stated that when he asked to see a gray suit, the sales worker Komarov showed him a "poor-quality" one that was not his size and informed him that there were no others available in his size. After he left the counter, however, Vasin said that he witnessed "a citizen in a nice coat" approach the manager and converse briefly with him. Vasin watched as the manager descended into the basement three times, each time returning with a different suit, which the citizen tried on. When this customer left the store without purchasing the suit, which, it turned out, had a hole in the lapel, Vasin reported that a "comrade" then approached the counter and asked to try on the same suit. According to Vasin, the seller Komarov demurred, "It won't do for you. It's not your size and it's defective," to which the comrade countered, "I'll take it with the hole," to which the seller parried, "We don't have permission to sell defective merchandise." Vasin stated that he again approached Komarov and asked him to show him a gray suit and that Komarov again asserted that there were none. This response infuriated Vasin, who accused Komarov of selling to his acquaintances, and he threatened to "make a scene" (*podnimat' skandal*) in the store. Only after a lengthy exchange with the manager in which Vasin accused him of "selling suits from the basement," did Komarov show Vasin a suit, although the seller still attempted to dissuade Vasin from buying it. Vasin's indictment of GUM rested on his conviction that preferential treatment amounted to dishonesty, corruption, and double-talk, and, ultimately the obstruction of his access to high-quality clothing. In making this charge, he noted his job as a factory worker, a position that made the violation of his rights all the more regrettable. He also assigned the shorthand labels "comrade" and "citizen," apparently on the basis of appearance, to argue that GUM routinely denied access to workers but provided it to less worthy consumers. Vasin further assumed from the citizen's fine coat that he might be "some kind of NEPman." Mincing no words, he declared that this kind of "swindling reigns in our state stores" and that it amounted to selling good merchandise to "those whom it ought not be [sold]" and depriving workers of being able to buy something a "little better."[83] An inspector, however, explained away Vasin's accusation of favoritism, stating that although the sales clerk Komarov had erred in showing suits that had not yet been priced, the assumption that the customer in question was a NEPman was false; in fact, he claimed, the man was a party member who worked at Dukat factory.[84]

Complainants like Vasin who presented themselves as responsible working-class citizens often assigned an undesirable persona to the perceived wrong-doer. "NEPman" was an ambiguous but highly charged label that could refer to types as disparate as wealthy merchant-industrialists and petty traders, or anyone who simply looked like they could play either of these roles. Those who labeled someone a NEPman understood the potency of the term and applied it to insinuate that the accused was taking more than was rightfully theirs and profiting at the expense of honest workers. Some complaint writers also conjured up the specter of the NEPman to point out that, in the absence of a strong state retail network, they would fall prey to private traders through no fault of their own. Acknowledging that they themselves chose, albeit against their better judgment, to patronize private stores, these consumers maintained they had no choice. Complaining about GUM's inept three-queue system, which wasted "the housewife's time," one (male) consumer claimed that he and other customers were driven from GUM's stores to the shops of private merchants.[85] One customer, who lived outside of Moscow, wrote to *Pravda* to inform party officials of the effect of GUM's inability to live up to its task. He reported that after traveling to Moscow three times in the previous six months to buy various items at GUM, including a cast-iron frying pan and a kettle, and returning home empty-handed, he had been "forced to line the pockets of the Sukharev trader."[86]

GUM's employees sometimes admitted that they favored certain customers, although they justified their actions by arguing that those who received privileges were more deserving. In Vasin's case, the inspector's justification of selling to a party member and factory worker rendered Vasin's accusation less compelling. Ekaterina Vernuchina found herself similarly outflanked by a soviet representative. She recorded in the complaint book that complete "chaos" broke out at the Vindavskii GUM when the manager declared that no one besides those already in line would be allowed entry to the store but then permitted a man who had not been waiting to enter and receive fabric. She protested that someone who had not waited his turn was issued four meters of fabric, while she, a wife and mother of two, could not even get one piece of cloth to make a pair of trousers for her husband. In her opinion, such actions were "disgraceful." The manager denied Vernuchina's charge, although at the same time he admitted that one and a half meters of fabric had been issued to one citizen out of turn, adding in his defense that the two "citizenesses" who had protested lived nearby and could get merchandise any time. The customer served out of turn, a worker and member of the raion soviet, did not have time to wait in line. Therefore, he concluded, the two protesting shoppers were "wrong."[87] As the manager saw it, the customer, a man dedicated to the work of governing, deserved special treatment. The two women, who presumably did not work outside of the home, made no productive contribution to society and, therefore, were less deserving. His reply was compatible with the imperative of inverting class and gender dynamics, with its distinction between the politically active worker and the nonaffiliated, nonworker and its contrast between the man as a purposeful consumer and the two women as shoppers with free time. The investigator upheld the manager's rationale, reasoning that, since Vernuchina's account "does not correspond to reality," the only conclusion to be reached is that her complaint is nothing more than the "dissatisfaction of a speculator."[88]

As Vernuchina's case illustrates, conventional gender stereotypes sometimes provided a framework for complaints and counter-complaints. The image of the spoiled consumer was deeply imbedded, powerful, and, in the 1920s, grounded in material shortages. It was also rhetorically linked to anxieties about the moral degradation of the bourgeoisie and women. As depicted in literature, cartoons, and social commentary in the decades prior to the 1920s, the spoiled consumer was a vain, self-absorbed, middle- or upper-class female who displayed a perverse, uncontrollable desire for material goods. In her quest to fulfill her desires, she made a nuisance of herself in department stores and shops, demanding indulgence of her whims, pestering and abusing shop assistants, and creating scenes. After 1917, popular publications and didactic literature such as Aleksandr Tarasov-Rodionov's 1922 novel *Chocolate* presented anxieties about women's supposed craving for material goods as threats to the revolution. *Chocolate,* set in the politically tense years of the civil war, told the cautionary tale of Zudin, an old Bolshevik and chairman of the provincial Cheka, and the consequences of his relationships with two women obsessed with material goods. Yelena Valts, a former ballet dancer, exhibits a weakness for luxuries, melting at the very thought of expensive chocolates given to her by a handsome young British agent. Lisa, Zudin's wife, also displays a fondness luxury items, succumbing to her longings by accepting gifts of chocolate and silk stockings from Yelena. Despite Zudin's devotion to revolutionary principles, revealed in a lecture to Yelena about the dangers of "our inner yearnings for the habits of the past," his association with these two women, both unable to control their

consuming desires, leads to his implication in a plot against Russia and his execution. The moral of the story was that self-indulgence, or even proximity to
it, weakened communists and jeopardized their victory.[89]

In the NEP era, tensions arising from shortages, speculation, and capitalist encirclement aligned themselves with pre-existing concerns about women's
physical desires, producing an antifeminine bias that revealed itself in ideological and literary works as a preoccupation with the female body. A shapely female form, for example, signified old-fashioned views and suggested excesses in
eating and sexual behavior. By contrast, a slender, androgynous body type was
endowed with ideological purity, and it symbolized restraint.[90] The figure of
the spoiled, consuming woman coincided with these anxieties, merging long-
held fears about women with contemporary concerns. In newspaper reportage,
popular stories, and cartoons, disorderly consumers often assumed a shapely
female form suggestive of decadence or of unwarranted access to consumer
goods.

A newspaper account of an incident that reportedly occurred in GUM's
grocery store in Orel captured the subversive threat that the spoiled female consumer posed. Nikitin, a Komsomol member, reported that a "garishly dressed
lady" wrapped in a fur entered the store, approached the counter, and, leaning
close to the shop assistant, took his hand. The assistant abandoned the customers
waiting in line and began to whisper with the woman. Then aloud he asked her,
"What would you like?" to which she replied, "Cookies and candy of the best
sort."[91] Workers standing in line reportedly became indignant at this obsequious show of preferential treatment, and one of them, a man, stepped out of the
line and yelled, "Hey, you! . . . Yeah, you, who do you think you are?" Indignantly, the woman left the store, leaving in her wake a chastened shop assistant.
The waiting customers reportedly lauded the outspoken worker for putting the
woman in her place and showing the shop assistant that all customers should
receive equal treatment. Even if Nikitin's piece was partly fictional, it nonetheless highlighted a set of appearances, attitudes, and behaviors perceived as
self-indulgent and, therefore, illegitimate. The woman's ostentatious clothing,
coy entreaty for pricey cookies and candy, symbols of the sweet life, identified
her as a decadent female who used her looks, sexuality, and wealth to satisfy
her cravings. Her demand to be served out of turn and her expectation that her
demand would be honored showed flagrant disregard for the other consumers,
who had been waiting their turn and may have lacked the means to pamper
themselves. Her obnoxious assertion of her desires, over the interests of the rest
of society, demonstrated that the woman did not know, or perhaps did not care,
about policies of queuing and the principle of equal access. Significantly, in the
story it is a male worker who disrupts her vulgar display of perverse femininity

and wayward attempt at consumption, thereby righting order in the store and in society.

When retail employees invoked the image of the spoiled consumer, they depicted consumers whose trifling requests and condescending attitude toward workers, other consumers, and the store's regimen violated the socialist principles upon which they understood a state store to operate. The manager's rebuke to the female consumer who wanted to buy enough calico for two dresses, for example, rendered her demand that of a voracious woman who aspired to fill her closet with more clothes than she needed. He even went so far as to argue that the Soviet constitution forbade owning more than one dress, an erroneous assertion that reflected his own misunderstanding or convenient misapplication of the principle of egalitarianism. In the case of the female worker Ermolaeva, employees also evoked the image of the spoiled female shopper. Ermolaeva presented herself as a decent, compliant consumer who, despite observing store protocol, nonetheless suffered abuse. According to her complaint, she waited in line, requested that a worker cut a piece of fabric, and paid for it, but when she tried to retrieve the piece, one of the workers reportedly told her to "go to hell." As the manager told the story, "some citizeness" who did not want to wait in line went directly to the cashier and paid a sum of money. When she tried to claim a piece of fabric, however, there was none left. Upon hearing this bad news, he reported that Ermolaeva "went into hysterics," cursing him and the other sellers in vulgar, abusive language.[92] In the manager's telling, she appeared as a woman who believed that rules did not apply to her. When her attempt to get around them failed, she threw a fit. As a conclusion, the manager asked GUM's board to inform Ermolaeva that retail workers were not in the least interested in witnessing such ill-mannered displays.

The image of the spoiled shopper was not reserved solely for women. Male complainants were also sometimes depicted as self-interested, overdemanding consumers, although their unacceptable behaviors were usually ascribed not to incorrigible material desires but to violent impulses and political opposition. When the customer Burkin complained that employees at GUM's store on Tverskaia Street had refused to issue him fabric, the manager depicted him as a disruptive, aggressive customer who entered the store and forced his way to the counter to demand fabric. When a female member of the Moscow soviet, who was on hand to help verify the identity of buyers, also turned down his request, the manager attested that Burkin raised "a complete scandal," insulting the soviet representative with indecent language, waving his ration book in her face, and then beating her on the arms.[93] Regarding his actions as "intolerable," the manager called the police, who reestablished order. The inspector assigned to Zhivotovskii's case, cited above, likewise discredited his complaint by depicting Zhivotovskii as a subversive hooligan who, in refusing to comply with the soviet's decree and thus to respect the rights of workers, had "violated the internal order of the store" and threatened the safety of employees.[94] According to the inspector's version of events, Zhivotovskii had forcibly burst into the store demanding service and, despite the manager's explanation of store protocol, continued to "make a fuss." Deeming his complaint "groundless," the inspector recommended that GUM's board call Zhivotovskii to account in order to protect workers from such incidents in the future.[95]

Routine inspections of GUM's stores confirmed the existence of the problems consumers described in their complaints. Among the flaws one inspector noted in his 1927 examination of the Vindavskii store, for example, was the dirty, unattractive grocery section (bereft of merchandise), which, in his opinion, more resembled a rural co-op than a department store.[96] The Danilovskii GUM was likewise derided as a "little *magazinchika* dimly lit by sunlight," with poor ventilation, dirty floors, and dusty merchandise.[97] When visiting the GUM branch in the Sretenka neighborhood, near Sukharev Market, an inspector found a spacious, well-lit store but a lack of the "most sought-after kinds of goods."[98] Besides the physical and operational defects inspectors found, they also discovered that employees lacked training or responsible management. Even the Red Square store was cited for defects. Inspections of the three GUM haberdashery stores there revealed crowded sales floors and underqualified sales workers in need of both discipline and cultural-educational training.[99] GUM's board chairman, named Goldberg, reproached the directors of the Red Square complex after his personal examination in 1928 revealed what he termed a lack of the "proprietary touch."[100] By contrast, Goldberg gave the Baumanskii department store high marks for its cleanliness, tidiness, and handling of customers during busy hours.[101]

What is most clear in all of these complaints and counter-complaints is that both consumers and retail employees blamed each other for circumstances that were beyond their control. Whether or not Zhivotovskii or any of the other complainants belonged to a privileged group, a ring of speculators, or a gang of hooligans or harbored anti-Soviet sentiments is beside the point. Whether the worker Smirnov innocently erred in striving to treat all customers equally is mostly irrelevant. When faced with chronic shortages and long lines, shoppers understandably became upset and took out their frustrations on workers who presented the only readily accessible target. They also frequently objected to other consumers' behaviors that prevented or made more onerous their attempts to obtain goods. Employees, irritated by working in such trying circumstances and faced with the same material hardships in their own lives, perhaps tormented customers as a way of relieving stress or punished those who made their jobs more difficult. Despite their commitment to workers, commercial and trade union officials surely did not want customers to feel abused or badgered, yet that was often the effect. Many customers who left state and cooperative stores feeling harassed and wronged belonged to the working classes, the very groups that the state hoped to better by revolutionizing the retail sector.

The legacy of the prerevolutionary retail sector is also evident. Still-lingering expectations of customer service and personal, potentially adversarial interaction intersected with the revolutionary demand for egalitarian treatment and access, all of which created an atmosphere in which retail workers and consumers constantly tested and monitored each other's behaviors. Many complaints, especially the rather long, complicated ones, unmistakably recall the haggling matches that merchants and consumers engaged in prior to the revolution. The inventory of performative behaviors—the mutual suspicion, intimidation, subterfuge and evasion, demands and counter-demands, retorts and counter-retorts—owed much to the traditional roles that merchants and consumers had customarily assumed in sales transactions. The scripts required of retail employees and of consumers, however, were in flux. Both were searching for the correct discursive register, the terminologies, personae, and tone, but some stock phrases and characteristic motifs were clearly emerging.

To be sure, there were substantive differences between the pre- and postrevolutionary eras. Consumers no longer dealt with merchants but with employees of state-sponsored and cooperative enterprises. Merchants and consumers no longer haggled over prices but over access to goods. Previously, anyone could enter a haggling match, but often only those with connections could strike a deal with a sales worker in a state store. Still, consumers had internalized the idea that they were entitled to the goods and services the state had promised, and their determination to outwit the employees of state retailers and the corrupt and incompetent officials that managed them, whether through a complaint, cunning, connections, bribery, or some other means, governed the retail exchange.

Given these deplorable conditions, one might wonder why the state continued to operate the retail enterprise. The reason, as stated in several inspectors' reports, was that despite inadequate funding, mismanagement, and chronic problems of supply and employee training, state retailers needed to maintain a presence in the commercial sphere. GUM's management team realized that no matter how tenuous its stake in the market, the state could not surrender it without giving up the commitment to a socialist economy and society. One inspector, remarking on the significance of the Baumanskii store, observed that from a strictly commercial point of view, the store's location, next to the German market and near an MSPO store and a range of private specialty stores, was not "expedient." From a socioeconomic view, however, he deemed the store "absolutely expedient," since it nonetheless stood the chance of restricting the business of nearby private retailers.[102] The best hope of the firm's executive team was that GUM would be able to struggle on until mistakes could be corrected. And, thus, poorly supplied, small, dirty shops and stores were left to carry the banner of class struggle in the marketplace.

Complaints of defective goods, rude retorts, and arbitrary procedures and aggressive, misbehaving customers reveal a retail marketplace full of anxiety and conflict and largely devoid of the abundance, efficiency, and pleasures promoted by state and cooperative enterprises in their advertisements. Obviously, these complaints contradicted the state's claims about constructing an egalitarian retail network, and they also highlighted the gap between consumers' demands for basic goods and services and the state's ability and willingness to provide them. While the NEP-era regime tried to create a mass market through the establishment of model stores and ads that invited men and women, workers, peasants, and other citizens all across the Soviet Union to join a constituency of consumer-citizens, the decision to prioritize heavy over light industrial production ultimately made that goal unattainable. GUM's dismal performance then glaringly pointed up the state's reneging on one of the revolution's central promises: to redistribute wealth and resources or, at the very least, to democratize access. While consumers enjoyed the right to complain about the price of tea, dirty sugar cubes, and uncooperative workers and employees possessed the right to defend themselves against impertinent demands and violent outbursts, the few indications of resolution suggest that the state's commercial officials regarded such grumblings as relatively trivial. And although some letters to the editor and complaints in complaint books evinced faith in the state's assurance of consumers' and workers' rights, others betrayed an already deeply embedded skepticism, and even cynicism and distrust. While the mass-circulation newspapers were more responsive in giving complainants some satisfaction, if only by publishing grievances and publicly shaming retailers, the defensiveness found in GUM's inspection reports, in particular the recurrent resort to dismissive stock phrases such as "unfounded" and "the consumer's account does not correspond to reality," suggests a tendency to deny problems and place the blame on consumers.

Despite the voiding of their complaints, however, consumers created their own counter-discourse that challenged official versions of reality. Their stock phrases asserted the right to access consumer goods and the immorality of rudeness and asserting one's interests above those of others. Although complaining may have been small comfort, it did serve as a nagging reminder to the state of its failure to provide everything for everybody. Furthermore, despite what appears to be a conflict between two oppositional groups, complaints and counter-complaints show a process of individuals trying to define appropriate behaviors and practices and to set limits on what a Soviet citizen, whether worker or consumer, could be expected to tolerate.

In a larger sense, the complaint process highlights the cultural transformation that the Soviet state was trying to effect in the retail sector, particularly the shift from a retail culture that stressed personal interaction between buyer and seller (be that a romancing or jousting) and a reliance on personality, the skill of persuasion, and sociability, underwritten by the private merchant classes, to a culture based on the collective rights of workers and consumers, utility, and codified procedures, guaranteed by a mediating state. The limitations of the cultural transformation in the retail sector, central to the transformation of the state, economy, and society, left a legacy of mistrust that lingered as the state tried again in the 1930s to remake Soviet citizens into citizen-consumers.

Epilogue

Model retailers such as GUM failed to deliver what the Soviet government promised with its version of modern retailing: abundance, comfort, efficiency, and respect for workers and consumers. Shopping was no longer a pleasure, a sport, or even a routine task but a humiliating, exacting chore. The significance of the state's failure in the retail sector was that the failure to make available things like sugar, galoshes, chisels, and frying pans transgressed a basic principle of socialism: improving the material condition of the formerly disenfranchised working classes. The seemingly small currency of these kinds of goods only pointed out more glaringly the inability of the regime to fulfill its larger promise.

Seriously underfunded from the start, GUM and other state enterprises also suffered from a lack of experienced personnel, gross mismanagement, corruption at all levels, and problems maintaining a healthy inventory, the last a result of production problems at state manufacturing enterprises and better-positioned private merchants. Although GUM turned a profit in some years, its defects hampered the mission of taking a vanguard position in the marketplace and besting private merchants.[1] Sovnarkom dismantled GUM in 1931, with the closure following the launch of the party's industrialization and collectivization campaigns and the final offensive to eliminate the NEPman. In 1927–1930, the state addressed the NEPman problem by imposing higher taxes on "superprofits," businesses, and income and by denying them food rations and housing. By late 1929, most private shops and stores had been closed, although private trade did not become officially illegal until 1932. The experiment in competition among various retail rivals ended as opponents of the NEPmen quelled the opposition instead of driving them out of business through superior performance.[2]

Another campaign to establish "Soviet trade" or "cultured Soviet trade" began in 1931–1932, gaining momentum in 1935 when rationing ended.[3] During these years, the Stalinist regime advanced the ideal of a mass consumer society, as reflected in a discourse that promoted the realization of the material promises of socialism and repositioned retailing and consumption as integral to the agenda of the 1930s. This highly publicized campaign sought to legitimate consumerism, mobilize consumers to carry out reforms in the retail sector, and promote "appropriate" norms of socialist consumption, thereby transforming attitudes and behaviors. Stalin and other political leaders distinguished the new campaign from the 1920s campaign by deeming it a campaign for Soviet trade without the NEPman, bureaucratism, corruption, or profiteering. In this iteration, they argued, formal stores with civilized, modern methods would replace trading rows and customary practices like haggling and retail workers would attend to customers' needs instead of simply issuing products.[4] As one *Izvestiia* journalist portrayed it, the state had dealt a "crippling blow" to "unhealthy tendencies" and defined a path to the future development of the Soviet retail sector, which would not be guided by "leftish" tendencies that had led state and co-op retail workers to perform a "mechanical distribution of goods" and completely disregard the interests of consumers. Arguing that, since industrial production had increased over 1932 levels and an expansion of the retail network should follow, he called for the mass of workers to involve themselves in the "struggle for cultured Soviet trade."[5]

The campaign to build socialist, cultured retailing brought considerable change to the retail sector. Private stores and shops, of course, disappeared, but so too did cooperative retail enterprises. The co-ops fell victim to the decision to identify socialist retailing with the modern, capitalist model and to emphasize luxury goods and customer service over the cooperative tradition, which had not stressed a store's appearance, merchandising, or advertising but had focused on the sale of staple goods. Some cooperative retail stores survived, primarily in the countryside, but most eventually closed. By 1937, rural co-ops accounted for only 20 percent of retail turnover. In place of private and co-op stores, thousands of new stores and stalls opened; thousands more were renovated and supplied with heat and new equipment.[6]

A couple of retail formats, one new and the other an innovation of the 1920s, defined the campaign of the 1930s. Torgsin stores, founded in 1930, sold primarily luxury or hard-to-get goods for foreign currency at prices set to benefit the industrialization drive. Initially, these stores limited access to foreign consumers, but Soviet citizens who traded foreign currency, gold, antiques, jewelry, and other valuables actually became Torgsin's primary customers.[7] Glavosobtorg stores, operated by the main commercial agency from 1930 to 1934, sold goods for rubles at very high prices. Like Torgsin, these stores were initially established to serve elites, but they ended up mostly retailing cotton textiles, vodka, sugar, and other basic goods to ordinary citizens, especially those who did not have a place in the rationing system. Both Torgsin and Glavosobtorg stores aimed to provide a pleasant shopping experience and attentive customer service. The Torgsin stores in Moscow and Leningrad impressed observers with their showcase wares, but most were apparently "dirty little shops" where customers suffered very long queues, rude retail workers, and other kinds of uncultured behaviors.[8] Most Glavosobtorg shops did not achieve the ideal of cultured trade either.[9] The disparity between rhetoric and practice shows that Soviet officials had not only inherited the ideals of cultured trade but also that they continued to struggle with the ideological and practical problems of implementing them and with reconciling their conflicting attitudes about retailing and consumption, all of which complicated the campaign.

Model retail stores in urban centers, like those established in the NEP era, were intended to serve as flagships of Soviet cultured trade. The Central Department Store (TsUM), housed in the building of the former Mostorg and Muir & Mirrielees, and Leningrad's Passazh department store, as well as six other model department stores, were set up by 1935. Gastronome No. 1, a model food emporium set up in the former Kommunar co-op and Eliseev's, displayed a wide variety of expensive food items. Although Gastronome No. 1 reportedly served tens of thousands of consumers a day, TsUM and the Passazh department store suffered from complaints of long lines and did not achieve many of the goals set for them. Despite their flaws, these stores were paragons of Soviet retailing, and many of them endured throughout the Soviet era. Still, the overwhelming majority of retail shops and stores in the 1930s were not model units but venues that were small, poorly stocked, and poorly equipped.[10]

Oddly, neither the Red Square arcade nor GUM was resurrected in the 1930s. Throughout the Stalinist era, the arcade housed government offices. A singular hostility was apparently reserved for the giant structure, perhaps because of its provenance in the late imperial era or because of its disappointing performance in the 1920s and association with the ills of the NEP. Even in the 1940s, government officials still viewed it with disdain. In 1947, the Committee of Architectural Affairs held discussions about erecting on Red Square a monument to the Soviet Union's victory in World War II. At one of the committee meetings, someone raised the issue of GUM's presence. Some members of the committee suggested removing "this unpleasant stain," which "disrupts Red Square," but because doing so would have involved considerable time and expense, they abandoned the idea.[11]

Despite the Stalinist state's emphasis on large, modern retail venues, open-air markets persisted. Realizing their necessity, but wanting to tie them to collectivization and state farms, the state recast the outdoor markets as *kolkhoz* markets in the late 1920s and authorized collective farmers and independent peasants to sell their agricultural products there at regulated prices. The markets ultimately became dominated by independent farmers and private vendors, who often engaged in illegal activities, a circumstance that led the state to closely police them. Nonetheless, these peasant markets, which constituted a private sector in a state-planned economy, played a crucial role in supplying Soviet citizens with foodstuffs for the rest of the century.[12]

The 1930s campaign for a cultured socialist retail sector owed much to the previous two attempts to install a new retail economy and culture in Russia. The model of large, attractive, comfortable stores that stocked a wide assortment of merchandise sold at fixed prices by professional, courteous retail workers had animated the campaigns launched by a section of the prerevolutionary merchant elite and the Bolsheviks' NEP-era campaign. Just as these two campaigns sought to revolutionize the ways in which goods were bought and sold and to reeducate retail workers and consumers in restrained, civil behavioral norms, so the Stalinist campaign endorsed modern retailing, furthering, as one historian puts it, "processes of socio-economic modernization that had already been underway."[13]

To be sure, there were substantive differences and outcomes among the three campaigns, and the revolution inspired new directions. The motives that guided the prerevolutionary elite merchants included a desire to be taken seriously in a society that largely devalued their skills and wealth, and theirs was as much a campaign to promote their leadership potential and to critique what they believed were oppressive and archaic political and social structures, as it was a crusade to transform the culture and daily life of the subjects of the Russian Empire. In the NEP-era campaign, political goals dovetailed with transformational impulses, blending the revolutionary objective of raising the material standard of life for the working classes with teaching workers and consumers to behave in restrained, constructive ways. Socialist revolution inspired the creation of new retail formats such as the state model store and the infusion of concepts of class struggle, workers' rights, consumer complaint and entitlement, and purposeful consumption. The 1930s campaign to rapidly construct socialism in the industrial, agricultural, and commercial sectors merged with the desire to educate workers in the tenets of customer service and consumers in taste and style. In this phase of the campaign, women entered the retail labor force in large numbers, their roles as retail workers making them eligible to achieve the status of labor hero and to receive material rewards.[14]

The role of the retail sector also changed dramatically after 1917. Prior to the Bolshevik revolution, the retail sector largely represented a vital, functional sector of society that incorporated participants into local communities through personal interaction, ritual, and spectacle, as well as through the exchange of goods for money. Consumers encountered in lavkas, markets, stores, and arcades familiar, ingratiating shop assistants and colorful, if crafty and pushy, merchants, a panoply of goods, and street spectacles, all of which made up part of the urban experience. Although Soviet retail officials tried to recreate some of the color and excitement of the late imperial commercial community, and even to improve on it by updating the appearance of stores, product packages, and advertisements, the state's model retailers did not gain the widespread loyalty or affection that many pre-Soviet retail venues had garnered. Instead, officials created a world mostly devoid of pleasure, visual appeal, and conviviality, and anxiety-ridden consumers perceived the Soviet stores as barren places staffed by indifferent workers. Furthermore, the state assumed many of the noncommercial functions of the retail sector, such as organizing public spectacles, leaving retailers with only the unenviable task of selling goods in chronically short supply.

To be fair, the commercial sphere of the late empire also had its share of dirty shops and rude, dishonest merchants and shop assistants, and the methods of modern retailing had not reached or engaged everyone. Soviet officials had to work to against the defects of the pre-1917 retail sector, as well as against Russia's relatively low level of industrial development and standard of living. To overcome those legacies in the span of a decade would be too much to expect. The devastation of the economy during the civil war produced conditions of extreme scarcity that lasted until the mid-1920s and reappeared at the end of the decade as the state encountered difficulties collecting grain from the peasants in order to finance industrialization. These kinds of problems, along with the state's continued prioritization of industry, not only created financial hardships for consumers but also undercut the efforts of the state's model retailers.

The rhetoric and daily practices that became attached to retailing and consumption after 1917 also transformed social identities. Some of the ways that consumers had understood their identities as urban dwellers or members of the middle class in the late empire derived from everyday behaviors learned in shops, stores, and markets, the consumption of certain items, or patronage of particular firms. The Soviet commercial regime instituted new social identities that carried specific rights. As evidenced by the complaints lodged against

GUM, Soviet consumers recognized themselves as citizen-consumers who had rights in the marketplace guaranteed by a benevolent socialist state. A culture of entitlement developed under the influence of a regime that promised material betterment and dignity for the previously disenfranchised. The socialist championing of the worker, however, undercut the rights of the consumer-citizen, leaving the two at odds over their rights and responsibilities in the marketplace.

There is disagreement about the extent to which a mass consumer society or a Soviet consumer emerged. The disagreement turns on whether a consumer is defined by the quantity and quality of purchases or by identification and preoccupation with consumption and engagement with issues of retailing and consumption. One interpretation holds that most Soviet citizens purchased basic, necessary goods, rather than those designed for leisure or pleasure. In this view, the Soviet Union did not constitute a mass consumer society.[15] The new Soviet elite, including the well-paid and rewarded political and cultural elites and shock workers, defined by their access to better housing, stores, and education, however, suggests a different model of a Soviet consumer.[16] Amy Randall offers another view, identifying a "new Soviet consumer" as one who recognized his or her status as a consumer and not just a worker, who participated in consultations and conferences about quality and quantity, thus helping to shape production, and who resorted to the complaint book more frequently and wrote more letters to the editor. In short, the new Soviet consumer was an individual who identified himself or herself as a consumer, who participated in addressing the problems associated with retailing and consumption, and who articulated expectations but did not necessarily indulge in the pleasures of shopping or consume in conspicuous ways on a regular basis.[17] In Elena Osokina's interpretation, Soviet life was organized primarily around issues of consumption, with a social structure denoted by a hierarchy of rationing, privileges, and entitlements.[18] In her view, Soviet citizens were consumed by consumption. As these works and this book have sought to make clear, issues relating to retailing and consumption were at the center of debates and central to the transformations taking place in the late imperial and early Soviet eras. They also defined the ways in which subjects and citizens understood themselves and their place in society. It seems less important that the Russian case fit terms devised to explain a particular, although related, set of developments in the West, than to illuminate the ways that retailing and consumption defined and helped constitute late imperial and then Soviet society.

Despite the varying ideological positions of the merchant elite, NEP advocates, and supporters of the Stalinist economic agenda and the various accomplishments and failures of the retail reform campaigns, a line of continuity is clear throughout the entire period of 1880 to 1930. Each campaign sought to restructure the retail economy, redefine the retail trade, and retrain the population to live in a modern, industrial, consumer-oriented, cultured society. In addition, those who sought to influence the direction of the economy endorsed the optimistic creed of modern mass retailing as the way to a better society. Finally, issues connected to retailing and consumption continued to serve as flashpoints for discussions of how a modern, just, more civil and democratic society should be constructed even after the 1930s.

The late imperial and early Soviet retail spheres were hybrid creations that juxtaposed numerous competing institutions, discourses, ideals, symbols, and practices. The conflicts and reciprocity among these diverse elements were reproduced in the blessing with holy water of an iron-and-glass retail arcade adorned with seventeenth-century architectural motifs and in constructivist-inspired advertisements for Red October's Easter chocolates on sale at state retail stores. The syncretic urban culture that had developed in Russia supported and absorbed the changes wrought by the introduction of modern retailing and by the October revolution, at the same time that it retained some established elements. While the abandonment of NEP eliminated many of the options that had sustained the variegated commercial sphere, the idea that modes of buying and selling structured and signified political, social, and cultural life persisted. It is testament to the fundamental role that retailing and consumption played that, in the 1950s, the state once again signaled its intention to pay more attention to consumers' needs. In 1953, GUM—the State Department Store—opened once again for business in the arcade on Red Square, another phase in the history of this centuries-old commercial site that awaits its historian.

Notes

Introduction

1. Georg Simmel, *The Philosophy of Money* (London: Routledge, 1978), 174–75. See also Kenneth Pomeranz and Steven Topik, *The World That Trade Created: Society, Culture, and the World Economy, 1400 to the Present* (Armonk, NY, and London: M. E. Sharpe, 1999), 3.

2. Works on retail trade in the West that proved most helpful in conceptualizing this project include Michael Miller, *The Bon Marché: Bourgeois Culture and the Department Store, 1869–1920* (Princeton: Princeton University Press, 1981); Victoria de Grazia, ed., with Ellen Furlough, *The Sex of Things: Gender and Consumption in Historical Perspective* (Berkeley: University of California Press, 1996); Susan Porter Benson, *Counter Cultures: Saleswomen, Managers, and Customers in American Department Stores, 1890–1940* (Urbana: University of Illinois Press, 1988); Rita Felski, *The Gender of Modernity* (Cambridge, MA: Harvard University Press, 1995); Jennifer Jones, "Repackaging Rousseau: Femininity and Fashion in Old Regime France," *French Historical Studies* 18:4 (fall 1994): 939–67; and Amanda Vickery, "Women and the World of Goods: A Lancashire Consumer and Her Possessions, 1751–81," in *Consumption and the World of Goods,* ed. John Brewer and Roy Porter (London: Routledge, 1993). Also instructive were Mary Louise Roberts, "Gender, Consumption, and Commodity Culture," *American Historical Review* 103:3 (June 1998): 817–44; and Matthew Hilton, "Class Consumption and the Public Sphere," *Journal of Contemporary History* 35:4 (2000): 655–66.

3. Louise McReynolds, *Russia at Play: Leisure Activities at the End of the Tsarist Era* (Ithaca: Cornell University Press, 2003), 7.

4. Sally West, *I Shop in Moscow: Advertising and the Creation of Consumer Culture in Late Tsarist Russia* (DeKalb: Northern Illinois University Press, 2011).

5. Christine Ruane, "Clothes Shopping in Imperial Russia: The Development of a Consumer Culture," *Journal of Social History* 28 (summer 1995): 777.

6. Christine Ruane, *The Empire's New Clothes: A History of the Russian Fashion Industry, 1700–1917* (New Haven: Yale University Press, 2009).

7. Alan M. Ball, *Russia's Last Capitalists: The Nepmen, 1921–1929* (Berkeley: University of California Press, 1987).

8. Elena Osokina, *Za fasada Stalinskogo izobiliia: raspredelenie i rynok v snabzhenii naseleniia v gody industrializatsii, 1927–1941* (Moscow: Rosspen, 1999).

9. Julie Hessler, *A Social History of Soviet Trade* (Princeton: Princeton University Press, 2004).

10. Amy Randall, *The Soviet Dream World of Retail Trade and Consumption in the 1930s* (New York: Palgrave Macmillan, 2008). See also Jukka Gronow, *Caviar with Champagne: Common Luxury and the Ideals of the Good Life in Stalin's Russia* (New York: Berg, 2003). An earlier study of the symbolic significance of bourgeois material culture in the late Stalinist era is Vera S. Dunham, *In Stalin's Time: Middleclass Values in Soviet Fiction* (New York: Cambridge University Press, 1976).

11. Anne E. Gorsuch and Diane P. Koenker, ed., *Turizm: The Russian and East European Tourist under Capitalism and Socialism* (Ithaca: Cornell University Press, 2006); Susan E. Reid, "Cold War in the Kitchen: Gender and the De-Stalinization of Consumer Taste in the Soviet Union under Khrushchev," *Slavic Review* 61:2 (summer 2002): 211–52. See also Susan E. Reid and David Crowley, eds., *Style and Socialism: Modernity and Material Culture in Post-War Eastern Europe* (New York: Berg, 2000).

12. Elena Osokina, for instance, argues that the NEP era should not be idealized as a time of relative prosperity, pointing out that the standard of living was consistently low. Osokina, *Our Daily Bread: Socialist Distribution and the Art of Survival in Stalin's Russia, 1927–1941* (Armonk, NY: M. E. Sharpe, 2000), 3.

13. William G. Rosenberg, "Introduction," in *Russia in the Era of NEP: Explorations in Soviet Society and Culture,* ed. Sheila Fitzpatrick, Alexander Rabinowitch, and Richard Stites (Bloomington: Indiana University Press, 1991), 3.

14. Hessler, *Social History of Soviet Trade,* 197–98.

15. Definition adapted from the introduction to de Grazia, with Furlough, *Sex of Things;* Neil McKendrick, John Brewer, and J. H. Plumb, *The Birth of a Consumer Society: The Commercialization of Eighteenth-Century England* (Bloomington: Indiana University Press, 1982), 1–30; Rosalind H. Williams, *Dream Worlds: Mass Consumption in Late Nineteenth-Century France* (Berkeley: University of California Press, 1982), 3–10; and David Crowley, "Warsaw's Shops, Stalinism and the Thaw," in *Style and Socialism,* ed. Reid and Crowley.

16. *Exchange culture* is Hessler's term, which more closely approximates my meaning. Hessler, *Social History of Soviet Trade,* 20.

17. Jürgen Habermas formulated the idea of the "liberal public sphere" of the late eighteenth and early nineteenth century. He suggests that this sphere comprised organizations and institutions that existed in a space between the state and private individuals and that mediated between the two. He also argues that this public sphere gave way to mass communications and consumption in the latter part of the nineteenth century. Jürgen Habermas, *The Structural Transformation of the Public Sphere: An Inquiry into a Category of Bourgeois Society,* trans. T. Burger (Cambridge, MA: MIT Press, 1989).

18. Alfred Rieber, *Merchants and Entrepreneurs in Imperial Russia* (Chapel Hill: University of North Carolina Press, 1982); Thomas C. Owen, *The Corporation under Russian Law, 1800–1917: A Study in Tsarist Economic Policy* (New York: Cambridge University Press, 1991); Jo Ann Ruckman, *The Moscow Business Elite: A Social and Cultural Portrait of Two Generations, 1840–1905* (DeKalb: Northern Illinois University Press, 1984); and Edith W. Clowes, Samuel D. Kassow, and James L. West, eds., *Between Tsar and People: Educated Society and the Quest for Public Identity in Late Imperial Russia* (Princeton: Princeton University Press, 1991).

19. James L. West, "Merchant Moscow in Historical Context," in *Merchant Moscow:*

Images of Russia's Vanished Bourgeoisie, ed. James L. West and Iurii A. Petrov (Princeton: Princeton University Press, 1998), 5.

20. Joseph Bradley's discussion of the problem of defining the terms *public sphere* and *civil society* and his review of the historiography of these two concepts in European, Russian, and U.S. history argues that voluntary associations grew in number and scope under Russian autocracy, providing a framework for the development of public opinion and helping subjects learn to become citizens. Joseph Bradley, "Subjects into Citizens: Societies, Civil Society, and Autocracy in Tsarist Russia," *American Historical Review* 107:4 (October 2002): 1094–1123; Bradley, "Pictures at an Exhibition: Science, Patriotism, and Civil Society in Imperial Russia," *Slavic Review* 67:4 (winter 2008): 943. A discussion of the problems with characterizing civil society as a democratic force is in Philip Nord's introduction to *Civil Society before Democracy: Lessons from Nineteenth-Century Europe,* ed. Nancy Bermeo and Philip Nord (Lanham, MD: Rowman & Littlefield, 2000), xiii–xiv. See also Clowes, Kassow, and West, introduction to *Between Tsar and People,* 6.

21. Roshanna Sylvester identifies the influence of Russia's middle classes, in particular the Jewish middle class, in the products of mass culture. Roshanna Sylvester, *Tales of Old Odessa: Crime and Civility in a City of Thieves* (DeKalb: Northern Illinois University Press, 2005), 5, 14.

22. West, *I Shop in Moscow,* chap. 2. In his exegesis of the diary of an eighteenth-century merchant, David Ransel refutes the stereotypes of the merchant, which Russia's intelligentsia had generated, and urges historians to reach beyond them for more complicated assessments of the roles and activities of merchants and their relationship to state power. David Ransel, ed., *A Russian Merchant's Tale: The Life and Adventures of Ivan Alekseevich Tolchënov, Based on His Diary* (Bloomington: Indiana University Press, 2009), xii–xxv.

23. Laura Engelstein finds that nineteenth-century Russians were embedded within a notion of society as composed of state, *narod* (people), and the public. Engelstein, "The Dream of Civil Society in Tsarist Russia," in *Civil Society before Democracy,* ed. Bermeo and Nord, 25.

24. Stephen White, *The Bolshevik Poster* (New Haven: Yale University Press, 1988), 8–17.

25. Judith Walkowitz, *City of Dreadful Delight: Narratives of Sexual Danger in Late-Victorian London* (Chicago: University of Chicago Press, 1992).

26. Felski, *Gender of Modernity,* 4–5.

27. Mary Louise Roberts discusses the reasons why acts of consumption have largely been represented as feminine, both in the cultural imagination and in the scholarly literature. See Roberts, "Gender, Consumption, and Commodity Culture," 818. See a similar discussion in Margot Finn, "Men's Things: Masculine Possession in the Consumer Revolution," *Social History* 25:2 (May 2000): 134. Finn's examination of the diaries of four English male consumers documents a variety of consuming behaviors and possessions among "highly acquisitive" men.

28. The English middle-class male's adoption of simple, black three-piece suits in the late eighteenth and early nineteenth centuries has been labeled "the great masculine renunciation" and "the triumph of black," descriptions that signify inconspicuous consumption and sober control. This sartorial transition, however, was the result of struggles for political power. See David Kuchta, "The Making of the Self-Made Man: Class, Clothing,

and English Masculinity, 1688–1832," in *Sex of Things,* ed. De Grazia with Furlough, 54–55; and Philippe Perrot, *Fashioning the Bourgeoisie: A History of Clothing in the Nineteenth Century,* trans. Richard Bienvenu (Princeton: Princeton University Press, 1994), 29–34. Leora Auslander has identified consuming personas of nineteenth-century French men, including the dandy and the collector—images of masculine consumption that exhibited an individuated purpose. Leora Auslander, "The Gendering of Consumer Practices in Nineteenth-Century France," in *Sex of Things,* ed. De Grazia with Furlough, 79.

29. Randi Barnes-Cox has also noted the conspicuous presence of the male worker-consumer in NEP-era ads. Randi Barnes-Cox, "The Creation of the Socialist Consumer: Advertising, Citizenship, and NEP" (PhD diss., Indiana University), 2000.

30. Sally West, "The Material Promised Land: Advertising's Modern Agenda in Late Imperial Russia," *Russian Review* 57:3 (July 1998): 345–63.

31. Sylvester, *Tales of Old Odessa,* 14.

Chapter 1. Russia's Retail Landscape, 1860s–1890s

1. N. V. Davydov, "Moskva piatidesiatye i shestidesiatye gody XIX stoletiia," in *Ushedshaia Moskva: vospominaniia sovremennikov o Moskve vtoroi poloviny XIX veka,* ed. N. S. Ashukina (Moscow, 1964), 22.

2. Ibid., 29.

3. Peter N. Stearns, *Consumerism in World History: The Global Transformation of Desire* (New York: Routledge, 2006), 9–11, 16–18.

4. B. N. Mironov, *Vnutrennyi rynok Rossii v vtoroi polovine XVIII–pervoi polovine XIX v.* (Leningrad, 1981), 71–72, 243.

5. Stearns, *Consumerism in World History,* chaps. 2, 4.

6. From 1885 to 1899, the number of trade enterprises in Russia grew from 575,700 to 845,300. G. A. Dikhtiar, *Vnutrenniaia torgovlia v dorevoliutsionnoi Rossii* (Moscow, 1960), 26.

7. In the mid-nineteenth century, more than 90 percent of merchants registered in the third guild, a category designated for petty domestic trade and manufacturing. William L. Blackwell, *The Beginnings of Russian Industrialization, 1800–1860* (Princeton: Princeton University Press, 1968), 97.

8. I. A. Slonov, *Iz zhizn' torgovoi Moskvy (polveka nazad)* (Moscow, 1914); A. P. Polovnikov, *Torgovlia v staroi Rossii* (Moscow, 1958), 80–81; Robert Gohstand, "The Internal Geography of Trade in Moscow from the Mid-Nineteenth Century to the First World War" (PhD diss., University of California, Berkeley, 1973), 28–32, 55; Ruane, *Empire's New Clothes,* 767.

9. Gohstand, "Internal Geography of Trade in Moscow," 155.

10. V. Giliarovskii, *Moskva i Moskvichi: ocherki staromoskovskogo byta* (Moscow, 1959), 45.

11. I. Avdenko, *Putevoditel' po Odesse i eia okrestnostiiam na 1912 goda* (Odessa, 1912), 59.

12. *Istoriia Moskvy,* vol. 4 (Moscow: Akademiia Nauk SSSR, 1954), 184. Gohstand disputes the higher figures, arguing that the number of street vendors remained fairly constant between 1882 and 1902, ranging from 4,440 in 1882 to 4,352 in 1902. Gohstand, "Internal Geography of Trade in Moscow," 605–6.

13. Stearns, *Consumerism in World History,* chaps. 2, 5; McKendrick, Brewer, and Plumb, *Birth of a Consumer Society,* 1–29.

14. Jennifer Jones, "Coquettes and Grisettes: Women Buying and Selling in Ancien Régime Paris," in *Sex of Things,* ed. De Grazia with Furlough, 33.

15. M. I. Pyliaev, *Staraia Moskva: rasskazy iz byloi zhizni pervoprestol'noi stolitsy* (Moscow, 1990), 255; *Istoriia Moskvy,* vol. 4, 170.

16. Grigorii Moskvich, *Illiustrirovannyi prakticheskii putevoditel' po Odesse* (Odessa, 1907), 105–12.

17. Thomas Owen, *Russian Corporate Capitalism from Peter the Great to Perestroika* (New York: Oxford University Press, 2005), 182.

18. Walter Benjamin, *The Arcades Project,* trans. Howard Eiland and Kevin McLaughlin (Cambridge, MA: Belknap Press of Harvard University Press, 1999), 15–16; Susan Buck-Morss, *The Dialectics of Seeing: Walter Benjamin and the Arcades Project* (Cambridge, MA: MIT Press, 1993), 39–40, 83–86. On retail arcades in Russia and commercial architecture more generally, see William Craft Brumfield, *A History of Russian Architecture* (New York: Cambridge University Press, 1993), 261, 405; Brumfield, "Aesthetics and Commerce: The Architecture of Merchant Moscow, 1890–1917," in *Merchant Moscow,* ed. West and Petrov, 120. See also *Istoriia Moskvy,* vol. 4, 170; Grigorii Moskvich, *Putevoditel' po Moskve* (Moscow, 1903), 27; and Gohstand, "Internal Geography of Trade in Moscow," 614–15.

19. McReynolds, *Russia at Play,* 5–10. On the transformation of the West End of Mayfair and St. James in late-nineteenth-century London, see Walkowitz, *City of Dreadful Delight,* 24–25.

20. The rise of the fancy goods and department store and a discussion of the characteristics of modern retailing are outlined in Miller, *Bon Marché,* chap. 1; Perrot, *Fashioning the Bourgeoisie,* chaps. 4, 5; Erika Diane Rappaport, *Shopping for Pleasure: Women in the Making of London's West End* (Princeton: Princeton University Press, 2001); Benson, *Counter Cultures,* chap. 1; and Williams, *Dream Worlds,* 66–67.

21. Harvey Pitcher, *Muir & Mirrielees: The Scottish Partnership That Became a Household Name in Russia* (Cromer, England: Swallow House Books, 1994); *Torgovlia, promylshennost' i tekhnika,* no. 2 (December 10, 1909): 2–3.

22. On the rebuilding of the store, see William Craft Brumfield, *The Origins of Modernism in Russian Architecture* (Berkeley: University of California Press, 1991), 116.

23. Muir & Mirrielees *preis-kuranty* (catalogs), Fine Arts Section, Russian State Library (Russkaia gosudarstvennaia biblioteka, Izobrazitel'nyi otdel, Moscow [hereafter, RGB IZO]).

24. Russkii gosudarstvennyi istoricheskii arkhiv (hereafter, RGIA), f. 23, opis' 24, d. 598, l. 77.

25. Profits detailed in the Muir & Mirrielees annual reports in RGIA, f. 23, opis' 24, d. 598, ll. 183–4; and f. 23, opis' 14, d. 699, ll. 22–23.

26. In 1896, the owner, Evstrati Mikhailovich Petrokokino, built the new store on Greek Street to take the place of the earlier structure. Departments included perfume, foreign cigars and smoking supplies, luggage, Russian- and foreign-made toys, Chinese and Japanese handcrafted items, housewares and gardening tools, and seasonal goods such as those for Easter and Christmas. *Torgovo-promyshlennaia Odessa,* July 9, 1914, 2; advertisement for Petrokokino Brothers in *Iuzhno-Russkii almanakh za 1898 g.* (Odessa, 1898), 26.

27. Dikhtiar, *Vnutrenniaia torgovlia,* 82.

28. Ibid., 93.

29. Ibid., 90.

30. Business cards preserved in Gosudarstvennyi istoricheskii muzei, Otdel pis'mennykh istochnikov (hereafter, GIM OPI), f. 402, opis' 1, d. 227.

31. I. Beliaev, "Obozrenie Moskvy. Vneshnii vid stolitsy," in *Moskovskii arkhiv: istoriko-kraevedcheskii al'manakh* (Moscow 1996), 417. This article was originally published in *Rodnaia Rech'* in 1897.

32. One former Moscow merchant detailed the variety and persistence of biases against the commercial-industrial classes in his memoir: P. A. Buryshkin, *Moskva kupecheskaia* (New York, 1954), 11–54.

33. Theodore H. von Laue, *Sergei Witte and the Industrialization of Russia* (New York: Atheneum, 1973), 95–99, 277–90; Ruth AmEnde Roosa, *Russian Industrialists in an Era of Revolution: The Association of Industry and Trade, 1906–1917,* ed. Thomas C. Owen (Armonk, NY: M. E. Sharpe, 1997), 42–53.

34. Joseph Bradley, *Muzhik i Muscovite: Urbanization in Late Imperial Russia* (Berkeley: University of California Press, 1985), 79; R. W. Davies, "Introduction: from Tsarism to NEP," in *From Tsarism to the New Economic Policy: Continuity and Change in the Economy of the USSR,* ed. R.W. Davies (Ithaca: Cornell University Press, 1991), 11–12.

35. Roosa, *Russian Industrialists,* 105–8.

36. Ruckman, *Moscow Business Elite,* 51–52; James L. West, "The Fate of Merchant Moscow," in *Merchant Moscow,* ed. West and Petrov, 173–75; Thomas C. Owen, *Capitalism and Politics in Russia: A Social History of the Moscow Merchants, 1855–1905* (New York: Cambridge University Press, 1981); Buryshkin, *Moskva kupecheskaia,* 247; Roosa, *Russian Industrialists,* 158–60.

37. Catriona Kelly and Vadim Volkov, "Directed Desires: *Kul'turnost'* and Consumption," in *Constructing Russian Culture in the Age of Revolution,1881–1940,* ed. Catriona Kelly and Vadim Volkov (New York: Oxford University Press, 1998), 121.

38. Edith W. Clowes, "Merchants on Stage and in Life: Theatricality and Public Consciousness," in *Merchant Moscow,* ed. West and Petrov; McReynolds, *Russia at Play,* 30–33, 63–64.

39. Laurie Manchester, *Holy Fathers, Secular Sons: Clergy, Intelligentsia, and the Modern Self in Revolutionary Russia* (DeKalb: Northern Illinois University Press, 2008), 63–67.

40. N. Teleshov, *Zapiski pisatelia: vospominaniia i rasskazy o proshlom* (Moscow, 1980), 246–47.

41. See also Davydov, "Moskva piatidesiatye i shestidesiatye gody," 30–32; I. A. Belousov, "Ushedshaia Moskva," in *Ushedshaia Moskva,* ed. Ashukina; and the memoir by the Row merchant Slonov, *Iz zhizn' torgovoi Moskvy.*

42. The word *listok* might also be rendered as "rag," hence *The Moscow Rag,* a translation that captures publishers' intent to create a less formal newspaper specializing in urban gossip, sensational stories, and humor.

43. Daniel R. Brower, "The Penny Press and Its Readers," in *Cultures in Flux: Lower-Class Values, Practices, and Resistance in Late Imperial Russia,* ed. Stephen P. Frank and Mark D. Steinberg (Princeton: Princeton University Press, 1994), 152–59; Louise McReynolds, "V. M. Doroshevich: The Newspaper Journalist and the Development of Public Opinion in Civil Society," in *Between Tsar and People,* ed. Clowes, Kassow, and West.

44. *Moskovksii listok,* January 31, 1896, 3.

45. *Moskovksii listok,* February 18, 1896, 3.

46. *Moskovksii listok,* February 22, 1889, 2; January 7, 1889, 2.

47. *Odesskaia mysl',* September 21, 1909, 2–3.

48. *Odesskie novosti,* June 1, 1895, 3.

49. *Moskovksii listok,* November 2, 1888. A similar report appeared on November 14, 1888, 2.

50. *Odesskie novosti,* January 26, 1900, 3.

51. *Odesskie novosti,* January 25, 1900, 3.

52. See discussion of the "Robinisti" and atmosphere at the two cafés in Sylvester, *Tales of Old Odessa,* 113–18. See also an earlier satirical critique in *Odesskii listok,* August 12, 1898, 3.

53. Peter Fritzsche interprets Berlin's boulevard press as schooling readers in a "metropolitan literacy," which gave them the ability to "read the city." Fritzsche, *Reading Berlin 1900* (Cambridge, MA: Harvard University Press, 1996), 89–90.

54. See, for example, *Moskovksii listok,* March 14, 1896, 2; *Odesskie novosti,* February 1, 1901, 3, January 6, 1901, 4, and April 17, 1901, 3; *Odesskii listok,* April 20, 1896, 3, January 29, 1900, 3, and April 13, 1896, 3.

55. *Odesskie novosti,* January 3, 1898, 3; *Odesskaia gazeta,* January 10, 1898, 3, January 24, 1898, 3.

Chapter 2. Palaces of Retailing and Consumption

1. Rieber, *Merchants and Entrepreneurs,* 416–21; Thomas C. Owen, "Impediments to a Bourgeois Consciousness in Russia, 1880–1905: The Estate Structure, Ethnic Diversity, and Economic Regionalism," in *Between Tsar and People,* ed. Clowes, Kassow, and West.

2. Documents pertaining to the construction of Odessa's Passazh have not been preserved in the archives. However, reports in the city's newspapers, as well as city guides and other sources, provide a considerable amount of information.

3. As chief clerk of the Upper Trading Rows Corporation, the joint-stock company formed to finance the rebuilding, Razmadze chronicled the history and rebuilding of the Upper Rows. A. S. Razmadze, *Torgovye riady na Krasnoi ploshchadi v Moskve* (Kiev, 1893).

4. *Istoriia Moskvy,* vol. 1, 428–36; M. V. Dovnar-Zapol'skii, "Torgovlia i promyshlennost' Moskvy XVI–XVII vv.," in *Moskva v ee proshlom i nastoiashchem,* vol. 6 (Moscow, 1911), 35–38; M. N. Tikhomirov, *Rossiia v XVI stoletii* (Moscow: Akademiia Nauk, 1962); Gohstand, "Internal Geography of Trade in Moscow," 86–115.

5. Slonov, *Iz zhizn' torgovoi Moskvy,* 100–139; Teleshov, *Zapiski pisatelia,* 245–48; P. V. Sytin, *Iz istorii Moskovskikh ulits* (Moscow, 1958), 73–77.

6. Gohstand, "Internal Geography of Trade in Moscow," 699–700; Irina Potkina, "Moscow's Commercial Mosaic," in *Merchant Moscow,* ed. West and Petrov, 39; William Craft Brumfield, "From the Lower Depths to the Upper Trading Rows: The Design of Retail Shopping Centers in Moscow," in *Commerce in Russian Urban Culture, 1861–1914,* ed. William Craft Brumfield, Boris V. Anan'ich, and Yuri A. Petrov (Washington, DC: Woodrow Wilson Center Press; Baltimore: Johns Hopkins University Press, 2001), 167.

7. Irina Paltusova, "Krupneishii passazh Rossii," *Mir muzeia,* no. 6 (1993): 18.

8. E. I. Kirichenko, *Moskva na rubezhe stoletii* (Moscow, 1977), 42.

9. Brumfield, "Aesthetics and Commerce," 121.

10. Joseph Bradley argues for a similar kind of complementarity in his study of the 1872 Polytechnical Exposition, orchestrated by the Moscow Society of Friends of Natural History, Anthropology, and Ethnography, which "juxtaposed the modern and the foreign with the traditional and the Russian" and demonstrated the desire to showcase Russia's

scientific and technical developments while retaining the country's cultural distinctiveness. Bradley, "Pictures at an Exhibition," 935.

11. Other cities also rebuilt their central rows several times. On the history of St. Petersburg's Gostinyi Dvor, see I. A. Bogdanov, *Gostinyi Dvor* (Leningrad, 1988). See also L. A. Kovaleva, "Kostromskie torgovye riady v pervoi polovine XVII v.," in *Torgovlia, kupechestvo i tamozhennoe delo v Rossii v XVI–XVII vv.* (St. Petersburg: St. Petersburg University, 2001).

12. This account of the origins and evolution of the Rows relies primarily on Razmadze, *Torgovye riady na Krasnoi ploshchadi,* 5–33; and Gohstand, "Internal Geography of Trade in Moscow," 86–98. See also Slonov, *Iz zhizn' torgovoi Moskvy,* 104–21; and Teleshov, *Zapiski pisatelia,* 245–48.

13. Samuel H. Baron, trans. and ed., *The Travels of Olearius in Seventeenth-Century Russia* (Stanford: Stanford University Press, 1967), 114–15. Summaries of other foreign visitors' impressions are in Dovnar-Zapol'skii, "Torgovlia i promyshlennost' Moskvy," 36.

14. Dovnar-Zapol'skii, "Torgovlia i promyshlennost' Moskvy," 39; *Istoriia Moskvy,* vol. 1, 431–33; Tikhomirov, *Rossiia v XVI stoletii,* 92.

15. On the 1789–1805 rebuilding, see Brumfield, *History of Russian Architecture,* 339; Slonov, *Iz zhizn' torgovoi Moskvy,* 116; and *Istoriia Moskvy,* vol. 4, 166.

16. Judging from photographs of market squares in other Russian cities, including smaller ones such as Torzhok and Mozhaisk, lavka rows united by a façade was common. I thank Mikhail Zolotarev for generously sharing with me his collection of photographs of commerce, including those of Torzhok's and Mozhaisk's trading rows.

17. Dovnar-Zapol'skii, "Torgovlia i promyshlennost' Moskvy," 39–45.

18. My figures do not reflect the number of different tenants, as some overlap existed. For example, one Mar'ia Dekhtereva sold haberdashery items from a cupboard on the Knife Row and maintained a boot shop on the Cotton and Knife Row. Likewise, Fedor Molchanov's icon shop on the Icon Row had an adjoining warehouse, listed as a separate space under his wife's name. *Topograficheskii kupecheskii riadskii kalendar'* (Moscow, 1862).

19. Map from 1875, Tsentral'nyi istoricheskii arkhiv Moskvy (hereafter, TsIAM), f. 173, opis' 1, d. 2, l. 25; K. Nustrem, *Spetsial'noe obozrenie Moskvy* (Moscow, 1846); M. Rudolf, *Ukazatel' mestnosti v Kremle i Kitai Gorode stolichnogo goroda Moskvy* (Moscow, 1846).

20. Teleshov, *Zapiski pisatelia,* 246.

21. G. Vasilich, "Moskva 1850–1910," in *Moskva v ee proshlom i nastoiashchem,* vol. 11 (Moscow, 1912), 8.

22. N. A. Varentsov, *Slyshannoe. Vidennoe. Peredymannoe. Perezhitoe* (Moscow, 1999), 357.

23. Slonov, *Iz zhizn' torgovoi Moskvy,* 116.

24. V. N. Kharuzina, *Proshloe: vospominaniia detskikh i otrocheskikh let* (Moscow, 1999), 69. Kharuzina (1866–1931) grew up in Moscow in a wealthy merchant family. She wrote her memoirs in 1912.

25. Slonov, *Iz zhizn' torgovoi Moskvy,* 135.

26. Teleshov, *Zapiski pisatelia,* 246–47.

27. Photographs published in *Moskva: vidy nekotorykh mestnstei, khramov, primechatel'nykh zdanii i drugikh sooruzhenii* (Moscow, 1888).

28. Slonov, *Iz zhizn' torgovoi Moskvy,* 149.

29. Kharuzina, *Proshloe,* 69.

30. G. Vasilich, "Moskva, 1850–1910," 9.

31. *Topograficheskii kupecheskii riadskii kalendar'*.

32. Gohstand, "Internal Geography of Trade in Moscow," 113–15; *Topograficheskii kupecheskii riadskii kalendar'*.

33. Gohstand, "Internal Geography of Trade in Moscow," 140–42. See also G. T. Lowth, *Around the Kremlin* (London: Hurst and Blacklett, 1868), 233–34, for an Englishman's description from an earlier period of the camaraderie he observed among Row merchants.

34. Kharuzina, *Proshloe*, 68.

35. Peasants and working-class males treated each other to drinks as part of a rite of initiation into adulthood and thereafter to cement work relationships. Christine Worobec, "Masculinity in Late-Imperial Russian Peasant Society," in *Russian Masculinities in History and Culture*, ed. Barbara Evans Clements, Rebecca Friedman, and Dan Healey (New York: Palgrave, 2002), 80–81; Mark Steinberg, *Moral Communities: The Culture of Class Relations in the Russian Printing Industry* (Berkeley: University of California Press, 1992), chap. 3.

36. Galina N. Ulianova, "Old Believers and New Entrepreneurs: Religious Belief and Ritual in Merchant Moscow," in *Merchant Moscow*, ed. West and Petrov.

37. Slonov, *Iz zhizn' torgovoi Moskvy*, 134–35.

38. Ibid., 150, 180.

39. The various rebuilding proposals are in the archives of the Moscow Governor-General, TsIAM, f. 16, opis' 27, d. 932, and summarized in Razmadze, *Torgovye riady na Krasnoi ploshchadi*, 34–35.

40. Petitions in TsIAM, f. 16, opis' 27, d. 932, l. 30.

41. "Doklad po osmotru torgovykh gorodskikh riadov," TsIAM, f. 16, opis' 27, d. 930, l. 15.

42. Alekseev (1852–1893) was a member of a prominent entrepreneurial family and a Hereditary Honored Citizen. Under Alekseev's leadership, a new city hall was built, and the duma took steps to extend public water service and create a sewage system. Alekseev also spearheaded improvements in the organization of city hospitals and expanded Moscow's school system. Critics excoriated him for his despotic methods and his disregard of the duma's role in municipal affairs. *Moskva:entsiklopediia*, ed. S. O. Shmidt (Moscow, 1997), 280–81. See also JoAnn Ruckman, *The Moscow Business Elite: A Social and Cultural Portrait of Two Generations, 1840–1905* (DeKalb: Northern Illinois University Press, 1984), 116–17.

43. Remarks of Dolgorukii and other officials in "Zapiska po delu o zakrytii . . . Moskovskikh gorodskikh riadakh," TsIAM, f. 16, opis' 27, d. 929, ll. 1–2, 6–60b.

44. Report on meeting of lavka proprietors in TsIAM, f. 16, opis' 27, d. 930, ll. 30–300b; and Razmadze, *Torgovye riady na Krasnoi ploshchadi*, 35.

45. Newspaper announcement in archives of Moscow Merchants Board, TsIAM, f. 3, opis' 1, d. 1807, l. 1.

46. The third inspection team cited fire and safety hazards, including dilapidated wooden floors, stone and tile passageways with uneven wear patterns and many holes, and steep, narrow, decrepit wooden staircases. Also, they also noted a lack of sufficient light and ventilation, cramped conditions, and untidy housekeeping, which, the inspectors asserted, created great quantities of dust in the air. "Protokol no. 1," TsIAM, f. 16, opis' 27, d. 930, ll. 60–600b.

47. "Zapiska po delu o zakrytii," TsIAM, f. 16, opis' 27, d. 929, l. 6 ob, 36–38.

48. Slonov, *Iz zhizn' torgovoi Moskvy,* 122.

49. Ibid. The incident was also reported in *Russkie vedomosti,* October 13, 1886.

50. Razmadze, *Torgovye riady na Krasnoi ploshchadi,* 37.

51. "Zapiska po delu o zakrytii," TsIAM, f. 16, opis' 27, d. 929, l. 210.

52. Walter Hanchett, "Moscow in the Late Nineteenth Century: A Study in Municipal Self-Government" (PhD diss., University of Chicago, 1964), 316–17.

53. Petition, in TsIAM, f. 3, opis' 1, d. 1807, ll. 24–25.

54. Petition, in TsIAM, f. 3, opis' 1, d. 1807, l. 31.

55. TsIAM, f. 16, opis' 27, d. 932, l. 163.

56. The Telepeevs, for example, received one hundred rubles.

57. TsIAM, f. 3, opis' 1, d. 1807, ll. 21–210b.

58. Both quotations from TsIAM, f. 16, opis' 27, d. 932, l. 44.

59. A copy of the statutes is preserved in TsIAM, f. 173, opis' 1, d. 3, ll. 4–15.

60. TsIAM, f. 173, opis' 1, d. 3, ll. 4–5, 6, 9, 12, 14, 15.

61. Razmadze, *Torgovye riady na Krasnoi ploshchadi,* 44–46.

62. Information compiled from 1894 and 1901 listings of shareholders. Comparisons of three lists from 1894, 1901, and 1912 show many continuities among top shareholders. List from 1894 in RGIA, f. 23, opis' 24, d. 57, ll. 174–79; list from 1901 in RGIA, f. 23, opis' 24, d. 57, ll. 273–291; list from 1912 in *Spisok aktsionerov obshchestva verkhnikh torgovykh riadov na Krasnoi ploshchadi v Moskve na 11 fevralia 1912 goda* (Moscow, 1912).

63. Five to ten shares were required to be a council member. Statutes of the Upper Trading Rows Corporation, TsIAM, f. 173, opis' 1, d. 3, ll. 9, 12.

64. Shareholders also elected P. V. Shchapov to be chairman of the council, and the council members elected were Pavel M. Tret'iakov (of the linen industrialist family and patron of Tret'iakov Art Museum), V. P. Vishniakov, M. P. Shcherbachev, V. M. Mikhailov, S. M. Musorin, V. V. Shchenkov, and Row merchant N. S. Sergeev. Profiles of most of these men are in *Spravochnaia kniga o litsakh poluchivshikh na 1894 goda kupecheskiia svidetel'stva po 1-i i 2-i gil' diiam v Moskve* (Moscow, 1894). There were changes in the composition of the company's board and council in the first few years. By 1895, S. A. Bulochkin occupied the chairman of the board position, and Kalashnikov and A. S. Izergin were serving as board members. That same year, P. P. Beldiartsev held the position of chairman of the council. During these intervening years, Tret'iakov also left his position and Shchapov died. Razmadze, *Torgovye riady na Krasnoi ploshchadi,* 39.

65. Razmadze, *Torgovye riady na Krasnoi ploshchadi,* 41.

66. TsIAM, f. 3, opis' 1, d. 1807, ll. 130–300b.

67. TsIAM, f. 3, opis' 1, d. 1807, l. 135; 139–390b.

68. TsIAM, f. 16, opis' 27, d. 932, l. 458.

69. Account of demolition in *Moskovskie vedomosti,* September 21, 1883, 3.

70. Brumfield, "Aesthetics and Commerce," 119–20.

71. Richard Wortman, *Scenarios of Power: Myth and Ceremony in Russian Monarchy,* vol. 2 (Princeton: Princeton University Press, 2000), chaps. 5, 6.

72. In 1882, *Nedeli stroitelia* (Construction Weekly) reported that the tsar wished the Cathedral of the Resurrection of Christ in St. Petersburg, which was in its planning stages, to be executed in the "Russian style." Wortman, *Scenarios of Power,* 244–45.

73. Brumfield, "Aesthetics and Commerce," 120–21; Wortman, *Scenarios of Power,* 244–56.

74. TsIAM, f. 173, opis' 1, d. 1, ll. 7–70b; Razmadze, *Torgovye riady na Krasnoi ploshchadi,* 42–44.

75. Razmadze, *Torgovye riady na Krasnoi ploshchadi,* 40.

76. *Konkurs na proektu zdanii Verkhnykh torgovykh riadov na Krasnoi ploshchadi v Moskve* (Moscow, 1889), 7, 20–21.

77. Ibid., 19, 25, 41.

78. Descriptions in Razmadze, *Torgovye riady na Krasnoi ploshchadi,* 45–50; *Moskovksii listok,* December 3, 1893, 4; *Russkie vedomosti,* December 3, 1893, 2; Grigorii Moskvich, *Illiustrirovannyi prakticheskii putevoditel' po Moskve,* 27; *Putevoditel' po verkhnym torgovym riadam na Krasnoi ploshchadi v Moskve* (Moscow, 1895), 10–12; Paltusova, "Krupneishii passazh Rossii," 14–20; Gohstand, "Internal Geography of Trade in Moscow," 503–5.

79. Razmadze, *Torgovye riady na Krasnoi ploshchadi,* 52.

80. "Novye torgovye riady," *Moskovskie vedomosti,* December 3, 1893, 4.

81. *1000 let Russkogo predprinimatel'stva* (Moscow 1995), 296–301.

82. *Moskovksii listok,* May 13, 1896, 2–3.

83. Kazan' Row may have been intended as a tribute to the city of Kazan' or to Ivan the Terrible's victory over the Kazan' khanate in 1552, an event that occasioned the building of St. Basil's Cathedral. Vladimir may have referred to the ancient town of Vladimir, Vladimir Monomakh, the Grand Prince of Kievan Rus', or Vladimir I, the ruler who adopted Christianity in 988. The names Minin and Pozharskii honored the merchant and prince who organized resistance in Moscow to Polish occupation in 1612. A statue to the two, built to commemorate the two-hundredth anniversary of the events, stood in front of the Rows for nearly one hundred years.

84. List of *shkafchiki* in *Putevoditel' po verkhnym torgovym riadam,* 37–38; Razmadze, *Torgovye riady na Krasnoi ploshchadi,* 48.

85. During the Soviet era, the Nikolai and the Kazan' Mother of God icons were plastered over. These icons have since been restored and reset into the building. The whereabouts of the icon of the Savior are unknown. A. Strekalov, "Ikony na zdanii verkhnykh torgovykh riadov," in *Moskovskii arkhiv: istorikokraevedcheskii al'manakh* (Moscow, 1996), 495–97.

86. Grand opening ceremonies are detailed in *Moskovskie vedomosti,* December 3, 1893, 4; *Russkie vedomosti,* December 3, 1893, 2; "O polozhenii predpriiatiia verkhnykh riadov," TsIAM, f. 173, opis' 1, d. 1, ll. 71–710b; and *Putevoditel' po verkhnym torgovym riadam,* 13. A gilt-edged, engraved invitation is preserved in GIM OPI, f. 402, opis' 1, d. 227.

87. Statutes preserved in TsIAM, f. 173, opis' 1, d. 3, ll. 7–70b.

88. The concept of activization comes from M. Gavlin, "Evreiskoe predprinimatel'stvo v Moskve v 60–90e gody XIX veka," *Vestnik Evreiskogo Universiteta v Moskve* 3:16 (1997): 11. Benjamin Nathans employs the term *selective integration* to describe the process by which "useful" Jews, including merchants, were allowed to settle in St. Petersburg and other major cities in the late nineteenth century. Benjamin Nathans, *Beyond the Pale: The Jewish Encounter with Late Imperial Russia* (Berkeley: University of California Press, 2002), 78.

89. Gavlin, "Evreiskoe predprinimatel'stvo," 11–12; Nathans, *Beyond the Pale,* 59, 83–86. A decree issued in 1861 gave permission to relocate to Jews having diplomas from scientific institutions and to those who were physicians and surgeons. In 1879, another decree gave the same right to Jews with a higher education, as well as pharmacists, dentists, *fel'dshuri*

(medical assistants), and midwives. See V. Kel'ner, "Evrei, kotorye zhili v Rossii," in *Evrei v Rossii: XIX vek* (Moscow: Novoe literaturnoe obozrenie, 2000), 17.

90. By 1915, Jews accounted for 50 percent of first-guild and 27 percent of second-guild merchants. Gavlin, "Evreiskoe predprinimatel'stvo," 15.

91. Nathans, *Beyond the Pale,* 31–39, 45–56.

92. Gavlin, "Evreiskoe predprinimatel'stvo," 17–18, 21–22.

93. TsIAM, f. 3, opis' 1, d. 1982, l. 1.

94. This assessment of Aleksandr's influence is advanced by John Klier, who argues that the tsar's reign "ushered in a generalized attack on many of the accomplishments of the Reform Era." Klier, "State Policies and the Conversion of Jews in Imperial Russia," in *Of Religion and Empire: Missions, Conversions, and Tolerance in Tsarist Russia,* ed. Robert P. Geraci and Michael Khodarkovsky (Ithaca: Cornell University Press, 2001), 105–6.

95. Gavlin, "Evreiskoe predprinimatel'stvo," 21–22; Owen, *Corporation under Russian Law,* 118–23.

96. I. Rozental', "Moskva nachala XX veka: Evrei, vlast', obshchestvo," *Vestnik Evreiskogo Universiteta,* no. 1 (1999): 96, 99.

97. In 1892, the year after Gresser's death, the number of Jews in the city rose significantly. Nathans, *Beyond the Pale,* 99–100, 106.

98. Vasilii Orlik, *Moi zametki na proekt ustava obshchestva torgovykh riadov na Krasnoi ploshchadi v Moskve* (Moscow 1886), 4 (original emphasis). Orlik's choice of terms is worth noting. Legally, Jews were classified as *inorodtsy,* a word that denotes a non-Russian. "*Chuzdyi dlia nas*" not only indicates that Jews were not Russian but also suggests that they were a group of people alien to or unconnected to Russia and Russians.

99. Theodore R. Weeks, *Nation and State in Late Imperial Russia: Nationalism and Russification on the Western Frontier, 1863–1914* (DeKalb: Northern Illinois University Press, 1996), 42.

100. Razmadze, *Torgovye riady na Krasnoi ploshchadi,* 5–8.

101. *Mysli o gorodskikh riadakh starogo obyvatelia g. Moskvy* (Moscow, 1887), 5–6.

102. Ibid., 7.

103. *Moskovskie vedomosti,* December 3, 1893, 3–4.

104. RGIA, f. 23, opis' 24, d. 57, l. 216.

105. RGIA, f. 23, opis' 24, d. 57, ll. 191–910b, 192–93.

106. RGIA, f. 23, opis' 24, d. 57, l. 220.

107. RGIA, f. 23, opis' 24, d. 57, l. 2990b.

108. RGIA, f. 23, opis' 24, d. 57, ll. 341–410b.

109. This estimate is based on a listing of tenants in "Spisok arendatorov verkhnykh torgovykh riadov" (1895), preserved in TsIAM, f. 173, opis' 1, d. 1, ll. 128–310b.

110. Figures based on my own calculations from lists of tenants in *Putevoditel' po verkhnym torgovym riadam.*

111. TsIAM, f. 173, opis' 1, d. 1, l. 47.

112. "Doklad no. 30: o plane deistvii na tekushchii 1895 g.," TsIAM, f. 173, opis' 1, d. 1, l. 93.

113. "O plane deistvii na 1896," TsIAM, f. 173, opis' 1, d. 1, l. 1360b.

114. Ibid., 134–340b, 136–360b. The number of occupants differs slightly, depending on sources. See *Putevoditel' po verkhnym torgovym riadam;* and "Spisok arendatorov," TsIAM, f. 173, opis' 1, d. 1, ll. 128–310b.

115. In 1902, approximately 790 spaces representing 332 firms were occupied, 280 on the first floor, 216 on the second, and 188 on the third. Figures calculated from a 1902 list of Row merchants. TsIAM, f. 173, opis' 1, d. 16, ll. 2–20b.

116. Gohstand, "Internal Geography of Trade in Moscow," 495.

117. Slonov, *Iz zhizn' torgovoi Moskvy,* 120–21.

118. Ibid., 121.

119. Ibid.

120. Provisions in "Dogovory" [Agreements], TsIAM, f. 173, opis' 1, d. 21, l. 74.

121. *Moskovksii listok,* January 31, 1896, 3.

122. "O plane deistvii na 1896," TsIAM, f. 173, opis' 1, d. 1, ll. 136–360b.

123. "Doklad no. 14: o deiatelnosti za 1896 g.," TsIAM, f. 173, opis' 1, d. 1, ll. 173–730b.

124. *Moskovksii listok,* March 18, 1896, 3.

125. Slonov, *Iz zhizn' torgovoi Moskvy,* 121.

126. Company's annual financial statements for 1895, 1904, and 1909, in TsIAM, f. 173, opis' 1, d. 1, ll. 22–24; d. 17, ll. 2–3; d. 18, ll. 2–3; d. 20, l. 35.

127. Patricia Herlihy, *Odessa: A History, 1794–1914* (Cambridge, MA: Harvard University Press, 1986), 270.

128. *Odessa, 1794–1894: izdanie gorodskogo obshchestvennogo upravleniia k stoletiiu goroda* (Odessa, 1895), 145–51, 182.

129. Comments of English and French visitors and officials reported in Herlihy, *Odessa,* 7, 12, 26, 174–77, 210–11.

130. Roshanna P. Sylvester, "Making an Appearance: Urban 'Types' and the Creation of Respectability in Odessa's Popular Press, 1912–1914," *Slavic Review* 59:4 (winter 2000): 802–3.

131. *Sovremennaia Rossiia: ocherki nashei gosudarstvennoi i obshchesstvennoi zhizni,* vol. 2 (St. Petersburg, 1891), 52.

132. Serhy Yekelchyk, *Ukraine: Birth of a Modern Nation* (New York: Oxford University Press, 2007), 14–15, 25–31, 34–35; Herlihy, *Odessa,* 13–17, 44, 255–56.

133. Herlihy, *Odessa,* 241; Stephen J. Zipperstein, *The Jews of Odessa: A Cultural History, 1794–1881* (Stanford: Stanford University Press, 1985), 34–39, 43. The 1897 census found that Jews were concentrated in the middle classes, filling positions in commerce, retail, and the professions, although they were not numerous in industry.

134. During Aleksandr III's reign, the proportion of seats Jews could hold was reduced to one-fifth, even though Jews constituted a third of the city's population. Herlihy, *Odessa,* 152, 251–53.

135. Herlihy, *Odessa,* 12–21; Herlihy, "Commerce and Architecture in Late Imperial Russia," in *Commerce in Russian Urban Culture, 1861–1914,* ed. William Craft Brumfield, Boris V. Anan'ich, and Yuri A. Petrov (Washington, DC: Woodrow Wilson Center Press; Baltimore: Johns Hopkins University Press, 2001).

136. The arcade cost 1.3 million rubles to build. Descriptions in D. I. Vainer, *Illius-trirovannyi putevoditel' "Odessa" na 1900 g.* (Odessa, 1900), 51, 53; Moskvich, *Illiustrirovannyi prakticheskii putevoditel' po Odesse,* 149–50.

137. Of the more than twenty-five retailers listed in the ad, only five or six carried ethnically Russian names. *Odesskie novosti,* January 12, 1900, 4.

138. Ads in *Odesskie novosti,* March 15, 1900, 1; March 24, 1900, 1; March 25, 1900, 3.

139. A first offense against the rule brought a fine of one hundred rubles, a second

infraction, two hundred rubles, and a third violation, five hundred rubles. *Odesskie novosti,* March 18, 1900, 1.

140. *Odesskie novosti,* January 24, 1900, 2.

141. Vainer, *Illiustrirovannyi putevoditel' "Odessa" na 1900 g.* 51 (first quote); Moskvich, *Illiustrirovannyi prakticheskii putevoditel' po Odesse,* 149 (remaining quotes).

142. Moskvich, *Illiustrirovannyi prakticheskii putevoditel' po Odesse,* 150.

143. Quotes from *Odesskie novosti* (evening extra), April 27, 1901, 2. Other accounts in *Odesskie novosti,* April 26, 1901, 3; April 27, 1901, 2; and April 29, 1901, 2.

144. *Odesskie novosti,* January 24, 1900, 2–3; January 24, 1900, 3.

145. Benjamin Nathans's call to "bring the empire back in" provided the inspiration and interpretive angle for my interpretation of the Passazh as a project of the Russian Empire.

146. Despite these patterns, he argues that while Jews and non-Jews maintained business relationships, social segregation remained firmly in place. Zipperstein, *Jews of Odessa,* 21, 36–39, 65–66.

147. Nathans, *Beyond the Pale,* 121.

148. Ibid., 50, 67–68.

149. Zipperstein, *Jews of Odessa,* 131.

150. Klier, "State Policies and the Conversion of Jews," 93.

151. See Nathans, *Beyond the Pale,* 155–61, for a fascinating analysis of the decades-long project to build the synagogue.

152. Reports of the blaze in *Odesskie novosti,* October 31, 1901, 2–3; November 2, 1901, 3; *Odesskie novosti* (evening extra), November 2, 1901, 2.

153. I. M. Radetskii's letter, *Odesskie novosti,* November 4, 1901, 4.

154. Vasilii Oltin's letter, in *Odesskie novosti,* November 4, 1901, 4.

157. *Odesskie novosti,* October 31, 1901, 3.

156. *Odesskie novosti,* November 4, 1901, 1; December 2, 1901, 2; evening extra, November 6, 1901, 3; November 19, 1901, 1.

Chapter 3. For God, Tsar, and Consumerism

1. Giliarovskii, *Moskva i Moskvichi,* 212–14. Description of Eliseev's store and history of the family and firm in *Torgovyi Dom "Brat'ia Eliseevy" (vne konkursa),* vol. 1 (St. Petersburg, 1900); P. A. Primachenko, *Torgovo-promyshlennyi mir* (Moscow, 1993), 230–36; and Viktor Gerasimov, "Saga o kuptsakh Eliseevykh," *Otchizna,* no. 7 (1991): 10–16.

2. Vera Shevzov, *Russian Orthodoxy on the Eve of Revolution* (New York: Oxford University Press, 2004), 112.

3. The literature on consumer culture provides ample evidence of the rendering of various ideas, trends, persons, and institutions—even those believed to be in opposition to the values of mass society—into commodities. One provocative study argues that the counterculture of the 1960s has been packaged and sold to American consumers. Joseph Heath and Andrew Potter, *Nation of Rebels: Why Counterculture Became Consumer Culture* (New York: Harper, 2004).

4. Rondo Cameron, *A Concise Economic History of the World: From Paleolithic Times to the Present,* 3rd ed. (New York: Oxford University Press, 1997), 130–33. See also John Thornton, *Africa and Africans in the Making of the Atlantic World, 1400–1800,* 2nd ed. (New York: Cambridge University Press, 1998), 53–71.

5. Paul Bushkovitch, *The Merchants of Moscow, 1580–1650* (New York: Cambridge University Press, 1980), 151–58; Samuel H. Baron, "Sixteenth/Seventeenth-Century Russia," in *Entrepreneurship in Imperial Russia and the Soviet Union,* ed. Gregory Guroff and Fred V. Carstensen (Princeton: Princeton University Press, 1983).

6. Robert Gohstand, "The Shaping of Moscow by Trade," in *The City in Russian History,* ed. Michael F. Hamm (Lexington: University Press of Kentucky, 1982), 162–64.

7. As early as 1775, St. Petersburg police and Prince Aleksandr Golitsyn, as military governor-general and field marshal, endeavored to keep bread prices down and thus avert social disorder, but they could not persuade merchants to lower the price of rye flour. See Ransel, *Russian Merchant's Tale,* 56–58. In 1908, one Moscow newspaper reported that municipal officials had failed to force private entrepreneurs to charge reasonable prices for bread. *Russkoe slovo,* July 15, 1908, 5.

8. Owen, *Corporation under Russian Law,* 60–61.

9. Some minor amendments were made to the law during the reign of Nicholas I. Owen, *Corporation under Russian Law,* 18–25.

10. Ibid., 118–20.

11. West, *I Shop in Moscow,* chap. 2. My thanks to Sally for sharing her manuscript with me.

12. Police confiscated more than thirteen hundred copies of the picture of the tsarevich and twenty-eight of the postcards. Correspondence between inspector and Odessa police in Gosudarstvennyi arkhiv Odesskoi oblasti (hereafter, GAOO), f. 13, opis' 1, d. 199, ll. 1, 5.

13. The legal age for street vending was fourteen. Street vending was prohibited at permanent commercial enterprises on Cathedral Square, on the steps of Nikolaevsk bulvar', and in Aleksandrovskii Park. *Adres-kalendar' Odesskogo gradonachal'stva na 1897 g.* (Odessa, 1897), 154–57.

14. *Istoriia Moskvy,* vol. 4, 172–74.

15. Owen, *Corporation under Russian Law,* 18–22.

16. Bushkovitch, *Merchants of Moscow,* 173.

17. Ransel, *Russian Merchant's Tale,* 58.

18. "Binding Decree on Business Hours of Commercial-Industrial Establishment on Sundays and Holidays," in *Adres-kalendar' Odesskogo gradonachal'stva,* 231–32. Some of Russia's leading merchants banded together to advertise that their stores would be closed on Sundays or have shortened workdays. Advertisements in *Odesskie novosti,* June 2, 1901, 1.

19. Sally West, "Constructing Consumer Culture: Advertising in Imperial Russia to 1914" (PhD diss., University of Illinois, 1995), 56–66.

20. Merchants could also be awarded titles such as "Purveyor to the Court of the Grand Duchess" or purveyors to other royal family members. West, "Constructing Consumer Culture," 76–81.

21. Valentin Katayev, *A Mosaic of Life or the Magic Horn of Oberon: Memoirs of a Russian Childhood* (Chicago: J. Philip O'Hara, 1976), 391.

22. From Einem's 1916 catalog, preserved in RGB IZO, Papka Y9 (28) 425.51.

23. Advertisement in *Damskii mir,* January 1912.

24. Advertisement for the cologne in *Damskii mir,* April 1912. Tin on display at Muzei upakovki, Moscow, 2000. A group of Moscow haberdashers offered commemorative

shawls with images of the leaders and events of 1812. See advertisement in *Vechernaia pochta,* January 1, 1912, 2.

25. *Zolotoi iubilei k piatidesiatiletiiu so dnia osnovaniia T-va Brokar i Ko* (Moscow, 1914), 64–66.

26. Wortman, *Scenarios of Power,* 481–84; advertisement for Sunshine of Russia in *Odesskie novosti,* June 27, 1913, 1.

27. The British royal ceremony, marked by greater skill of presentation and positive reception, was also reinvented. David Cannadine, "Splendor Out of Court: Royal Spectacle and Pageantry in Modern Britain, c. 1820–1977," in *Rites of Power: Symbolism, Ritual, and Politics since the Middle Ages,* ed. Sean Wilentz (Philadelphia: University of Pennsylvania, 1985), 222. Tori Smith notes that the skillful presentation and successful reception were largely achieved through commercial involvement. See Tori Smith, "'Almost Pathetic . . . but Also Very Glorious': The Consumer Spectacle of the Diamond Jubilee," *Histoire sociale/ Social History* 58 (November 1996): 333–56.

28. *Odesskie novosti,* May 15, 1896, 2–3.

29. *Moskovskii listok,* May 8, 1896, 3.

30. Shevzov, *Russian Orthodoxy on the Eve of Revolution,* 112.

31. *Moskovskii listok,* November 1888, 2. The merchants of Zaitsev market, along with local residents, also organized a thanksgiving service. *Moskovskii listok,* November 4, 1888, 2.

32. Of the proceeds from the sale of the lithographs, 10 percent went to the procurement of additional beds in the surgical unit at St. George's Hospital. Advertisement in *Moskovskii listok,* February 21, 1889, 4.

33. Georg Simmel's theory of fashion change postulates that fashions are first adopted by the upper class and later by the middle and lower classes. Georg Simmel, "Fashion," *American Journal of Sociology* 63 (May 1958): 541–58. Veblen's classic model of "conspicuous consumption" postulates that the upper classes consume goods in order to display their social status. Thorstein Veblen, *The Theory of the Leisure Class* (New York: Macmillan, 1899). For a concise discussion of the development of theories on consumption, see Diana Crane, *Fashion and Its Social Agendas: Class, Gender, and Identity in Clothing* (Chicago: University of Chicago Press, 2000), 6–15.

34. Daniel Bell, *The Cultural Contradictions of Capitalism* (New York: Basic Books, 1976); Robert Bocock, *Consumption* (New York: Routledge, 1993). See also de Grazia, introduction to *Sex of Things,* ed. de Grazia with Furlough; and Grant McCracken, *Culture and Consumption: New Approaches to the Symbolic Character of Consumer Goods and Activities* (Bloomington: Indiana University Press, 1988).

35. West, *I Shop in Moscow,* 13, 303; McReynolds, *Russia at Play,* 4–7; Irina Paltusova, *Uvlekatel'nyi mir Moskovskoi reklamy XIX–nachala XX veka* (Moscow 1996); Barbara Alpern Engel, *Between the Fields and the City: Women, Work, and Family in Russia, 1861–1914* (New York: Cambridge University Press, 1994), 81–82, 117–18, 155–58; Jeffrey Burds, *Peasant Dreams and Market Politics: Labor Migration and the Russian Village, 1861–1905* (Pittsburgh: University of Pittsburgh Press, 1998), 144–71; Laura Engelstein, *The Keys to Happiness: Sex and the Search for Modernity in Fin-de-Siècle Russia* (Ithaca: Cornell University Press, 1992), 359–403; Jeffrey Brooks, *When Russia Learned to Read: Literacy and Popular Literature, 1861–1917* (Princeton: Princeton University Press, 1985).

36. Abrikosov's 1911 catalog, RGB IZO, Papka Y9 (28) 425.51; Brocard's products,

Zolotoi iubilei, 58–62, 116; Krakhmalnikov's candy wrappers, Nicolas V. Iljine, ed., *Odessa Memories* (Seattle: University of Washington Press, 2003), 82–83.

37. Giliarovskii, *Moskva i Moskvichi,* 207, 211–14; Gerasimov, "Saga o kuptsakh Eliseevykh," 12.

38. Floral became one of Brocard's best-selling items. *Zolotoi iubilei,* 60–61, 68–69, 72–73.

39. *K stoletiiu chainoi firmy "V. Perlov s synov'iami" (1787 g. – 1887 g.): istoriko-statisticheskii ocherk* (Moscow, 1898), 133–42.

40. Information on newspapers and reader profiles in Brower, "Penny Press and Its Readers," 152–53; Brooks, *When Russia Learned to Read,* 128–29; and Louise McReynolds, *The News under Russia's Old Regime: The Development of a Mass Circulation Press* (Princeton: Princeton University Press, 1991), 102.

41. *Moskovskii listok,* August 4, 1889, 4.

42. *Moskovskii listok,* August 9, 1889, 4.

43. Moskvich, *Illiustrirovannyi prakticheskii putevoditel' po Odesse,* 155.

44. *Moskovskii listok,* June 4, 1889, 4; *Russkoe slovo,* October 13, 1907, 6; *Russkie vedomosti,* August 23, 1908, 4.

45. Advertisement for Petrokokino Brothers in *Iuzhno-Russkii a'manakh za 1898 g.,* 2. Muir & Mirrielees's policies on delivery and COD outlined in various catalogs. See, for example, spring 1897 catalogs in the collection at RGB IZO, Papka Y9 (28) 425.52.

46. Max Weber, *The Protestant Ethic and the Spirit of Capitalism* (New York: Charles Scribner's Sons, 1958).

47. See, for example, essays in Hartmut Lehmann and Guenther Roth, eds., *The Protestant Ethic: Origins, Evidence, Contexts* (Cambridge: Cambridge University Press, 1993).

48. William Leach, *Land of Desire: Merchants, Power, and the Rise of a New American Culture* (New York: Pantheon Books, 1993), 211–13.

49. Ibid., 34–35.

50. James L. West, "The Riabushinskii Circle: *Burzhuaziia* and *Obshchestvennost'* in Late Imperial Russia," in *Between Tsar and People,* ed. Clowes, Kassow, and West; Rieber, *Merchants and Entrepreneurs,* 139–65.

51. Rieber, *Merchants and Entrepreneurs,* 419; Ulianova, "Old Believers and New Entrepreneurs," 24–31.

52. Vasilich, "Moskva 1850–1910 gg," 14, 22.

53. Ruckman, *Moscow Business Elite,* 155–63; P A. Buryshkin, *Moskva kupecheskaia,* 112–220.

54. Teleshov, *Zapiski pisatelia,* 246–47.

55. "Vospominaniia starogo prodavtsa," Gosudarstvennyi arkhiv Russkoi federatsiia, Moscow (hereafter, GARF), f. 6875, opis' 1, d. 525, ll. 1–2.

56. Ulianova, "Old Believers and New Entrepreneurs," 65.

57. *Moskovskie vedomosti,* September 8, 1888, 3; September 12, 1888, 2; September 13, 1888, 2.

58. Reports of various merchant groups' services in *Moskovskie vedomosti,* September 8, 1888, 3; September 12, 1888, 2; September 23, 1888, 3; September 27, 1888, 2.

59. *Moskovskie vedomosti,* June 11, 1913, 3.

60. Slonov, *Iz zhizn' torgovoi Moskvy,* 135–36.

61. M. D. Shevchenko, *Dukhovnaia kul'tura zapadnoi Evropy i Rossii* (Moscow, 1999),

68–69; M. M. Gromyko, "Sluzhby vne khrama," in *Pravoslavnaia zhizn' russkikh krest'ian xix–xx vekov* (Moscow, 2001), 103, 112–16; Shevzov, *Russian Orthodoxy on the Eve of Revolution,* 142–47.

62. Chris J. Chulos, *Converging Worlds: Religion and Community in Peasant Russia, 1861–1917* (DeKalb: Northern Illinois University Press, 2003), 17.

63. Carolyn Johnston Pouncy, ed., *The Domostroi: Rules for Russian Households in the Time of Ivan the Terrible* (Ithaca: Cornell University Press, 1994), 75.

64. Chulos, *Converging Worlds,* 46.

65. In the eighteenth century, the Holy Synod tried to maintain control by requiring worshipers to apply for permission to organize annual processions of the cross, but villagers apparently ignored the requirement and independently made oral agreements with parish priests. Shevzov, *Russian Orthodoxy on the Eve of Revolution,* 145.

66. Calendar preserved in GIM OPI, f. 402, opis' 1, d. 227.

67. Saint Catherine of Alexandria was noted for, among other things, her learning, and she was venerated as the patroness of female students. Advertisements in *Russkie vedomosti,* November 22, 1908, 8; *Russkoe slovo,* September 14, 1906, 1.

68. *Odesskoe slovo,* March 23, 1909, 1; *Novaia Odesskaia gazeta,* September 7, 1908, 1.

69. West, *I Shop in Moscow,* chap. 2.

70. A police supervisor demanded that the offending picture be removed from the display, but the owners did not comply with his request. The case ended up in court, where a justice of the peace fined the Prostakov brothers twenty rubles each. *Odesskie novosti,* April 16, 1901, 33.

71. Only one merchant's merchandise was confiscated. Orders and reports from police stations to police chief in GAOO, f. 2, opis' 1, d. 349, ll. 6–39.

72. I. I. Shneider, *Zapiski starogo Moskvicha* (Moscow, 1970), 91.

73. Ibid., 91–92. *Baby* (meaning "peasant women") confections were taller and more elaborate than the kuliches. They were decorated with sugar clouds, pink and light blue silk banners, and sugar canes topped by small doll heads representing peasant women.

74. Whitney Walton, *France at the Crystal Palace: Bourgeois Taste and Artisan Manufacture in the Nineteenth Century* (Berkeley: University of California Press, 1992), 12.

75. Miller, *Bon Marché,* 19–20.

76. *Chicago Tribune,* October 13, 1868, 4. Taking obvious pride in the construction of the magnificent retail store, the journalist remarked that "New York cannot boast of such a gorgeous palace for the display of dry goods." Ibid.

77. Michael Miller finds a similar tendency among French retail merchants, who also struggled to overcome a generally unsavory image. To counteract it, the Boucicaut family worked diligently to market the Bon Marché to its clientele by cultivating an image of middle-class morality and probity and by dispelling perceptions of the store as an immoral, ruthless place of business. See Miller, *Bon Marché,* chap. 6. Mark Steinberg has examined the impulse among employers in the Russian printing industry to present themselves as entrepreneurs dedicated to traditional values. Moral norms and the calculation of self-interest became intertwined as entrepreneurs sought profit yet strove to improve workers' lives. See Steinberg, *Moral Communities,* chap. 2. Louise McReynolds's interpretation of the "entrepreneurs of the new culture industry," however, diverges from my and these two interpretations. She argues that the various branches of the commercial

entertainment industry depended on the "imagination of men eager to begin new traditions because they had no stake in the old ones." McReynolds, *Russia at Play,* 207.

78. Clifford Geertz, "Centers, Kings, and Charisma: Reflections on the Symbolics of Power," in *Culture and Its Creators: Essays in Honor of Edward Shils,* ed. Joseph Ben-David and Terry Nicholas Clark (Chicago: University of Chicago Press, 1977), 151.

79. In her memoirs, Ekaterina Andreevna-Bal'mont signaled her family's position by dropping the names of prestigious retailers throughout a description of the family home. She recalled that the rooms were furnished by "Mssr. Pascale" and that all of the bronze items were ordered from Shneider's store on Kuznetskii Most. E. A. Andreevna-Bal'mont, *Vospominaniia* (Moscow, 1996), 110.

80. In the mid- to late 1930s, event organizers aimed to provide both entertainment and instruction in the new public political holidays instituted by the Soviet Union. Rosalinde Sartorti, "Stalinism and Carnival: Organisation and Aesthetics of Political Holidays," in *The Culture of the Stalin Period,* ed. Hans Gunther (New York: St. Martin's Press, 1990), 44.

81. Cannadine attributes this trend to the rise of the popular press, international rivalries, and the change in royal image making that presented the monarch as the head of the nation as well as the state. Cannadine, "Splendor Out of Court," 213–19.

82. Wortman, *Scenarios of Power,* 13.

83. Max Rheinstein, ed., *Max Weber on Law in Economy and Society* (New York: Simon & Schuster, 1967), 335–37; Max Weber, *The Sociology of Religion* (Boston: Beacon Press, 1963), 106–7.

84. Wortman, *Scenarios of Power,* 1.

85. Geertz, "Centers, Kings, and Charisma," 152–53; Robert Bocock, *Ritual in Industrial Society: A Sociological Analysis of Ritualism in Modern England* (London: Allen & Unwin, 1974), 9.

86. *Odesskii listok,* June 8, 1896, 2; *Odesskie novosti,* June 8, 1896, 3. These press accounts closely resemble accounts of other large-scale ritual blessing ceremonies. Other retail firms and enterprises for which I have located reportage on opening or anniversary ceremonies include the Upper Trading Rows on Red Square, Postnikov Passazh, Lubianka Passazh, Golofteev Passazh, Filippov's, V. Perlov & Sons, Pavel Sorokoumovskii & Sons Furriers, Brocard & Company, and R. R. Keller.

87. Advertisement in *Iuzhno-Russkii a'lmanakh,* 26; Moskvich, *Illiustrirovannyi prakticheskii putevoditel' po Odesse,* 153–55; *Torgovo-promyshlennaia Odessa,* July 9, 1914, 2; *Adres-kalendar' Odesskogo gradonachal'stva,* 276.

88. For a similar observation about the role of newspapers in early Bolshevik festivals, see James von Geldern, *Bolshevik Festivals, 1917–1920* (Berkeley: University of California Press, 1993). See also the discussion of framing in Diana Crane, *The Production of Culture: Media and the Urban Arts* (Newbury Park, CA: Sage Publications, 1992), 79.

89. This ideal was formally elaborated and circulated in the trade press, especially in *Torgovoe delo* and *Torgovyi mir.*

90. *Odesskii listok,* June 8, 1896, 2.

91. Ibid.

92. Pictures of the south courtyard views of the Louvre, built in 1546, show visual similarities. Horst de la Croix and Richard G. Tansey, eds., *Gardner's Art through the Ages,* 6th ed. (New York: Harcourt Brace Jovanovich, 1975), 573–76.

93. The desire to present customers with refined interiors and aesthetic experiences was not unique to Russia. The dome of the rotunda in the Marshall Field's State Street store, built in Chicago in 1907, featured an illuminated mosaic of Tiffany glass. Jay Pridmore, *Marshall Field's* (San Francisco: Pomegranate, 2002), 41. The Bon Marché exhibited paintings on its main floor and offered in-store concerts. See Miller, *Bon Marché,* chap. 5.

94. Employees of various fur companies in Moscow made a similar presentation to Petr Pavlovich Sorokoumovskii on the occasion of the one-hundredth anniversary of his firm. They presented him with a leather portfolio that contained a written proclamation lauding him for his energy and initiative, kindness of heart, tolerance, humanity, and honesty. Irina Paltusova, "Urok Rossiiskim predprinimateliam," *Mir muzeia,* no. 6 (November–December 1995): 46–48.

95. The term *moral community* is from Steinberg, *Moral Communities.* On the presentation rite, see ibid., 61–66. For a discussion of the paternal policies of the owners of the Bon Marché, see Miller, *Bon Marché,* 87–112.

96. Steinberg also makes this point in his reading of the rituals of the workplace. See Steinberg, *Moral Communities,* 248–49.

97. A photograph from one of the ritual blessings held during the reconstruction of the Upper Trading Rows in Moscow shows very few women among the dignitaries gathered near the front or among the workers standing on the edges of the crowd and above. Photo from Razmadze, *Torgovye riady na Krasnoi ploshchadi.*

98. Advertisement for the bazaar in *Moskovskie vedomosti,* December 3, 1893, 1.

99. *Odesskie novosti* reported that more than six thousand people attended the bazaar, which raised thirty-two hundred rubles. *Odesskie novosti,* April 27, 1901, 2; April 28, 1901, 3.

100. Merchant banks in Moscow gave a "tithe" of 10 percent of their earnings to merchants' charities each year. Adele Lindenmeyr, *Poverty Is Not a Vice: Charity, Society, and the State in Imperial Russia* (Princeton: Princeton University Press, 1996), 58. See also discussion of women's roles in charitable organizations in ibid., 13, 111–26, 149–51; and G. N. Ulianova, *Blagotvoritel'nost' Moskovskikh predprinimatelei, 1860–1914* (Moscow, 1999), 271.

101. *Moskovskii listok,* November 9, 1888, 2.

102. *Odesskii listok,* June 8, 1896, 2.

103. *Odesskie novosti,* January 24, 1900, 3.

104. *K stoletiiu chainoi firmy "V. Perlov s synov'iami,"* 95–102.

105. *Kormchii,* August 16, 1908, 404–5.

106. *Odesskii listok,* June 8, 1896, 2; *Odesskie novosti,* June 8, 1896, 3.

107. Primachenko, *Torgovo-promyshlennyi mir,* 236.

108. Attitudes toward foreign investment in Russia are explored in John P. McKay, *Pioneers for Profit: Foreign Entrepreneurship and Russian Industrialization, 1885–1913* (Chicago: University of Chicago Press, 1970), 268–86.

109. Pitcher, *Muir & Mirrielees,* 161–62.

110. *Moskovskie vedomosti,* May 8, 1889, 3.

111. *K stoletiiu chainoi firmy "V. Perlov s synov'iami,"* 129–31.

112. *Odesskie novosti,* April 16, 1901, 3.

113. *Moskovskii listok,* April 15, 1896, 2.

114. *Zolotoi iubilei,* 89, 112.

115. *Moskovskie vedomosti*, December 3, 1893, 4.

116. *Odesskie novosti*, January 24, 1900, 2–3.

117. *Moskovskie vedomosti*, September 26, 1888, 2; August 30, 1908, 2.

Chapter 4. Visions of Modernity

1. Many professional groups embarked on campaigns to revive and reform Russia in the years after 1905. For an example dealing with physicians, lawyers, and the definition of the modern "sexual regime," see Engelstein, *Keys to Happiness*. For a study that explores the anxieties about behavior among the lower classes in the 1905 era, see Joan Neuberger, *Hooliganism: Crime, Culture, and Power in St. Petersburg, 1900–1914* (Berkeley: University of California Press, 1993).

2. James L. West, "Visions of Russia's Entrepreneurial Future: Pavel Riabushinskii's Utopian Capitalism," in *Merchant Moscow*, ed. West and Petrov.

3. *Torgovyi mir*, September 1910, 2.

4. *Torgovyi mir*, February 1910, 1–3.

5. *Torgovo-promyshlennaia Rossiia*, January 1907, 11–12.

6. *Torgovyi mir*, February 1910, 3.

7. Circulation figures are available only for *Torgovoe delo*, which in 1914 printed thirty-five hundred copies.

8. Barbara Evans Clements, introduction to *Russian Masculinities in History and Culture*, ed. Clements, Friedman, and Healey, 5–10; R. W. Connell, *Masculinities* (Berkeley: University of California Press, 1995), 190–91.

9. Catriona Kelly, "The Education of the Will: Advice Literature, *Zakal*, and Manliness in Early Twentieth Century Russia," in *Russian Masculinities*, ed. Clements, Friedman, and Healey, 141.

10. Michael S. Kimmel, *Manhood in America: A Cultural History* (New York: Free Press, 1996), 5–6; Connell, *Masculinities*, 77–79; Judith Kegan Gardiner, introduction to *Masculinity Studies & Feminist Theory: New Directions*, ed. Judith Kegan Gardiner (New York: Columbia University Press, 2002), 11–12.

11. S. A. Smith, "Masculinity in Transition: Peasant Migrants to Late Imperial St. Petersburg," in *Russian Masculinities*, ed. Clements, Friedman, and Healey, 100–101.

12. Clements, introduction to *Russian Masculinities*, 5. Michael Kimmel refers to a similar set of traits and values as "marketplace manhood." Michael S. Kimmel, *The History of Men: Essays on the History of American and British Masculinities* (Albany: State University of New York Press, 2005), 38.

13. Kelly, "Education of the Will."

14. Ideas of power relations between men and women and of male dominance are, of course, central tenets of gender studies. Joan Wallach Scott, *Gender and the Politics of History* (New York: Columbia University Press, 1988), 2; Connell, *Masculinities*, 68. In a recent essay, Calvin Thomas even argued that masculinity studies should be about the effect of masculinity construction on women. Calvin Thomas, "Reenfleshing the Bright Boys; or, How Male Bodies Matter to Feminist Theory," in *Masculinity Studies & Feminist Theory*, ed. Gardiner, 62. Kimmel, however, argues that American men define masculinity less in relation to women than in relation to each other, yet he states that "women are not incidental to masculinity." The "idea" of women or femininity, and particularly the

perception of effeminacy by other men, inspires constructions of masculinity. Kimmel, *Manhood in America*, 7.

15. Robyn Weigman, "Unmaking: Men and Masculinity in Feminist Theory," in *Masculinity Studies & Feminist Theory*, ed. Gardiner, 43.

16. *Pervaia vseobshchaia perepis' naseleniia Rossiiskoi Imperii, 1897 g.*, vol. 47 (St. Petersburg, 1899–1905).

17. An exception to the tendency to portray only men as merchants can be found in a serialized feuilleton, "The Department Store," which appeared in *Torgovoe delo*. In this tale, a *prikazchik* (shop assistant), with the help of his energetic wife, decides to leave his post at a busy, thriving store to open his own store. The merchant's wife acts as a helpmeet who partners with her husband to create a modern retail store. A. Riazantsev, "Universal'nyi magazin," *Torgovoe delo*, January, February, and March, 1909.

18. *Torgovoe delo*, January 20, 1907, 1–2.

19. Ibid.

20. *Torgovyi mir*, October 4, 1909, 2.

21. Ibid. Kit Kitych is the name of a merchant character in Aleksandr Ostrovskii's play *Shouldering Another's Trouble*. The character's name was commonly used thereafter to refer to a provincial, tyrannical, greedy merchant.

22. *Torgovlia, promyshlennost' i tekhnika*, November 29, 1909, 1.

23. Ibid.

24. Novus, "Iz nabliudenie," *Torgovoe delo*, February 15, 1911, 13–14.

25. Ibid.

26. "Uspekh v zhizni," *Torgovoe delo*, January 20, 1907, 4–5; "Kupecheskii dukh," *Torgovoe delo*, March 20, 1908, 67–68; "Energiia i schast'e v torgovle," *Torgovoe delo*, December 20, 1908, 358–60; "Universal'nyi magazin," *Torgovoe delo*, January, February, and March 1909; *Torgovyi mir*, March 1, 1911, 1; "Iz opyta," *Torgovyi mir*, February 15, 1911, 13–14.

27. This view is expressed in many articles, including *Torgovoe delo*, March 20, 1907, 1–3; May 20, 1908, 5; September 20, 1908, 259–60; *Torgovyi mir*, April 1, 1911, 3–5.

28. "Bez zaprosa," *Torgovoe delo*, July 20, 1908, 198.

29. Ibid.

30. *Torgovyi mir*, March 1, 1911, 3–6; March 15, 1911, 2–4; *Torgovoe delo*, October 20, 1908, 297–98.

31. *Torgovoe delo*, February 20, 1908, 37–38. Many articles devoted themselves to window dressing, including "Vitrina," *Torgovyi mir*, October 1909, 16; "Proekt reklamy," *Torgovoe delo*, February 20, 1907, 18; and "Dekorirovka magazinnykh okon," *Torgovoe delo*, January 15, 1913, 44–49.

32. *Torgovyi mir*, March 1, 1911, 3–4.

33. Novus, "Kupets i pokupatel'," *Torgovoe delo*, June 20, 1908, 163.

34. Ibid.

35. *Torgovyi mir*, September 1909, 19–20.

36. *Torgovoe delo*, June 25, 1907, 7–8.

37. *Torgovoe delo*, July 20, 1907, 7–8.

38. *Torgovyi mir*, February 15, 1911, 13–14.

39. *Torgovlia, promyshlennost', i tekhnika*, December 24, 1909, 3.

40. Sobolev published various books and articles on the economy and commerce at the turn of the century, including *Essays on the World History of Commerce* and *The Commercial*

Geography of Russia. He was recognized in his field and merited inclusion in *The Encyclopedic Dictionary* (1900), where a brief profile of his career and works may be found. *Entsiklope-dichesskii slovar'*, vol. 30 (St. Petersburg, 1900), 646.

41. M. Sobolev, "Universal'nye magaziny i bazary, kak iavlenie noveishago torgovago oborota," *Mir Bozhii*, no. 4 (April 1900): 114–30; M. Sobolev, "Konkurrentsiia, kak dvigatel' sovremennoi ekonomicheskoi zhizni," *Mir Bozhii*, no. 9 (September 1900): 1–22.

42. Sobolev, "Universal'nye magaziny i bazary," 115–22. Many of the same arguments in favor of the department store are also discussed in P. Kh. Spasskii, ed., *Istoriia torgovli i promyshlennosti v Rossii*, vol. 1 (St. Petersburg, 1910), 72–73. Commentators in other countries advanced similar points. Two French observers, Henri Garrigues and Leon Duclos, regarded the department store as a great step toward progress, although Garrigues viewed its employees as cogs in a great machine and Duclos regarded mass production and distribution as forces that imposed uniformity "without a thought and without character." Henri Garrigues's *Les grands magasins de nouveautés et le petit commerce de détail* (1898), Leon Duclos's *Des transformations du commerce de détail en France au XIXème siècle* (1902), and the ideas of French observers and critics are discussed in Miller, *Bon Marché*, 191–97.

43. Some advocates of modern retailing acknowledged this problem. One source claimed that department stores took the place of between one thousand and two thousand small magazins. Spasskii, *Istoriia torgovli i promyshlennosti v Rossii*, 72.

44. Biographical sketch of Elets in *Voennaia entsiklopediia* (St. Petersburg, 1912), 322. Besides contributing articles on military issues to various newspapers and journals, Elets wrote a novel, *The Disease of the Century,* an essay titled "From Life," and a collection of stories titled *O, Women!* He also composed poetry, some of which appeared in the women's magazine *Damkskii mir.*

45. Iu. L. Elets, *Poval'noe bezumie (k sverzheniiu iga mod)* (St. Petersburg, 1914). Christine Ruane analyzes this text as an example of the way that clothes shopping was constructed as a Western, urban, feminine phenomenon and ultimately rejected in Russia. Ruane, "Clothes Shopping in Imperial Russia," 773–77.

46. The perception of the department store as a disorderly female space populated by voracious consuming women was most vividly developed in *Au bonheur des dames.* European, American, and Russian critics of modern retailing, as well as scholars of consumer culture, built on this perception. The warnings of French critics Pierre Giffard and Alphonse Pontmartin about the deleterious effects of women's irrational desires for clothing and fashionable goods are discussed in Miller, *Bon Marché*, 192–93; and Leila Whittemore, "Theatre of the Bazaar: Women and the Architecture of Fashion in 19th-Century Paris," *A/R/C: Architecture, Research, Criticism* 1 (1994–1995): 18. Feminist readings of Zola's and Dreiser's novels are in Felski, *Gender of Modernity*, 65–75; and Rachel Bowlby, *Just Looking: Consumer Culture in Dreiser, Gissing, and Zola* (New York: Methuen, 1985), 72–84, 95–116. See also Benson, *Counter Cultures*, chap. 3; and Elaine Abelson, *When Ladies Go A-Thieving: Middle-Class Shoplifters in the Victorian Department Store* (New York: Oxford University Press, 1989), 13–14.

47. Elets, *Poval'noe bezumie,* 47–49, 271–72.

48. Ibid., 6.

49. Ibid., 273–74.

50. G. Vasilich, "Ulitsy i liudi sovremennoi Moskvy," in *Moskva v ee proshlom i nastoiashchem,* vol. 12 (Moscow, 1912), 6.

51. Ibid., 274.

52. Ibid., 17. Similar comments appear in ibid., 8, 39–42.

53. Ibid., 300–308.

54. As discussed earlier, Slonov and his partner remained in the Upper Trading Rows after the building was refashioned as a modern, luxurious arcade in 1893, when many other Row merchants moved elsewhere. They did move out several years later, however, complaining of the arcade's impractical design.

55. Slonov, *Iz zhizn' torgovoi Moskvy,* 95.

56. Ibid., 94–96.

57. Ibid., 99.

58. Dan Healey, *Homosexual Desire in Revolutionary Russia: The Regulation of Sexual and Gender Dissent* (Chicago: University of Chicago Press, 2001), 31.

59. Contemporary descriptions of the harsh life of apprentices and shop assistants can be found in Slonov's comments on his own apprenticeship. See Slonov, *Iz zhizn' torgovoi Moskvy,* 65–66; A. Gudvan, *Ocherki po istorii dvizheniia sluzhashchikh v Rossii (chast' pervaia)* (Moscow, 1925), 125–27, 138–39; and I. Amirov, "Klass torgovo-promyshlennykh sluzhashchikh i ego blizhaishiia zadachi," *Russkaia mysl',* no. 7 (July 1908).

60. Al'bin M. Konechnyi, "Shows for the People: Public Amusement Parks in Nineteenth-Century St. Petersburg," in *Cultures in Flux,* ed. Frank and Steinberg.

61. See Slonov, *Iz zhizn' torgovoi Moskvy,* 134–40; Vasilich, "Moskva 1850–1910," 8–9; and Teleshov, *Zapiski pisatelia,* 246–47.

62. "Ia khochu goluboe plat'e," *Odesskie novosti,* March 2, 1900, 3; *Vecherniaia pochta,* April 17, 1912, 2.

Chapter 5. Consuming the City

1. Regarding how consumers create social relationships, see Caroline Humphrey and Stephen Hugh-Jones, introduction to *Barter, Exchange and Value: An Anthropological Approach,* ed. Caroline Humphrey and Stephen Hugh-Jones (New York: Cambridge University Press, 1992), 2–17. Their essay is on the culture of barter, which, although a different system of exchange, shares some commonalities with the retail transaction.

2. Two works that detail consumption patterns among Russian workers and peasants are Engel, *Between the Fields and the City;* and Burds, *Peasant Dreams and Market Politics,* esp. 153–80. See also McReynolds, *Russia at Play.*

3. *Torgovoe delo,* May 20, 1908, 131–32.

4. McReynolds, *Russia at Play,* 96–100.

5. Katayev, *Mosaic of Life,* 31.

6. Richard Coe, *When the Grass Was Taller: Autobiography and the Experience of Childhood* (New Haven: Yale University Press, 1984), 2.

7. Dandies and dandyism were first noted in Russia in the late eighteenth and early nineteenth centuries. They exhibited some traits distinct from their Western counterparts, including the wearing of two watches. See Olga Vainshtein, "Russian Dandyism: Constructing a Man of Fashion," in *Russian Masculinities,* ed. Clements, Friedman, and Healey. On the rational collector and French example of the dandy, see Auslander, "Gendering of Consumer Practices."

8. Kuchta, "Making of the Self-Made Man," 62–70.

9. In this regard, Amanda Vickery's and Lorna Weatherill's studies on nonextraor-

dinary modes of male consumption and ownership have been instrumental. Amanda Vickery, "Women and the World of Goods: A Lancashire Consumer and Her Possessions, 1751–81"; Lorna Weatherill, "The Meaning of Consumer Behavior in Late-Seventeenth- and Early-Eighteenth-Century England," both in *Consumption and the World of Goods,* ed. Brewer and Porter.

10. Ilya Ehrenburg, *People and Life,* trans. Anna Bostock and Yvonne Kapp (London: Macgibbon & Lee, 1961), 27.

11. Isaak Babel', "Detstvo u babushki," *Probuzhdenie: ocherki, rasskazy, kinopovest', p'esa* (Tbilisi, 1989), 388–89.

12. Andreeva-Bal'mont, *Vospominaniia,* 62.

13. Mikhail Segal, "Odessa moei molodosti," from a file of uncataloged newspaper clippings at Istoriko-Kraevedcheskii muzei, Odessa.

14. Shneider, *Zapiski starogo Moskvicha,* 81–82.

15. Kharuzina, *Proshloe,* 179.

16. Ivan Mikhailovich Filippov (1824–1878) founded the firm. His son took over upon Ivan's death and rebuilt the store in 1896, expanding the bakery and opening a restaurant. By 1913, Filippov's operated seventeen bakeries and annual production generated 4.5 million rubles. See Irina Potkina, *Delovaia Moskva: ocherki po istorii predprinimatel'stva* (Moscow, 1997), 3–31; Moskvich, *Putevoditel' po Moskve,* 16; and Giliarovskii, *Moskva i Moskvichi,* 144–45.

17. Ivan Shmelev, "Imeniny," *Sobranie sochinenii,* vol. 4 (Moscow, 1998), 186–209.

18. Quoted in Giliarovskii, *Moskva i Moskvichi,* 144.

19. Teleshov, *Zapiski pisatelia,* 247.

20. Anastasiia Tsvetaeva, *Vospominaniia* (Moscow, 1974), 21.

21. Ibid., 21–22.

22. Ibid., 22.

23. Vera Broido, *Daughter of Revolution: A Russian Girlhood Remembered* (London: Constable, 1998), 40.

24. Kharuzina, *Proshloe,* 67.

25. Katayev, *Mosaic of Life,* 386–88.

26. Walkowitz, *City of Dreadful Delight,* 15.

27. Kharuzina, *Proshloe,* 68; Broido, *Daughter of Revolution,* 41.

28. Babel, "Detstvo u babushki," 389.

29. Giliarovskii, *Moskva i Moskvichi,* 48.

30. Ibid., 109–13.

31. Quoted in Sylvester, *Tales of Old Odessa,* 114.

32. Andreeva-Bal'mont, *Vospominaniia,* 62–63.

33. M. Neil Browne, "If Markets Are So Wonderful, Why Can't I Find Friends at the Store?" *American Journal of Economics and Sociology* 61:4 (October 2002): 793.

34. Lowth, *Around the Kremlin,* 235–36.

35. Vasilich, "Moskva 1850–1910," 9.

36. Davydov, "Moskva piatidesiatye i shestidesiatye gody," 30.

37. P. P. Semenov, ed., *Zhivopisnaia Rossiia: otechestvo nashe,* vol. 7 (Moscow 1898), 290–91.

38. Vasilich, "Moskva 1850–1910," 9.

39. Davydov, "Moskva piatidesiatye i shestidesiatye gody," 30–31.

40. Vasilich, "Moskva 1850–1910," 9.

41. Terms adapted from Steven Salop and Joseph Stiglitz, "Bargains and Ripoffs: A Model of Monopolistically Competitive Price Dispersion," *Review of Economic Studies* 44 (October 1977): 493–510.

42. Vasilich, "Ulitsy i liudi," 8.

43. *Moskovskii listok,* December 23, 1888, 3.

44. Leonid Utesov, "Odessa moego detstva," in *Spasibo serdtse* (Moscow, 1976), 69.

45. Walkowitz, *City of Dreadful Delight,* 15–17. See also Susan Buck-Morss, "The Flaneur, the Sandwichman, and the Whore: The Politics of Loitering," *New German Critique* 13:39 (1986): 99–142.

46. Walkowitz, *City of Dreadful Delight,* 16.

47. *Vecherniaia pochta,* April 14, 1912, 2.

48. Ibid.

49. Slonov, *Iz zhizn' torgovoi Moskvy,* 70.

50. Vasilich, "Moskva 1850–1910," 9.

51. Varentsov, *Slyshannoe. Vidennoe,* 436.

52. Quoted in Oleg Gubar', "Postavshchik imperatorskogo dvora," *Delovaia Odessa,* no. 23, December 7, 1990, 7.

53. Giliarovskii, *Moskva i Moskvichi,* 55. A similar view of middle-class confidence is also expressed in Davydov, "Moskva piatidesiatye i shestidesiatye gody," 30.

54. Giliarovskii, *Moskva i Moskvichi,* 110.

55. *Damskii mir,* no. 3, March 1908, 8–12.

56. Kharuzina, *Proshloe,* 56.

57. Broido, *Daughter of Revolution,* 65.

58. Utesov, "Odessa moego detstva," 18.

59. *Moskovskii listok,* December 23, 1888, 3.

60. The stories contained in a compilation of women's recollections about their childhood and young adulthood, along with the tales and narratives discussed above, suggest this conclusion. In this collection, women wrote of the meaning that certain items had in their lives but not about shopping for them. See Toby W. Clyman and Judith Vowles, eds., *Russia through Women's Eyes: Autobiographies from Tsarist Russia* (New Haven: Yale University Press, 1996).

61. The intelligentsia also showed hostility toward behaviors seen as aggressive or backward, including dueling. Kelly, "Education of the Will," 137–40.

62. *Khoroshii ton:sbornik pravil, nastavlenii i sovetov, kak sleduet vesti sebia v raznykh sluchaiakh domashnei i obshchestvennoi zhizni* (Moscow, 1911), 3.

63. Ibid., 72–109, 170–72.

64. Kharuzina, *Proshloe,* 56.

65. Ibid., 69–70.

66. "Vospominaniia starogo prodavtsa," GARF, f. 6875, opis' 1, d. 525, l. 1–2.

67. Giliarovskii, *Moskva i Moskvichi,* 54–55.

68. Ibid., 55.

69. Walkowitz, *City of Dreadful Delight,* 45–50.

70. Vasilich, "Ulitsy i liudi," 6–7.

71. Ibid.

Chapter 6. War and Revolution in the Marketplace, 1914–1921

1. Lars Lih, *Bread and Authority in Russia, 1914–1921* (Berkeley: University of California Press, 1990), 1.

2. Peter Holquist, *Making War, Forging Revolution: Russia's Continuum of Crisis, 1914–1921* (New York: Cambridge University Press, 2002), 2–3.

3. Peter Gatrell, *Russia's First World War: A Social and Economic History* (London: Pearson, 2005), 2; Eric Lohr, *Nationalizing the Russian Empire: The Campaign against Enemy Aliens during World War I* (Cambridge, MA: Harvard University Press, 2003), 9. In her exploration of private entrepreneurship in the pharmaceutical industry during the New Economic Policy (NEP) era, Mary Conroy finds that World War I was a critical turning point in the gradual transition from tsarist to Soviet industry. Mary Conroy, "Chastniki nepovskoi Rossii: krest'iane-proizvoditeli lekarstvennykh rastenii, kustari-izgotoviteli farmatsevticheskikh sresdstv i farmatsevty," in *Bubliki dlia respubliki: istoricheskii profil' NEPmanov,* ed. R. A. Khaziev (Ufa: RIO BashGU, 2005). Hubertus Jahn identifies links between changes in the depictions of nationalism and patriotism in wartime culture, a circumstance that, he argues, played a role in a "dispersion of loyalties" and contributed to the 1917 revolutions. Hubertus F. Jahn, *Patriotic Culture in Russia during World War I* (Ithaca: Cornell University Press, 1995), 177.

4. Hessler, *Social History of Soviet Trade,* 19.

5. Lohr, *Nationalizing the Russian Empire,* 83.

6. Gatrell, *Russia's First World War,* 2, 25, 125; Hessler, *Social History of Soviet Trade,* 22–23.

7. Gatrell, *Russia's First World War,* 96–97, 168.

8. Ibid., 72–75, 144.

9. Lohr, *Nationalizing the Russian Empire,* 9. Some evidence indicates that in the early stages of civil war, the White governments also liquidated some German firms. Ibid., 82.

10. Leaders throughout Europe and in the United States marshaled resources under a single authority and intervened in the economy in exceptional ways, including planned production and distribution, rationing, and campaigns against enemy subjects and citizens, as well as minorities. Lohr, *Nationalizing the Russian Empire,* 1, 62.

11. Boris Nolde, *Russia in the Economic War* (New Haven: Yale University Press, 1928), 8.

12. Ibid., 9–11.

13. Lohr, *Nationalizing the Russian Empire,* 23–30, 61–63; Gatrell, *Russia's First World War,* 177–80.

14. This order resulted in the deportation of tens of thousands of individuals accused of spying and in the confiscation of their property, even when there was no proof of their guilt. Lohr, *Nationalizing the Russian Empire,* 63.

15. Nolde, *Russia in the Economic War,* 11–13.

16. Copy of decree in GAOO, f. 20, opis' 1, d. 22, l. 2. A handbill published by Moscow's Supreme Commander to inform the public of the law is preserved in GIM OPI, f. 402, opis' 1, d. 254. If a firm had been founded in an enemy country, it was considered to belong to an enemy national. If founded under Russian law, it was considered Russian. Jews and Muslims who were Russian subjects were sometimes also targeted, although to a lesser extent than were Germans and Austrians. Lohr, *Nationalizing the Russian Empire,* 83.

17. Nolde, *Russia in the Economic War*, 8; Lohr, *Nationalizing the Russian Empire,* 67.

18. See, for example, the *doverennost'* (power of attorney) giving the manager, Albert Karlovich Stiglits, the power to act in the name of the firm. GAOO, f, 20, opis' 1, d. 22, l. 2.

19. GAOO, f. 20, opis' 1, d. 22, ll. 29–87, 143–72.

20. Prompted by an anonymous denunciation alleging that Dattan was the head of a spy ring, a raid was carried out on the Kunst & Al'bers headquarters in September 1914. Dattan and other enemy subject employees were arrested. Another raid, conducted in January 1915, ended in Dattan's arrest and deportation to Narym. Lohr, *Nationalizing the Russian Empire,* 77–78. After army headquarters issued a circular in December 1914 claiming that Singer was a German company, several hundred of the firm's branches were searched and more than five hundred stores closed. Singer's assets and accounts were also frozen. In late 1915, the state allowed many of the stores to reopen, but only under a state inspector's control. Ibid., 79–81.

21. See Hessler, *Social History of Soviet Trade,* 54; Gatrell, *Russia's First World War,* 167–72.

22. Gatrell, *Russia's First World War,* 24–25, 145–46; Jahn, *Patriotic Culture in Russia,* 91–92.

23. Lih, *Bread and Authority in Russia,* 13.

24. Barbara Alpern Engel, "Not by Bread Alone: Subsistence Riots in Russia during World War I," *Journal of Modern History* 69 (December 1997): 696–721.

25. Ibid., 714.

26. Gatrell, *Russia's First World War,* 66.

27. Engel, "Not by Bread Alone," 706.

28. Lohr, *Nationalizing the Russian Empire,* 67–69, 82–83.

29. *Sobranie uzakonenii i rasporiazhenii raboche-krest'ianskogo pravitel'stva RSFSR* (Moscow, 1917–1923), 7–8.

30. *Krasnaia Moskva, 1917–1920 gg.* (Moscow: Publication of the Moscow Soviet, 1920), 288–91; Ball, *Russia's Last Capitalists,* 5–7; Hessler, *Social History of Soviet Trade,* 24–25.

31. Cities in other provinces, for example, Arkangel'sk, Penza, and Chernigov, saw fewer businesses, if any, nationalized or municipalized in this period. Hessler, *Social History of Soviet Trade,* 26.

32. Decrees on retailing in *Sobranie uzakonenii i rasporiazhenii, 1917–1949* (Moscow, 1920–1950), 1917–1918, no. 83, art. 879. Information on other measures in *Krasnaia Moskva,* 288–91; *Izvestiia,* November 21, 1918, 4. List of perfume/cosmetics stores to be municipalized in Tsentral'nyi arkhiv goroda Moskvy (hereafter, TsAGM), f. 499, opis' 2, d. 44, ll. 13. See also Ball, *Russia's Last Capitalists,* 1–6; Hessler, *Social History of Soviet Trade,* 25–26. A general discussion of the confiscation of private property from October 1917 through the civil war can be found in K. V. Kharchenko, *Vlast', imushchestvo, chelovek: peredel sobstvennosti v bol'shevistskoi Rossii, 1917–nachala 1921 gg.* (Moscow: Russkii dvor, 2000).

33. *Krasnaia Moskva,* 291–92.

34. *Vestnik narodnogo kommisariata torgovli i promyshlennosti,* November 1918, 21–22. See also Alec Nove, *An Economic History of the USSR, 1917–1991* (New York: Penguin Books, 1992), 46–47.

35. The Provisions Section of the Moscow soviet warned the furriers that if they continued to obstruct the inventory process, their merchandise would be removed and the merchant subjected to "all strictness of revolutionary law." *Izvestiia,* December 5, 1918, 4.

36. *Izvestiia,* December 26, 1918, 4.

37. *Izvestiia,* November 21, 1918, 4.

38. *Izvestiia,* February 1919, 5.

39. Report in Russkii gosudarstvennyi arkhiv ekonomiki (hereafter, RGAE), f. 3429, opis' 2, d. 1452, ll. 1–2. *Izvestiia* reported on the Cheka's discovery that at Alenov's warehouse in the Upper Rows, a site that had already been inventoried, there was speculation in textiles being conducted. Another notice reported that seven persons were carrying out a speculation operation in a church cellar on Bolshaia Lubianka. *Izvestiia,* July 20, 1918, 5; August 8, 1918, 7.

40. Decree of the Moscow soviet published in *Izvestiia,* November 20, 1918, 4.

41. Rental agreements in TsIAM, f. 173, opis' 1, d. 21, ll. 114–15, 121, 126.

42. *Izvestiia,* November 9, 1918, 2.

43. "V Golofteevskom passazhe (Moskovskie vpechatleniia)," *Izvestiia,* December 10, 1918, 4.

44. Ibid.

45. Richard Stites, "Iconoclastic Currents in the Russian Revolution: Destroying and Preserving the Past," in *Bolshevik Culture: Experiment and Order in the Russian Revolution,* ed. Abbott Gleason, Peter Kenez, and Richard Stites (Bloomington: Indiana University Press, 1985).

46. Mark von Hagen argues that the civil war experience molded the men who assumed leading posts in politics and the economy, a situation that led to the "militarization" of Soviet society. von Hagen, *Soldiers in the Proletarian Dictatorship: The Red Army and the Soviet Socialist State, 1917–1930* (Ithaca: Cornell University Press, 1990). See also Barbara Clements, *Bolshevik Women* (New York: Cambridge University Press, 1997).

47. Victoria Bonnell, "The Representation of Women in Early Soviet Political Art," *Russian Review* 50:3 (1991): 267–88.

48. Quoted in V. S. Aksel'rod, *Kak my uchilis' torgovat'* (Moscow, 1986), 28.

49. Mauricio Borrero, *Hungry Moscow: Scarcity and Urban Society in the Russian Civil War* (New York: Peter Lang, 2003), 185. The scene at Sukharev's closing is recounted in a letter, dated 1927, sent by members of the Sukharev Market's committee to a municipal commercial official. TsAGM, f. 1275, opis' 1, d. 95, l. 42.

50. Walter Duranty, *I Write as I Please* (London: Hamish Hamilton, 1935), 108–9.

51. K. Paustovskii, *Nachalo nevedomogo veka: vremia bol'shikh ozhidanii* (Kiev, 1985), 197.

52. *Izvestiia,* January 19, 1919, 4.

53. *Krasnaia Moskva,* 295.

54. Ibid., 294–95, 298–300.

55. M. M. Zhirmunskii, *Chastnyi kapital v tovarooborote* (Moscow, 1924), 3–4; R. W. Davies, "Industry," in *The Economic Transformation of the Soviet Union, 1913–1945,* ed. R. W. Davies, Mark Harrison, and S. G. Wheatcroft (New York: Cambridge University Press, 1994), 135.

56. Daniel K. Brower, "'The City in Danger': The Civil War and the Russian Urban Population," in *Party, State, and Society in the Russian Civil War,* ed. Diane P. Koenker, William G. Rosenberg, and Ronald Grigor Suny (Bloomington: Indiana University Press, 1989).

57. Borrero, *Hungry Moscow,* 117–25, 130–36.

58. Ibid., 130–36, 188.

59. I. I. Soia-Serko, an employee in GUM's advertising department during the 1920s, sketched people on the streets selling "fragments of the past," including a glass perfume bottle, candelabra, a lady's hat with a veil, and binoculars. Soia-Serko, "Moskva moei molodosti," *Moskovskii zhurnal*, no. 7, (1998).

60. Discussion of bag men, widespread corruption, and the rise of the black market from Ball, *Russia's Last Capitalists*, 6–9, 33–34, 88, 110–18; and Arup Banerji, *Merchants and Markets in Revolutionary Russia, 1917–1930* (New York: St. Martin's Press, 1997), 25–34. See also Mauricio Borrero, "Hunger and Society in Civil War Moscow, 1917–1921" (PhD diss., Indiana University, 1992); and Nove, *Economic History of the USSR*, 54–55. The diary of Alexis Babine is especially revealing about material conditions and consumers' efforts to obtain food and provisions. See Donald J. Raleigh, ed., *A Russian Civil War Diary: Alexis Babine in Saratov, 1917–1922* (Durham: Duke University Press, 1988), 34.

61. Terence Emmons, trans. and ed., *Time of Troubles: The Diary of Iurii Vladimirovich Got'e* (Princeton: Princeton University Press, 1988), 232–33, 286–87.

62. Raleigh, ed., *Russian Civil War Diary*, 36.

63. Ibid., 120–21.

64. Ibid., 141. He eventually located some milk and a loaf of bread.

65. Ibid., 150, 168, 170, 182, 184–85.

66. Arjun Appadurai, among others, has pointed out that material objects circulate in different *"regimes of value* in space and time" (original emphasis). Appadurai, *The Social Life of Things: Commodities in Cultural Perspective* (New York: Cambridge University Press, 1988), 4.

67. *Ekonomicheskaia zhizn'*, November 3, 1918, 2. Babine lamented on numerous occasions the barley coffee that had become an unvarying part of his diet. Raleigh, ed., *Russian Civil War Diary*, 122.

68. Irina Sergeevna Tidmarsh and Valentin Kataev both remembered tea brewed from carrots. Tidmarsh information from Anna Horsbrugh-Porter, ed., *Memories of Revolution: Russian Women Remember* (New York: Routledge, 1993), 61–62; Valentin Kataev, *Almaznyi moi venets* (Moscow, 1990), 81–82. Descriptions of bread from Tidmarsh in Horsbrugh-Porter, ed., *Memories of Revolution*, 62; Dorothy Russell in ibid., 42–43; K. Paustovskii, *Nachalo nevedomogo veka*, 217; and Emmons, ed., *Time of Troubles*, 75.

69. Duranty, *I Write as I Please*, 107–9.

70. *Ekonomicheskaia zhizn'*, November 28, 1918, 4.

71. Iurii Got'e confided to his diary his concern that, even though rooms in the family's apartment had been appropriated to house other individuals and families, he and his family would eventually be evicted. He began moving furniture to the museum where he was employed. He and his family took up residence there in March 1919 following their eviction and began sharing a makeshift apartment with another professor. Emmons, ed., *Time of Troubles*, 241, 251.

72. Vladimir Galitskii, *Odesskii byli* (St. Petersburg, 1994), 19.

73. Tidmarsh in Horsbrugh-Porter, ed., *Memories of Revolution*, 62; Marguerite E. Harrison, *Marooned in Moscow: The Story of am American Woman Imprisoned in Russia* (London: Thornton Butterworth, 1921), 97.

74. Ia. M. Belitskii, *Zabytaia Moskva* (Moscow, 1994), 56–57.

75. Harrison, *Marooned in Moscow*, 150–51.

76. Babine recorded this incident on December 18, 1918. Raleigh, ed., *Russian Civil War Diary,* 126.

77. Raleigh, ed., *Russian Civil War Diary,* 153–54.

78. Ibid., 154.

Chapter 7. Retailing the Revolution

An earlier version of this chapter appeared as "Retailing the Revolution: the State Department Store (GUM) and Soviet Society in the 1920s," in the *Journal of Social History* 37, no. 4 (summer 2004): 939–64.

1. N. Kal'ma, "Pod stekliannym nebom GUM'a," *Vecherniaia Moskva,* November 4, 1926, preserved in a clippings file on GUM in TsAGM, f. 474, opis' 3, d. 204, l. 9.

2. The workers' credit program enabled low-income individuals to buy "basic necessities," such as fabric, clothing, shoes, coats, linens, and furniture, on installment at designated state stores. Apparently, terms were renegotiated each year. At the time that the newspaper ran this story, credit was extended to workers and employees who earned no more than seventy rubles per month. The credit line was not to exceed half a month's salary, and a 10 percent down payment was required. The total amount due was to be paid within five months. Several state enterprises participated in the program, including the Moscow Union of Consumer Societies stores, GUM, and the ready-to-wear trust, Moskvoshvei. *Izvestiia,* November 20, 1926; *Pravda,* December 16, 1926; *Vecherniaia Moskva,* October 16, 1926, GUM clippings file, TsAGM, f. 474, opis' 3, d. 204, l. 50b, 8, 140b.

3. Peter Kenez has pointed out the Bolsheviks' use of various popular media, including films, books, and posters, in their agitational efforts. Peter Kenez, *The Birth of the Propaganda State: Soviet Methods of Mass Mobilization, 1917–1929* (New York: Cambridge University Press, 1985). For an excellent comparative discussion of the simultaneous rise of the modern interventionist state and a culture of mass consumption, see Randall, *Soviet Dream World of Retail Trade,* chap. 7.

4. Ball, *Russia's Last Capitalists;* Anne Gorsuch, *Youth in Revolutionary Russia: Enthusiasts, Bohemians, Delinquents* (Bloomington: Indiana University Press, 2000).

5. Fitzpatrick, Rabinowitch, and Stites, *Russia in the Era of NEP;* Lewis Siegelbaum, *Soviet State and Society between Revolutions, 1918–1929* (New York: Cambridge University Press, 1992). Hessler presents a darker picture of the 1920s, one that stresses the distrust and "native impulse" of state policy makers to repress private business owners. Hessler, *Social History of Soviet Trade,* 137–38.

6. Siegelbaum, *Soviet State and Society between Revolutions,* chap. 3; Nove, *Economic History of the USSR,* chaps. 4–6; E. H. Carr, *The Bolshevik Revolution, 1917–1923,* 3 vols. (New York: Norton, 1980), 2:269–360; Ball, *Russia's Last Capitalists,* 16–20.

7. Ball, *Russia's Last Capitalists,* 21–24, 90–91.

8. M. A. Bulgakov, "Torgovyi renessans (Moskva v nachale 1922 goda)," reprinted in *Sotsiologicheskie issledovaniia,* no. 1 (1988): 137–38.

9. *Rabochaia Moskva,* January 7, 1925, 7; *Pravda,* February 11, 1925, 4.

10. Inflation, however, continued to concern Got'e, as evidenced by his notation of the price of basic foodstuffs without any further commentary. Emmons, ed., *Time of Troubles,* 424, 442.

11. Ball, *Russia's Last Capitalists,* 16.

12. Alexandre Barmine, *One Who Survived: The Life Story of a Russian under the Soviets* (New York: G. P. Putnam's Sons, 1945), 124–25.

13. Ibid., 125.

14. Ball, *Russia's Last Capitalists,* 44–55; Siegelbaum, *Soviet State and Society between Revolutions,* chap. 3.

15. Hessler, *Social History of Soviet Trade,* 113–19; Ball, *Russia's Last Capitalists,* 38–44, 56–60.

16. Leon Trotsky, *Problems of Everyday Life, and Other Writings on Culture and Science* (New York: Pathfinder Press, 1973).

17. Kollontai's wardrobe impressed the *Baltimore Sun* correspondent Marguerite Harrison, who considered her "chic and charming." Harrison reported that when Kollontai received her at home, she was wearing an "exquisite" green velvet boudoir gown trimmed with sable and had matching velvet slippers. Harrison, *Marooned in Moscow,* 178.

18. Kollontai's statements from 1918 in Rossiiskii gosudarstvennyi arkhiv sotsial'no-politicheskoi istorii (hereafter, RGASPI), f. 134, opis' 1, d. 144, ll. 1–3, 8–9. Sofiia Smidovich's 1924 statement, made in response to the Thirteenth Party Congress's resolution on the tasks of the Zhenotdel, in RGASPI, f. 17, opis' 10, d. 137, Ll. 4–10. The editor of the journal *Rabotnitsa* reported that issues of everyday life "interest and stir *rabotnitsi* [workers] more than all others." *Rabotnitsa,* December 1926, 15.

19. Protocol from 1923 session of the Central Bureau of Women Workers on issues of everyday life in RGASPI, f. 17, opis' 10, d. 92, ll. 56–58. Also on this point, see Beatrice Farnsworth, "Village Women Experience the Revolution," in *Bolshevik Culture,* ed. Gleason, Kenez, and Stites, 245–54.

20. Posters preserved at RGB IZO, Papka 25, P2; Papka 30, P2.X; Papka 71, P3 XV.3.

21. RGB IZO, Papka 28, P8 XXII.

22. The number of outlets that Mossel'prom maintained varied throughout the 1920s. In 1926, the trust operated 37 stores, 135 kiosks, 62 beer halls, and 3,000 hawkers' stands. By 1929, figures rose to 44 stores and 272 kiosks. *Vecherniaia Moskva,* March 10, 1925, 2; March 16, 1925, 2; *Rabochaia Moskva,* July 28, 1926, 4.

23. *Rabochaia Moskva,* August 14, 1926, 4.

24. Some GUM offices and outlets were in operation as early as December 1921. Advertisements for GUM's opening in *Rabochaia Moskva,* March 22, 1922, 8; and *Ekonomicheskaia zhizn',* March 25, 1922, 4. See also A. M. Kochurov, *GUM: vchera, segodnia, zavtra* (Moscow, 1974); and "Historical Background," TsAGM, f. 474, opis' 1. Information on Mostorg in "Historical Background," TsAGM, f. 1953, opis' 1; Georgii Ivanovich Fokin, *Flagman sovetskoi torgovli* (Moscow, 1968), 3; and *Doklad chrezvychainomu obshchemu sobraniiu aktsionerov "Mostorg" o deiatel'nosti obshchestva za polugodie: Noiabr' 1923 g. – Aprel' 1924 g.* (Moscow, 1924), 11. The original goal of Larek was to collect funds to aid homeless children and the hungry, but, after 1922, the company widened its circle of shareholders and expanded its retail network, becoming a purely retail organization. V. A. Arkhipov and L. F. Morozov, *Bor'ba protiv kapitalisticheskikh elementov v promyshlennosti i torgovle* (Moscow, 1978), 66–67; *Vseukrainskoe paevoe torgovoe t-vo "Larek" Otchet pravleniia za 1924–25 gg.* (n.p., n.d.), 6–7, 14–16.

25. This store was not affiliated with GUM Moscow. In fact, upon the opening of the Odessa store, the chairman of Moscow GUM showed up to lodge a complaint. Asserting

that the store's name was too close to the Moscow original, he argued that retailers trading on the name *GUM* would damage the state retailer's image, especially if such businesses reneged on their debts or went out of business. Moscow GUM requested that the Odessa store add the word *Odessa* to its name to distinguish itself. *Vechernye izvestiia,* December 24, 1926, preserved in TsAGM, f. 474, opis' 3, d. 204, l. 3.

26. Potkina, *Delovaia Moskva,* 30–35, 46; A. V. Mikhalkov, *Ocherki iz istorii Moskovskogo kupechestva:ch'i predpriiatia sluzhili Moskve posle revoliutsii* (Moscow 1996), 10–15, 38–47; *Vsia Moskva v karmane na 1924–25* (Moscow, 1924), 271. See also M. M. Gorinov, "Moskve v 20-x godakh," *Otechestvennaia istoriia,* no. 5 (1996): 5–6.

27. Babaev and TEZhE wrappers and labels preserved in GIM OPI, f. 402, opis' 1, d. 853. Bolshevik Confectioners' 1927 *preis-kurant* at RGB IZO, Papka Y9 (2) 421.512.1.

28. Advertisement reprinted in Selim O. Khan-Magomedov, *Rodchenko: The Complete Work* (Cambridge, MA: MIT Press, 1987), 151.

29. Advertisement reprinted in Mikhail Anikst, *Soviet Commercial Design of the Twenties* (London: Thames and Hudson, 1987), 94.

30. As late as 1925, one journalist asserted that all Moscow residents, when asked to name the remarkable building located at 40 Tverskaia Street, at the corner of Kozitskii, would still reply that it was Eliseev's gastronome. *Vecherniaia Moskva,* February 19, 1925, 2.

31. *Ekonomicheskaia zhizn',* February 18, 1922, 1. For similar discussion, see D. Mar, "Univermagy," *Ekonomicheskaia zhizn',* January 17, 1922, 1.

32. Leonidov based his recommendations on the findings of delegates who had spent time abroad studying the retail trade. *Vecherniaia Moskva,* July 31, 1928, 2.

33. Haggling nevertheless persisted in markets and some private stores. A feuilleton titled "The New Sukharevka" suggests that while the appearance of that market had changed, practices and customs remained the same. *Vecherniaia Moskva,* February 28, 1925, 2. Even some private merchants were trying to eliminate the practice of "calling." See *Vecherniaia Moskva,* October 12, 1927, 2, regarding a convention of Mosgubtorgotdel and private merchants where this issue was discussed. A 1927 complaint of bargaining in an Odessa artel addressed to the Odessa city soviet's Workers' and Peasants' Inspectorate may be indicative of a wider trend. GAOO, F. R-1234, opis' 1, d. 642, ll. 198–980b. Other mentions of haggling in private stores and markets are in *Khar'kovskii proletarii,* May 26, preserved in TsAGM, f. 474, opis' 3, d. 204, l. 330b, and in Soia-Serko, "Moskva moei molodosti," 29. Some NEPmen in the Siberian region, facing pressure from the state, tried to present themselves as responsible and respectable and to stand by the traditions of prerevolutionary merchants. A convention of Krasnoiarsk private merchants also discussed how to stop petty traders from cheating customers. E. V. Demchik, "Sibirskie nepmany: predprinimateli i moshenniki," *Bubliki dlia respubliki: istoricheskii profil' NEPmanov,* ed. R. A. Khaziev (Ufa: RIO, 2005), 168–69, 245.

34. V. I. Lenin, *Polnoe sobranie sochinenii,* 5th ed. (Moscow, 1958–65), vol. 44, 167.

35. This seems to have been the case in not only European Russia but also eastern Russia. In Siberia, only about 15 percent of former entrepreneurs were able to reconstitute their businesses. Demchik, "Sibirskie nepmany," 152.

36. Former Muir & Mirrielees chairman of the board Walter Philip and managing director Willie Cazalet were arrested in late summer or early fall of 1918. Both were eventually released. Cazalet returned to England. Philip worked for a short time for the Control Committee set up to run the store, designated as Store No. 1, before he was

dismissed in 1919. He fell ill and died the following June. Pitcher, *Muir & Mirrielees*, 178–83. The new directors of the former Brocard & Company turned to the heirs of the previous owner and his main specialist for help. Mikhalkov, *Ocherki iz istorii Moskovskogo kupechestva*, 41.

37. Newspaper reports of Burshtein's trial for "economic counterrevolution" include details of his career. The press excoriated him for being a "speculator on a grand scale." Press clippings preserved in TsAGM, f. 474, opis' 3, d. 204, ll. 84–6. Semen Pliatskii, previously a millionaire metal trader, also worked for the Soviet state after the revolution, and, in the 1920s, he set up his own business to supply state enterprises. Ball, *Russia's Last Capitalists*, 91–92.

38. Similarly, in Siberia in the 1920s, more than half of businessmen were former shop employees. Demchik, "Sibirskie nepmany," 152.

39. *Ekonomicheskaia zhizn'*, January 17, 1922, 1.

40. *Vecherniaia Moskva*, February 19, 1922, 2.

41. Camilla Gray, *The Russian Experiment in Art, 1863–1922* (New York: Thames and Hudson, 1962), 245–76; Anikst, *Soviet Commercial Design*, 18–29; Elena Barkhatova, ed., *Russian Constructivist Posters* (Moscow 1992), 3–9; White, *Bolshevik Poster*.

42. Rodchenko's sketches in Khan-Magomedov, *Rodchenko*, 40–41.

43. Anikst, *Soviet Commercial Design*, 27; Khan-Magomedov, *Rodchenko*, 143, 151; *Vsia Moskva v karmane* (Moscow-Leningrad, 1926), 91; *Vecherniaia Moskva*, January 15, 1925, 2. The building still stands in Moscow, although it has been converted into an apartment complex.

44. *Vecherniaia Moskva*, October 1, 1926, 4; Khan-Magomedov, *Rodchenko*, 256. Mel'nikov also designed the Soviet pavilion for the 1925 International Exhibition of Decorative Arts in Paris and several workers' clubs in Moscow. Blair Ruble, "Moscow's Avant-Garde Architecture of the 1920s: A Tour," in *Architecture and the New Urban Environment: Western Influences on Modernism in Russia and the USSR* (Washington, DC: Kennan Institute for Advanced Russian Studies, 1988).

45. Richard Stites, *Revolutionary Dreams: Utopian Vision and Experimental Life in the Russian Revolution* (New York: Oxford University Press, 1989), 149–56.

46. *Vecherniaia Moskva*, October 20, 1927, 2; November 24, 1927, 2. Kommunar did not implement many of Orgstroi's recommendations, and the store was not ready to open in time for the ten-year anniversary. Ibid., December 23, 1927, 2.

47. See Ellen Furlough, *Consumer Cooperation in France: The Politics of Consumption, 1834–1930* (Ithaca: Cornell University Press, 1991); Yanni Kotsonis, *Making Peasants Backward: Agricultural Cooperatives and the Agrarian Question in Russia, 1861–1914* (New York: St. Martin's Press, 1999); Alexander Dillon, "The Forgotten Movement: Cooperatives and Cooperative Networks in Ukraine and Imperial Russia," *Harvard Ukrainian Studies* 23:1–2 (1999): 129–43; and S. V. Veselov, "Kooperatsiia i Sovetskaia vlast': period 'Voennogo Kommunizma,'" *Voprosy istorii*, no. 9–10 (1991): 25–37.

48. Hessler, *Social History of Soviet Trade*, 54.

49. *Ekonomicheskaia zhizn'*, February 19, 1925, 4.

50. Hessler, *Social History of Soviet Trade*, 56–61 (quotes, 61).

51. *Pravila vnutrennogo rasporiadka dlia sluzhashchikh Gosudarstvennogo Universal'nogo Magazina GUM* (Moscow, 1925), 5.

52. K. Remtzen and V. Tsuberbiller, *Organizatsiia roznichnoi torgovli* (Moscow, 1925),

81–83. Worker correspondents circulated similar ideas in popular newspapers. See, for example, the piece in Odessa's *Vechernye izvestiia,* March 7, 1927, 2.

53. GUM's founding and mission, TsAGM, f. 474, opis' 3, d. 24, ll. 2, 5. GUM's sources, ibid., l. 28. List of holdings, TsAGM, f. 474, opis' 3, d. 204, ll. 25, 55. Other divisions and branches, ibid., d. 200, ll. 200b–220b. The New York office closed in 1924. Ibid., d. 2, ll. 64–640b. GUM opening-day advertisements, *Rabochaia Moskva,* March 22, 1922, 8; *Ekonomicheskaia zhizn',* March 25, 1922, 4. Sovnarkom initially formed the Interdepartmental Department Store (Mezhduvedomstvennyi universal'nyi magazin or MUM) in October 1921. In December, it recast MUM as GUM. By 1927, the number of departments had expanded to more than twenty-five and included, in addition to those already listed, luggage, musical instruments, stationery, tea, ladies' hats, and clearance items. TsAGM, f. 474, opis' 3, d. 213, ll. 77–80.

54. Copy of GUM's statutes, signed by Lenin, RGAE, f. 3429, opis' 2, d. 2584, ll. 1–2. Board members, "Postanovlenie," TsAGM, f. 474, opis 3, d. 24, l. 2. Management team *Ekonomicheskaia zhizn',* February 28, 1922, 1, 53; March 6, 1922, 4. On capital and financial and operational problems, see RGAE, f. 3429, d. 2586, opis' 2, ll. 1–2, 4-ob; TsAGM, f. 474, opis' 3, d. 24, ll. 5–50b; d. 205, ll. 69–70.

55. TsAGM, f. 474, opis' 3, d. 200, l. 132.

56. "Dokladnaia zapiska: po voprosu o reorganizatsii GUM'a," TsAGM, f. 474, opis' 3, d. 205, l. 71.

57. TsAGM, f. 474, opis' 3, d. 205, ll. 59, 73–730b.

58. TsAGM, f. 474, opis' 3, d. 205, l. 71.

59. Survey of provincial stores, October 1927–1928, TsAGM, f. 474, opis' 3, d. 200, ll. 178–830b.

60. TsAGM, f. 474, opis' 3, d. 205, ll. 690b–74; d. 221, ll. 35–350b.

61. Advertisements from 1926, TsAGM, f. 474, opis' 3, d. 204, ll. 42, 450b, 47, 58.

62. Advertisement for Dvigatel', *Ekonomicheskaia zhizn',* February 13, 1925, 6.

63. *Zhurnalist* was a publication of Rabotnik prosveshchenie, an organ of the central soviet section of the workers' press. D. I. Reitynberg, "Nigde krome . . . ," *Zhurnalist,* October 26, 1925, 60; V. Gaus, "Reklama v gazette," *Zhurnalist,* November 27, 1925, 64–65.

64. Maiakovskii first put his talents to work during World War I, creating anti-German *lubki* (woodcuts) for various publications. During the civil war, he drew political cartoons for the Russian Telegraph Agency (ROSTA), and later, at Glavpolitprosvet, he produced agitational texts for posters. Rodchenko worked in the art studio of the Moscow soviet during the civil war. Jahn, *Patriotic Culture in Russia,* 14–17.

65. V. Maiakovskii, "Agitatsiia i reklama," *Polnoe sobranie sochinenii,* vol. 12 (Moscow, 1959), 60.

66. Anikst, *Soviet Commercial Design,* 25.

67. "Vse, chto trebuet zheludok, telo, ili, um–vse cheloveku predostavliaet GUM." Kochurov, *GUM,* 7.

68. "Khvataites' za etot spasatel'nyi krug! Dobrokachestvenno, deshevo, i pervykh ruk!" Advertisement reprinted in Anikst, *Soviet Commercial Design,* 54.

69. "Kupish' v Mostorge—budesh v vostorge!" Belitskii, *Zabytaia Moskva,* 142.

70. *Rabochaia Moskva,* February 25, 1922, 4; *Izvestiia,* March 8, 1922, 4.

71. "Chelovek—tol'ko s chasami. Chasy tol'ko Mozera. Mozer tol'ko u GUMa." Advertisement (1923) reprinted in Anikst, *Soviet Commercial Design,* 55.

72. Advertisement reprinted in Khan-Magomedov, *Rodchenko,* 149.

73. Maiakovskii and Rodchenko advertisements reproduced in V. N. Liakhov, *Sovetskii reklamnyi plakaty* (Moscow: Sovetskii Khudozhnik, 1972), 21.

74. The complete text is in an advertisement in *Vechernye izvestiia,* June 29, 1924, 4.

75. *Vechernye izvestiia,* December 28, 1924, 4.

76. Advertisement, TsAGM, f. 474, opis' 3, d. 204, l. 8.

77. *Rabochaia Moskva,* September 4, 1922, 8.

78. Advertisement for the opening of the Voronezh GUM, RGB IZO, P2 IV.2.

79. Advertisement reprinted in Anikst, *Soviet Commercial Design,* 98. This point is made in Randi Barnes-Cox, "'All This Can Be Yours!': Soviet Commercial Advertising and the Social Construction of Space, 1928–1956," in *The Landscape of Stalinism: The Art and Ideology of Soviet Space,* ed. Evgeny Dobrenko and Eric Naiman (Seattle: University of Washington Press, 2003), 132.

80. Victoria Bonnell, "The Representation of Women in Early Soviet Political Art," *Russian Review* 50 (1991): 267–88.

81. Advertisement in *Prozhektor,* no. 6 (1924), inside cover.

82. Advertisements preserved in RGB IZO, P2 IV.2.

83. Advertisements preserved in RGB IZO, P2 IV.1.

84. Advertisement preserved in RGB IZO, P2 IV.1.

85. TsAGM f. 474, opis' 3, d. 200, ll. 128–32.

86. Figures from the 1924–1925 operating year, for example, show that the Red Square stores averaged monthly sales of 1 million rubles, out of a total of 1.8 million. TsAGM, f. 474, opis' 3, d. 204, ll. 71, 73.

87. *Krasnyi put',* August 14, 1926, preserved in TsAGM, f. 474, opis' 3, d. 204, l. 170b.

88. Khan-Magomedov, *Rodchenko,* 150. For an analysis of this type of male-centered advertising, which was frequently used prior to 1917, see Sally West, "Imperial Russia's Masculine Consumer: Advertising to Men in the Feminized Arena of Early Consumer Culture," paper presented at the AAASS annual meeting, New Orleans, Louisiana, November 15–18, 2007.

89. Khan-Magomedov, *Rodchenko,* 150.

90. RGB IZO, P2 IV.1, P2 IV.2.

91. Ad for Rezinotrest reprinted in Anikst, *Soviet Commercial Design,* 97.

92. RGB IZO, P2.XI.3, P3 XXVI.7.

93. RGB IZO, P2 XI.3.

94. For example, "*Rabotnitsa-Khoziaka!* You Are the Main Consumer. Join the Cooperative." RGB IZO, P2 XI.3.

95. Several posters highlight this theme, including two with the slogans "*Rabotnitsi* and *Krest'ianki* Join Cooperatives" and "Women! Join the Cooperative!" in RGB IZO, P2 XI.3, and "*Krest'ianka!* Join the Dairy Cooperative. It Helps Rebuild the Economy in a Cultured Way," in ibid., P3 XXVI.7.

96. Many of these textiles were displayed at the Soviet Textiles in Everyday Life exhibit in 1928. Agit-textiles, however, were not produced in large quantities and ultimately failed to find a wide consuming public. Tatiana Strizhenova, *Soviet Costumes and Textiles, 1917–1945* (Moscow, 1991), 133–42, 190–200.

97. *Pravda,* February 22, 1925, 4.

98. State Mail-Order Company catalogs for 1928 and 1929, RGB IZO, Papka Sborniki, 1920–31. Lantern brochure, RGB IZO, P3.II.

99. Many of these high-priced pieces were exhibited abroad and sold in special stores in Leningrad and Moscow. Nina Lobanov-Rostovsky, *Revolutionary Ceramics: Soviet Porcelain, 1917–1927* (New York: Rizzoli, 1990), 13, 26–28, 32–33, 57.

100. Photographs of wrappers and the mobile candy wrapper in Anikst, *Soviet Commercial Design*, 41–43, 93–94. Tractor and metric system wrappers on display at Maiakovskii House, Moscow.

101. *Rabochaia Moskva,* December 3, 1926, 3; December 28, 1926, 3.

102. Fall bazaar advertisements in *Vecherniaia Moskva,* August 25, 1926, August 22, 1926, TsAGM, f. 474, opis' 3, d. 204, ll. 9, 23. Spring bazaar advertisement in *Vecherniaia Moskva,* March 22, 1926, March 25, 1926, TsAGM, f. 474, opis' 3, d. 204, ll. 48ob–49.

103. *Vecherniaia Moskva,* May 6, 1926, 1; May 12, 1926, 2; May 14, 1926, 2; May 22, 1926, 2.

104. Advertisement in *Vecherniaia Moskva,* March 9, 1925, 2.

105. Holiday sales advertised in *Vechernye izvestiia,* November 6, 1924, 5; *Rabochaia gazeta,* November 3, 7, 1926. Larek contest announced in *Rabochaia gazeta,* November 13, 1924, 4. It is not clear how many, if any, parents claimed prizes. Although Larek promised to publish the names of those who received gifts, a list never appeared in the newspaper, an indication either that the fashion of giving revolutionary names to children was not particularly popular in Odessa or that no children of committed communists happened to be born on that day. Advertisement for Treasure campaign reprinted in Anikst, *Soviet Commercial Design,* 38–39.

106. GUM's chairman of the board discussed the goals of the bazaar in *Vecherniaia Moskva,* August 25, 1926.

107. Nove, *Economic History of the USSR,* 88–91.

108. Paul R. Gregory, "National Income," in *From Tsarism to the New Economic Policy,* ed. Davies, 247; Mark Harrison, "National Income," and R. W. Davies, "Industry," both in *Economic Transformation of the Soviet Union,* ed. Davies, Harrison, and Wheatcroft, 110–14, and 136, respectively; Osokina, *Our Daily Bread,* chaps. 1, 2.

109. *Rabochaia gazeta,* December 1926 (undated), clippings file, TsAGM, f. 474, opis' 3, d. 204, l. 25.

110. *Pravda,* September 17, 1925, 3.

111. *Rabochaia Moskva,* December 25, 1926, 3.

112. This list was compiled in 1925. TsAGM, f. 2156, opis' 7, d. 93, l. 69.

113. *Pravda,* December 16, 1926, clipping in TsAGM, f. R-474, opis' 3, d. 204, l. 50b.

114. A. Radchenko, *Domovodstvo,* vol. 1, *Kak pravil'no vesti svoi dom* (Moscow, 1928), 20–21, 30, 32–35.

115. Birgitta Ingemanson, "The Political Function of Domestic Objects in the Fiction of Aleksandra Kollontai," *Slavic Review* 48:1 (spring 1989): 71–82.

116. TsAGM, f. 2156, opis' 7, d. 89, l. 24.

117. *Rabochaia Moskva,* April 9, 1924, 4.

118. *Rabotnitsa,* January 1924, 13. *Delegatka,* another journal devoted to women's issues, reported on a meeting of women workers who discussed, among other things, the use of rouge and the practice of curling and fixing their hair. *Delegatka,* May 1926, 12.

119. Il'ia Lin, "V Chem Krasota," *Rabotnitsa,* September 1927, 15.

120. Ibid.

121. Ibid., 16.

122. Mariia Il'ina, "V Chem Krasota," *Rabotnitsa,* December 1927, 15.

123. Ibid. The writer acknowledged that many readers, including several Komsomol members, had asked a version of this question.

124. Mariia Il'ina, "V Chem Krasota," *Rabotnitsa,* December 1927, 16.

125. Malte Rolf, "A Hall of Mirrors: Sovietizing Culture under Stalinism," *Slavic Review* 68:3 (fall 2009): 604–5, 627.

126. Walter Benjamin reported that at Sukharev Market, he bought tree decorations and saw stands selling images of the saints. He also reported tree decorations on sale at shops on Tverskaia, Tverskaia-Iamskaia, and other main streets. Walter Benjamin, *Moscow Diary,* ed. Gary Smith, trans. Richard Sieburth (Cambridge, MA: Harvard University Press, 1986), 18–20, 68.

127. *Vecherniaia Moskva,* April 23, 1924, 2.

128. Ibid. In the same article, the vice-president of the Moscow Workers' Co-op called these practices "intolerable crimes" and remarked that cooperatives that employed rabbis were a disgrace.

129. Advertisements in *Vechernye izvestiia,* December 15, 1924, 4; December 22, 1924, 4.

130. *Vecherniaia Moskva,* April 6, 1925, 4.

131. Mosgubvnutorg (Moscow Guberniia Internal Commerce) ordered all co-op and state organizations to deliver an adequate supply of goods to Moscow before the beginning of pre-holiday demand. *Rabochaia Moskva,* December 10, 1926, 3.

132. Babaev advertisement, *Vechernye izvestiia,* December 1924, 4. Red October and State Factory catalogs, RGB IZO, Papka Y(2) 421.512.1.

133. *Vecherniaia Moskva,* April 25, 1924, 2. The investigator also stated that the vendor had the proper registration certificates from Narkomfin. Complaint and investigator's report, TsAGM, f. 1275, opis' 1, d. 114, ll. 30b–4.

134. GIM OPI, f. 402, opis' 1, d. 853.

135. William Husband, *"Godless Communists": Atheism and Society in Soviet Russia, 1917–1932* (DeKalb: Northern Illinois University Press, 2000); Daniel Peris, *Storming the Heavens: The Soviet League of the Militant Godless* (Ithaca: Cornell University Press, 1998).

136. Holding services outside of a church and inviting a priest to bless a home or other premises were prohibited. Gromyko, "Sluzhby vne khrama," 17; Chulos, *Converging Worlds,* 111.

137. *Kommunar* (Tula), March 10, 1925, in TsAGM, f. 474, opis' 3, d. 204, l. 102.

138. TsAGM, f. 474, opis' 1, d. 229, l. 402.

139. Nina Tumarkin, *Lenin Lives! The Lenin Cult in Soviet Russia* (Cambridge, MA: Harvard University Press, 1997), 126–27, 221–24.

140. See Richard Stites, "Bolshevik Ritual Building in the 1920s," in *Russia in the Era of NEP,* ed. Fitzpatrick, Rabinowitch, and Stites, 295–309.

141. Hessler, *Social History of Soviet Trade,* 202.

142. Nove, *Economic History of the USSR,* 99. R. W. Davies estimates that, by 1926, the state held more than half of all "organized" retail trade, excluding street vending and peasant markets, in its hands. Davies, *From Tsarism to the New Economic Policy,* 13.

Chapter 8. The Customer Is Always Wrong

An earlier version of this chapter appeared as "The Customer is Always Wrong: Consumer Complaint in Late-NEP Russia," in the *Russian Review* 68, no. 1 (January 2009): 1–25.

1. More than two hundred complaints from GUM's books, dating from 1927 to 1929, are preserved in several files at TsAGM. My survey of complaints in the mass-circulation press dated from 1925 to 1929; the publications that printed the complaints had a readership of urban working-class and middling groups and included *Rabochaia Moskva, Rabochaia gazeta, Vecherniaia Moskva,* and Odessa's *Vechernye izvestiia.*

2. Articles informing readers about the infractions discovered at private retail venues ran frequently. One typical piece reported that a survey of 248 private shopkeepers and market vendors in Moscow's Sokolniki area found that 68 percent of them regularly cheated and shortchanged consumers when weighing products. The report cited the vendor Sklovskii at Sukharev Market, who allegedly affixed to the underside of his scales a five-kopek piece. Several co-ops were also cited. *Rabochaia Moskva,* April 29, 1926, 4.

3. Jeffrey Brooks has noted the existence of a kind of restricted, popular public culture based on the popular press in the 1920s. In this sphere, active readers exchanged opinions, evaluated policies, identified abuses, and superimposed values on the realities of daily life. Jeffrey Brooks, "Public and Private Values in the Soviet Press, 1921–1928," *Slavic Review* 48:1 (spring 1989): 16–35.

4. Richard Hellie, "The Origins of Denunciation in Muscovy," *Russian History/Histoire russe* 24:1–2 (spring–summer 1997): 11–26.

5. For an examination of how Russians contemplated the relationship between a man's socioeconomic status and military service in the late imperial era, see Josh Sanborn, "Conscription, Correspondence, and Politics in Late Imperial Russia," *Russian History/ Histoire russe* 24:1–2 (spring–summer 1997): 27–40. For an exploration of Russians' articulation of their experiences and aspirations during 1917, see Mark Steinberg, *Voices of Revolution, 1917* (New Haven: Yale University Press, 2001).

6. For an argument that a contestation of the "self" and the "social" was framed by larger "public narratives about the proper behavior of workers and state servants," see Lewis Siegelbaum, "Narratives of Appeal and the Appeal of Narratives: Labor Discipline and Its Contestation in the Early Soviet Period," *Russian History/Histoire russe* 24:1–2 (spring–summer 1997): 65–87. Regarding how petitions from the disenfranchised for reinstatement of their rights in the 1920s and 1930s illustrate an older discourse of victimization and a new political discourse of the enemy, see Golfo Alexopoulos, "Victim Talk: Defense Testimony and Denunciation under Stalin," in *Russian Modernity: Politics, Knowledge, Practices,* ed. David L. Hoffmann and Yanni Kotsonis (New York: St. Martin's Press, 2000). For a finding that denunciations and complaints from the 1930s mixed pre-Soviet and Soviet conventions, blending "comradeship and supplication," see Sheila Fitzpatrick's "Suppliants and Citizens: Public Letter-Writing in Soviet Russia in the 1930s," *Slavic Review* 55:1 (spring 1996): 78–105; and "Signals from Below: Soviet Letters of Denunciation of the 1930s," *Journal of Modern History* 68:4 (December 1996): 831–66.

7. Osokina, *Za fasada Stalinskogo izobiliia;* Hessler, *Social History of Soviet Trade.*

8. Hessler identifies the 1930s as a turning point in the invention of socialist trade and, more particularly, the inauguration of a Soviet "exchange culture." Hessler, *Social History*

of Soviet Trade, 197–98. Amy Randall also characterizes the Stalinist campaign of the 1930s as a "new approach to trade and consumption." Randall, *Soviet Dream World of Retail Trade,* 11.

9. The power of discourses to construct meaning and difference is well established in the theoretical literature. This analysis recognizes that the process of making meaning occurs in specific political, social, economic, and cultural contexts and that subjects do not simply receive language and symbols; they also shape, appropriate, and reconstruct them. Discourse is defined as a site of struggle, a space in which meanings are produced and challenged through language and experience. Speaking and labeling people, places, and things are active forces within this site. Kathleen Canning, "Feminist History after the Linguistic Turn: Historicizing Discourse and Experience," *Signs* 19:2 (winter 1994): 368–404; Nancy Ries, *Russian Talk: Culture and Conversation during Perestroika* (Ithaca: Cornell University Press, 1997), 3–5.

10. Benson, *Counter Cultures,* 91.

11. A. Gudvan dedicated himself to work among commercial employees, and many of his works detail their harsh working and living conditions. Gudvan, *Ocherki po istorii dvizheniia sluzhashchikh,* 125–39. The merchant I. A. Slonov recounted the regimen of retail apprentices in his memoirs. Slonov, *Iz zhizn' torgovoi Moskvy,* 65–66.

12. Gudvan, *Ocherki po istorii dvizheniia sluzhashchikh,* 10–21, 25–48, 63–70. For evidence that merchants ignored the decrees against Sunday commerce, see *Odesskie novosti,* July 7, 1901, 3; August 15, 1901, 4. Gudvan, along with the police, rounded up thirteen lavka proprietors from the Novyi Bazaar area for operating on Sunday. Each was fined twenty rubles or seven days for the infraction.

13. "Iz zhizn'," *Vestnik torgovykh sluzhashchikh,* November 24, 1907, 14–15.

14. The Union of Soviet and Commercial Employees had 1.2 million members by 1926. On the position of sales workers vis-à-vis industrial workers, see Daniel Orlovsky, "The Hidden Class: White-Collar Workers in the Soviet 1920s," in *Making Workers Soviet: Power, Class, and Identity,* ed. Lewis H. Siegelbaum and Ronald Grigor Suny (Ithaca: Cornell University Press, 1994).

15. *Pravila vnutrennogo rasporiadka,* 5. See also Alexander Wicksteed, *Life under the Soviets* (London: John Lane, 1928), 6–7.

16. *Pravda,* September 17, 1925, 3.

17. Ibid.

18. *Golos rabotnika,* May 31, 1924, 5. See also Remtzen and Tsuberbiller, *Organizatsiia roznichnoi torgovli,* 81–83.

19. *Pravila vnutrennogo rasporiadka,* 4–5.

20. Personnel files (*ankety*) of GUM's employees from 1921 to 1931, TsAGM, f. 474, opis' 4, d. 1-3952. My cursory examination of these files reveals social diversity and widely varying levels of experience among the workers. There was also an influx of 150 young "Red merchants" at GUM and an active Komsomol unit. See Aksel'rod, *Kak my uchilis' torgovat',* 41–42.

21. Volzhanin, "Bol'she vnimaniia pokupateliu i . . . prodavtsy," *Golos rabotnika,* May 15, 1924, 8.

22. Ibid.

23. Letter preserved in TsAGM, f. 2156, opis' 7, d. 93, ll. 126–27.

24. *Golos rabotnika,* May 31, 1924, 5. For other comments about the state's unresponsive-

ness, see S. M. Malyshev, *"Mostorg" Opyt statistiko-ekonomicheskogo issledovaniia universal'nogo optovo-roznichnogo predpriiatiia* (Moscow, 1923), 180; and *Rabochaia Moskva,* December 5, 1926, 3.

25. "Sudebnoe delo o sotrudnike Belov," TsAGM, f. 474, opis' 3, d. 4, ll. 100–20.

26. Newspaper clippings covering the trial in TsAGM, f. 474, opis' 3, d. 204, ll. 84–86. In 1926, Sergei Chernysh, a former Red Army soldier and assistant manager of the Moscow GUM's controller's office, was tried for embezzlement. Press coverage of the trial in TsAGM, f. 474, opis' 3, d. 204, l. 230b, 17, 36, and 38.

27. The state charged several of GUM's tailors and garment workers with forgery and accepting money for orders of custom-made clothing that were never sewn. *Vecherniaia Moskva,* April 2, 1926, 2. See, for example, inspection reports of GUM branch stores in TsAGM, f. 474, opis' 3, d. 14, l. 3; d. 17, l. 52; d. 200, ll. 178–83ob; and d. 218, ll. 8–18.

28. Subsidies for newspapers were common in the 1920s. Jeffrey Brooks, "The Press and Its Messages: Images of America in the 1920s and 1930s," in *Russia in the Era of NEP,* ed. Fitzpatrick, Rabinowitch, and Stites, 232.

29. The total number of entries received was not disclosed, but the newspaper featured approximately ten for each of the five weeks that the contest ran. *Rabochaia Moskva,* April 22, 1926, 3. Similar contests were instituted in other realms of society. See Diane Koenker's examination of *Pravda's* 1922 contest for best and worst factory directors in Diane P. Koenker, "Factory Tales: Narratives of Industrial Relations in the Transition to NEP," *Russian Review* 55:3 (July 1996): 384–411.

30. Michael S. Gorham, "Tongue-Tied Writers: The *Rabsel'kor* Movement and the Voice of the 'New Intelligentsia' in Early Soviet Russia," *Russian Review* 55 (July 1996): 412–29; Brooks, "Public and Private Values," 23–24; Regine Robin, "Popular Literature of the 1920s," in *Russia in the Era of NEP,* ed. Fitzpatrick, Rabinowitch, and Stites, 255.

31. My thanks to Amy Randall for sharing her findings on the origins of the complaint book. According to Randall, one of the earliest literary references to the complaint book is in Anton Chekhov's 1884 short story "Complaint Book." See A. P. Chekhov, *Sobranie sochineneii,* vol. 2 (Moscow, 1960), 199–200, 566. Thus far, I have found no references to complaint books in the retail industry in the West. In many department stores in the United States, dissatisfied customers who complained on the sales floor or wrote a letter of complaint were referred to an executive or "diplomat." See Benson, *Counter Cultures,* 94–96; and Leach, *Land of Desire,* 133–34. The Bon Marché in Paris had a "complaints service," which resolved complaints on the spot. Complaint letters received via mail would have been received by the correspondence bureau and likely passed on to an executive. Miller, *Bon Marché,* 63–64.

32. Retailers and vendors with little capital, particularly those who operated booths and stalls, were temporarily exempt from keeping a complaint book. All kinds of institutions, such as theaters, were also required to maintain complaint books. See rules as set forth in *Pravila vnutrennogo rasporiadka,* 5. Guidelines may be found inside most complaint books preserved in the archives of GUM and other enterprises. Discussion of the Narkomtorg decree in *Vecherniaia Moskva,* July 10, 1928, 2.

33. *Vecherniaia Moskva,* July 16, 1928, 2.

34. *Vecherniaia Moskva,* July 10, 1928, 2.

35. Criteria for defining class in the 1920s were not precisely defined, and dislocations in occupation, residence, and status following the revolution often made determining a

person's true social class difficult. See Sheila Fitzpatrick, "Ascribing Class: The Construction of Social Identity in Soviet Russia," *Journal of Modern History* 65 (December 1993): 749–58.

36. Kenez, *Birth of the Propaganda State,* 157.

37. Women increasingly joined the party in the 1920s, but they constituted only a small percentage of the total membership: only 7.8 percent in 1922 and 12.1 percent in 1927. T. H. Rigby, *Communist Party Membership in the U.S.S.R., 1917–1967* (Princeton: Princeton University Press, 1968), 361.

38. Ries, *Russian Talk,* 52–56.

39. *Rabochaia Moskva,* June 6, 1926, 4. A similar tale of misfortune appeared in the February 5, 1929, issue.

40. *Rabochaia Moskva,* June 6, 1926, 4.

41. *Rabochaia gazeta* clipping, TsAGM, f. 474, opis' 1, d. 229, l. 395.

42. Ibid.

43. *Rabochaia gazeta* clipping, TsAGM, f. 474, opis' 1, d. 229, ll. 393–930b.

44. *Rabochaia gazeta* clipping, TsAGM, f. 474, opis' 1, d. 229, l. 398.

45. *Rabochaia Moskva,* November 14, 1926, 3; August 20, 1926, 4; May 11, 1926, 4.

46. *Rabochaia Moskva,* May 28, 1926, 4.

47. *Rabochaia Moskva,* May 11, 1926, 4; May 28, 1926, 4.

48. *Rabochaia Moskva,* June 6, 1926, 4.

49. *Rabochaia Moskva,* May 14, 1926, 4; June 6, 1926, 4.

50. *Rabochaia Moskva,* May 18, 1926, 4; June 6, 1926, 4.

51. *Vechernye izvestiia,* March 7, 1927, 2.

52. TsAGM, f. 474, opis' 1, d. 229, ll. 447, 449.

53. TsAGM, f. 474, opis' 1, d. 229, l. 103. Another claim from a customer about poor-quality gloves bought at this same store is in ibid., l. 107. His complaint was also rejected as one that "does not conform to reality." Ibid., l. 108.

54. TsAGM, f. 474, opis' 1, d. 229, l. 33.

55. *Rabochaia Moskva,* May 11, 1926, 4.

56. *Rabochaia Moskva,* June 6, 1926, 4.

57. *Rabochaia Moskva,* November 14, 1926, 3.

58. *Rabochaia Moskva,* May 14, 1926, 4.

59. *Rabochaia Moskva,* May 18, 1926, 4. Comparisons between private shops and state and co-op stores were common. One from an earlier period had contrasted the "courteous treatment" received from a private trader with the indifference of a co-op worker, who the writer referred to as an "expediter of the counter." *Rabochaia Moskva,* June 20, 1924, 6.

60. *Rabochaia Moskva,* May 25, 1926, 4.

61. *Rabochaia Moskva,* May 11, 1926, 4. Another complaint about the sale of sugar in kilos is in *Rabochaia Moskva,* November 26, 1926, 3.

62. *Rabochaia Moskva,* May 11, 1926, 4.

63. TsAGM, f. 474, opis' 3, d. 213, l. 232.

64. TsAGM, f. 474, opis' 1, d. 229, l. 699.

65. TsAGM, f. 474, opis' 3, d. 218, ll. 99–100; d. 225, l. 5; d. 213, ll. 187–870b; opis' 1, d. 229, ll. 92–940b.

66. TsAGM, f. 474, opis' 1, d. 229, l. 301.

67. TsAGM, f. 474, opis' 1, d. 229, l. 302.

68. TsAGM, f. 474, opis' 1, d. 229, l. 319.

69. TsAGM, f. 474, opis' 1, d. 229, l. 320.

70. TsAGM, f. 474, opis' 1, d. 229, l. 598.

71. TsAGM, f. 474, opis' 1, d. 229, l. 5980b.

72. TsAGM, f. 474, opis' 1, d. 229, l. 599.

73. TsAGM, f. 474, opis' 1, d. 229, l. 106.

74. TsAGM, f. 474, opis' 1, d. 229, l. 104.

75. TsAGM, f. 474, opis' 1, d. 229, l. 197. Two similar complaints of early closing and unlawful denial of access are in ibid., d. 229, ll. 477, 755.

76. TsAGM, f. 474, opis' 1, d. 229, l. 198.

77. TsAGM, f. 474, opis' 1, d. 229, l. 700–701.

78. TsAGM, f. 474, opis' 1, d. 229, l. 437. Other customers complained that they were questioned about their place of employment, the intended purpose for the fabric, and quantity of fabric requested; see ibid., ll. 435, 440–41.

79. TsAGM, f. 474, opis' 1, d. 229, l. 752. In a similar incident, the customer Burkin accused GUM's employees of not following identification procedures, thereby privileging some customers over others. A bystander seconded his accusation, stating that he watched as a woman went up to the counter and showed a party card but answered incorrectly when asked to give her date of birth. She nevertheless received fabric, while Burkin, who also had a rationing book, was denied merchandise. Ibid.

80. TsAGM, f. 474, opis' 1, d. 229, l. 437.

81. Fitzpatrick, "Ascribing Class," 755–58.

82. TsAGM, f. 474, opis' 3, d. 213, ll. 95–950b.

83. TsAGM f. 474, opis' 1, d. 229, ll. 649–490b.

84. TsAGM, f. 474, opis' 1, d. 229, l. 644.

85. TsAGM, f. 474, opis' 3, d. 229, ll. 350–51.

86. TsAGM, f. 474, opis' 3, d. 25, ll. 171–72.

87. TsAGM, f. 474, opis' 1, d. 229, l. 602. An attached complaint verified Vernuchina's account.

88. TsAGM, f. 474, opis' 1, d. 229, l. 6020b.

89. Although Tarasov-Rodionov's novel was later criticized for ideological errors, the novel struck a chord among Communist youth. Aleksandr Tarasov-Rodionov, *Chocolate,* trans. Charles Malamuth (New York: Doubleday, Doran, 1932).

90. See "NEP as Female Complaint (II): Revolutionary Anorexia," which is chapter 6 in Eric Naiman, *Sex in Public: The Incarnation of Early Soviet Ideology* (Princeton: Princeton University Press, 1997).

91. *Orlovskaia Pravda,* March 28, 1925, preserved in TsAGM, f. 474, opis' 3, d. 204, l. 95.

92. TsAGM, f. 474, opis' 1, d. 229, l. 761.

93. TsAGM, f. 474, opis' 1, d. 229, ll. 474–76.

94. TsAGM, f. 474, opis' 1, d. 229, l. 199.

95. Ibid.

96. TsAGM, f. 474, opis' 3, d. 218, ll. 157–60.

97. TsAGM, f. 474, opis' 3, d. 218, ll. 126–29.

98. TsAGM, f. 474, opis' 3, d. 218, ll. 107–9.

99. TsAGM, f. 474, opis' 1, d. 229, ll. 92–940b.

100. His communication to the directors stated that despite repeated warnings and

instructions to the employees, the displays of the stores facing the square were in an "abominable condition." He singled out Haberdashery Store No. 3 for its slovenliness; dust covered the store fixtures and boxes for starched linens, and copper spittoons in the corners had turned a moldy green. TsAGM, f. 474, opis' 3, d. 14, ll. 68–69. The Arbat store was singled out for its good condition. Ibid., d. 28, l. 101.

101. TsAGM, f. 474, opis' 3, d. 213, l. 179; d. 218, l. 101.

102. TsAGM, f. 474, opis' 3, d. 218, ll. 120–22.

Epilogue

1. Profits for 1924 equaled 184,000 rubles and in 1926, 1.1 million rubles. Profit statements in TsAGM, f. 474, opis' 3, d. 5, ll. 2, 54.

2. Ball, *Russia's Last Capitalists,* chap. 3; Hessler, *Social History of Soviet Trade,* chap. 5; Osokina, *Our Daily Bread,* chaps. 2–3.

3. Quoted phrases from Randall, *Soviet Dream World of Retail Trade,* 18; and Hessler, *Social History of Soviet Trade,* 198, respectively.

4. Randall, *Soviet Dream World of Retail Trade,* 17–22.

5. *Izvestiia,* January 29, 1932, 1.

6. On the decision to phase out cooperatives, see Hessler, *Social History of Soviet Trade,* 19; and Randall, *Soviet Dream World of Retail Trade,* 3, 27–28.

7. Hessler, *Social History of Soviet Trade,* 207–9; Elena Osokina, "Za zerkal'noi dver'iu Torgsina," *Otechestvennaia istoriia,* no. 2 (April 1995): 86–104.

8. Osokina, "Za zerkal'noi dver'iu Torgsina."

9. Hessler, *Social History of Soviet Trade,* 201.

10. Ibid., 205–7.

11. S. Sorokin, *Sto let na Krasnoi ploshchadi* (Moscow, 1993), 51–53.

12. Randall, *Soviet Dream World of Retail Trade,* 28–29.

13. Acknowledging the legacy of the NEP, Hessler nonetheless treats the campaign of the 1930s as novel, referring to the campaign as a "new departure" and to the model of Western-style retailing as a "new model." Hessler, *Social History of Soviet Trade,* 222. Randall likewise terms the Stalinist-era campaign a "new direction for social and economic policy." Randall, *Soviet Dream World of Retail Trade,* 3.

14. Randall, *Soviet Dream World of Retail Trade,* 68–69.

15. Hessler, *Social History of Soviet Trade,* 229.

16. Dunham, *In Stalin's Time.*

17. Randall, *Soviet Dream World of Retail Trade,* 134–51.

18. Osokina, *Za fasada Stalinskogo izobilia,* 12.

Bibliography

Primary Sources

Archival Collections

Gosudarstvennyi arkhiv Odesskoi oblasti (GAOO), Odessa
Gosudarstvennyi arkhiv Russkoi federatsiia (GARF), Moscow
Rossiiskii gosudarstvennyi arkhiv po ekonomike (RGAE), Moscow
Rossiiskii gosudarstvennyi arkhiv sotsial'no-politicheskoi istorii (RGASPI), Moscow
Russkii gosudarstvennyi istoricheskii arkhiv (RGIA), St. Petersburg
Tsentral'nyi arkhiv goroda Moskvy (TsAGM), Moscow
Tsentral'nyi istoricheskii arkhiv Moskvy (TsIAM), Moscow

Library and Museum Collections

Gosudarstvennyi istoricheskii muzei, Otdel pis'mennykh istochnikov (GIM OPI), Moscow
Istoriko-Kraevedcheskii muzei, Odessa
Muzei istorii goroda Moskvy, Moscow
Muzei upakovki, Moscow
Russkaia gosudarstvennaia biblioteka, Izobrazitel'nyi otdel (RGB IZO), Moscow

Journals and Newspapers

Damskii mir	*Odesskie novosti*	*Torgovo-promyshlennaia Odessa*
Delegatka	*Odesskii listok*	*Torgovo-promyshlennaia Rossiia*
Ekonomicheskaia zhizn'	*Odesskoe slovo*	*Torgovoe delo*
Golos rabotnika	*Pravda*	*Torgovyi mir*
Izvestiia	*Prozhektor*	*Vecherniaia Moskva*
Kormchii	*Rabochaia gazeta*	*Vecherniaia pochta*
Moskovskie vedomosti	*Rabochaia Moskva*	*Vechernye izvestiia*
Moskovskii listok	*Rabotnitsa*	*Vestnik narodnogo kommissariata*
Novaia Odesskaia gazeta	*Russkie vedomosti*	*torgovli i promyshlennosti*
Odesskaia gazeta	*Russkoe slovo*	*Vestnik torgovykh sluzhashchikh*
Odesskaia mysl'	*Torgovlia, promyshlennost',*	*Zhurnalist*
	i tekhnika	

Published Collections of Laws and Decrees, Statistical Sources, Corporate and Merchant Publications, and Other Informational Guides

Adres-kalendar' Odesskogo gradonachal'stva na 1905 g. Odessa, 1905.

Doklad chrezvychainomu obshchemu sobraniiu aktsionerov "Mostorg" o deiatel'nosti obshchestva za polugodie: Noiabr' 1923 g. – Aprel' 1924 g. Moscow, 1924.

Entsiklopedichesskii slovar'. St. Petersburg, 1900.

Iuzhno-Russkii almanakh za 1898 g. Odessa, 1898.

Khoroshii ton: sbornik pravil, nastavlenii i sovetov, kak sleduet vesti sebia v raznykh sluchaiakh domashnei i obshchestvennoi zhizni. Moscow, 1911.

Konkurs na proektu zdanii Verkhnykh torgovykh riadov na Krasnoi ploshchadi v Moskve. Moscow, 1889.

Krasnaia Moskva, 1917–1920 gg. Moscow: Publication of the Moscow Soviet, 1920.

K stoletiiu chainoi firmy "V. Perlov s synov'iami" (1787g. – 1887 g.): istoriko-statisticheskii ocherk. Moscow, 1898.

Moskva: entsiklopediia. Edited by S. O. Shmidt. Moscow, 1997.

Moskva: vidy nekotorykh mestnostei, khramov, primechatel'nykh zdanii i drugikh sooruzhenii. Moscow, 1888.

Novorossiiskii kalendar' na 1891 g. Odessa, 1891.

Odessa, 1794–1894: izdanie gorodskogo obshchestvennogo upravleniia k stoletiiu goroda. Odessa, 1895.

Odessa i eia okrestnosti: istoricheskii ocherk i illiustrirovannyi putevoditel' na 1894. Odessa, 1894.

Pervaia vseobshchaia perepis' naseleniia Rossiiskoi Imperii, 1897 g. Vol. 47. St. Petersburg, 1899–1905.

Pravila vnutrennogo rasporiadka dlia sluzhashchikh Gosudarstvennogo Universal'nogo Magazina GUM. Moscow, 1925.

Putevoditel' po verkhnym torgovym riadam na Krasnoi ploshchadi v Moskve. Moscow, 1895.

Sobranie uzakonenii i rasporiazhenii, 1917–1949. Moscow, 1920–1950.

Sobranie uzakonenii i rasporiazhenii raboche-krest'ianskogo pravitel'stva RSFSR. Moscow, 1917–1923.

Sovremennaia Rossiia: ocherki nashei gosudarstvennoi i obshchestvennoi zhizni. Vol. 2. St. Petersburg, 1891.

Spisok aktsionerov obshchestva verkhnikh torgovykh riadov na Krasnoi ploshchadi v Moskve na 11 febralia 1912 goda. Moscow, 1912.

Spisok Odesskikh kuptsov i voobshche litsi uchrezhdenii torgovo-promyshlennogo klass po gorodu Odessa na 1909 god. Odessa, 1909.

Spisok torgovykh domov i kupechestva g. Odessy na 1894 god. Odessa, 1894.

Spravochnaia kniga o litsakh poluchivshikh na 1894 goda kupecheskie svidetel'stva po 1-i i 2-i gil'diiam v Moskve. Moscow, 1894.

Spravochnaia kniga o litsakh poluchivshikh na 1898 god kupecheskie svidetel'stva po 1-i i 2-i gil'diiam v Moskve. Moscow, 1898.

Topograficheskii kupecheskii riadskii kalendar'. Moscow, 1862.

Torgovo-promyshlennaia Odessa: Adresnaia kniga na 1908 g. Odessa, 1907.

Torgovyi Dom "Brat'ia Eliseevy" (vne konkursa). Vol. 1. St. Petersburg, 1900.

Voennaia entsiklopediia. St. Petersburg, 1912.

Vseukrainskoe paevoe torgovoe t-vo "Larek" Otchet pravleniia za 1924–25 gg. N.p., n.d.

Vsia Moskva v karmane na 1924–25. Moscow, 1924.

Vsia Moskva v karmane. Moscow-Leningrad, 1926.

Vsia torgovo-promyshlennaia Odessa: adresnaia-spravochnaia kniga na 1914 god. Odessa, 1914.

Zolotoi iubilei k piatidesiatiletiiu so dnia osnovaniia T-va Brokar i Ko. Moscow, 1914.

Books, Articles, and Collections

Avdenko, I. *Putevoditel' po Odesse i eia okrestnostiiam na 1912 goda.* Odessa, 1912.

Amirov, I. "Klass torgovo-promyshlennykh sluzhashchikh i ego blizhaishiia zadachi." *Russkaia mysl',* no. 7 (July 1908): 41–52.

Andreeva-Bal'mont, E. A. *Vospominaniia.* Moscow, 1996.

Babel', Isaak. *Probuzhdenie: ocherki, rasskazy, kinopovest', p'esa.* Tbilisi, 1989.

Barmine, Alexander. *One Who Survived: The Life Story of a Russian under the Soviets.* New York: G. P. Putnam's Sons, 1945.

Baron, Samuel, trans. and ed. *The Travels of Olearius in Seventeenth-Century Russia.* Stanford: Stanford University Press, 1967.

Beliaev, I. "Obozrenie Moskvy: vneshnii vid stolitsy." In *Moskovskii arkhiv: istoriko-kraevedcheskii al'manakh.* Moscow, 1996.

Belitskii, Ia. M. *Zabytaia Moskva.* N.p., 1994.

Belousov, I. A. "Ushedshaia Moskva." In *Ushedshaia Moskva: vospominaniia sovremennikov o Moskve vtoroi poloviny XIX veka,* edited by N. S. Ashukina. Moscow, 1964.

Benjamin, Walter. *The Arcades Project.* Translated by Howard Eiland and Kevin McLaughlin. Cambridge, MA: Belknap Press of Harvard University Press, 1999.

———. *Moscow Diary.* Edited by Gary Smith. Translated by Richard Sieburth. Cambridge, MA: Harvard University Press, 1986.

Broido, Vera. *Daughter of Revolution: A Russian Girlhood Remembered.* London: Constable, 1998.

Bulgakov, M. A. "Torgovyi renessans: Moskva v nachale 1922 goda." Reprinted in *Sotsiologicheskie issledovaniia,* no. 1 (1988): 137–38.

Buryshkin, P. A. *Moskva kupecheskaia.* New York, 1954.

Chekhov, A. P. *Sobranie sochineneii.* Vol. 2. Moscow, 1960.

Davydov, N. V. "Moskva piatidesiatye i shestidesiatye gody XIX stoletiia." In *Ushedshaia Moskva: vospominaniia sovremennikov o Moskve vtoroi poloviny XIX veka,* edited by N. S. Ashukina. Moscow, 1964.

Duranty, Walter. *I Write as I Please.* London: Hamish Hamilton, 1935.

Ehrenburg, Ilya. *People and Life.* Translated by Anna Bostock and Yvonne Kapp. London: Macgibbon & Lee, 1961.

Elets, Iu. L. *Poval'noe bezumie (k sverzheniiu iga mod).* St. Petersburg, 1914.

Emmons, Terence, trans. and ed. *Time of Troubles: The Diary of Iurii Vladimirovich Got'e.* Princeton: Princeton University Press, 1988.

Galitskii, Vladimir. *Odesskii byli.* St. Petersburg, 1994.

Giliarovskii, V. *Moskva i Moskvichi: ocherki staromoskovskogo byta.* Moscow, 1959.

Gudvan, A. *Ocherki po istorii dvizheniia sluzhashchikh v Rossii (chast' pervaia).* Moscow, 1925.

Harrison, Marguerite. *Marooned in Moscow: The Story of an American Woman Imprisoned in Russia.* London: Thornton Butterworth, 1921.

Horsbrugh-Porter, Anna, ed. *Memories of Revolution: Russian Women Remember.* New York: Routledge, 1993.

Katayev, Valentin. *A Mosaic of Life or the Magic Horn of Oberon: Memoirs of a Russian Childhood.* Chicago: J. Philip O'Hara, 1976.

———. *Almaznyi moi venets.* Moscow, 1990.

Kharuzina, V. N. *Proshloe: vospominaniia detskikh i otrocheskikh let.* Moscow, 1999.

Kra__vskii, Al. *Mozhno-li v Moskve torgavat' chestno? Sovremennye zametki.* Moscow, 1886.

Lenin, V. I. *Polnoe sobranie sochinenii.* 5th ed. Moscow, 1958–1965.

Lowth, G. T. *Around the Kremlin.* London: Hurst and Blacklett, 1868.

Maiakovskii, V. *Polnoe sobranie sochinenii.* Vol. 12. Moscow, 1959.

Malyshev, S. M. *"Mostorg" Opyt statistiko-ekonomicheskogo issledovaniia universal'nogo optovo-roznichnogo predpriiatiia.* Moscow, 1923.

Moskvich, Grigorii. *Illiustrirovannyi prakticheskii putevoditel' po Odesse.* Odessa, 1907.

———. *Putevoditel' po Moskve.* Moscow, 1903.

Mysli o gorodskikh riadov starogo obyvatelia g. Moskvy. Moscow, 1887.

Nolde, Boris. *Russia in the Economic War.* New Haven: Yale University Press, 1928.

Nustrem, K. *Spetsial'noe obozrenia Moskvy.* Moscow, 1846.

Paustovskii, K. *Nachalo nevedomogo veka: vremia bol'shikh ozhidanii.* Kiev, 1985.

Pouncy, Carolyn Johnston, ed. *The Domostroi: Rules for Russian Households in the Time of Ivan the Terrible.* Ithaca: Cornell University Press, 1994.

Pyliaev, M. I. *Staraia Moskva: rasskazy iz byloi zhizni pervoprestol'noi stolitsy.* Moscow, 1990.

Radchenko, A. *Domovodstvo.* Vol. 1. *Kak pravil'no vesti svoi dom.* Moscow 1928.

Raleigh, Donald J., ed. *A Russian Civil War Diary: Alexis Babine in Saratov, 1917–1922.* Durham: Duke University Press, 1988.

Razmadze, A. S. *Torgovye riady na Krasnoi ploshchadi v Moskve.* Kiev, 1893.

Remtzen, K., and V. Tsuberbiller. *Organizatsiia roznichnoi torgovli.* Moscow, 1925.

Rudolf, M. *Ukazatel' mestnosti v Kremle i Kitai Gorode stolichnogo goroda Moskvy.* Moscow, 1846.

Segal, Mikhail. "Odessa moei molodosti." Uncataloged clipping in Istoriko-Kraevedcheskii muzei, Odessa.

Semenov, P. P., ed. *Zhivopisnaia Rossiia: otechestvo nashe.* Vol. 7. Moscow, 1898.

Shmelev, Ivan. *Sobranie sochinenii.* Vol. 4. Moscow, 1998.

Shneider, I. I. *Zapiski starogo Moskvicha.* Moscow, 1970.

Slonov, I. A. *Iz zhizn' torgovoi Moskvy (polveka nazad).* Moscow, 1914.

Sobolev, M. "Konkurrentsiia, kak dvigatel' sovremennoi ekonomicheskoi zhizni." *Mir Bozhii,* no. 9 (September 1900): 1–22.

———. "Universal'nye magaziny i bazary, kak iavlenie noveishago torgovago oborota." *Mir Bozhii,* no. 4 (April 1900): 114–30.

Soia-Serko, I. I. "Moskva moei molodosti." *Moskovskii zhurnal,* no. 7 (1998): 28–36.

Spasskii, P. Kh., ed. *Istoriia torgovli i promyshlennosti v Rossii.* Vol. 1. St. Petersburg, 1910.

Tarasov-Rodionov, Aleksandr. *Chocolate.* Translated by Charles Malamuth. New York: Doubleday, Doran, 1932.

Teleshov, N. *Zapiski pisatelia: vospominaniia i rasskazy o proshlom.* Moscow, 1980.

Trotsky, Leon. *Problems of Everyday Life, and Other Writings on Culture and Science.* New York: Pathfinder Press, 1973.

Tsvetaeva, Anastasiia. *Vospominaniia.* Moscow, 1974.

Utesov, Leonid. *Spasibo serdtse.* Moscow, 1976.

Vainer, D. I. *Illiustrirovannyi putevoditel' "Odessa" na 1900 g.* Odessa, 1900.

Varentsov, N. A. *Slyshannoe. Vidennoe. Peredymannoe. Perezhitoe.* Moscow, 1999.

Vasilich, G. "Moskva 1850–1910." In *Moskva v ee proshlom i nastoiashchem.* Vol. 11. Moscow, 1912.

———. "Ulitsy i liudi sovremennoi Moskvy. In *Moskva v ee proshlom i nastoiashchem.* Vol. 12. Moscow, 1912.

Wicksteed, Alexander. *Life under the Soviets.* London: John Lane, 1928.

Zhirmunskii, M. M. *Chastnyi kapital v tovarooborote.* Moscow, 1924.

Zola, Émile. *The Ladies' Paradise.* Translated by Brian Nelson. New York: Oxford University Press, 1995.

Selected Secondary Sources

Abelson, Elaine S. *When Ladies Go A-Thieving: Middle-Class Shoplifters in the Victorian Department Store.* New York: Oxford University Press, 1989.

Aksel'rod, V. S. *Kak my uchilis' torgovat'.* Moscow, 1986.

Alexopoulos, Golfo. "Victim Talk: Defense Testimony and Denunciation under Stalin." In *Russian Modernity: Politics, Knowledge, Practices,* edited by David L. Hoffmann and Yanni Kotsonis. New York: St. Martin's Press, 2000.

Anikst, Mikhail. *Soviet Commercial Design of the Twenties.* London: Thames and Hudson, 1987.

Appadurai, Arjun. *The Social Life of Things: Commodities in Cultural Perspective.* New York: Cambridge University Press, 1988.

Arkhipov, V. A., and L. F. Morozov. *Bor'ba protiv kapitalisticheskikh elementov v promyshlennosti i torgovle.* Moscow, 1978.

Auslander, Leora. "The Gendering of Consumer Practices in Nineteenth-Century France." In *The Sex of Things: Gender and Consumption in Historical Perspective,* edited by Victoria de Grazia with Ellen Furlough. Berkeley: University of California Press, 1996.

Ball, Alan M. *Russia's Last Capitalists: The Nepmen, 1921–1929.* Berkeley: University of California Press, 1987.

Banerji, Arup. *Merchants and Markets in Revolutionary Russia, 1917–1930.* New York: St. Martin's Press, 1997.

Barkhatova, Elena, ed. *Russian Constructivist Posters.* Moscow, 1992.

Barnes-Cox, Randi. "'All This Can Be Yours!': Soviet Commercial Advertising and the Social Construction of Space, 1928–1956." In *The Landscape of Stalinism: The Art and Ideology of Soviet Space,* edited by Evgeny Dobrenko and Eric Naiman. Seattle: University of Washington Press, 2003.

———. "The Creation of the Socialist Consumer: Advertising, Citizenship, and NEP." PhD dissertation, Indiana University, 2000.

Baron, Samuel H. "Sixteenth/Seventeenth-Century Russia." In *Entrepreneurship in Imperial Russia and the Soviet Union,* edited by Gregory Guroff and Fred V. Carstensen. Princeton: Princeton University Press, 1983.

Bell, Daniel. *The Cultural Contradictions of Capitalism.* New York: Basic Books, 1976.

Benson, Susan Porter. *Counter Cultures: Saleswomen, Managers, and Customers in American Department Stores, 1890–1940.* Urbana: University of Illinois Press, 1988.

Bermeo, Nancy, and Philip Nord, eds. *Civil Society before Democracy: Lessons from Nineteenth-Century Europe.* Lanham, MD: Rowman & Littlefield, 2000.

Blackwell, William L. *The Beginnings of Russian Industrialization, 1800–1860.* Princeton: Princeton University Press, 1968.

Bocock, Robert. *Consumption.* New York: Routledge, 1993.

———. *Ritual in Industrial Society: A Sociological Analysis of Ritualism in Modern England.* London: George Allen & Unwin, 1974.

Bogdanov, I. A. *Gostinyi Dvor.* Leningrad, 1988.

Bonnell, Victoria. "The Representation of Women in Early Soviet Political Art." *Russian Review* 50:3 (1991): 267–88.

Borrero, Mauricio. "Hunger and Society in Civil War Moscow, 1917–1921." PhD dissertation, Indiana University, 1992.

———. *Hungry Moscow: Scarcity and Urban Society in the Russian Civil War.* New York: Peter Lang, 2003.

Bowlby, Rachel. *Just Looking: Consumer Culture in Dreiser, Gissing, and Zola.* New York: Methuen, 1985.

Bradley, Joseph. *Muzhik i Muscovite: Urbanization in Late Imperial Russia.* Berkeley: University of California Press, 1985.

———. "Pictures at an Exhibition: Science, Patriotism, and Civil Society in Imperial Russia." *Slavic Review* 67:4 (winter 2008): 934–66.

———. "Subjects into Citizens: Societies, Civil Society, and Autocracy in Tsarist Russia." *American Historical Review* 107:4 (October 2002): 1094–1123.

Brewer, John, and Roy Porter. *Consumption and the World of Goods.* London: Routledge, 1993.

Brooks, Jeffrey. "The Press and Its Messages: Images of America in the 1920s and 1930s." In *Russia in the Era of NEP: Explorations in Soviet Society and Culture,* edited by Sheila Fitzpatrick, Alexander Rabinowitch, and Richard Stites. Bloomington: Indiana University Press, 1991.

———. "Public and Private Values in the Soviet Press, 1921–1928." *Slavic Review* 48:1 (spring 1989): 16–35.

———. *When Russia Learned to Read: Literacy and Popular Literature, 1861–1917.* Princeton: Princeton University Press, 1985.

Brower, Daniel K. "'The City in Danger': The Civil War and the Russian Urban Population." In *Party, State, and Society in the Russian Civil War,* edited by Diane P. Koenker, William G. Rosenberg, and Ronald Grigor Suny. Bloomington: Indiana University Press, 1989.

———. "The Penny Press and Its Readers." In *Cultures in Flux: Lower-Class Values, Practices, and Resistance in Late Imperial Russia,* edited by Stephen P. Frank and Mark D. Steinberg. Princeton: Princeton University Press, 1994.

Browne, M. Neil. "If Markets Are So Wonderful, Why Can't I Find Friends at the Store?" *American Journal of Economics and Sociology* 61:4 (October 2002): 787–800.

Brumfield, William. "Aesthetics and Commerce: The Architecture of Merchant Moscow, 1890–1917." In *Merchant Moscow: Images of Russia's Vanished Bourgeoisie,* edited by James L. West and Iurii A. Petrov. Princeton: Princeton University Press, 1998.

———. "From the Lower Depths to the Upper Trading Rows: The Design of Retail Shopping Centers in Moscow." In *Commerce in Russian Urban Culture, 1861–1914,* edited by William Craft Brumfield, Boris V. Anan'ich, and Yuri A. Petrov. Washington, DC: Woodrow Wilson Center Press; Baltimore: Johns Hopkins University Press, 2001.

————. *A History of Russian Architecture*. New York: Cambridge University Press, 1993.

————. *The Origins of Modernism in Russian Architecture*. Berkeley: University of California Press, 1991.

Buck-Morss, Susan. *The Dialectics of Seeing: Walter Benjamin and the Arcades Project*. Cambridge, MA: MIT Press, 1993.

————. "The Flaneur, the Sandwichman, and the Whore: The Politics of Loitering." *New German Critique* 13:39 (1986): 99–142.

Burds, Jeffrey. *Peasant Dreams and Market Politics: Labor Migration and the Russian Village, 1861–1905*. Pittsburgh: University of Pittsburgh Press, 1998.

Bushkovitch, Paul. *The Merchants of Moscow, 1580–1650*. New York: Cambridge University Press, 1980.

Cameron, Rondo. *A Concise Economic History of the World: From Paleolithic Times to the Present*. 3rd ed. New York: Oxford University Press, 1997.

Cannadine, David. "Splendor Out of Court: Royal Spectacle and Pageantry in Modern Britain, c. 1820–1977." In *Rites of Power: Symbolism, Ritual, and Politics since the Middle Ages*, edited by Sean Wilentz. Philadelphia: University of Pennsylvania Press, 1985.

Canning, Kathleen. "Feminist History after the Linguistic Turn: Historicizing Discourse and Experience." *Signs* 19:2 (winter 1994): 368–404.

Carr, E. H. *The Bolshevik Revolution, 1917–1923*. 3 vols. New York: Norton, 1980.

Chulos, Chris J. *Converging Worlds: Religion and Community in Peasant Russia, 1861–1917*. DeKalb: Northern Illinois University Press, 2003.

Clements, Barbara Evans. *Bolshevik Women*. New York: Cambridge University Press, 1997.

————. Introduction to *Russian Masculinities in History and Culture*, edited by Barbara Evans Clements, Rebecca Friedman, and Dan Healey. New York: Palgrave, 2001.

Clowes, Edith. "Merchants on Stage and in Life: Theatricality and Public Consciousness." In *Merchant Moscow: Images of Russia's Vanished Bourgeoisie*, edited by James L. West and Iurii A. Petrov. Princeton: Princeton University Press, 1998.

————, Samuel D. Kassow, and James L. West, eds. *Between Tsar and People: Educated Society and the Quest for Public Identity in Late Imperial Russia*. Princeton: Princeton University Press, 1991.

Clyman, Toby W., and Judith Vowles, eds. *Russia through Women's Eyes: Autobiographies from Tsarist Russia*. New Haven: Yale University Press, 1996.

Coe, Richard. *When the Grass Was Taller: Autobiography and the Experience of Childhood*. New Haven: Yale University Press, 1984.

Connell, R. W. *Masculinities*. Berkeley: University of California Press, 1995.

Conroy, Mary. "Chastniki nepovskoi Rossii: krest'iane-proizvoditeli lekarstvennykh rastenii, kustari-izgotoviteli farmatsevticheskikh sresdstv i farmatsevty." In *Bubliki dlia respubliki: istoricheskii profil' NEPmanov*, edited by R. A. Khaziev. Ufa: RIO BashGU, 2005.

Crane, Diana. *Fashion and Its Social Agendas: Class, Gender, and Identity in Clothing*. Chicago: University of Chicago Press, 2000.

————. *The Production of Culture: Media and the Urban Arts*. Newbury Park, CA: Sage Publications, 1992.

Davies, R. W., ed. *From Tsarism to the New Economic Policy: Continuity and Change in the Economy of the USSR*. Ithaca: Cornell University Press, 1991.

——, Mark Harrison, and S. G. Wheatcroft, eds. *The Economic Transformation of the Soviet Union, 1913–1945*. New York: Cambridge University Press, 1994.

de Grazia, Victoria, ed., with Ellen Furlough. *The Sex of Things: Gender and Consumption in Historical Perspective*. Berkeley: University of California Press, 1996.

de la Croix, Horst, and Richard G. Tansey. *Gardner's Art through the Ages*. 6th ed. New York: Harcourt Brace Jovanovich, 1975.

Demchik, E. V. "Sibirskie nepmany: predprinimateli i moshenniki." In *Bubliki dlia respubliki: istoricheskii profil' NEPmanov*, edited by R. A. Khaziev. Ufa: RIO, 2005.

Dikhtiar, G. A. *Vnutrenniaia torgovlia v dorevoliutsionnoi Rossii*. Moscow, 1960.

Dillon, Alexander. "The Forgotten Movement: Cooperatives and Cooperative Networks in Ukraine and Imperial Russia." *Harvard Ukrainian Studies* 23:1–2 (1999): 129–43.

Dorokhova, Nina. "Zhizn' byla slashche." *Stolitsa*, no. 3 (1994): 29–31.

Dovnar-Zapol'skii, M. V. "Torgovlia i promyshlennost' Moskvy XVI–XVII vv." In *Moskva v ee proshlom i nastoiashchem*. Vol. 6. Moscow, 1911.

Dunham, Vera S. *In Stalin's Time: Middleclass Values in Soviet Fiction*. New York: Cambridge University Press, 1976.

Engel, Barbara Alpern. *Between the Fields and the City: Women, Work, and Family in Russia, 1861–1914*. New York: Cambridge University Press, 1994.

——. "Not by Bread Alone: Subsistence Riots in Russia during World War I." *Journal of Modern History* 69 (December 1997): 696–721.

Engelstein, Laura. *The Keys to Happiness: Sex and the Search for Modernity in Fin-de-Siècle Russia*. Ithaca: Cornell University Press, 1992.

Farnsworth, Beatrice. "Village Women Experience the Revolution." In *Bolshevik Culture: Experiment and Order in the Russian Revolution,* edited by Abbott Gleason, Peter Kenez, and Richard Stites. Bloomington: Indiana University Press, 1985.

Felski, Rita. *The Gender of Modernity*. Cambridge, MA: Harvard University Press, 1995.

Finn, Margot. "Men's Things: Masculine Possession in the Consumer Revolution." *Social History* 25:2 (May 2000): 133–55.

Fitzpatrick, Sheila. "Ascribing Class: The Construction of Social Identity in Soviet Russia." *Journal of Modern History* 65 (December 1993): 745–70.

——. "Signals from Below: Soviet Letters of Denunciation of the 1930s." *Journal of Modern History* 68:4 (December 1996): 831–66.

——. "Supplicants and Citizens: Public Letter-Writing in Soviet Russia in the 1930s." *Slavic Review* 55:1 (spring 1996): 78–105.

Fitzpatrick, Sheila, Alexander Rabinowitch, and Richard Stites, eds. *Russia in the Era of NEP: Explorations in Soviet Society and Culture*. Bloomington: Indiana University Press, 1991.

Fokin, Georgii Ivanovich. *Flagman sovetskoi torgovli*. Moscow, 1968.

Fritzsche, Peter. *Reading Berlin 1900*. Cambridge, MA: Harvard University Press, 1996.

Furlough, Ellen. *Consumer Cooperation in France: The Politics of Consumption, 1834–1930*. Ithaca: Cornell University Press, 1991.

Gardiner, Judith Kegan, ed. *Masculinity Studies & Feminist Theory: New Directions*. New York: Columbia University Press, 2002.

Gatrell, Peter. *Russia's First World War: A Social and Economic History*. London: Pearson, 2005.

Gavlin, M. "Evreiskoe predprinimatel'stvo v Moskve v 60–90e gody XIV veka." *Vestnik Evreiskogo Universiteta v Moskve*, 3:16 (1997): 11–26.

Geertz, Clifford. "Centers, Kings, and Charisma: Reflections on the Symbolics of Power." In *Culture and Its Creators: Essays in Honor of Edward Shils,* edited by Joseph Ben-David and Terry Nicholas Clark. Chicago: University of Chicago Press, 1977.

Gerasimov, Viktor. "Saga o kuptsakh Eliseevykh." *Otchizna,* no. 7 (1991): 10–16.

Gohstand, Robert. "The Internal Geography of Trade in Moscow from the Mid-Nineteenth Century to the First World War." PhD dissertation, University of California, Berkeley, 1973.

———. "The Shaping of Moscow by Trade." In *The City in Russian History,* edited by Michael F. Hamm. Lexington: University Press of Kentucky, 1982.

Gorham, Michael S. "Tongue-Tied Writers: The *Rabsel'kor* Movement and the Voice of the 'New Intelligentsia' in Early Soviet Russia." *Russian Review* 55 (July 1996): 412–29.

Gorinov, M. M. "*Moskve v 20-x godakh.*" *Otechestvennaia istoriia,* no. 5 (1996): 3–17.

Gorsuch, Anne. *Youth in Revolutionary Russia: Enthusiasts, Bohemians, Delinquents.* Bloomington: Indiana University Press, 2000.

———, and Diane P. Koenker, eds. *Turizm: The Russian and East European Tourist under Capitalism and Socialism.* Ithaca: Cornell University Press, 2006.

Gray, Camilla. *The Russian Experiment in Art, 1863–1922.* New York: Thames and Hudson, 1962.

Gromyko, M. M. "Sluzhby vne khrama." In *Pravoslavnaia zhizn' russkikh krest'ian xix–xx vekov.* Moscow, 2001.

Gronow, Jukka. *Caviar with Champagne: Common Luxury and the Ideals of the Good Life in Stalin's Russia.* New York: Berg, 2003.

Gubar', Oleg. "Postavshchik imperatorskogo dvora." *Delovaia Odessa,* no. 23, December 7, 1990.

Habermas, Jürgen. *The Structural Transformation of the Public Sphere: An Inquiry into a Category of Bourgeois Society.* Translated by T. Burger. Cambridge, MA: MIT Press, 1989.

Hanchett, Walter S. "Moscow in the Late Nineteenth Century: A Study in Municipal Self-Government." PhD dissertation, University of Chicago, 1964.

Healey, Dan. *Homosexual Desire in Revolutionary Russia: The Regulation of Sexual and Gender Dissent.* Chicago: University of Chicago Press, 2001.

Heath, Joseph, and Andrew Potter. *Nation of Rebels: Why Counterculture Became Consumer Culture.* New York: Harper, 2004.

Hellie, Richard. "The Origins of Denunciation in Muscovy." *Russian History/Histoire russe* 24:1–2 (spring–summer 1997): 11–26.

Herlihy, Patricia. "Commerce and Architecture in Late Imperial Russia." In *Commerce in Russian Urban Culture, 1861–1914,* edited by William Craft Brumfield, Boris V. Anan'ich, and Yuri A. Petrov. Washington, DC: Woodrow Wilson Center Press; Baltimore: Johns Hopkins University Press, 2001.

———. *Odessa: A History, 1794–1914.* Cambridge, MA: Harvard University Press, 1986.

Hessler, Julie. *A Social History of Soviet Trade.* Princeton: Princeton University Press, 2004.

Hilton, Matthew. "Class, Consumption, and the Public Sphere." *Journal of Contemporary History* 35:4 (2000): 655–66.

Holquist, Peter. *Making War, Forging Revolution: Russia's Continuum of Crisis, 1914–1921.* New York: Cambridge University Press, 2002.

Humphrey, Caroline, and Stephen Hugh-Jones, eds. *Barter, Exchange and Value: An Anthropological Approach.* New York: Cambridge University Press, 1992.

Husband, William. *"Godless Communists": Atheism and Society in Soviet Russia, 1917–1932.*
   DeKalb: Northern Illinois University Press, 2000.
Iljine, Nicolas V., ed. *Odessa Memories.* Seattle: University of Washington Press, 2003.
Ingemanson, Birgitta. "The Political Function of Domestic Objects in the Fiction of
   Aleksandra Kollontai." *Slavic Review* 48:1 (spring 1989): 71–82.
Istoriia Moskvy. Vols. 1, 4. Moscow: Akademiia Nauk SSSR, 1954.
Jahn, Hubertus F. *Patriotic Culture in Russia during World War I.* Ithaca: Cornell University
   Press, 1995.
Jones, Jennifer. "Coquettes and Grisettes: Women Buying and Selling in Ancien Régime
   Paris." In *The Sex of Things: Gender and Consumption in Historical Perspective,* edited by
   Victoria de Grazia with Ellen Furlough. Berkeley: University of California Press, 1996.
————. "Repackaging Rousseau: Femininity and Fashion in Old Regime France." *French
   Historical Studies* 18:4 (fall 1994): 939–67.
Kelly, Catriona. "The Education of the Will: Advice Literature, *Zakal,* and Manliness
   in Early Twentieth Century Russia." In *Russian Masculinities in History and Culture,*
   edited by Barbara Evans Clements, Rebecca Friedman, and Dan Healey. New York:
   Palgrave, 2001.
————, and Vadim Volkov, eds. *Constructing Russian Culture in the Age of Revolution,
   1881–1940.* New York: Oxford University Press, 1998.
Kel'ner, V. "Evrei, kotorye zhili v Rossii." In *Evrei v Rossii: XIX vek.* Moscow: Novoe
   literaturnoe obozrenie, 2000.
Kenez, Peter. *The Birth of the Propaganda State: Soviet Methods of Mass Mobilization, 1917–1929.*
   New York: Cambridge University Press, 1985.
Khan-Magomedov, Selim O. *Rodchenko: The Complete Work.* Cambridge, MA: MIT Press,
   1987.
Kharchenko, K. V. *Vlast', imushchestvo, chelovek: peredel sobstvennosti v bol'shevistskoi Rossii,
   1917–nachala 1921 gg.* Moscow: Russkii dvor, 2000.
Kimmel, Michael S. *The History of Men: Essays on the History of American and British
   Masculinities.* New York: Oxford University Press, 2005.
————. *Manhood in America: A Cultural History.* New York: Free Press, 1996.
Kirichenko, E. I. *Moskva na rubezhe stoletii.* Moscow, 1977.
Klier, John. "State Policies and the Conversion of Jews in Imperial Russia." In *Of Religion
   and Empire: Missions, Conversions, and Tolerance in Tsarist Russia,* edited by Robert P.
   Geraci and Michael Khodarkovsky. Ithaca: Cornell University Press, 2001.
Kochurov, A. M. *GUM: vchera, segodnia, zavtra.* Moscow, 1974.
Koenker, Diane P. "Factory Tales: Narratives of Industrial Relations in the Transition to
   NEP." *Russian Review* 55:3 (July 1996): 384–411.
Konechnyi, Al'bin M. "Shows for the People: Public Amusement Parks in Nineteenth-
   Century St. Petersburg." In *Cultures in Flux: Lower-Class Values, Practices, and Resistance
   in Late Imperial Russia,* edited by Stephen P. Frank and Mark D. Steinberg. Princeton:
   Princeton University Press, 1994.
Kotsonis, Yanni. *Making Peasants Backward: Agricultural Cooperatives and the Agrarian Question
   in Russia, 1861–1914.* New York: St. Martin's Press, 1999.
Kovaleva, L. A. "Kostromskie torgovye riady v pervoi polovine XVII v." In *Torgovlia,
   kupechestvo i tamozhennoe delo v Rossii v XVI–XVII vv.* St. Petersburg: St. Petersburg
   University, 2001.

Kuchta, David. "The Making of the Self-Made Man: Class, Clothing, and English Masculinity, 1688–1832." In *The Sex of Things: Gender and Consumption in Historical Perspective,* edited by Victoria de Grazia with Ellen Furlough. Berkeley: University of California Press, 1996.

Leach, William. *Land of Desire: Merchants, Power, and the Rise of a New American Culture.* New York: Pantheon Books, 1993.

Lehmann, Hartmut, and Guenther Roth, eds. *The Protestant Ethic: Origins, Evidence, Contexts.* Cambridge: Cambridge University Press, 1993.

Liakhov, V. N. *Sovetskii reklamnyi plakaty.* Moscow: Sovetskii Khudozhnik, 1972.

Lih, Lars. *Bread and Authority in Russia, 1914–1921.* Berkeley: University of California Press, 1990.

Lindenmeyr, Adele. *Poverty Is Not a Vice: Charity, Society, and the State in Imperial Russia.* Princeton: Princeton University Press, 1996.

Lobanov-Rostovsky, Nina. *Revolutionary Ceramics: Soviet Porcelain, 1917–1927.* New York: Rizzoli, 1990.

Lohr, Eric. *Nationalizing the Russian Empire: The Campaign against Enemy Aliens during World War I.* Cambridge, MA: Harvard University Press, 2003.

Manchester, Laurie. *Holy Fathers, Secular Sons: Clergy, Intelligentsia, and the Modern Self in Revolutionary Russia.* DeKalb: Northern Illinois University Press, 2008.

McCracken, Grant. *Culture and Consumption: New Approaches to the Symbolic Character of Consumer Goods and Activities.* Bloomington: Indiana University Press, 1988.

McKay, John P. *Pioneers for Profit: Foreign Entrepreneurship and Russian Industrialization, 1885–1913.* Chicago: University of Chicago Press, 1970.

McKendrick, Neil, John Brewer, and J. H. Plumb. *The Birth of a Consumer Society: The Commercialization of Eighteenth-Century England.* Bloomington: Indiana University Press, 1982.

McReynolds, Louise. *The News under Russia's Old Regime: The Development of a Mass Circulation Press.* Princeton: Princeton University Press, 1991.

———. *Russia at Play: Leisure Activities at the End of the Tsarist Era.* Ithaca: Cornell University Press, 2003.

———. "V. M. Doroshevich: The Newspaper Journalist and the Development of Public Opinion in Civil Society." In *Between Tsar and People: Educated Society and the Quest for Public Identity in Late Imperial Russia,* edited by Edith W. Clowes, Samuel D. Kassow, and James L. West. Princeton: Princeton University Press, 1991.

Mikhalkov, A. V. *Ocherki iz istorii Moskovskogo kupechestva: ch'i predpriiatia sluzhili Moskve posle revoliutsii.* Moscow, 1996.

Miller, Michael. *The Bon Marché: Bourgeois Culture and the Department Store, 1869–1920.* Princeton: Princeton University Press, 1981.

Mironov, Boris. *Vnutrennyi rynok Rossii v vtoroi polovine XVIII–pervoi polovine XIX v.* Leningrad, 1981.

Naiman, Eric. *Sex in Public: The Incarnation of Early Soviet Ideology.* Princeton: Princeton University Press, 1997.

Nathans, Benjamin. *Beyond the Pale: The Jewish Encounter with Late Imperial Russia.* Berkeley: University of California Press, 2002.

Neuberger, Joan. *Crime, Culture, and Power in St. Petersburg, 1900–1914.* Berkeley: University of California Press, 1993.

Nord, Philip. Introduction to *Civil Society before Democracy: Lessons from Nineteenth-Century Europe,* edited by Nancy Bermeo and Philip Nord. Lanham, MD: Rowman & Littlefield Publishers, Inc., 2000.

Nove, Alec. *An Economic History of the USSR, 1917–1991.* New York: Penguin Books, 1992.

Orlik, Vasilii. *Moi zametki na proekt ustava obshchestva torgovykh riadov na Krasnoi ploshchadi v Moskve.* Moscow, 1886.

Orlovsky, Daniel. "The Hidden Class: White-Collar Workers in the Soviet 1920s." In *Making Workers Soviet: Power, Class, and Identity,* edited by Lewis H. Siegelbaum and Ronald Grigor Suny. Ithaca: Cornell University Press, 1994.

Osokina, Elena. *Our Daily Bread: Socialist Distribution and the Art of Survival in Stalin's Russia, 1927–1941.* Armonk, NY: M. E. Sharpe, 2000.

———. *Za fasada Stalinskogo izobilia: raspredelenie i rynok v snabzhenii naseleniia v gody industrializatsii, 1927–1941.* Moscow: Rosspen, 1999.

———. "Za zerkal'noi dver'iu Torgsina." *Otechestvennaia istoriia,* no. 2 (April 1995): 86–104.

Owen, Thomas C. *Capitalism and Politics in Russia: A Social History of the Moscow Merchants, 1855–1905.* New York: Cambridge University Press, 1981.

———. *The Corporation under Russian Law, 1800–1917: A Study in Tsarist Economic Policy.* New York: Cambridge University Press, 1991.

———. "Doing Business in Merchant Moscow." In *Merchant Moscow: Images of Russia's Vanished Bourgeoisie,* edited by James L. West and Iurii A. Petrov. Princeton: Princeton University Press, 1998.

———. "Impediments to a Bourgeois Consciousness in Russia, 1880–1905: The Estate Structure, Ethnic Diversity, and Economic Regionalism." In *Between Tsar and People: Educated Society and the Quest for Public Identity in Late Imperial Russia,* edited by Edith W. Clowes, Samuel D. Kassow, and James L. West. Princeton: Princeton University Press, 1991.

———. *Russian Corporate Capitalism from Peter the Great to Perestroika.* New York: Oxford University Press, 2005.

Paltusova, Irina. "Krupneishii passazh Rossii." *Mir muzeia,* no. 6 (1993): 14–20.

———. "Urok Rossiisskim predprinimateliam." *Mir muzeia,* no. 6 (November–December 1995): 46–48.

———. *Uvlekatel'nyi mir Moskovskoi reklamy XIX–nachala XX veka.* Moscow, 1996.

Peris, Daniel. *Storming the Heavens: The Soviet League of the Militant Godless.* Ithaca: Cornell University Press, 1998.

Perrot, Philippe. *Fashioning the Bourgeoisie: A History of Clothing in the Nineteenth Century.* Translated by Richard Bienvenu. Princeton: Princeton University Press, 1994.

Pitcher, Harvey. *Muir & Mirrielees: The Scottish Partnership That Became a Household Name in Russia.* Cromer, England: Swallow House Books, 1994.

Polovnikov, A. P. *Torgovlia v staroi Rossii.* Moscow, 1958.

Pomeranz, Kenneth, and Steven Topik. *The World That Trade Created: Society, Culture, and the World Economy, 1400 to the Present.* Armonk, NY, and London: M. E. Sharpe, 1999.

Potkina, Irina. *Delovaia Moskva: ocherki po istorii predprinimatel'stva.* Moscow, 1997.

———. "Moscow's Commercial Mosaic." In *Merchant Moscow: Images of Russia's Vanished Bourgeoisie,* edited by James L. West and Iurii A. Petrov. Princeton: Princeton University Press, 1998.

Pridmore, Jay. *Marshall Field's.* San Francisco: Pomegranate, 2002.

Primachenko, P. A. *Torgovo-promyshlennyi mir.* Moscow, 1993.

Randall, Amy E. *The Soviet Dream World of Retail Trade and Consumption in the 1930s.* New York: Palgrave Macmillan, 2008.

Ransel, David L. *A Russian Merchant's Tale: The Life and Adventures of Ivan Alekseevich Tolchënov, Based on His Diary.* Bloomington: Indiana University Press, 2009.

Rappaport, Erika Diane. *Shopping for Pleasure: Women in the Making of London's West End.* Princeton: Princeton University Press, 2001.

Reid, Susan E. "Cold War in the Kitchen: Gender and the De-Stalinization of Consumer Taste in the Soviet Union under Khrushchev." *Slavic Review* 61:2 (summer 2002): 211–52.

———, and David Crowley, eds. *Style and Socialism: Modernity and Material Culture in Post-War Eastern Europe.* New York: Berg, 2000.

Rheinstein, Max, ed. *Max Weber on Law in Economy and Society.* New York: Simon & Schuster, 1967.

Rieber, Alfred J. *Merchants and Entrepreneurs in Imperial Russia.* Chapel Hill: University of North Carolina Press, 1982.

Ries, Nancy. *Russian Talk: Culture and Conversation during Perestroika.* Ithaca: Cornell University Press, 1997.

Rigby, T. H. *Communist Party Membership in the U.S.S.R., 1917–1967.* Princeton: Princeton University Press, 1968.

Roberts, Mary Louise. "Gender, Consumption, and Commodity Culture." *American Historical Review* 103:3 (June 1998): 817–44.

Robin, Regine. "Popular Literature of the 1920s." In *Russia in the Era of NEP: Explorations in Soviet Society and Culture,* edited by Sheila Fitzpatrick, Alexander Rabinowitch, and Richard Stites. Bloomington: Indiana University Press, 1991.

Rolf, Malte. "A Hall of Mirrors: Sovietizing Culture under Stalinism." *Slavic Review* 68:3 (fall 2009): 601–30.

Roosa, Ruth AmEnde. *Russian Industrialists in an Era of Revolution: The Association of Industry and Trade, 1906–1917,* edited by Thomas C. Owen. Armonk, NY: M. E. Sharpe, 1997.

Rozental', I. "Moskva nachala XX veka: Evrei, vlast', obshchestvo." *Vestnik Evreiskogo Universiteta,* no. 1 (1999): 95–119.

Ruane, Christine. "Clothes Shopping in Imperial Russia: The Development of a Consumer Culture." *Journal of Social History* 28 (summer 1995): 765–82.

———. *The Empire's New Clothes: A History of the Russian Fashion Industry, 1700–1917.* New Haven: Yale University Press, 2009.

Ruble, Blair. "Moscow's Avant-Garde Architecture of the 1920s: A Tour." In *Architecture and the New Urban Environment: Western Influences on Modernism in Russia and the USSR.* Washington, DC: Kennan Institute for Advanced Russian Studies, 1988.

Ruckman, JoAnn. *The Moscow Business Elite: A Social and Cultural Portrait of Two Generations, 1840–1905.* DeKalb: Northern Illinois University Press, 1984.

Salop, Steven, and Joseph Stiglitz. "Bargains and Ripoffs: A Model of Monopolistically Competitive Price Dispersion." *Review of Economic Studies* 44 (October 1977): 493–510.

Sanborn, Josh. "Conscription, Correspondence, and Politics in Late Imperial Russia." *Russian History/Histoire russe* 24:1–2 (spring 1997): 27–40.

Sartorti, Rosalinde. "Stalinism and Carnival: Organisation and Aesthetics of Political Holidays." In *The Culture of the Stalin Period,* edited by Hans Gunther. New York: St. Martin's Press, 1990.

Scott, Joan Wallach. *Gender and the Politics of History*. New York: Columbia University Press, 1988.

Shevchenko, M. D. *Dukhovnaia kul'tura zapadnoi Evropy i Rossii*. Moscow, 1999.

Shevzov, Vera. *Russian Orthodoxy on the Eve of Revolution*. New York: Oxford University Press, 2004.

Siegelbaum, Lewis. "Narratives of Appeal and the Appeal of Narratives: Labor Discipline and Its Contestation in the Early Soviet Period." *Russian History/Histoire russe* 24:1–2 (spring 1997): 65–87.

———. *Soviet State and Society between Revolutions, 1918–1929*. New York: Cambridge University Press, 1992.

Simmel, Georg. "Fashion." *American Journal of Sociology* 63 (May 1958): 541–58.

———. *The Philosophy of Money*. London: Routledge, 1978.

Smith, S. A. "Masculinity in Transition: Peasant Migrants to Late Imperial St. Petersburg." In *Russian Masculinities in History and Culture*, edited by Barbara Evans Clements, Rebecca Friedman, and Dan Healey. New York: Palgrave, 2001.

Smith, Tori. "'Almost Pathetic . . . but Also Very Glorious': The Consumer Spectacle of the Diamond Jubilee." *Histoire sociale/Social History* 58 (November 1996): 333–56.

Sorokin, S. *Sto let na Krasnoi ploshchadi*. Moscow, 1993.

Stearns, Peter N. *Consumerism in World History: The Global Transformation of Desire*. New York: Routledge, 2006.

Steinberg, Mark. *Moral Communities: The Culture of Class Relations in the Russian Printing Industry*. Berkeley: University of California Press, 1992.

———. *Voices of Revolution, 1917*. New Haven: Yale University Press, 2001.

Stites, Richard. "Bolshevik Ritual Building in the 1920s." In *Russia in the Era of NEP: Explorations in Soviet Society and Culture*, edited by Sheila Fitzpatrick, Alexander Rabinowitch, and Richard Stites. Bloomington: Indiana University Press, 1991.

———. "Iconoclastic Currents in the Russian Revolution: Destroying and Preserving the Past." In *Bolshevik Culture: Experiment and Order in the Russian Revolution*, edited by Abbott Gleason, Peter Kenez, and Richard Stites. Bloomington: Indiana University Press, 1985.

———. *Revolutionary Dreams: Utopian Vision and Experimental Life in the Russian Revolution*. New York: Oxford University Press, 1989.

Strekalov, A. "Ikony na zdanii verkhnykh torgovykh riadov." In *Moskovskii arkhiv: istorikokraevedcheskii al'manakh*. Moscow, 1996.

Strizhenova, Tatiana. *Soviet Costumes and Textiles, 1917–1945*. Moscow, 1991.

Sylvester, Roshanna. "Making an Appearance: Urban 'Types' and the Creation of Respectability in Odessa's Popular Press, 1912–1914." *Slavic Review* 59:4 (winter 2000): 802–23.

———. *Tales of Old Odessa: Crime and Civility in a City of Thieves*. DeKalb: Northern Illinois University Press, 2005.

Sytin, P. V. *Iz istorii Moskovskikh ulits*. Moscow, 1958.

Thomas, Calvin. "Reenfleshing the Bright Boys; or, How Male Bodies Matter to Feminist Theory." In *Masculinity Studies & Feminist Theory: New Directions*, edited by Judith Kegan Gardiner. New York: Columbia University Press, 2002.

Thornton, John. *Africa and Africans in the Making of the Atlantic World, 1400–1800*. 2nd ed. New York: Cambridge University Press, 1998.

Tikhomirov, M. N. *Rossiia v XVI stoletii*. Moscow: Akademiia Nauk, 1962.

Tumarkin, Nina. *Lenin Lives! The Lenin Cult in Soviet Russia*. Cambridge, MA: Harvard University Press, 1997.

1000 let Russkogo predprinimatel'stva. Moscow, 1995.

Ulianova, Galina N. *Blagotvoritel'nost' Moskovskikh predprinimatelei, 1860–1914*. Moscow, 1999.

———. "Old Believers and New Entrepreneurs: Religious Belief and Ritual in Merchant Moscow." In *Merchant Moscow: Images of Russia's Vanished Bourgeoisie*, edited by James L. West and Iurii A. Petrov. Princeton: Princeton University Press, 1998.

Vainshtein, Olga. "Russian Dandyism: Constructing a Man of Fashion." In *Russian Masculinities in History and Culture*, edited by Barbara Evans Clements, Rebecca Friedman, and Dan Healey. New York: Palgrave, 2001.

Val'din, Anton. "Sladkaia slava Rossii: put' Tovarishchestva A. I. Abrikosova Synovei." *Tsentr*, no. 7–8 (1993): 59–61.

Veblen, Thorstein. *The Theory of the Leisure Class*. New York: Macmillan, 1899.

Veselov, S. V. "*Kooperatsiia i Sovetskaia vlast: period "Voennogo Kommunizma.*" *Voprosy istorii*, no. 9–10 (1991): 25–37.

Vickery, Amanda. "Women and the World of Goods: A Lancashire Consumer and Her Possessions, 1751–81." In *Consumption and the World of Goods*, edited by John Brewer and Roy Porter. London: Routledge, 1993.

von Geldern, James. *Bolshevik Festivals, 1917–1920*. Berkeley: University of California Press, 1993.

von Hagen, Mark. *Soldiers in the Proletarian Dictatorship: The Red Army and the Soviet Socialist State, 1917–1930*. Ithaca: Cornell University Press, 1990.

von Laue, Theodore H. *Sergei Witte and the Industrialization of Russia*. New York: Atheneum, 1973.

Walkowitz, Judith. *City of Dreadful Delight: Narratives of Sexual Danger in Late-Victorian London*. Chicago: University of Chicago Press, 1992.

Walton, Whitney. *France at the Crystal Palace: Bourgeois Taste and Artisan Manufacture in the Nineteenth Century*. Berkeley: University of California Press, 1992.

Weatherill, Lorna. "The Meaning of Consumer Behavior in Late-Seventeenth- and Early-Eighteenth-Century England." In *Consumption and the World of Goods*, edited by John Brewer and Roy Porter. London: Routledge, 1993.

Weber, Max. *The Protestant Ethic and the Spirit of Capitalism*. New York: Charles Scribner's Sons, 1958.

———. *The Sociology of Religion*. Boston: Beacon Press, 1963.

Weeks, Theodore R. *Nation and State in Late Imperial Russia: Nationalism and Russification on the Western Frontier, 1863–1914*. DeKalb: Northern Illinois University Press, 1996.

Weigman, Robyn. "Unmaking: Men and Masculinity in Feminist Theory." In *Masculinity Studies & Feminist Theory: New Directions*, edited by Judith Kegan Gardiner. New York: Columbia University Press, 2002.

West, James L. "The Fate of Merchant Moscow." In *Merchant Moscow: Images of Russia's Vanished Bourgeoisie*, edited by James L. West and Iurii A. Petrov. Princeton: Princeton University Press, 1998.

———. "Merchant Moscow in Historical Context." In *Merchant Moscow: Images of Russia's Vanished Bourgeoisie*, edited by James L. West and Iurii A. Petrov. Princeton: Princeton University Press, 1998.

———. "The Riabushinsky Circle: *Burzhuaziia* and *Obshchestvennost'* in Late Imperial Russia." In *Between Tsar and People: Educated Society and the Quest for Public Identity in Late Imperial Russia,* edited by Edith W. Clowes, Samuel D. Kassow, and James L. West. Princeton: Princeton University Press, 1991.

———. "Visions of Russia's Entrepreneurial Future: Pavel Riabushinskii's Utopian Capitalism." In *Merchant Moscow: Images of Russia's Vanished Bourgeoisie,* edited by James L. West and Iurii A. Petrov. Princeton: Princeton University Press, 1998.

West, Sally. "Constructing Consumer Culture: Advertising in Imperial Russia to 1914." PhD dissertation, University of Illinois, 1995.

———. *I Shop in Moscow: Advertising and the Creation of Consumer Culture in Late Tsarist Russia.* DeKalb: Northern Illinois University Press, 2011.

———. "The Material Promised Land: Advertising's Modern Agenda in Late Imperial Russia." *Russian Review* 57:3 (July 1998): 345–63.

White, Stephen. *The Bolshevik Poster.* New Haven: Yale University Press, 1988.

Whittemore, Leila. "Theatre of the Bazaar: Women and the Architecture of Fashion in 19th-Century Paris." *A/R/C: Architecture, Research, Criticism* 1 (1994–1995): 14–25.

Williams, Rosalind H. *Dream Worlds: Mass Consumption in Late Nineteenth-Century France.* Berkeley: University of California Press, 1982.

Worobec, Christine. "Masculinity in Late-Imperial Russian Peasant Society." In *Russian Masculinities in History and Culture,* edited by Barbara Evans Clements, Rebecca Friedman, and Dan Healey. New York: Palgrave, 2001.

Wortman, Richard. *Scenarios of Power: Myth and Ceremony in Russian Monarchy.* Vol. 2. Princeton: Princeton University Press, 2000.

Yekelchyk, Serhy. *Ukraine: Birth of a Modern Nation.* New York: Oxford University Press, 2007.

Zipperstein, Stephen J. *The Jews of Odessa: A Cultural History, 1794–1881.* Stanford: Stanford University Press, 1985.

Index